INTERNATIONAL OPERATIONS MANAGEMENT

A SELECTION OF IMEDE CASES

INTERNATIONAL OPERATIONS MANAGEMENT
A SELECTION OF IMEDE CASES

D. Clay Whybark
Indiana University

IMEDE

1989

BPI
IRWIN
Homewood, IL 60430
Boston, MA 02116

Sponsoring editor: Richard T. Hercher, Jr.
Project editor: Waivah Clement
Production manager: Stephen K. Emry
Cover designer: Paula Lang
Compositor: Compset Inc.
Typeface: 11/13 Times Roman
Printer: R. R. Donnelley & Sons Company

LIBRARY OF CONGRESS
Library of Congress Cataloging-in-Publication Data

Whybark, D. Clay.
    International operations management: a selection of IMEDE cases / D. Clay Whybark.
        p.   cm.
    ISBN 0-256-07410-0 (pbk.)
    1. International business enterprises—Management—Case studies.
    I. Title.
    HD62.4.W58   1989
    658'.049—dc19   88–21971
                                                                              CIP

Printed in the United States of America
1 2 3 4 5 6 7 8 9 0 DO 6 5 4 3 2 1 0 9

Dedicated to Jean and Janine Gambarini

FOREWORD

Here in Europe we have seen manufacturing operations assume an increasingly important role in the affairs of successful firms. The challenge of the changes in the European Economic Community, increased competition from outside the community and advancing technology have all played a part in reshaping manufacturing. Indeed, many companies would not have their current market share or be able to participate in global markets if their management had not taken an aggressive position on integrating manufacturing into their strategic plans.

In the service sector, as well, a revolution of sorts has occurred in the operating activities. Improving the service delivery process, improving efficiencies and reducing the costs of services are all receiving more top management attention. The processes for making these improvements in the service sector have also been applied to the indirect activities of manufacturing firms as the pressure mounts for better control of overhead costs.

Managing operations has always been viewed as a technically difficult task. As firms become more international, the job becomes more complex and more important. In an effort to confront this management need, Clay Whybark has compiled this collection of IMEDE cases which depicts executives in different parts of the world addressing key operations questions. The issues range from basic concerns like determining capacity requirements, through planning and managing global facilities, to determining the appropriate operations strategy for the enterprise.

We have already seen the impact of these cases in our classes at IMEDE and I am pleased that they will now be more widely disseminated. In our efforts to provide quality programs for general managers around the world, we recognize the need for a continual stream of such quality teaching material. I am proud of IMEDE's role in developing these cases and am sure they will provide you an exciting glimpse into the management of an important area.

Derek F. Abell, Dean

PREFACE

This collection of cases has been assembled to bring an international dimension to operations management. The business world is now characterized by multinational firms, global markets, offshore manufacturing, and managers who move from nation to nation. Terms like "world class manufacturing" and "global standards" have become part of the business vocabulary. In this environment it is important for every student of operations to have some understanding of the impact of the international dimension on functional and general management. These cases are provided to help gain that understanding.

The title is "operations" management for a reason. The cases cover a much broader scope of management activities than just manufacturing. The broad definition of operations that is used here includes functions like purchasing, logistics (physical distribution and supply), and strategy. There are also cases involving service organizations and the indirect activities of manufacturing firms. Thus the perspective is not only global, but functionally broad.

The cases cover many countries, issues, company sizes, and industries. Most come from Europe, but countries as diverse as the People's Republic of China and the United States are represented. The issues run from specific operating problems to questions of strategy in the global arena. They involve problems that arise because of the international character of the company to those that might be found in companies the world over. All require an understanding of the local situation for making viable suggestions for solutions.

The book has been organized in four sections, starting with general issues encountered in managing operations. The other sections cover topics from operations planning and control through materials management to strategic concerns. These run, roughly, from fairly focused problems to broad managerial issues. Unfortunately, the world does not divide itself neatly into these categories, and neither do the cases. The cases in all sections will contain a variety of management concerns that need to be taken into account. The introductory material at the beginning of each section provides a brief description of the role of the cases in that section. That may be a helpful starting point for analyzing the cases.

It has been a learning experience for me to write and teach these cases. I gain new insights each time a group of students discusses them. I hope your experience with them will be as rewarding as mine.

ACKNOWLEDGMENTS

Many people have contributed to the publication of this collection. I certainly owe a great deal of thanks to the two Deans with whom I've been associated the last couple of years. Dean Jack Wentworth at Indiana University graciously permitted me a long leave of absence to work overseas. I learned a great deal during the period. Dean Derek Abell of IMEDE (the international management school in Lausanne, Switzerland) was a key factor in that education. He supported the writing of all of the cases and provided the student body upon which they were tested. Professor Bob Britney, Western Ontario, made very insightful suggestions after reviewing the manuscript.

My colleagues at IMEDE made many contributions to the book. Bob Collins always provided help when needed and showed me many new insights into the material. Roger Schmenner was particularly skillful at making editorial suggestions and providing frameworks for the cases. Ivor Morgan and Linda Sprague provided great insights (and comic relief) when needed. A token marketing person, Jean-Pierre Jeannet, also helped in shaping the concept of the book. Their specific case contributions were as follows:

Robert S. Collins:	Maillefer SA (A)
	Olivetti—The Scarmagno Plant
	Stewart Instruments Ltd.
	Sunwind AB (A)
William K. Holstein:	Olivetti—The Scarmagno Plant
Jean-Pierre Jeannet:	Biral International (A)
Ivor P. Morgan:	Alpine Tobacco GmbH
	Inalfa BV (A)
Roger W. Schmenner:	International Plow
	Olivetti—The Scarmagno Plant
	Royal Clyde Biscuit Co., Ltd.
Linda G. Sprague:	North Sea Machine Tool Factory

Several research associates at IMEDE helped with individual cases. Owen Dempsey worked on Maillefer and Stewart Instruments, Juli Dixon helped with Crystalox and Olivetti, and Kevin O'Connell was involved with Inalfa. In China, several research associates helped with the North Sea Machine Tool Factory: Hugh Thomas, Sui Cheng Ben,

Kang Shu Sen, and Peter Kwok. Roberto Amodio, Hiroshi Fujii, Stephan Issenmann, Bengt Jansson, and Georges-Henri Meylan, all middle management program participants at IMEDE, worked on Frisbee Frozen Foods.

To my family, who missed some walks in the Alps on nice weekends, many thanks for your patience. To Cynthia Panettieri, who put up with my dictation, poor handwriting, editorial compulsion, and innumerable crises, thanks for your help.

Finally, and especially, anyone who has had the opportunity to visit IMEDE will understand that two people who have contributed enormously to the character of the place and have made sure that the torch passed gracefully from one group of faculty and students to the next are Jean and Janine Gambarini. This book is dedicated to them in thanks for the care and love they have given all of us.

D. Clay Whybark

CONTENTS

PART 1

MANAGING OPERATIONS

This section contains cases covering very general issues in the management of operations. The first case, The Geneva Technical Institute, introduces a variety of operating problems. Though set in a university office, the case raises questions of quality control, capacity management, priority setting, and job design. It presents a very common problem that requires both short-term actions and longer-term directions.

The introductory case is followed by Crystalox Limited, which describes a small company in England producing a technologically advanced product for research laboratories. The general manager must deal with a proposal to move manufacturing into a separate facility while trying to increase profitability. The role of operations in the company must be assessed before a clear course of action can be set.

In Alpine Tobacco GmbH, a subsidiary of a U.S. company, and the Central Tracing Agency of the Red Cross, the issue is one of productivity. In Alpine the concern is with factory productivity, including both equipment and people. In the Red Cross, the effective use of a professional staff that must respond to highly variable demands under very uncertain world conditions is of concern. In both cases, the role of the computer as a tool for increasing productivity is considered.

The last two cases take place on virtually opposite sides of the globe. In China, the North Sea Machine Tool Factory is concerned about reducing lead times to meet competition arising from the government's policy of opening up the economy to market forces. The case provides a glimpse into the difficulties faced by Chinese managers as they cope with significant changes in the rules of the game. In Royal Clyde Biscuit Co., Ltd., the concerns revolve around the lessons to be learned from a recently completed plant expansion and automation project. The role of the computer in improving plant productivity is raised again in this case.

The Geneva Technical Institute (A)

Dr. Richard Albu, chairman of the Physics Department at The Geneva Technical Institute, looked up from the letter on his desk at the clock on the wall. The letter had so many typing errors that he did not want to send it out without correction. It was already late in the afternoon and the secretaries were all gone. He knew that having his letter retyped in the morning would just make someone else's work late tomorrow. As he was trying to decide what to do, Dr. André Bucher burst into the office and said: "We simply must do something about the secretarial problem around here. I can't get anything done on time and when I do get it, it's full of mistakes. You must come up with something before the faculty meeting on Friday."

BACKGROUND

The Physics Department at The Geneva Technical Institute had grown quite rapidly in the last few years. Many of the faculty were known throughout the world for excellent scholarship. This had attracted increasing numbers of students, additional research and new specialties, all of which required additional faculty. The full-time members of the department had grown from 8 to 12 during the last five years, and there were often visiting scholars in residence as well. Dr. Albu was named department chairman two years ago in an effort to help "keep the administrative tasks off the backs of the professional faculty."

One of the first projects Dr. Albu undertook was to increase the secretarial staff from two to three people. This turned out to be very difficult. Budgets had been based on two secretaries per department and interdepartmental jealousies guarded the ratio very carefully. In addition, the funds for administrative support were very limited. Finally, Dr. Albu's arguments that the Physics Department was "different" and more productive than other departments prevailed and the third secretary was hired. Each secretary was nominally assigned to certain faculty members, with an informal understanding that peak loads would be shared.

As the number of professional staff and courses expanded, other changes were occurring that placed increased work on the secretaries.

3

Several new doctoral students joined the department. They had responsibility for teaching some of the classes as well as working on their doctoral studies. The increased research meant more manuscripts needed to be typed, and it was not long before the secretaries were complaining that they could not get all the work done in a normal day.

Most of the faculty felt the secretary's time was largely devoted to typing manuscripts, course outlines, research proposals and faculty correspondence. The secretaries, on the other hand, said that this was only a small part of their work and that the majority of their time was spent doing "errands." These errands involved getting copies of material from the duplicating center, distributing mail, providing supplies to the faculty, helping the doctoral students in the administrative activities associated with their teaching, answering the telephone, greeting visitors, and performing some of the administrative chores associated with the office. They also reported that the duplicating center had just replaced its high-speed duplicating and collating equipment with a slower, less costly piece of equipment in order to save money. This resulted in delays when rush jobs or peak loads occurred.

Several of the faculty members were complaining that the secretaries were not spending much time typing. They said the secretaries seemed to be spending a great deal of time talking with the doctoral students and visitors. Dr. Albu heard complaints other than about the quality of the typing or the long delays in getting work done. Some faculty had missed important phone calls and occasionally material that they had prepared was "lost" in duplication. There were even instances of friction between the secretaries as they quarrelled over priorities and jobs.

PREPARING FOR THE FACULTY MEETING

As Dr. Albu thought of all the complaints and the comment that he should do something before the faculty meeting, he concluded that the Friday meeting would be long and difficult. He already had several suggestions from members of the faculty. Some had suggested that the office needed word processing equipment, while others wanted to reassign the secretaries or put them into a common pool. One was concerned that the secretaries were not well trained. Many, of course, simply wanted to hire a fourth secretary. Each of these suggestions required time and/or money, both of which were limited.

EXHIBIT 1
THE GENEVA TECHNICAL INSTITUTE
Estimates of the Secretarial Use of Time

Category	Faculty Estimate* (in percent)	Work Sample†
Typing	74	28
On the phone	7	18
Writing/drawing	—	3
Talking to someone	—	23
Away from office	13	18
Distribution of papers, mail	5	6
In faculty offices	2	3

Note: The estimates may not total 100 percent due to rounding.
*An average of seven responses received from faculty members.
†Based on 43 observations over two days.

In preparing for the Friday faculty meeting, Dr. Albu asked some of the faculty to estimate how they felt the secretaries spent their time. He also conducted an informal work sampling of what they actually were doing in the days just before the meeting. (These are summarized in Exhibit 1.) He felt his responsibility was to provide support for the professional staff. He was concerned that they might get discouraged and look for jobs elsewhere. He knew that their professional reputations were so good that most of the faculty would have no difficulty in relocating if they wanted to. Finally, he turned to the task of organizing his thoughts for the meeting.

Crystalox Limited

Audun Boerve, managing director of Crystalox, Ltd., stopped off the airplane at London's Heathrow Airport after a quick trip to Switzerland. He had capitalized on a visit to a potential customer to stop at his alma mater, a well-known international management institute, to talk with some of the faculty about recent developments at his company. He was quite pleased with the progress that had been made since he had joined the company in 1985. Sales and sales potential had been increased, for example. He had also been successful in hiring a number of people to strengthen several areas of the company and in implementing a reorganization that would help them focus their efforts. He was still concerned, however, about the company's manufacturing efforts.

As a part of the reorganization, Mr. Boerve had arranged to have all manufacturing activities report directly to him. In the discussions about manufacturing, Graham Young, the manager of the Workshop, proposed that part of the manufacturing facilities be moved to another location and that a joint venture between him and Crystalox be created. Mr. Young felt that this would help Crystalox and that it would help him achieve a longstanding goal of having his own machine shop. He had just submitted a detailed written proposal on the idea for Crystalox's consideration. Mr. Boerve knew he would have to deal with the proposal as a part of his overall evaluation of the manufacturing activities. As he walked down the gateway, he mused, "What can I do to improve our manufacturing effectiveness and position us for future growth?" He was already trying to prioritize the actions he would take on arriving at the office the next morning.

BACKGROUND AND HISTORY

Crystalox was founded in 1970 by Dr. David Hukin, who holds a Ph.D. in physics. As a specialist in crystal "growth" techniques, he had developed equipment to produce high-purity crystals while serving as head of Materials Preparation at Clarendon Laboratories in Oxford. The remarkably successful use of silicon crystals for making microchips had spurred an interest in seeking other applications of silicon and in studying the properties of other crystals. Dr. Hukin's research colleagues around the world and the visitors to the laboratory convinced him there was a large potential market for machines that could produce high-purity crystals of various metals, so Crystalox was formed. (Some of the potential uses for the products which use these crystals are described in the Appendix.)

The first undertakings of the company involved technical consulting. The character of the company as a "problem solving" firm was set at this early stage. Dr. Hukin, working closely with the customers, designed specific machines to solve their crystal growing problems. Through his personal contacts and professional reputation, Dr. Hukin was able to meet many potential customers, and by the mid-1970s, he had two employees helping assemble machines from purchased and subcontracted components. Working from a small shed in Wantage, England, about 30 kilometers from Oxford, the company produced one or two machines a year for university, government, and industrial research laboratories around the world.

By 1982, the number of employees had increased to ten and Dr. Hukin found the time for his professional activities squeezed by the demands of managing the company. To leave him more time for the technical activities and to raise capital for expansion, Dr. Hukin sold a 75 percent interest in the company to a local property development firm. They agreed to construct a new building and to be responsible for the day-to-day management of the company. The building was built, but unfortunately, financial and other problems plagued the arrangement nearly from the beginning. The new managers didn't have experience in managing a manufacturing firm, nor did they have a good understanding of the technology upon which the company was based.

During this period, Crystalox was working on a project to build a special machine for Elkem AS., a Norwegian firm that produces silicon and other basic materials, products that had not been enjoying expanding markets. The Crystalox machine was to produce large silicon crystals for solar cells that would help Elkem enter new markets. As Elkem's management became aware of the deteriorating situation at Crystalox, they considered acquiring the company to protect their interest in the project. The acquisition offered Elkem some other advantages as well. It could expand the base of their business by providing access to advanced technology in a variety of materials and by providing forward integration into other processing activities.

With this in mind, negotiations commenced and, in 1985, Crystalox became a profit center in the Electronic Materials Division of the Elkem Group. Crystalox brought the technology to the new company, and Elkem supplied an infusion of funds plus management support. Audun

Boerve, for example, had been sales manager for silicon metal in Norway before being appointed as managing director, and Per Dybwad, a member of the Elkem acquisition team, provided financial consulting services.

Mr. Boerve's first activities as managing director were focused on finishing up two special machines that were in process (both of which were behind schedule when he arrived) in order to generate some cash for the company. While this was going on he spent some time identifying strengths and weaknesses of the company so he could develop a plan to position the firm for the future. During 1985, personnel were added and more contracts were sought, but the company recorded a loss. In 1986, his efforts began to pay off and the company made a profit for the first time since 1982 (see the financial statements in Exhibits 1 and 2).

During 1986, it became clear that it would be necessary to restructure the organization. Because of the difficulties prior to Elkem's arrival, Dr. Hukin had been spending time on virtually every aspect of the

EXHIBIT 1
CRYSTALOX LIMITED
Consolidated Profit and Loss Statement
(in pounds sterling)

	12 months to 31 December 1986	12 months to 31 December 1985
Sales	907,775*	342,045
Cost of goods sold		
Purchases	274,659	107,767
Labour	236,901	147,487
Materials	33,044	20,014
Subcontracting	28,323	17,244
Manufacturing overhead	25,304	15,395
	598,231	307,907
Gross Profit	309,544	34,138
Operating expenses		
Marketing expenses	89,792	54,687
General and administrative	219,720	193,889
Operating (loss)/profit	32	(214,438)

*Sales breakdown:

Subcontracting	49,214
Special machines	614,803
Standard products	243,758
Total	907,775

EXHIBIT 2
CRYSTALOX LIMITED
Balance Sheet as of December 31
(in pounds sterling)

	1986	1985
Current assets:		
Cash	52	(12)
Accounts receivable	132,502	10,566
Inventory	373,585*	185,740
Other	4,943	4,442
	511,082	200,736
Fixed assets:		
Land and buildings	340,555	302,366
Plant/machinery	67,210	32,343
Other	59,117	56,240
	466,882	390,949
Intangible assets	—	3,219
Total assets	977,964	594,904
Current liabilities:		
Bank note current	408,337	246,655
Accounts payable	217,724	121,465
Other	181,834	56,747
	807,895	424,867
Long-term liabilities:		
Loan from Elkem	399,928	399,928
Equity	(229,859)	(229,891)
Total equity and liabilities	977,964	594,904

*Raw materials and supplies	11,037
Work in process	362,548
	373,585

business, from initial customer contact to manufacturing and delivery problems. During 1986, as the size of the company increased to 30 employees, he still found it necessary to help out in a variety of areas, even though everyone realized that his contacts and technical knowledge were essential for reaching the market. At the same time, manufacturing coordination was becoming more complex as the volume of business increased.

The reorganization in early 1987 provided the structure for Dr. Hukin to focus his attention on the technical aspects of marketing and new product development. It also provided for direct involvement in manu-

EXHIBIT 3
CRYSTALOX LIMITED
Organization Chart

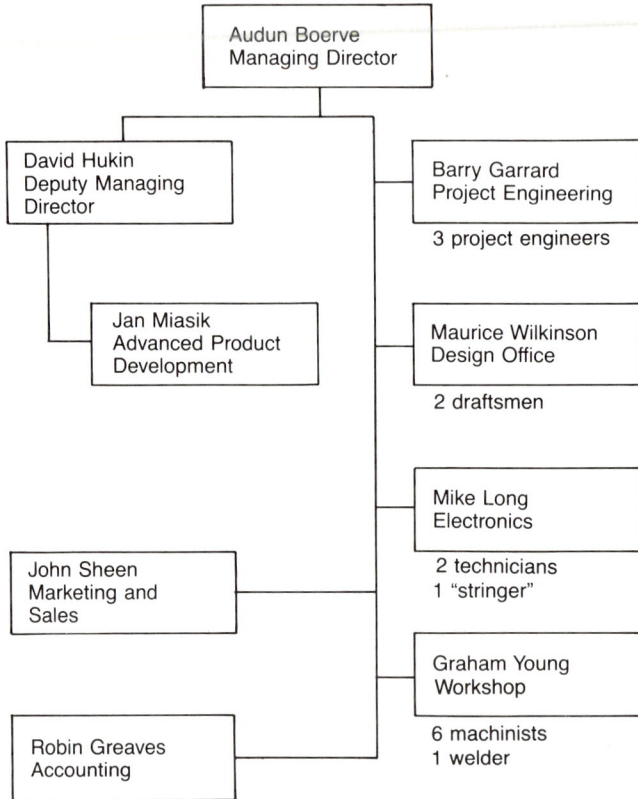

facturing by Mr. Boerve (an organization chart is shown in Exhibit 3). Mr. Boerve felt that the current organization would allow them to increase the output from the 6 special machines produced in 1986 to 9 to 11 machines in 1987.

THE MARKET

Crystalox's products are sold worldwide to research and development laboratories in both the private and public sectors. The company estimates that there are about 3,000 such laboratories in the world. For

Crystalox, the key persons in these institutes are the scientists who conduct the research and the administrators who approve the budgets for equipment. The scientists form a fairly close-knit community and many gather once a year or so to exchange information at professional meetings and conferences. Dr. Hukin's presence at these gatherings is an important mode of contact for the company. The administrators tend to get involved in the buying process only after the preliminary discussions on the technical aspects have taken place and the research proposals are being approved.

The buying decision often starts with a scientist who is conducting research for which crystals will be required. The scientist may involve Crystalox in answering some basic questions early in the process. For example, can a crystal that will meet the specifications for size, purity, and shape of the material required be grown, and what would be the approximate cost of a machine that could do it? If it appears feasible, Crystalox may be asked to submit a quotation for inclusion in the research proposal. Then the decision process moves to the administrators involved.

The research proposal approval process can take a long time, during which even the research scientist does not know if it will be approved. Sometimes a quote will be outstanding for a year or more before it is clear whether there will be a contract or not. Often the proposal is simply rejected. Occasionally the budget has been cut, and Crystalox is asked what they can do for a reduced amount of money. If the proposal is approved, however, Crystalox has a good chance to get the contract for the detail design and manufacturing of the machine. On average, about 25 percent of the quotes result in contracts.

Crystalox enjoys a unique niche in the market. Their competition is indirect, coming from firms that have different strategic objectives. There is a group of firms, for example, that sells components that the laboratories themselves can assemble into a machine. There is another group of companies, often competing on a cost basis, that make "production" machines. They sell in lots of 10 to 50 machines to companies that produce crystals commercially. There are no other companies that have the combination of scientific and other talent to offer uniquely designed "turnkey" machines to the research community.

The market for research crystals is constantly changing as new materials attract attention or as new properties become important. The research scientists appreciate being able to work with a company like Crystalox that "speaks their language" and understands the "leading edge" of the technology. The ability to offer solutions or intelligent alternatives to their problems is important to this community.

THE PRODUCTS

The product line consists of special machines that are designed and built for a specific customer and "standard" products that were designed as components of special machines but that are now sold separately. In addition, some subcontracting is done by the machine shop for local manufacturers. The special machines provided about two thirds of the 1986 revenue.

The special machines are built up from modules of components that perform the specific functions required to produce the kind of crystal the customer wants. All machines, however, perform several common basic functions. For example, all machines melt the material from which the crystal is to be made. This can require temperatures up to 2,000°C. They all have a means for growing the crystal. In the Czochralski process, for example, a "seed," around which the crystal is grown, is inserted into the melt. This is then rotated and pulled from the melt in such a way that the crystal size and shape is controlled. The pulling action has given rise to the name "crystal pullers" for machines of this type. In the Bridgeman-Stockbarger process, the crystal is grown around the seed in the melting vessel. Crystalox produces machines for both processes.

In addition to the functions performed by all machines, some may require a system for purifying the material before growing the crystal, or a vacuum system, or a means of injecting controlled amounts of additives, or even systems for surrounding the process with specific gases. Regardless of configuration, however, the whole process requires very close control. Each machine, therefore, has electronic equipment for monitoring all aspects of the process. All of the components are connected together and mounted in cabinets (a sample product is shown in Exhibit 4). Most special machines fall in a price range from £50,000–£200,000, with the average price currently about £100,000.

Most of the current standard products had first been designed as a component for a special machine. Many still are used on new machines, as well as being sold independently. The products range from parts like the crucible in which the material is melted or the chamber that sur-

EXHIBIT 4
CRYSTALOX LIMITED
Sample Product

The Crystalox CGS is designed for the Czochralski growth of

metals
semiconductors
oxides
halides

high purity, single crystals, up to 50 mm diameter.

RF induction heating is available with
programmed precision temperature control. Readout through
Thermocouples or Pyrometer.

The CGS comprises:
Growth chamber,
500 mm diameter A
Vacuum system B
Inert gas system B
Residual gas analysis B
RF power temperature
control C
allowing for
Remote computer control
and
fully microprocessor
controlled D
Digital pulling head
rotation and translation E
Digital crucible rotation or
crucible load cell monitoring F
ADC interface module

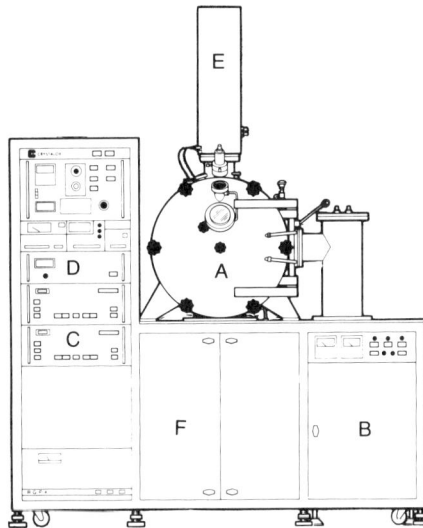

rounds the process, to complex electromechanical assemblies like the head which pulls the crystal from the melt. The Advanced Product Development group has been given the responsibility of developing new products that can be sold separately, whether or not they will be used on a special machine. Prototypes of some of these new products are being built now.

PROJECT ENGINEERING

Much of the responsibility for coordination of projects for special machines rests with the project engineers. They are involved throughout the life of the project, with special responsibilities at the beginning and the end. At the beginning, they are involved in the technical design issues and help determine the components to be purchased outside. At the end, they have responsibility for making sure the machine performs as the customer expects. In between, during design and manufacturing, they monitor, control, and coordinate the progress of the machines.

Before 1986, there was only one project engineer, Dr. Barry Garrard. During that year, Crystalox hired three more, two of whom had Ph.D.s. Dr. Garrard explained, "The focus of the project engineer is on the machine, a sort of champion for the customer here in the shop. He constantly reviews the design to make improvements or to rectify faults. Sometimes the theory doesn't translate into practice or something was missed and changes must be made. Since he knows that he must make the machine work during final test, he wants as few surprises as possible by the time it gets there."

The project engineer's job requires many skills. It requires technical knowledge to be able to modify and improve the design of the machine. It also requires organizational skills to perform the coordination needed to keep the machine on schedule. Finally, a great deal of inventiveness may be required when problems occur in final test. The greatest amount of the project engineer's time is spent in final test, but the general coordination activities take an average of 90 hours for each special machine.

GENERAL PROCESS

The general process from the receipt of a customer inquiry to the delivery of a special machine is shown in Exhibit 5. The activities are shown as occurring sequentially, but there is substantial interaction between all elements during the process. Each machine is assigned to a project engineer, usually at the preliminary design stage. The preliminary design is the basis for the quotation that goes out to the customer. The customer may request changes that might require more design work and negotiations with the customer. Once everything is agreed upon, the general design is finalized and the detailed drawings that are used to

EXHIBIT 5
CRYSTALOX LIMITED
General Process for a Special Machine

Responsibility	Steps

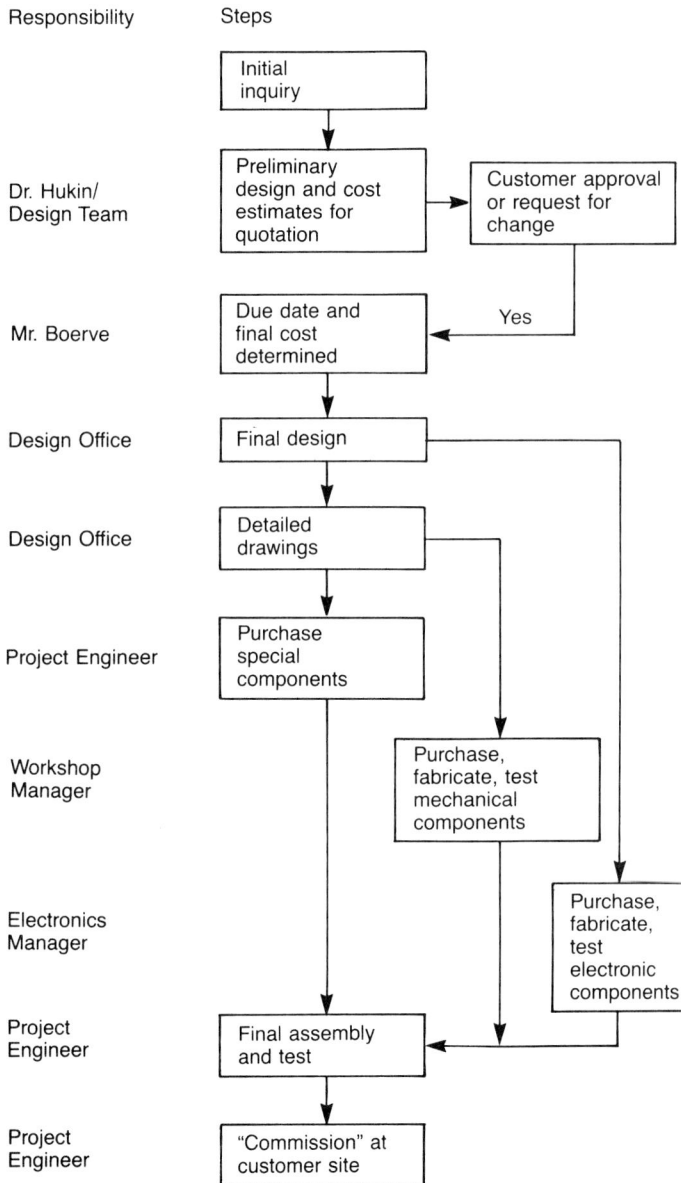

Responsibility / Steps flowchart:

- **Initial inquiry**
- **Dr. Hukin/ Design Team** — Preliminary design and cost estimates for quotation → Customer approval or request for change
- **Mr. Boerve** — Due date and final cost determined (← Yes)
- **Design Office** — Final design
- **Design Office** — Detailed drawings
- **Project Engineer** — Purchase special components
- **Workshop Manager** — Purchase, fabricate, test mechanical components
- **Electronics Manager** — Purchase, fabricate, test electronic components
- **Project Engineer** — Final assembly and test
- **Project Engineer** — "Commission" at customer site

build the machine are completed by the Design Office and sent to the Workshop.

The purchasing of specialized parts and components from outside suppliers is done by the project engineer. These would include such items as special vacuum pumps or gas analyzers. Graham Young, manager of the Workshop, is responsible for purchasing the raw material and components for making the mechanical parts of the machine. He would make, for example, the chamber which surrounds the crystal growing process, would subcontract manufacturing of some of the metal parts, and would purchase raw materials and components like sheet steel and ball bearings. Mike Long, manager of the Electronics Department, purchases cables and circuits, and fabricates, for example, control panels. Component testing is done in the individual departments, while final testing at the end of the process involves the project engineer.

MACHINE DESIGN

A customer's inquiry about a special machine leads to a preliminary design meeting attended by the managers of the Design Office, the Workshop, the Electronics Department, the project engineer, and Dr. Hukin, with others attending as needed. In this meeting they will develop the initial design specifications. Using these specifications, Maurice Wilkinson, manager of the Design Office, will prepare an initial drawing of the machine, something like that shown in Exhibit 4. The other departments will prepare labor and purchased-part cost estimates for the quotation to be sent to the customer. The quotation also states that the delivery date will be determined after the quotation is accepted.

When a quotation is accepted, the delivery date must be determined. This is influenced by the work in process and by the desires of the people involved. Discussions between the customer, Mr. Boerve, the project engineer, and others are used to set the date. Generally the customer wants the machine right away, the project engineer wants to have about 5 months (3 for manufacturing and 2 for final assembly and test), and Mr. Boerve wants to minimize the capital tied up in work in process. Usually the delivery dates for the special machines are established for 3 to 4 months from the time the machine can be started.

In the meantime, the final design specifications are set and the overall machine drawings prepared. The last step in the design effort is the drafting of detailed drawings and the development of the final list of purchased components. Some of the manufacturing work can be started as soon as the first detailed drawings are done. It can continue while the remaining detailed drawings are being completed.

The special machine activities of the Design Office and the range of time required for each are shown in Exhibit 6. The North American University machine was a typical product for the department. Mr. Wilkinson himself does the first two steps, although he can help in any of the other five. "Either of the two draftsmen can do any of the last five steps," he said. "Our job is not limited to the start of a special machine project, though. The project engineer will come to our office at any stage and ask for some changes. These may come from the customer,

EXHIBIT 6
CRYSTALOX LIMITED
Steps and Labor Hours Required in the Design Office
(special machines)

Step	North American University Machine (in hours)	Range (in hours)
1. Preliminary design specifications for cost estimates for quotation	25	2–100
2. Final design and drawings showing all views of the product, but not detailed enough to be used to manufacture the machine	75	30–300
3. Detailing—drawings of every part of the machine and the specification of the order in which the parts must be assembled	400	200–2000
4. Checking and correcting—ensures that parts all fit together	90	50–400
5. Bought out list (purchasing)—lists of all components and any materials to be purchased with the names of the suppliers specified and the assignment of the person who must do the purchasing of each part	30	15–150
6. Special drawings for the customer	10	5–30
7. Modifications—drawings of changes in the design suggested by the project engineer either while the product is being built or during the testing stage	30	20–175
	660	

or the project engineer may have found a problem or a better way to do something. We also spend about 10 hours a week on new product prototypes but almost nothing on the standard products. They have already been designed."

MECHANICAL PARTS

Graham Young, the manager of the Workshop, is responsible for the machine and welding shops, and for assembling and testing the mechanical aspects of the company's products. A layout of the shop is shown in Exhibit 7. Eight people are involved with this work. In addition to

EXHIBIT 7
CRYSTALOX LIMITED
Shop Layout

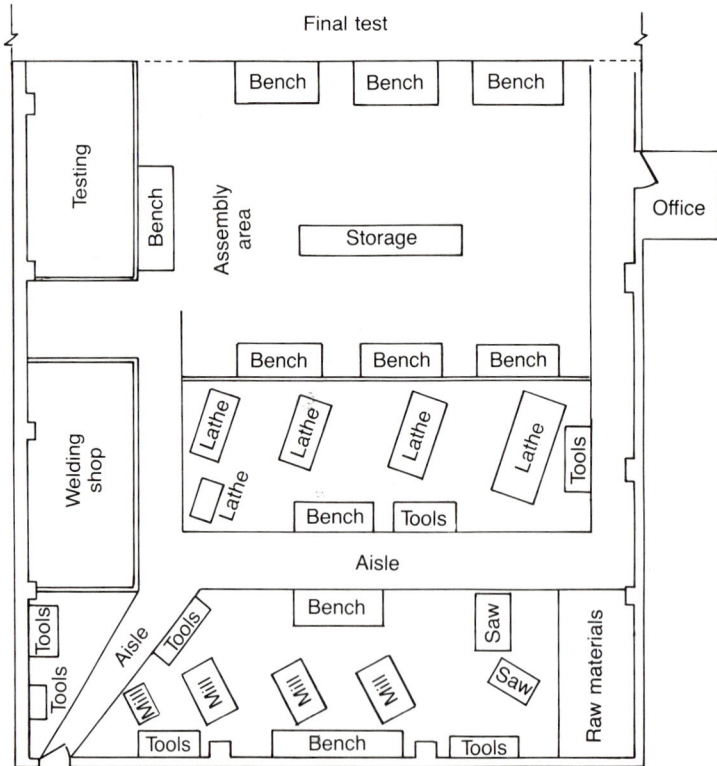

Mr. Young, there are six machinists and one welder. The workweek consists of five 7½ hour days, but they are now working about 4 hours a week overtime per person.

The special machines follow the sequence of steps and require the times presented in Exhibit 8. (The North American University machine was typical for the Workshop.) The six machinists perform all the machining (milling and lathe work) in steps 1 and 3. They can all operate each of the company's lathes and mills, so Mr. Young trys to assign them responsibility for all the machining necessary to produce an order, instead of assigning each person to a single milling machine or lathe. "This helps the people understand what they are making, gives them a greater sense of satisfaction and provides broadly trained people who give me flexibility. This will be possible as long as I have enough lathes and milling machines, as I do now," he explained.

The first machining starts with the preparation and cutting of raw materials and requires work on both the milling machines and lathes to produce parts. In the second step the parts are joined together by the welder, who is the only one who does this work. Mr. Young can do some welding, but rarely has time to help with any of the jobs in the shop. The second machining will be done on the welded parts. This step, like the first, requires work on both the milling machines and the lathes.

EXHIBIT 8
CRYSTALOX LIMITED
Steps and Labor Hours Required in the Workshop
(special machines)

Step	North American University Machine (in hours)	Range (in hours)
1. First machining		
Lathe	85	65–100
Mill	93	75–100
2. Welding	90	50–150
3. Second machining		
Lathe	235	180–270
Mill	257	225–300
4. Assembly	150	120–190
5. Test	60	40–90
	970*	

*In addition to these hours, the Workshop manager recorded a total of 86 hours for modifications to this project. The range for modifications is from 50 to 120 hours.

Crystalox subcontracts some of its work to outside machine shops. Some of it, like making the frames for the machines, could be done in-house, while such things as bending stainless steel and anodizing aluminum cannot. There is no problem finding subcontractors, although Mr. Young sometimes complains about their quality or cost. For instance, one recent set of frames was not "true" (square) and additional time was required in assembly because things didn't fit as well as they should. For purchased parts, Mr. Young uses several suppliers. "There are lots of suppliers for the common raw materials and I enjoy playing them off against one another to get the best prices," he says. "I really don't have any trouble with any of my suppliers. I can get most of the common things in 4–6 days and I just order the long lead time items as soon as we know we are going to build a machine."

Once all of the parts have been produced or received from suppliers, steps 4 and 5, the assembly and testing of the mechanical aspects of the machine, can be started. These steps consist of attaching the various parts to the frame and assuring that they can perform their intended function. For example, the vacuum system would be tested to see if it leaks and to see if it could reach the pressures required for the particular machine. The work is performed by two of the machinists with the occasional help of the welder.

Mr. Young explained: "We do more than build the special machines in here. We spend about 80 labor hours a week (50 in machining, 10 in welding, and 20 in assembly and test) on our standard products. We also have a department that is trying to develop new products. They currently require about 10 hours a week of our time for making prototypes. We also make parts for other firms.

"One Saturday, quite some time ago, a fellow walked by our shop and saw our big lathe. He came in, saw what we could do and asked us to bid on some work for him. I did and we have been doing some subcontracting for him ever since. Word of mouth about our quality and reliable delivery performance has brought us other customers as well. This business turns us a nice profit and uses my extra machine time. I get an average of £25 an hour for it, though I really sock it to a guy who needs something in a hurry. I think we could get a great deal more of this work. At the moment it's only taking about 30 hours a week in the machine shop and 10 in welding."

Mr. Young schedules the Workshop, the outside subcontracting, and the delivery of purchased components. He uses an overall estimate of 1,000 labor hours (plus 10 percent for contingencies) of Workshop time for each special machine. The schedule takes into account current work in process and the need to coordinate the production of some parts with the activities of other departments. The daily assignment of people to their jobs is in his head. "I've evolved a feeling for moving people around during my fourteen years in the business," he says. "Luckily, I was able to build up the number of people in the Workshop gradually so that I could develop my systems slowly. It's already getting a bit difficult, and I'm not sure that I'd be able to continue operating as I do now if I had to add more people. Besides, I don't know where I could put them if I had to."

He tries to adhere to the schedule but finds that it must be changed frequently. He describes the major problem as unforeseen interruptions. "The project engineers keep wanting to make changes that just weren't in the schedule. For example, we were just asked to remake some parts for a machine that we had completed last week. There was some problem in final test, and the project engineer wanted to make some changes. Now I'll have to help install those new parts as well. What they don't realize is that for every unscheduled hour they ask for, our schedule is set back two since I can't then do the work that is slotted into that time. There is additional set up time too."

"These changes can continue right up to the moment the machine is to go to the customer. The project engineers like to keep the machines around a long time so that they can fine tune them. I'm all for getting them out as soon as possible so that we can get some money in the bank. Besides, the more times a machine comes back on the shop floor after we think it's finished, the less interest people have in doing the work."

ELECTRONICS

Mike Long, manager of the Electronics Department, attends the design discussions at the beginning of a special machine project. He describes this stage as the "pinning down" phase, saying the project engineers must describe exactly what the machine specifications are so that he can design the control system and connections. He will do the detailed design of all the electronics himself. The project engineer will review the design and any required adjustments will be made before the detailed drawings are produced.

To schedule the Electronics Department's work, Mr. Long works backwards from the shipment date for the machine. For this purpose he uses a figure of 300 labor hours per special machine. The department's activities take much less time than those of the Workshop, but he must coordinate with the Workshop during the process, since some of the control equipment is mounted on parts produced by them. Exhibit 9 shows the process steps in the Electronics Department, along with the times required for each.

All subassemblies for the control system, which connect to the other systems (vacuum, heating, power, gas analysis, etc.), are produced in-house. In the Electronics Department, in addition to Mr. Long, there is one person who is employed especially to string the wires during assembly, and two persons for fabrication of subassemblies (who can also help on the assembly and test). All of the subassemblies will be tested individually before they are connected together. The recent installation of programmable logic in the control systems has allowed Mr. Long to increase flexibility and reduce the assembly time to its current value.

Mr. Long keeps several suppliers on tap and has never experienced trouble with any of them. For the everyday items he can get delivery in two days, and the suppliers are very price competitive. The purchased components are tested before being installed on a machine. The suppliers have never caused a delay for the department and, as Mr. Long says, "We usually get our special machine work done ahead of schedule now. We also work about 20 labor hours a week in subassembly fabrications and 5 hours a week in assembly and test on standard products, and about 1 hour a week on prototypes of new products."

EXHIBIT 9
CRYSTALOX LIMITED
Steps and Labor Hours Required in Electronics
(special machines)

Step	North American University Machine* (in hours)	Range (in hours)
1. Design	44.5	30–100
2. Fabrication of subassemblies	178.0	170–250
3. Assembly and test	7.5	5–80
	230.0	

*This project was not typical from the Electronics Department's standpoint. For planning purposes, the Electronics' manager uses 60 hours, 200 hours, and 40 hours for design, fabrication, and assembly/test, respectively.

FINAL TEST

Project engineers are responsible for final testing once final assembly is completed. The test involves checking the temperature profile, melt capabilities, growth mechanism, and so on. Sometimes the project engineers will even grow crystals on the machine. They also like to make very sure everything is right at this stage, since they often must go out to the customer's site to "commission" the machine. The average time in final test is about 220 labor hours, with a range from 100 to 600 (in addition to the 90 hours for general coordination). The project engineers also spend about 4 hours a week testing standard products.

According to Dr. Garrard, "The testing time we get is never as long as it should be. All the problems from Design, Workshop, and Electronics eat into the testing time. Problems often occur just because we're on the fringe of technology, and we must make changes to make the machine perform up to specifications. Often, we also find some ways to make real improvements in performance. But at times we're just squeezed. I remember one special machine that hadn't even been put up to the required temperature before the customer came for the acceptance test.

"What the shop people don't seem to understand is that we are making the changes to improve the product for the customer. These interruptions are part of our business and must be accepted." He continued, "The shipment date is like a brick wall. We can't usually extend it, so we get squeezed in final test." Exhibit 10 shows the delivery performance for some special machines and standard products.

The company has earned a fine reputation for quality products. Very rarely are there problems once they have been sent out. Most problems that do occur can usually be solved over the phone. Crystalox has occasionally sent someone out to do some work on products in the field, however. The project engineers argue that the quality image could be in jeopardy if final test continues to get squeezed for time.

IMPROVING PRODUCTION

Mr. Boerve has taken some initial steps in the process of improving the production activities. For instance, a time and cost reporting system has been implemented. An example of the breakdown of costs now possible is shown in Exhibit 11 for the North American University machine. The

EXHIBIT 10
CRYSTALOX LIMITED
Product Delivery Performance

	Due in Final Test	Arrive in Final Test	Shipment Promised	Actual Shipment
Special machines:				
1061	N.A.	N.A.	Oct 4, 1985	Oct 4, 1985
1098	Dec 1, 1985	Dec 19, 1985	Feb 10, 1986	Feb 10, 1986
1123*	Dec 5, 1986	Dec 19, 1986	Jan 19, 1987	Jan 14, 1987
1176	Dec 19, 1986	Jan 7, 1987	Feb 27, 1987	Feb 24, 1987
Standard products with project engineering:				
1152	Sept 28, 1986	Oct 10, 1986	Oct 30, 1986	Oct 28, 1986
Standard products with no project engineering:				
1024			Sept 9, 1986	Sept 8, 1986
1193			Sept 5, 1986	Sept 5, 1986

N.A. = Not available.
*North American University machine.

EXHIBIT 11
CRYSTALOX LIMITED
Costs Associated with North American University Machine*
(in pounds sterling)

Workshop:	
Materials	£ 4,500
Labour (at £ 9.43 per hour)	10,241
Parts purchased outside	11,925
Subcontracting	2,500
Electronics:	
Materials	3,796
Labour (at £15.48 per hour)	3,560
Parts purchased outside	3,721
Subcontracting	4,180
Design Office:	
Labour (at £13.44 per hour)	8,870
Project Engineering:	
Labour (at £16.25 per hour)	4,631
Parts purchased outside	27,204

*Revenue received for this project was £107,000.

reporting system has not helped explain the delays in getting to the final testing stage, however.

To meet the budget projections for the next year, production output will need to be increased. It would require producing about 10 special machines and the standard product business would need to increase by about 20 percent as well. Mr. Boerve said, "Production has got to produce—we have doubled the number of people in the last year, and our overheads are high. I would like to see sales increase to £1,400,000 next year to cover these costs. Production is going to have to perform."

He is hesitant to suggest subcontracting more work to outside firms because of possible delivery and quality problems. He also feels that Crystalox has developed some special manufacturing skills, and the ability of the Workshop to sell subcontracted parts seems to support this contention. Besides, he felt some production capacity was needed to support the project engineers. Dr. Hukin explained, "When a project engineer is having a difficult time with his machine in final test, he needs all the support he can get. We have a machine in final test right now that's a good example. It is right at the edge of technology and I know we can make it perform, but the project engineer is spending day and night trying to get it right. Each time he makes a change, he needs a couple of parts right away and we have to be able to supply him."

THE PROPOSAL

Mr. Boerve knows that he must deal with the proposal to move the machine shop out to a different location. The proposal recommends that all the machine tools and the welding equipment be moved to a different location several miles away. Graham Young feels that having some distance between Crystalox and the shop would mean fewer interruptions by the project engineers. He also feels that the current level of Crystalox special machines and standard products will serve as a solid business base for the enterprise, but that there is a great deal of other general machine shop business available to them. Per Dybwad, from Elkem, was enthusiastic about the idea. "This could be a way to absorb some of the increased overhead. We have already seen that there is a market for the service. Besides, what's wrong with filling up the extra capacity with cash-generating business? Of course, Crystalox would have to have priority for production time."

Mr. Boerve mused, "In the past our machine projects have required more brain power than machine power. But now I'm wondering if we are experiencing a shift in the type of business we are doing, with more of an emphasis on the machine power, and if this is putting a burden on production. Over the last year we have done some standardization, have sold some special machines similar to ones we'd made before, and have introduced our line of standard products. Maybe these factors are changing the manufacturing part." "It's clear the character of the place has changed," Dr. Hukin added. "The families of the workers used to come around and see the special machines before we shipped them off to the customers. They even wanted their pictures taken with the machines. That kind of thing is happening less frequently now."

APPENDIX

The crystal machines that are sold by Crystalox go into laboratories around the world. The research that is performed on the crystals that they produce is concerned with things like the electrical properties, the light transmission properties, and so on. In addition to the use of silicon crystals for microchips, other crystals have found use in night vision systems, laser beams in various wavelengths, and superconductive materials. The potential for future applications of crystals of various kinds is just being discovered, hence the research interest. The rapid and wide adaptation of glass fibre for transmission of information is an example of the potential. Lasers have great potential for transmission of energy in addition to information. The light transmitting and detecting properties of other materials have just begun to be understood. The potential uses, other than night vision systems, are still being explored, but include things like detecting various waves from outer space and transmission of great amounts of energy efficiently.

Great interest has been expressed in growing crystals in space to enhance their purity and symmetry. The space connection does not stop at increasing the purity attributes of the crystals, however. The use of ever purer crystals for detection and separation of various waves from space has great potential for improving human understanding of the universe. The military is involved, as well, looking for the strength, energy transmission, and detection capabilities of pure crystals. In some cases, impurities are introduced into the crystals to give them other properties. Much of the future for these kinds of materials is yet to be discovered.

Alpine Tobacco GmbH

Georg Bader, the director of engineering at Alpine Tobacco GmbH, sat in his office gazing out over the Austrian countryside. It was the fall of 1985 and Georg had just received news that the recent initiative to increase automation in the Innsbruck factory had received approval from the parent company of Alpine Tobacco, which was located in the southern part of the United States. This approval was for an investment of ASch. 250 million[1] and would permit a major overhaul of the secondary cigarette processes at the company. Georg doubted that Alpine had ever faced such a challenge. The investment program would mean a higher level of automation later and disruption on the shop floor as the equipment was installed. The program would result in the replacement of some of the existing cigarette machinery and further mechanical linkages of the cigarette makers with the packaging processes.

The automation investment was not the only program in manufacturing, however, because Georg Bader and his staff had also developed a plan for improving productivity through the implementation of a shop floor management information system dubbed the SIS. Many U.S. plants had already made substantial investments in shop floor information systems and the feeling in the U.S. Head Office Systems Group (HOSG) was that the European plants could take what was needed from the U.S. systems already developed. Georg Bader disagreed strongly with the HOSG viewpoint:

"My problem is that our markets and product mix are very different from those served by the U.S. plants. They serve large markets with few products. We deliver a large number of products to many markets, some of which are very small. We deal with as many as 70 different brands. On top of this, the quality demands for our products are much higher in Europe than in the United States. One small example of this is in filter specifications where our designs are much more complex than

---

[1] In 1985, the exchange rate was ASch. 21 per U.S. $.

those in the United States. The American suggestion that we use the management information systems they have already developed is all very well, but their systems were developed years ago and use outdated computing equipment. In addition, their management information systems operate in a batch mode, whereas we are aiming at real-time responses to improve operating efficiency."

"The pressure is on us to improve our productivity, and we have a good track record. Our operating costs in terms of cigarettes/manhour continue to decrease, yet our markets have declined (as shown in Exhibit 1). We have an excellent work force and make some of the best cigarettes in the business measured by objective industry criteria. But I get very frustrated with blockages to the logical continuation of our progress. And my frustration is not improved with the knowledge that as our operating costs decline, the costs of head office overhead, particularly HOSG, rise to offset all our efforts. To extract the best from our automation program, we need the shop floor management information system to highlight those areas where we can get the best returns from our efforts. The automation, by itself, will not give us any more information about the opportunities for further productivity improvements. We need the continuous monitoring of processes and an information system pulling the monitoring data together to do this."

EXHIBIT 1
ALPINE TOBACCO GmbH
Five-Year Trends 1980–1985

	1980	*1985*	
Volume of cigarettes sold	19 billion	12.5 billion	
Approximate number of different:			
Packaging specifications	150	150	Relatively
Brands	70	70	constant
Filters	50	50	
Quality index*	30	10	

*The scale was 0–100 with 0 the high end of quality; 20 was considered very good; some competitive brands were rated as low as 60.

ALPINE TOBACCO

Situated on the outskirts of Innsbruck, Austria, with excellent road and rail connections to the major centers of European commerce, Alpine Tobacco was one of several European manufacturing locations of a large North-American-based cigarette and tobacco manufacturer. The development of Europe into two major trading blocks, the European Economic Community (EEC) and the European Free Trade Area (EFTA), had virtually required that manufacturers of tobacco products have a presence in both. However, the changing membership patterns had created an increasingly large market within the EEC and EFTA members and others moved to join it. This large-scale restructuring of country alliances had very real implications for EFTA-based Alpine Tobacco; many of their traditional markets were now being supplied from plants within the EEC. Alpine Tobacco, therefore, supplied about 60 percent of its output to such non-EEC markets of Europe as Norway, Finland, and Sweden in Scandinavia, and Switzerland and Austria in Central Europe. Unfortunately these countries each had relatively small populations, and yet each required separate specifications for even common product brands. These individual specifications ranged from the packaging, which was in different languages for each of the countries, to content specifications, which differed according to the laws of each country, and even to blends and flavors, which often differed by country for the same brand. This accounted for a large number of packaging specifications in relation to the number of brands (Exhibit 1).

The reduced market possibilities within Western Europe had made it necessary for Alpine Tobacco to seek new markets in increasing numbers. These markets included Eastern Europe, Africa, and Asia. They had risen to account for about 30 percent of Alpine's current production output. However, though the plant had been designed to supply world markets, the net effect of the increased supply of the EEC market from within the EEC had been a decline in the overall business for Alpine Tobacco. Indeed, business had fallen from a 1980 high of 19 billion cigarettes to an expected volume of 12.5 billion in 1985.[2]

Alpine's reputation for quality was extremely high and there was a possibility that they could meet the requirements of the promising mar-

---

[2]One billion = one thousand million.

ket in Japan. A modest entry in this market would mean a substantial increase in volume for the company.

DEMAND MANAGEMENT

European demand profiles were far from constant. There were considerable seasonal variations in overall demand, particularly in the countries supplied by Alpine. These countries enjoyed substantial tourist traffic, and this resulted in seasonal demands in tobacco products which became particularly heavy during the summer months, and over the winter sports period starting in December.

The somewhat random nature of the visitor mix caused an additional problem for Alpine Tobacco, because the swings in demand were accompanied by unpredictable changes in product mix requirements. Demand in non-European countries followed an even less predictable pattern.

The difficulty of predicting demand even for relatively captive geographical markets meant that a supply of finished goods was necessary to ensure that stockouts were kept to a minimum. These were kept in a large warehouse on the plant site. In the fall of 1985, this inventory represented two months of production. There was a considerable incentive to keep this inventory small because a tax was paid to the Austrian government amounting to ASch. 8 per pack of 20 cigarettes on the manufacture of the cigarettes. This tax was recoverable later if the cigarettes were exported.

Filling the orders for Austria and other countries within EFTA had not proved to be a problem. Using inventory, these orders could normally be satisfied in one to two weeks. Orders from other areas were often large, and a single order could represent as much as 20 percent of the total annual European business supplied by Alpine. This made them more difficult to handle. Lead times for these orders were in the three- to six-month range, with shipments being made in batches over this time.

Senior management in the United States had set a goal of reducing the warehouse stocks at Alpine to one month's supply. To help in this process, a software package which had originally been developed to control inventories in the automobile industry was being implemented for both manufacturing and distribution inventory planning. Georg Bader felt that the management people in both manufacturing and distribution were currently "up to their eyes" in problems. They were trying to cope with implementing the new system for inventory control and yet at the same time were running the business using their traditional systems. These traditional systems were very rudimentary and used rough rules of thumb to set inventory levels, rather than using order status or knowledge of the manufacturing situation.

THE CIGARETTE MAKING PROCESS

The cigarette making process at Alpine Tobacco followed the classical pattern of the tobacco industry. The process had two stages, commonly referred to as the primary and secondary. The primary department contained all the processes dealing with the preparation of tobacco prior to the actual cigarette manufacture. The secondary stage dealt with manufacturing filters and cigarettes, and with packaging and preparation for shipping.

Primary

A detailed diagram of the primary process flow is given in Exhibit 2. The primary operations were essentially concerned with the conversion of raw tobacco leaves into a form suitable for assembly into a cigarette. During the primary processes, other ingredients were added to the raw tobacco. These were mainly flavorings which were added at various stages of the primary process.

There were several key steps in the primary operation. One was conditioning. The objective of conditioning was to maintain the tobacco at a predetermined temperature and moisture level to ensure maximum yield from the tobacco throughout the process. Approximately 20 tobacco grades were blended into the four basic generic types—Burley, Virginia, Maryland, and Oriental—that were used to make Alpine's brands. Evaluating the conditioning of the leaf for Alpine Tobacco's process involved substantial judgment by skilled workers.

Another important step in the primary operation was casing. Casing was the process through which such flavors as sugar, chocolate, or honey were added to the tobacco. After casing came some drying to fix the flavor to the leaf and then the application of "top flavor." The tobacco was then blended according to a particular recipe. Subsequently, it was conditioned further, cut, and dried.

EXHIBIT 2
ALPINE TOBACCO GmbH
The Primary Process

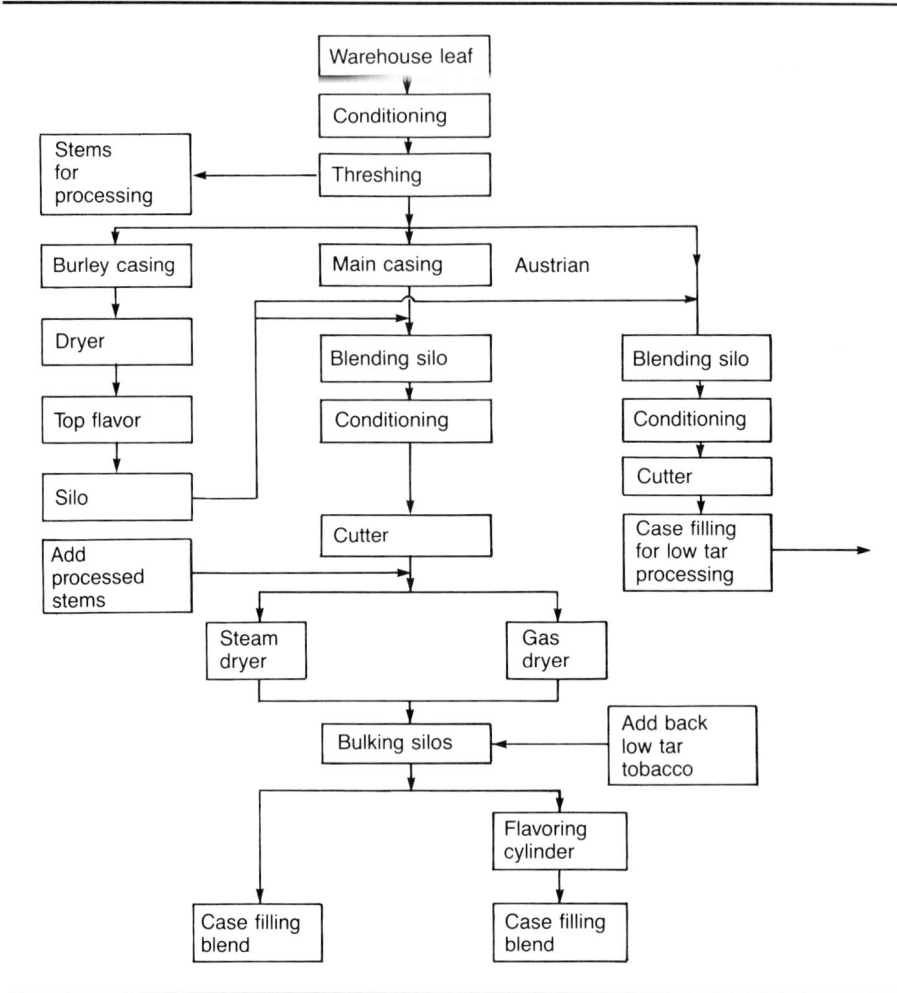

```
                           ┌─────────────────┐
                           │ Warehouse leaf  │
                           └────────┬────────┘
                                    ▼
                           ┌─────────────────┐
                           │  Conditioning   │
                           └────────┬────────┘
   ┌──────────────┐                 ▼
   │ Stems        │        ┌─────────────────┐
   │ for          │◄───────│   Threshing     │
   │ processing   │        └────────┬────────┘
   └──────────────┘                 │
   ┌──────────────┐        ┌─────────────────┐
   │ Burley casing│        │  Main casing    │  Austrian
   └──────┬───────┘        └────────┬────────┘
   ┌──────────────┐        ┌─────────────────┐   ┌─────────────────┐
   │ Dryer        │        │ Blending silo   │   │ Blending silo   │
   └──────┬───────┘        └────────┬────────┘   └────────┬────────┘
   ┌──────────────┐        ┌─────────────────┐   ┌─────────────────┐
   │ Top flavor   │        │  Conditioning   │   │  Conditioning   │
   └──────┬───────┘        └────────┬────────┘   └────────┬────────┘
   ┌──────────────┐                              ┌─────────────────┐
   │ Silo         │                              │   Cutter        │
   └──────┬───────┘        ┌─────────────────┐   └────────┬────────┘
   ┌──────────────┐        │   Cutter        │   ┌─────────────────┐
   │ Add          │        └────────┬────────┘   │ Case filling    │
   │ processed    │                              │ for low tar     │──►
   │ stems        │                              │ processing      │
   └──────────────┘                              └─────────────────┘
        ┌─────────────────┐       ┌─────────────────┐
        │ Steam           │       │ Gas             │
        │ dryer           │       │ dryer           │
        └────────┬────────┘       └────────┬────────┘
                 ┌─────────────────┐       ┌─────────────────┐
                 │ Bulking silos   │◄──────│ Add back        │
                 └────────┬────────┘       │ low tar         │
                          │                │ tobacco         │
                          │                └─────────────────┘
                          │       ┌─────────────────┐
                          │       │ Flavoring       │
                          │       │ cylinder        │
                          │       └────────┬────────┘
        ┌─────────────────┐       ┌─────────────────┐
        │ Case filling    │       │ Case filling    │
        │ blend           │       │ blend           │
        └─────────────────┘       └─────────────────┘
```

After processing, the cut, flavored, and blended tobacco was put into storage in cases. This case inventory amounted to 1 to 2 days of normal production. There could be about 40 different blends at this stage, though the normal number was closer to 25. One blend could make as many as ten brands, a brand being a particular combination of paper, filter and tobacco.

Tobacco accounted for roughly 60 percent of the standard total manufacturing cost of a cigarette. Other materials (e.g., filter, packaging, paper) amounted to about 25 percent, while operations costs accounted for the remainder. One kilogram of tobacco made approximately 1,200 cigarettes. The standard total manufacturing cost amounted to about ASch. 150 per 1,000 cigarettes, including packing.

Secondary

The overall flow of the secondary process is given in Exhibit 3. By and large, all the steps from filter making through cigarette making and the various stages of packing could be considered as independent operations. However, Alpine Tobacco had made some advances in automating and linking the operations of cigarette making, packing, and bundling into cartons. Increasing the number of linkages throughout the secondary process was the principal objective of the automation program at Alpine Tobacco.

EXHIBIT 3
ALPINE TOBACCO GmbH
The Secondary Process

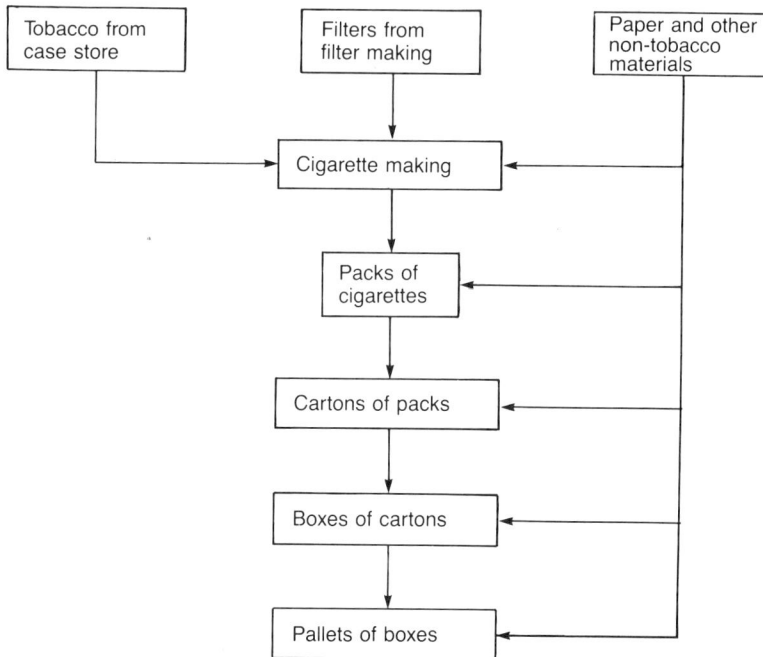

The secondary processes began with the making of filters. Alpine Tobacco made approximately 50 types of filters, and the operations people were continually pushing to reduce the number of filter varieties. Hans Lucien, Alpine Tobacco's chief project engineer, commented:

"We do make progress in gaining some standardization and we can get the company to cut back, say, six filters after much effort. But the problem is that R&D and then marketing come out with even more ideas for new products and we end up back where we started. The European market is the most complicated in the world. We make single, double, and even triple filters from a variety of materials."

The simplest filter made by Alpine Tobacco was of white acetate. This was made by a process which ended with a continuous rod sufficient for 6 cigarettes. Double and triple filters used other materials such as charcoal between the simple acetate filters to form the additional filters. The multifilter sets were also made into rods suitable for six cigarettes. The filters could not be used directly after being made, but required six hours to one day for hardening.

The filter machines came in two types: normal and combination. There were 7 machines which made white normal filters (80 percent utilization) and one which made semi-finished black normal filters (25–30 percent utilization). The other 12 machines in the filter making department made combinations (15–20 percent utilization).

The filter rods varied in length according to the specification of the cigarette brand. Filter variety depended therefore not only on the materials used, whether single, double, or triple, but also on the dimensions of the filter. The large variety of filters and long setup times on the machines for making a specific filter had led Alpine management to dedicate machines for the major filter varieties. An inventory of filters amounting to some six to seven months' supply was held in the company warehouse to ensure that the filter making process did not delay cigarette manufacture. Mr. Lucien commented:

"The low utilization levels of many of our filter making machines are considered important to preserve operating flexibility. While the setup time to change from one filter type to another with the same dimensions could be as little as two to four hours, a dimension change could take as long as one month. Utilization here is measured as run time divided by available machine time, where available machine time excludes maintenance and setup times. In spite of our apparent excess of machine capacity, we try not to keep an excess of manpower."

The heart of the secondary operation was undoubtedly the cigarette making machine itself. Here tobacco transported by pneumatic and conveyor systems was monitored carefully by automatic systems to form a uniform tobacco rod. The diameter of the rod approximated that of a cigarette. Paper was rolled around the tobacco and subsequently glued. The cigarette machine also printed the brand name on the cigarette paper. So critical was the weight of each cigarette that it was automatically monitored by a sophisticated control system employing Beta-radiation, and the cigarette paper was automatically checked for the degree of ventilation. The weight checking system monitored the amount of tobacco supplied to each cigarette. A readout of the average and standard deviation of the cigarette weights was provided and cigarettes not within control limits were rejected by the system. Cigarettes not meeting ventilation specifications were also rejected. Georg Bader estimated that the secondary process currently had about a 5 percent reject rate. The rejects were subsequently reprocessed but resulted in a scrap loss of all the non-tobacco materials and about 30 percent of the tobacco.

There were three generations of cigarette making machines at Alpine. The most modern machine operated at about 8,000 cigarettes per minute (cpm). Alpine had only one of these machines and operated it at close to maximum utilization. Alpine had 15 machines of the previous generation which could operate at 4,000–5,000 cpm. Ten of these were already linked to a packaging operation and operated at close to maximum capacity utilization. The remaining five of these machines were free-standing and their capacity utilizations varied from 25–80 percent. The oldest generation of cigarette machines at Alpine operated at 1,500–3,000 cpm. There were 20 such machines, some of which were kept as reserves. The highest capacity utilization of the oldest generation amounted to about 25 percent.

Linking a typical cigarette making machine directly to a packer had been made possible by upgrading the packer speed to that of the cigarette maker. The cost of linking two free-standing units together was approximately ASch. 2.5 million. This linking resulted in the saving of just over one operator out of eight on a two-shift basis (about ½ operator per shift). This saving was partly offset by a reduction in machine utilization caused by major breakdowns which affected both machines in the linked condition. A small amount of inventory was kept between the maker and packer for this eventuality, but it was insufficient to offset the utilization reduction entirely.

The setup time for changing brands on a cigarette maker was from two to four hours, provided dimensions remained unchanged. Dimension changes, such as incorporating a longer filter, could take several weeks, and thus were not often done. There was little difference between the setup times of the three equipment generations.

Packaging was a highly automated process. Finished cigarettes were fed into the packaging machines and combined into packs of cigarettes. The formation of the packs into bundles of 10 packs (cartons) was also part of the packing process. The packs were either soft or hard, and each type was made on different machinery. There were 6 machines for making soft packs and 10 machines for hard packs. A soft pack had an inner wrap (usually of foil) and a soft outer wrap of paper. A hard pack normally had an inner wrap, a cardboard box outer and then an outer see-through wrap in addition. The normal setup time for packers was considered to be about two days, but an extensive change involving size or count adjustments could require two weeks to a month. Small changes in setup, however, could take much less than two days. The utilization of packaging machinery varied widely. Machines dedicated to popular brands operated at close to maximum capacity, whereas those for low-demand brands operated at 5–10 percent capacity utilization.

The final stage of the packaging process was the packaging of cartons into boxes and the formation of pallets from boxes. This process had been already automated by Alpine Tobacco and was performed by a robot.

MANNING

The target manning at Alpine Tobacco was calculated using the planned annual output level of 12.5 billion cigarettes. This level could be produced by a total direct work force amounting to 450 workers. Each of these received an average of ASch. 400,000 a year (including social benefits). Manning of the primary required 95 people, and the secondary, 300 people. The remaining 55 workers were in the filter department. Calculation of primary manning was based on the assumption that a primary worker could process approximately 130,000 kilograms of tobacco per year. Actual manning was somewhat higher than the target levels. Mr. Lucien commented, "Our current performance is around 13,500 cigarettes/direct labor hour, which does not compare well with some of the high-volume plants with few brands which have 80 percent higher productivity than we do. We simply must work harder to improve our performance."

The primary and the secondary areas operated different shift systems. The primary operated a single shift from 07:00–16:00 hours with an hour off for lunch. The secondary operated a two-shift system—06:00–14:00 hours and 14:00–22:00 hours. Thus the primary capacity could be increased relatively simply by working overtime. Increasing secondary capacity would require the use of temporary workers or Saturday work. On this subject, Mr. Lucien stated:

"The recent decline in volume in this plant has brought this shift pattern about. However, we do not anticipate any problems with the work force should we receive a non-European order for, say, 1 billion cigarettes. The workers are aware that some 40 or so left the work force last year through natural attrition and were not replaced. They are anxious to maintain the company's success."

AUTOMATION AND TECHNOLOGICAL CHANGE

The drive for increased productivity had been an ever-present pressure at Alpine Tobacco. Mr. Bader:

"This is a very competitive industry but we feel this competition more than most. We are the subsidiary of a U.S. company and the loss of markets to the EEC has put increasing pressure on us to perform competitively worldwide. Because of this we have been quite innovative with our own processes. We have installed process control on one dryer, and have extensive computer support on the secondary shop floor to pinpoint operating system failures. In addition, we have developed our own automatic boxing system. We are also well advanced in linking individual systems together, particularly cigarette making and packing. This has been done by using expandable storage to link the processes to supply sufficient work-in-process inventory to see us through breakdowns. We are currently linking our highest speed cigarette maker with a packer. The recently approved automation plan is for similar linkages between other makers and packers.

"Our old cigarette making machines are the Mk 8 and Mk 9 models of a British manufacturer. The latest machine installed, however, has much better economic performance (see Exhibit 4 for a performance comparison and for the capital cost of the latest generation machinery). Indeed, the performance improvement of these machines has been remarkable over the past five years. But there is a real question of how these performance trends fit our business.

"We think that our current automation program provides an excel-

EXHIBIT 4
ALPINE TOBACCO GmbH
Performance of Cigarette Making Machines

Performance Comparison

MACHINE:	*Mk 9*	*Protos**
	(1980 technology)	(1985 technology)
Manning	9	7
Speed	4,000–5,000 cigs/min.	8,000 cigs/min.
Capacity/year	650 million	1,150 million†

Performance Trend in Machine Speed

1980: 5,000 cigs/min.
1983: 6,000 cigs/min.
1984: 7,000 cigs/min.
1985: 8,000 cigs/min.

Typical Capital Costs—Latest Equipment Generation

Cigarette maker	ASch. 14 million
Packer	ASch. 15 million
Automatic boxer	ASch. 2 million
Connection devices for automation	ASch. 13 million

*This is a West German machine. The manufacturer of the Mk 9 offered a new generation of machines with similar performance.
†Assumes 220 days per year, 14.5 hrs/day and 75 percent utilization.

lent opportunity for installing a shop floor reporting system to allow us to highlight unknown problem areas. These are the areas that are opportunities for us. Tobacco costs are $5–$6 per kilogram, so a saving of even 1 percent would be very substantial. Of course, our system is very good already, so a 1 percent overall saving would be hard to achieve. However, even a 0.25–0.50 percent saving would be very significant."

SHOP FLOOR MANAGEMENT INFORMATION

The Manufacturing Engineering Department gave the following trends as reasons for developing the new shop floor management information system (SIS) plans:

- As machines become more sophisticated, their high investment cost makes for increasingly expensive downtime.

- Higher speed production raises the need for constant quality monitoring.
- Reduction in manning requires more automation and automatic control.

The aim of the proposed SIS was to work toward perfect quality through better identification of the causes of production problems, be it in making or packaging, and through optimizing machine settings, improving machines and materials, and through training. Future material savings were thought possible only if the process was monitored and measured better. The deficiencies of the existing system were felt to be quite general, even though one process control computer was in place in the primary area and other systems monitored the cigarette making machines to allow quick diagnosis of failure. More accurate, complete, and timely information was felt necessary to achieve SIS objectives at a managerial level.

The SIS proposal also aimed at improving the level of information received by shop floor operators and supervisors. This would require sensor data or coupled signals from machines to be gathered by a microcomputer and then transferred to a central computer for overall data processing and production reporting. The data would be continuously recorded, allowing for a report of the overall production situation at any time. Output data, productivity analyses, rejects and the number of breakdowns (and their reasons) would be displayed on request. Major additional information would be yield and quality analysis.

One percent of the existing 5 percent scrap was judged to be avoidable with the SIS system. To achieve this, hardware modifications requiring approximately $1 million (ASch. 21 million) and a computer costing $500,000 would be necessary. Software estimated at $300,000 would also be necessary, but the cost of this could be defrayed by Alpine's sister European plants if they accepted the SIS concept.

USA

The presentation of Alpine's SIS proposal in the USA set some real uncertainties for Georg Bader. The traditional policy of the U.S. parent for worldwide standardization and compatibility with U.S. systems was driven by the many hundreds of computer programs which had been developed for managerial information in the United States. The company's central U.S. data processing department employed almost as many people as did Alpine in its factory. Though Alpine's Manufacturing Engineering Department felt that the U.S. management information systems were quite out of date, they recognized that the balance of power did not lie in their favor. Also, Alpine's management felt their needs to be substantially different from those of the U.S. plant requirements. In addition to product, volume, and quality differences, European reporting requirements for the shop floor would differ by the country's language—and hardware needs would vary by plant size. Thus Georg Bader wanted to make as strong a justification as possible.

THE NEXT STEP

As Georg Bader thought about submitting a capital request for the SIS, he thought of the problems ahead. Relationships were excellent between Manufacturing Engineering and Manufacturing, but the automation project would take a lot of energy and good will. The logistics function, which managed both supplies to Alpine Tobacco and the distribution of finished products, had always supported the plant's initiatives, but were very busy with the new inventory control software. In addition, due to a shortage of personnel, relationships had been difficult with the Information Systems Department at Alpine, and Georg felt they were unlikely to support SIS unless it was their project. On the other hand, the recent approval for Alpine's automation program demonstrated headquarter's support for the productivity drive at Alpine.

The reduction of factory volumes because of lost markets was a very sensitive issue, and it was clear to Georg that the way to ensure world market competitiveness was through being superior in both cost and quality. Only through such a strategy could Alpine Tobacco hope to gain entry into potentially major international markets. He wondered how he should frame the proposal to headquarters.

The Central Tracing Agency of the International Committee of the Red Cross

Mr. François Perez was appointed head of the Central Tracing Agency (the Agency) shortly after he returned from a nineteen-week executive program at a well-known European international management institute. During the period he was away a major reorganization of the Agency had been worked out, paving the way for him to apply some of the concepts he had acquired in the program. As he reflected on the challenge before him, he said: "I was aware of the reorganization, and felt that it would be more responsive to future needs. My job is to use the organization effectively. We have some very skilled and dedicated persons in the Agency and I must see to it that the changes don't diminish their goodwill."

Mr. Perez had chosen to focus his initial efforts on the activities at the home office in Geneva. The computer was located in Geneva, and improving the effectiveness of computer use was a high priority. The efforts in Geneva should have general application later to the activities in other areas of the world. Much of the work of the Agency involved close cooperation with the national Red Cross Societies in many countries of the world. To maintain the goodwill of these societies, Mr. Perez knew that the communication channels had to be kept open. Therefore, he was planning a seminar to discuss the developments in Geneva, and to help the national societies coordinate among themselves and with the Agency. Mr. Perez summed up the task ahead of him by saying, "We're trying to improve the productivity of a group of very skilled professional people who are providing a variety of services to a changing world where there is little prospect for certain planning."

BACKGROUND

The Red Cross is well known as an organization offering humanitarian services all over the world in times of international and non-international conflicts, internal disturbances, and natural disasters. The founding committee (the International Committee of the Red Cross, the ICRC) located in Geneva, Switzerland, provides its services in all locations of conflict. The Central Tracing Agency is part of the ICRC, as

EXHIBIT 1
THE CENTRAL TRACING AGENCY OF THE INTERNATIONAL COMMITTEE OF THE RED CROSS
The International Committee of the Red Cross Organization

```
                        ASSEMBLY
                        EXECUTIVE
                          BOARD

        Chief
        Medical         DIRECTORATE        Management
        Officer                            Controller

      General            Operational        Administrative
      Affairs            Activities         Affairs

              Principles              Central                    Finance
  Information  and      Operations    Tracing     Personnel      and
               Law                    Agency                     Administration
```

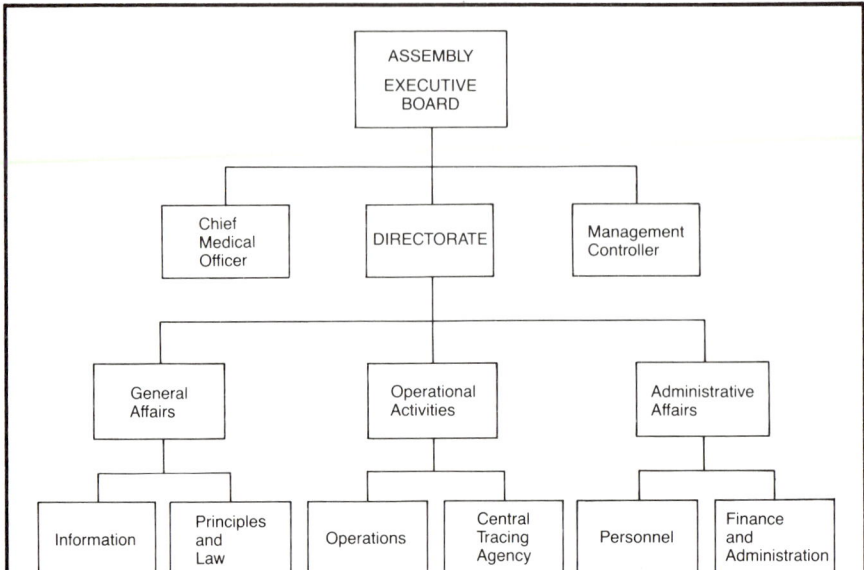

Don't be misled by the name—the *International Committee of the Red Cross is a private Swiss organization,* subject to Swiss law and made up of Swiss citizens. But it is quite independent of the Swiss, or any other government. It remains neutral regardless of political, ideological or religious considerations.

The international aspect of the ICRC is its field of action, and the way it gets its funds, mainly through voluntary contributions by governments and national Red Cross Societies.

The *Committee* itself is composed of prominent Swiss (maximum membership twenty-five) who share a respect for Red Cross principles and who have wide-ranging experience of international problems. They meet in *Assembly* about eight times a year. The Assembly is the supreme policy-making body; it lays down principles and general policy and supervises all ICRC activities.

The *Executive Board,* comprising up to seven members, is responsible for running the ICRC's affairs and supervising its administration. Both the Assembly and the Executive Board are chaired by the ICRC President.

The *Directorate,* which is responsible for management,is composed of three directors, each of whom is in charge of one of the following: General Affairs (covering the departments of Information and Principles and Law); Operational Activities (Operations Department and the Central Tracing Agency); Administrative Affairs (departments of Personnel and Finance and Administration). The Medical Division and that of International Organizations are both under the direction of Operational Activities, while the Financing Division is under Administrative Affairs.

seen in Exhibit 1. The National Red Cross and Red Crescent Societies operate primarily in their own countries, providing the disaster relief and other services for which the Red Cross is so well known. The relationships among the various organizations are shown in Exhibit 2.

Shortly after the establishment of the ICRC in 1863, the "Agency of Basel" was created to list, for the first time ever, the names of the prisoners of war (POWs) and to provide relief to the sick and wounded of the Franco-Prussian War of 1870–71. The list of POW names enabled them to provide information to the victims' families. This agency was the earliest predecessor to the Central Tracing Agency of today. Over the years the activities of the Agency have changed, and the name has changed as well. Aid to prisoners during World War I lead to the crea-

EXHIBIT 2
THE CENTRAL TRACING AGENCY OF THE INTERNATIONAL RED CROSS
The Red Cross Family

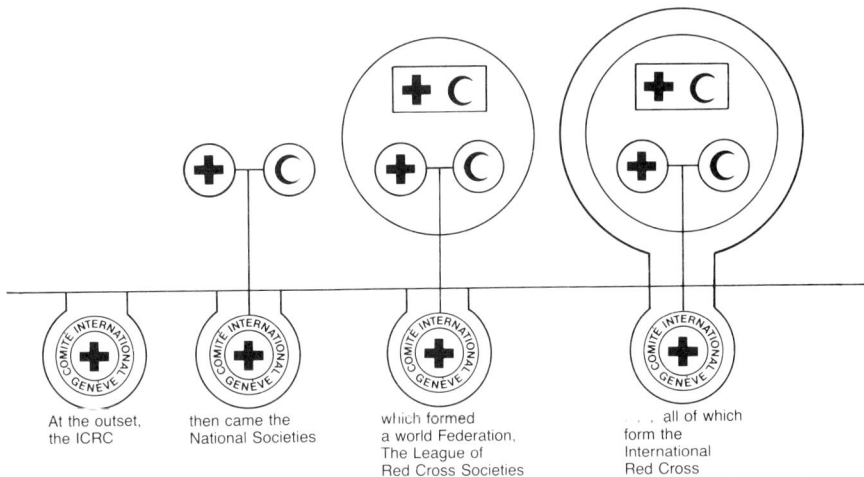

| At the outset, the ICRC | then came the National Societies | which formed a world Federation, The League of Red Cross Societies | . . , all of which form the International Red Cross |

Everybody has heard of "The Red Cross."
But how much do people know *about* the Red Cross?

We have seen that the ICRC was at the origin of the Red Cross movement. Next came the national Red Cross and Red Crescent Societies — a vast family whose members now number 230 million people of all races and creeds. Then there is the League of Red Cross and Red Crescent Societies.
Finally, we have the International Red Cross.
What is the difference between them all?

The *ICRC* as a neutral intermediary, carries out its work worldwide, mainly in times of armed conflicts, internal strife and other man-made disasters.
The *National Societies* work within their own countries and assist the public authorities. Their services include health and nursing care, relief programmes for victims of natural disasters and those in need, youth problems, spreading knowledge of Red Cross principles, blood donaton and similar activities. The Societies also take part in the Red Cross programmes of international aid.

The *League of Red Cross Societies* is the world federation of national societies and acts as their co-ordinating body. In particular, the League organizes, at international level, the despatch of Red Cross relief following natural disasters (floods, earthquakes, etc.), when damage to life and property reaches such proportions that the national society alone cannot cope. The League also helps the development of each national society.
The ICRC National Societies and League together form the *International Red Cross.*
The three bodies which make up the International Red Cross and the governments which have signed the Geneva Conventions meet every four years for an *International Red Cross Conference*—something like a parliament. The International Conference is the top decision-making body of the worldwide movement of the Red Cross. Its decisions and resolutions are binding on the entire Red Cross and on governments which have signed the Conventions.

tion of the International Prisoners of War Agency, and the Tracing Services was started in 1919. The Central Tracing Agency, which combined these activities, dates from 1960.

During World War II, the Agency reached a peak of activity as seen in Exhibit 3. The employment and communication activity have varied over time and the nature of the Agency's activities has evolved as the needs demanded. In recent times, events in the Far East and Africa have carried the services to new parts of the world and increased the work with refugees. Today about one third of the Agency's activities are associated with World War II and earlier conflicts, one third are associated with post-World War II conflicts as well as internal tensions since 1945, and the remaining one third are associated with on-going conflicts,

EXHIBIT 3
THE CENTRAL TRACING AGENCY OF THE INTERNATIONAL RED CROSS
Central Tracing Agency Comparative Statistics

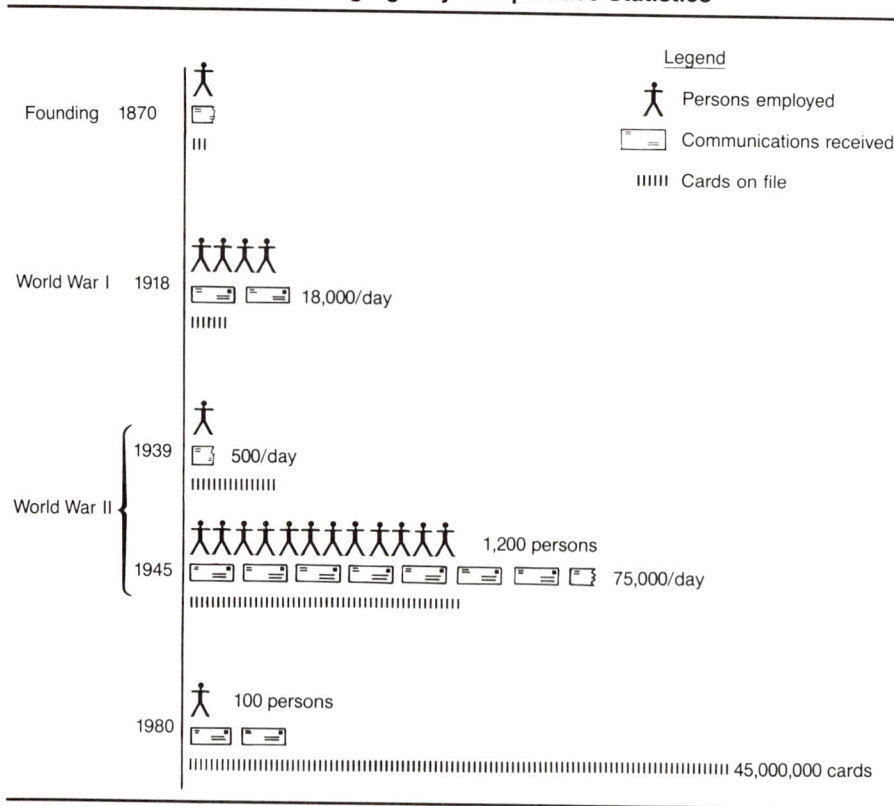

including problems of political detainees, refugees, and displaced persons.

As the Agency has evolved and the activity levels have changed, the information base has continued to expand. In 1982 there were over 55,000,000 cards on file containing information dating back to before the Agency's creation (the Prussia-Denmark war of 1864). These serve as the basic resource for responding to the Agency's current responsibilities:

1. To obtain, record, process, and, if need be, transmit all information required for the identification of persons in need of ICRC assistance, in the context of international conflicts, civil wars, and situations of internal unrest and tension.
2. To transmit correspondence between captives and their families, and between civilians separated from their relatives.
3. To search for missing persons.
4. To reunite families, organize transfers and repatriations.
5. To issue travel documents to persons without identity papers (refugees, displaced persons, political exiles) wishing to travel to a country willing to receive them or repatriate them and to provide capture, sickness or other certificates to persons who, in order to obtain pensions or assistance, must supply evidence.

ORGANIZATION

Prior to the reorganization, the Central Tracing Agency and the Operations Department were separate entities. To provide a better structure for conducting and coordinating activities, the two units were brought together under one director, as shown in Exhibit 1. The Operations Department is generally the field arm of the ICRC, coordinating people around the world who are evaluating conditions, gathering information, visiting prisoners and distributing relief. The Central Tracing Agency discharges its responsibilities primarily in Geneva.

The organization of the Central Tracing Agency is shown in Exhibit 4. The department is divided into three geographical divisions. Within each of these, the units generally are geographic also, although the microfilm service and the archives are functional units. The use of geographical subdivisions has linguistic advantages and parallels the Operations Department organization as well. A total of slightly more than

EXHIBIT 4
THE CENTRAL TRACING AGENCY OF THE INTERNATIONAL RED CROSS
Organization Chart of the Central Tracing Agency

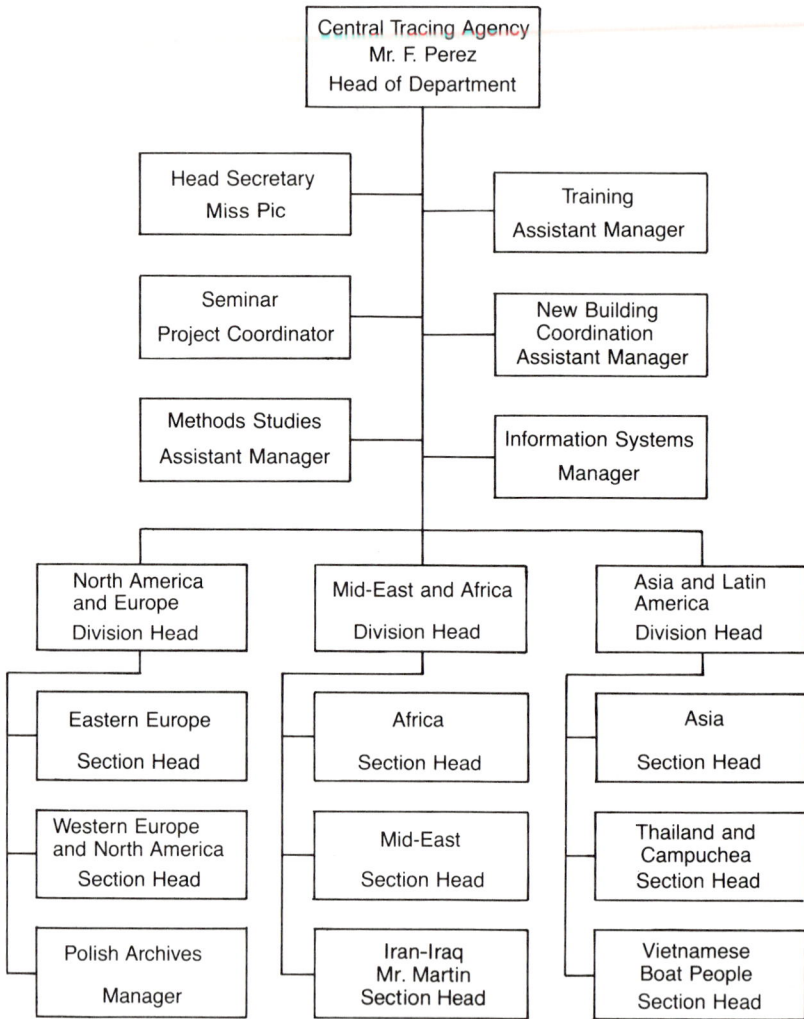

```
                         Central Tracing Agency
                              Mr. F. Perez
                           Head of Department

    Head Secretary                              Training
       Miss Pic                            Assistant Manager

       Seminar                              New Building
   Project Coordinator                      Coordination
                                          Assistant Manager

   Methods Studies                       Information Systems
   Assistant Manager                          Manager


  North America          Mid-East and Africa        Asia and Latin
  and Europe                                         America
  Division Head            Division Head             Division Head


  Eastern Europe              Africa                    Asia
  Section Head             Section Head              Section Head

  Western Europe             Mid-East             Thailand and
  and North America                               Campuchea
  Section Head             Section Head            Section Head

  Polish Archives           Iran-Iraq               Vietnamese
                            Mr. Martin              Boat People
    Manager               Section Head             Section Head
```

100 people are employed by the Agency in Geneva, of whom about 15 are engaged in the activities associated with the support functions.

The support functions of the Central Tracing Agency include the preparation of the seminar for the national societies and the coordination of computer activities. A move to a new building in the near future is being coordinated as a support function, as is an effort to unify some of the methods used in the Agency. The training function provides internal staff training and familiarizes the delegates (specially designated persons who represent the Red Cross's neutral and humanitarian activities in the field) with the Agency's procedures and requirements for information gathering.

CENTRAL TRACING AGENCY ACTIVITIES

As the concerns of the ICRC have changed and expanded, the Central Tracing Agency has developed new activities. These now include services for almost any category of victim of conflict, internal or international tension, or their consequences. This evolving role has taken the Central Tracing Agency into political and military conflicts around the globe.

This worldwide involvement makes it very difficult to predict where or what the next requirement for Agency services might be. Mr. Perez summarized this by saying, "We should be ready to react in days to both startups and shutdowns. For example, we must react quickly when a country like Poland invites us to come in and talk with detainees or when we are given permission to visit the prisoners of war in the Iran-Iraq conflict. On the other hand, we must evacuate and close down all formal activities within a very short period of time when a country like Uganda closes its door to us. Very little warning in such situations makes it difficult for us to prepare for the conduct of the activities for which we are responsible."

In very general terms the Agency's primary task is information management. The raw material of the Agency is information; it is the inventory of the organization, and is the basis for the services performed. Indeed, the first charge to the Agency is to gather information. The discharge of all the remaining tasks depends on what information has been gathered. The Agency functions break down into three main categories. The first of these, registration, has to do with recording and storing information on prisoners, wounded persons, refugees, etc. The second function is message forwarding for military and civilian prisoners and for civilians in case of breakdown of postal communications. This requires information (on locations), as do the remaining tasks of answering requests for information on people or providing documents.

One of the key sources of information is the registration of prisoners, displaced persons, refugees, and so on. In many cases the registration of their names also provides them a guarantee of safety. Many have commented that "The Red Cross gives me hope," or "Now I cannot simply disappear. Someone knows where I am." The registrations are based on official Red Cross delegate visits to the areas of disturbance and lists of POWs provided by the detaining power. In addition to these official sources, the agency occasionally receives informal information from the prisoners, escapees, returnees, etc. Only formal information (verified) becomes part of the official files, however. The registration file from these field sources is created by the Agency.

Historically, the Agency prepared registration cards which were then filed. Recently, however, the computer has been used in registration. Data entry clerks feed the information to the computer. In some applications they need to be able to read the language of the countries involved, since the basic registration forms can differ between country, delegate, and government lists. In some cases it is difficult to tell a person's name from a town name or a battlefield from a prison camp without knowing the language. The transcription situation has been helped somewhat by a standardized "capture card" which is used by internment or POW camp officials to register their prisoners. The informal information, however, can arrive at Geneva in virtually any form from scribbles on the back of a cigarette package to neatly typed columns of names.

The file not only needs to be created, but needs to be updated as changes occur. The delegates, on follow-up visits, record status changes (i.e., releases, changes of location, death, sickness, etc.) for the people they are seeing. These changes, and those which may come from the captors, need to be incorporated into the files. This is complicated by identical names, aliases, errors in recording identification numbers, and so on. The Agency has developed a great deal of experience with these kinds of problems in Europe, but is faced with new challenges as the activities expand all over the world.

The registration files are the basis for nearly all Agency activities. The transmission of detainee lists to the power (country) of origin, determining where to send correspondence, issuing verification certificates, and responding to requests for information all use the files. This means that the files need to be accessible for retrieving and matching information. File organization is complicated because it is difficult to envisage all possible future forms of request for information. The requests may come from inside the ICRC as well as outside. For example, the ICRC delegate's follow-up visits are facilitated when the current status of all the people to be visited is available. Even with the computer, it has not always been possible to provide this because of the shortness of time between the initial and follow-up visits.

The registration files also provide a basis for responding to requests for information from families and others concerned about a possible detainee (tracing). When requests are received, there is a need to acknowledge the request and to check and see if it contains any new information as well as to see if the request can be answered. If the case involves a current situation, then a check is made with the field for any current status changes or to get information if there is nothing in the files in Geneva. The requestor needs to be notified whether or not there is any information available. No information is given to the requestor without the permission of the sought person, however. Files are opened on the requests for which no information is available, in case relevant information is obtained later. The tracing activities can go on for decades after the conflict has ceased.

The forwarding of messages makes use of the files also. When the sender does not know the whereabouts of the prisoner, the file might provide the answer. A check for new information should be made before delivery to the field. If an answer to a message is received, it should be dispatched to the message originator.

In addition to the registration, tracing, and message delivery functions, one of the big tasks of the Agency management revolves around planning. This is very demanding, since exact forecasting is not possible. When a conflict develops, the ICRC may be invited or may send a delegate to make an independent assessment of the situation. This will involve making a clear statement of objectives for the ICRC and estimating the means to achieve the objectives. An estimate of the registration and tracing activities provides the basis for preparing the Agency budget necessary to support these objectives. The Agency budget process takes place in Geneva and a few weeks can elapse before it is completed and people can actually be assigned to the effort. In general, the professionals that will work in the tracing function of the new activity come from within the ICRC. The data entry clerks generally are hired from the outside. As overall activity levels increase at the ICRC, more professionals will be hired from the outside.

The impossibility of making very precise estimates early in a situation can lead to the need for additional resources later. These "extraordinary" needs are covered in supplementary budget requests which also require time to develop and approve. Although the budgeting process requires time, time is of the essence at the beginning of a conflict or entry into a political situation. For example, the early registration of detainees and preparation of status lists can greatly facilitate the field work of the ICRC. This prompted Mr. Dupont, who recently was made responsible for computer registration of Polish detainees, to remark, "I could have saved two or three weeks if some secretarial and computer help would have been available and supported by a budget immediately."

A SPECIFIC EXAMPLE

Although the individual activities at each of the geographical subdivisions of the Agency are different, there is a common thread that runs through them. The Iran-Iraq conflict will provide a specific example of the activities of the Central Tracing Agency. The Iran-Iraq "desk" (see Exhibit 4) is headed by Mr. Martin.

When the Red Cross was first involved in the Iran-Iraq conflict, the task was to register the direct casualties of the war: the dead, captured, wounded and so on. More categories, such as displaced civilians, were to be registered as the involvement of the Red Cross continued. To help with the registration task, the decision was made to use the computer. Initially the Agency's IBM Model 38 computer (used by all other desks) was used, but the Iran-Iraq desk changed to the NCR administrative equipment when capacity became severely limited on the IBM Model 38. To facilitate the computer registration in Geneva, the records are translated and put into a common format prior to data entry. Currently the registration is on the computer, while the tracing inquiries are handled in a separate manual system. The intention is to eventually use the computer for both tasks, but no conceptual framework was available in the beginning to accomplish that.

Originally the Iran-Iraq activity was combined with the Middle East desk. When it was separated, the group consisted of 8 persons. This increased to 11 persons when the number of victims to be registered increased substantially. The current staff still is insufficient to reduce the backlog of work as quickly as desired. A request for three more people is pending, but the forecasts of computer registration activity are constantly updated and uncertain. In fact, there was an increase in the estimates of the number of people to be registered after the request for new people had been submitted. A record of some of the Iran-Iraq activity is shown in Exhibit 5.

EXHIBIT 5
THE CENTRAL TRACING AGENCY OF THE INTERNATIONAL RED CROSS
Statistics on the Iran-Iraq Desk Activity
(cumulative totals as of month end)

Month	Staff	Computer Registration	Requests	Messages
June	8	6,000	500	53,000
December	7	9,500	650	196,000
February	8	10,000	700	262,000
April	11	25,000*	750	331,000

*These include both new and change requests. Only about 10,000 of these have been entered into the computer. An average of 7–8 registrations have been included on each communication received at the desk.

The Iran-Iraq group has both contract and temporary people. The data entry jobs tend to be the ones assigned to temporary persons. As the group has grown, the composition has changed as well. Of the initial 8 people, only 4 remain. Of the 4 replacements, only 2 remain. Only some of the people leave the Red Cross; others go to the field, change geographical areas, or leave for training. The current composition of the group is:

- *1 Desk Officer* coordinates field and Geneva, prepares budget requests, plans and monitors work flows, forecasts workloads.
- *2 Assistants* coordinate computer activity, help manage desk, perform special projects.
- *3 Executive Secretaries* carry out the tracing activities (case work) and message forwarding.
- *5 Data Entry Clerks* perform the computer registration and record status changes.

The data entry clerks can enter about 100 new computer registrations per day, but only about 20 changes in status (this results in an average of about 40 entries per day, since about three quarters of the activity concerns changes). The messages are processed about once a week and take about one half day (largely for gathering statistics) for one executive secretary. The executive secretaries can process about 10 tracing requests per day. The actual volume they process varies greatly, depending on the nature of the requests, number of messages, and what other activities are going on. An executive secretary's effectiveness in tracing improves greatly with practice. The more experienced persons not only perform their tasks more quickly, they can handle more complicated situations.

Communications destined for the Iran-Iraq desk arrive at the main building of the International Committee of the Red Cross in Geneva. An initial screening and distribution of the documents or telephone messages is made there for later distribution to the different departments. When the documents reach the Central Tracing Agency, Miss Pic, the head secretary, reads through them and decides which specific area should receive each. Almost everything in Arabic comes to a secretary for the Mid-East and Iran-Iraq desks. The secretary distributes the communications between the two desks.

When the information finally arrives at Mr. Martin's desk, he scans the documents in order to follow the trends for his desk. Somewhat more than 1,000 communications related to registration and tracing activities cross his desk a month. The documents will be assigned to an executive secretary or data entry clerk, although currently there is about 1½ months backlog of tracing requests at Mr. Martin's desk. An important first step is the recording of basic statistics on volumes. These are used for reporting back to the countries that support ICRC activities and to help organize and estimate workloads for the desk and division.

The tracing requests are entered into a log book that is maintained by everyone in the area, and an acknowledgement letter, prepared on the word processor by the executive secretary, is sent to the requestor. Next the computer registration list and the manual inquiry file are checked to make sure that no file has already been opened on the person involved in the request. If not, an index card is made with the information and a file is opened. Whether or not there is any information in the files, the executive secretaries follow up with the field. They check for newer information on anything that they have found in the files, and they request information if nothing is found. They make up request letters to the field, using the word processor. Recently they have had to schedule several days in advance in order to use one of the word processors.

The executive secretaries use the log book to follow up on requests that have been sent to the field. They check the log book periodically to communicate with any requestor that is still waiting and to make sure that no request gets lost in the system. When a response does come back from the field, a letter to the requestor is prepared by the executive secretary for Mr. Martin's signature. Even in cases where the response from the field is "no information available," a letter is sent out. In all instances the log book is closed out at this time, and no other follow up with the request is made.

One executive secretary and an assistant are assigned to a special project which occupies them full time. The other executive secretaries are given a variety of tracing and message forwarding work. An experienced executive secretary at one of the desks with a single file to consult can process 30 requests a day. As Mr. Martin says, "I try to give each person a variety. We tried to have them specialize on certain things before but it became very much like a factory and not very motivating for them. Of the communications I get each month, about 25 are requests for information, and, until recently, something like a 1,000 concerned registration. We forward about 30,000 family messages a month. We are hopeful that with the new people we will be able to get on top of the registrations. We have not been able to develop the system to enter the inquiries into the computer but intend to do that as well. We know all the advantages."

PLANS FOR THE FUTURE

Mr. Perez discussed his objectives for the Agency, "It is one of my real desires to make the organization more professional administratively. We have grown very quickly and have greatly changed the mix of our work. The computer is still new to us and we are still having difficulties learning how to use it effectively. It is time to rationalize our procedures. We need some well-defined methods in some of our activities and a comprehensive training of the people responsible for carrying out the jobs. We must be able to respond quickly and efficiently to changing and unpredictable situations, perhaps with a special cadre of persons. The real questions that I need to address now are how to focus the resources of the organization on the objectives and where to concentrate my efforts to begin to make improvements."

North Sea Machine Tool Factory

Bei Hai Ji Chuang Chang

In late September 1980, management at the North Sea Machine Tool factory (NSMT) were worried by the fact that their 1981 order books for NSMT's special order tool/transfer complex (TTC) line were far from full. Although the TTC line accounted for only 10 percent of the number of units sold by the factory, it generated about 60 percent of revenue. With the implementation of the "expansion of autonomy" program nationwide planned for 1981, NSMT's management and workers expected to have to bear the brunt of any profit reductions. Shi Pu Lan, director of the Production and Planning Department, was studying the factory's operations seeking improvements which could brighten NSMT's prospects, if not for 1981, at least for subsequent years.

BACKGROUND

NSMT was established as a state-owned enterprise in 1948 by consolidating 15 small iron-working plants. Initially the factory produced only small replacement parts for machinery. In 1957 the factory became one of the first in China to produce machine tools. Within a few years NSMT had gained substantial expertise in the custom design and manufacture of special-purpose machine tools.

In the early 1960s, the National #1 Machinery Ministry transferred most of NSMT's designers to a newly created National Specialized Machine Tool Research Institute located in the same city as NSMT. For the rest of the decade, NSMT relied on this institute to design its special-purpose machine tools.

During the 1960s, the number of other factories throughout China which relied on the National Institute's design capability increased. By the early 1970s, the NSMT had decided that its design needs could no longer be met by the National Institute; NSMT redeveloped its own design capability by creating its own Factory Research Institute (essentially a design department). By 1975, NSMT no longer maintained any connection with the National Institute. This had the effect of providing China with two separate institutes with the ability to design special-purpose machine tools and tool complexes meeting international standards.

In 1978 the National Research Institute had entered into a long-term joint agreement with five other manufacturers for machine tools located throughout China. While NSMT did not know the details of this agreement, it was obvious it had the warm support of the #1 Machinery Ministry. NSMT management believed that they would, as a result of this agreement, face competition from these smaller factories which now had the National Institute's design capability at their disposal.

In 1980 NSMT was undergoing external organizational change. Originally the factory had reported to the Bureau of Machine Tools, a national bureau under the leadership of the #1 Machinery Ministry. For a short period, NSMT had been transferred to the Provincial Machinery Bureau. Then, in the late 1970s, it was under the Municipal Machinery Bureau. In 1980, that bureau was abolished and a new Municipal Machine Tools Company was being formed. Within that company, NSMT would be the largest factory, and the only one producing specialized machine tools and tool/transfer complexes.

In 1980 NSMT employed 5,600 workers, used 800 pieces of equipment (about 30% of which the factory had built), and sold five product lines:

1. Tool/transfer complexes—special-order systems of machine tools and transfer/handling equipment.
2. Universal lathes.
3. Relieving lathes.
4. Hydraulic semi-automatic chucking lathes (multitooled).
5. Numerically controlled machine tools.

Exhibit 1 shows an example of a special-purpose machine tool manufactured by NSMT. Tool/transfer complexes (TTCs) ranged in size from two machine tools (both general and special-purpose machine tools were used) joined by a single transfer machine through sets of more than a dozen machine tool stations meshed with transfer equipment; these large systems sold for well over ¥1 million. The TTC line was sold directly to customers; all other product lines were produced to the state plan with only production in excess of the plan's quota sold directly to customers.

NSMT's 1980 sales volume was ¥40[1] million, with ¥7 million

---

[1] In 1980 the yuan (¥) was valued at approximately $.67 (U.S.).

EXHIBIT 1
NORTH SEA MACHINE TOOL FACTORY
Product Examples: Special-Purpose Machine Tools/Transfer Lines

BX-7 Transfer Machine for Cylinder Blocks

This transfer machine is a part of the system designed for manufacturing cylinder blocks. It consists of 6 metal cutting pieces of equipment and produces cylinder blocks at the rate of 47 pieces per hour at 100% efficiency. The major operations performed by this machine are:

1. Drilling and tapping holes on end faces
2. Drilling and reaming locating pin holes
3. Drilling oil gallery hole
4. Countersinking dowel holes
5. Counterboring cam and cover holes

BX-16 Transfer Machine for Axle Housing

This machine is designed for the manufacture of automobile housings (including the front, middle and rear axle housings). It performs boring, turning, drilling, counterboring, and tapping operations and its output is 61 pieces per hour at 100% efficiency. This machine is composed of 9 metal cutting machines configured in line by the sequence of operations. The main conveyor is divided into two sections by its own hydraulic cylinder; the pallet returns from a conveyor interlinked with the main conveyors which makes the transfer system a closed loop. At the end of the machining operations, a washing is carried out.

BU-477 Special Purpose Machine with Changeable Spindle Heads

This is a special-purpose machine for automobile augmentor bodies. The main feature of the machine is that a workpiece can be machined completely in one clamping setup, with one power unit, by changing 11 spindle heads automatically. This machine is primarily for a specific workpiece; however, the user can choose the appropriate spindle heads on a part-family basis, so it is economical for medium batch production.

BU-73 Special Purpose Machine for Rear Axle Housing

This is a special-purpose machine for rough boring on two ends of a rear axle housing. It produces workpieces at a rate of 19 pieces per hour at 100% efficiency. All operations of this machine are achieved automatically except loading and unloading of the workpiece. This machine consists of modular units, such as wing base, power slide, reduction gear box, and specially designed units such as the fixture spindle, box, tools, etc. The fixture is mounted on the center base. The workpiece is positioned by V-blocks and clamped by hydraulic power.

Source: NSMT 1980 Catalogue.

EXHIBIT 1 (concluded)
NORTH SEA MACHINE TOOL FACTORY
Parts of a Special-Purpose Machine Tool: A One-Position Horizontal
Boring Mill—Single Machine
(for boring piston holes in engine blocks)

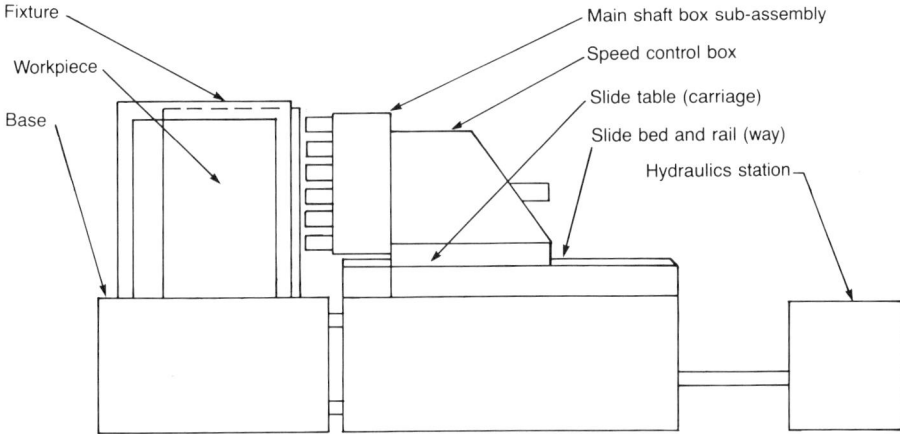

Fixture

Workpiece

Base

Main shaft box sub-assembly

Speed control box

Slide table (carriage)

Slide bed and rail (way)

Hydraulics station

profit. Exhibit 2 is a summary of NSMT's financial situation; Exhibit 3 lists NSMT's organizational entities.

TTCs were custom designed and manufactured, so the scheduling and control of TTC production required more effort than that used for the lathe lines. Shi estimated that about 80 percent of management's time was devoted to TTC design and manufacture. The numerically controlled tools were a new line, introduced in 1980; only one had been sold.

In terms of unit volume, universal lathes were NSMT's most important; the factory had the capacity to produce 3,000 units per year. Relieving lathes were produced continuously at a rate of about 30 per month. Chucking lathes were produced in small lots. Exhibit 4 shows the general work flow at NSMT.

Exhibit 5 shows the steps from receipt of the customer's order to shipment of the finished product involved in manufacture of a TTC using general purpose tools. The process took from 16 to 22 months and was, in Shi's estimation, far longer than the lead times for several developed countries. Exhibit 6 was prepared by members of the Production and Planning Department from general industry reference material.

EXHIBIT 2
NORTH SEA MACHINE TOOL FACTORY
Financial Statements
Balance sheet as of December 31
(¥1,000,000)

	1975	1976	1977	1978	1979	1980 1st Qtr.	1980 2nd Qtr.
Assigned (approved)							
Current assets:	29.44	30.87	38.61	32.19	30.01	33.54	32.72
Raw materials	15.86	15.47	17.53	14.99	11.72	12.80	12.21
W.I.P.	7.68	6.76	15.48	13.76	12.99	13.45	13.37
Finished goods	5.90	8.64	5.60	3.44	3.40	5.39	4.99
Obsolete inventory					1.90	1.90	2.15
Gross fixed assets	50.83	52.87	56.91	60.25	63.94	63.87	63.49
Net fixed assets	27.67	27.85	30.08	31.19	32.78	32.10	31.24
Total Assets	57.11	58.72	68.69	63.38	62.79	65.64	63.96
State funds:							
(for fixed assets)	27.67	27.85	30.08	31.19	32.78	32.10	31.24
(for current assets)	17.70	17.70	17.70	17.70	17.70	17.70	18.27
Bank loans:							
Within plan	10.28	12.43	17.51	16.19	14.12	5.58	5.58
Over plan						2.05	4.01
Overstock						6.60	5.00
Other funds	1.46	.74	3.40	(1.70)	(1.81)	1.61	(.14)
Total Funds	57.11	58.72	68.69	63.38	62.79	65.64	63.96

EXHIBIT 2 (concluded)
Income Statements
(¥1,000,000)

	1975	1976	1977	1978	1979	1980 1st Quarter	1980 2nd Quarter
Sales	43.57	42.36	32.20	39.15	40.15	9.48	9.60
Cost of goods sold	28.14	26.32	21.03	27.27	28.74	6.59	7.05
Taxes	2.17	2.13	1.60	1.94	1.99	.47	.47
Income from operation	13.26	13.91	9.57	9.94	9.42	2.42	2.08
Other income (loss)	(.50)	(.20)	.02	(.56)	(2.81)	(.03)	(.17)
Net income	12.76	13.71	9.59	9.38	6.61	2.39	1.91

Cost breakdown for the special-purpose machine tool:

Materials	48.3%
Administration	27.6
Workshop expenses	14.7
Workshop tools	4.7
Wages	4.7
	1C0.0%

EXHIBIT 3
NORTH SEA MACHINE TOOL FACTORY
Departments and Offices

Accounting Department
Checking Department
   Measurement Office
   Special Testing Office
Education Department
Energy Office
Environmental Protection Department
Equipment Department
Factory Office
Foundry Department
Labor and Wages Department
Material Conservation Office
Office of the Chief Engineer
Political Affairs Department
Process Technology Department

Production and Planning Department
   Assembly Workshops
   Painting and Packing Workshop
   Processing (Machinery) Workshops
Quality Office
Research Institute
   5 Product Offices (by line)
   Machining Office
   Electronics Office
   Hydraulics Office
   Standardization Office
   Parts Commonality Office
Supply Department
Tools Department
Transportation Department
Workers' Housing Authority
Workers' Union
Young People's Office

TECHNICAL PREPARATIONS

Before a TTC began manufacture, a number of technical preparations were necessary—design, tool design and manufacture, standard setting, process planning, mold preparation, and so on. After a TTC was shipped, the design and plans were kept for reference although they were seldom used again; molds were scrapped.

The preliminary technical tasks were carried out by about 500 engineers and technicians in 10 technical departments and 3 preparation workshops. The Office of the Chief Engineer had established three principles to guide this preliminary work:

1. Parts standardization.
2. Parts commonality.
3. Product systematization.

Standard parts ranged from such nationally standardized parts as screws, nuts, and bolts to NSMT's own standardized parts. Standard parts were to be used wherever possible. About three quarters of NSMT's standard parts were nationally standardized; the balance were factory standard.

EXHIBIT 4
NORTH SEA MACHINE TOOL FACTORY
Organization of Work Flow

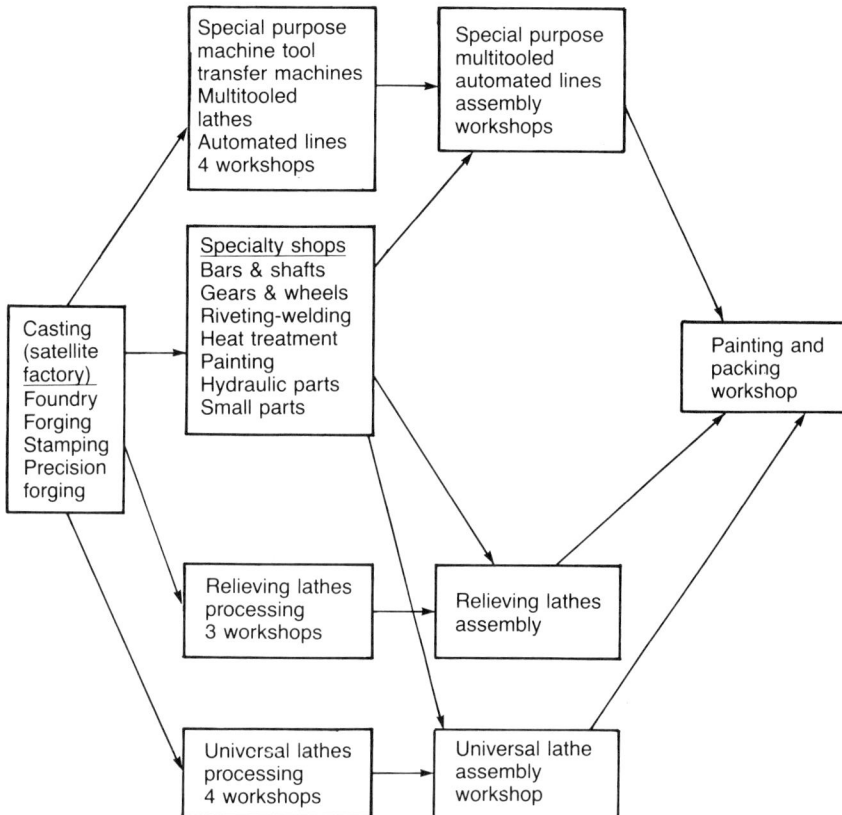

| Casting (satellite factory) Foundry Forging Stamping Precision forging |
| Special purpose machine tool transfer machines Multitooled lathes Automated lines 4 workshops |
| Special purpose multitooled automated lines assembly workshops |
| Specialty shops Bars & shafts Gears & wheels Riveting-welding Heat treatment Painting Hydraulic parts Small parts |
| Painting and packing workshop |
| Relieving lathes processing 3 workshops |
| Relieving lathes assembly |
| Universal lathes processing 4 workshops |
| Universal lathe assembly workshop |

I Foundry   II Machining   III Assembly   IV Painting and packing

Most of NSMT's common parts were factory common; some were common throughout China within a particular product line. In 1980, NSMT management was strongly supporting increasing parts commonality. (See Exhibit 7 for an analysis of the relationship between parts commonality and manufacturing lead time.) NSMT's Production and Planning Department estimated that the TTC line achieved about 55 percent parts commonality, calculated on the basis of labor time embodied in parts production. This figure was well below the 85 percent believed by factory technicians to be the norm in developed nations' factories.

EXHIBIT 5
NORTH SEA MACHINE TOOL FACTORY
Design and Manufacturing Program: Tool/Transfer Complex

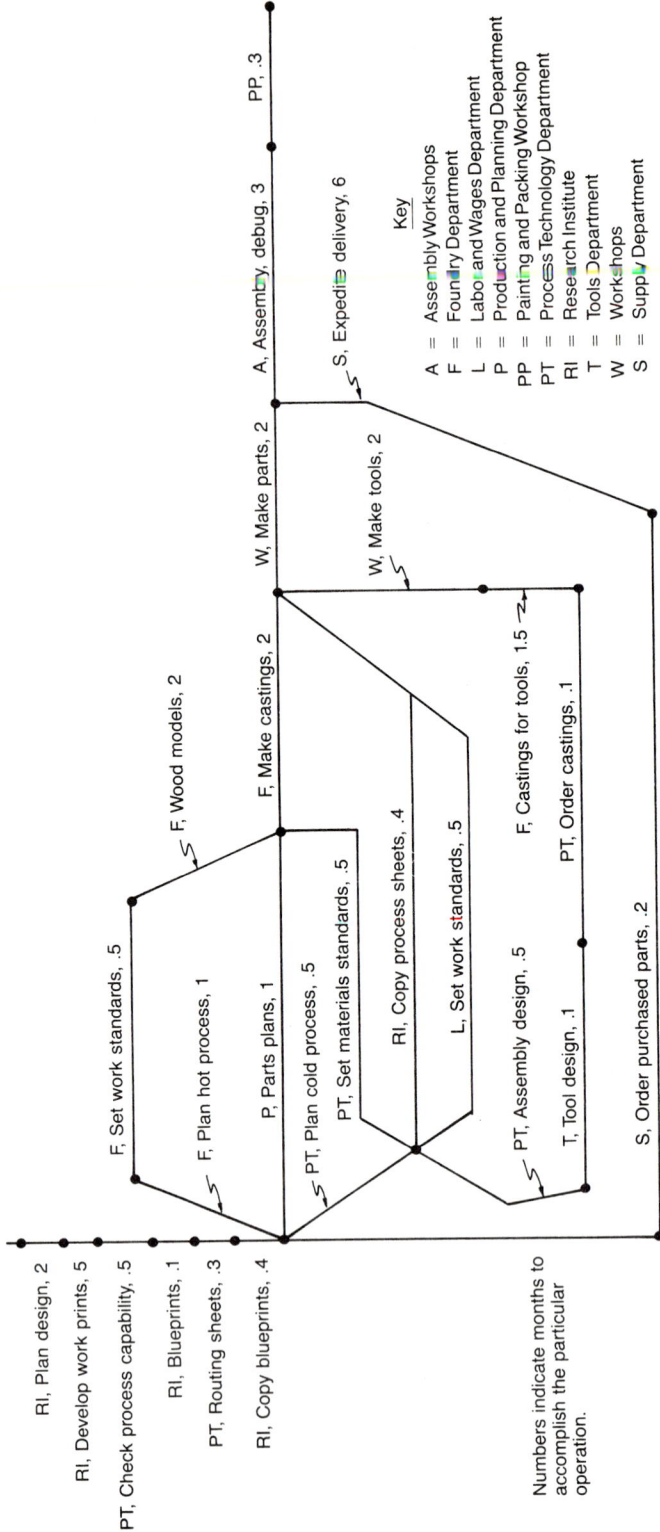

RI, Plan design, 2

RI, Develop work prints, 5

PT, Check process capability, .5

RI, Blueprints, .1

PT, Routing sheets, .3

RI, Copy blueprints, .4

F, Set work standards, .5

F, Plan hot process, 1

P, Parts plans, 1

PT, Plan cold process, .5

PT, Set materials standards, .5

RI, Copy process sheets, .4

L, Set work standards, .5

PT, Assembly design, .5

T, Tool design, .1

PT, Order castings, .1

S, Order purchased parts, .2

F, Wood models, 2

F, Make castings, 2

F, Castings for tools, 1.5

W, Make parts, 2

W, Make tools, 2

A, Assembly, debug, 3

S, Expedite delivery, 6

PP, .3

Numbers indicate months to accomplish the particular operation.

Key

A = Assembly Workshops
F = Foundry Department
L = Labor and Wages Department
P = Production and Planning Department
PP = Painting and Packing Workshop
PT = Process Technology Department
RI = Research Institute
T = Tools Department
W = Workshops
S = Supply Department

EXHIBIT 6
NORTH SEA MACHINE TOOL FACTORY
Comparative Manufacturing Lead Times for Special-Purpose Machine Tools
(months)

	Japan	Germany	USSR	USA	NSMT
Single machine	3–4	5–6	8–10	5–7	16
Transfer machine	8–12	12–14	12	9–15	20

Source: Intra-Industry reference material.

EXHIBIT 7
NORTH SEA MACHINE TOOL FACTORY
Relationship between Parts Commonality and Manufacturing Lead Time

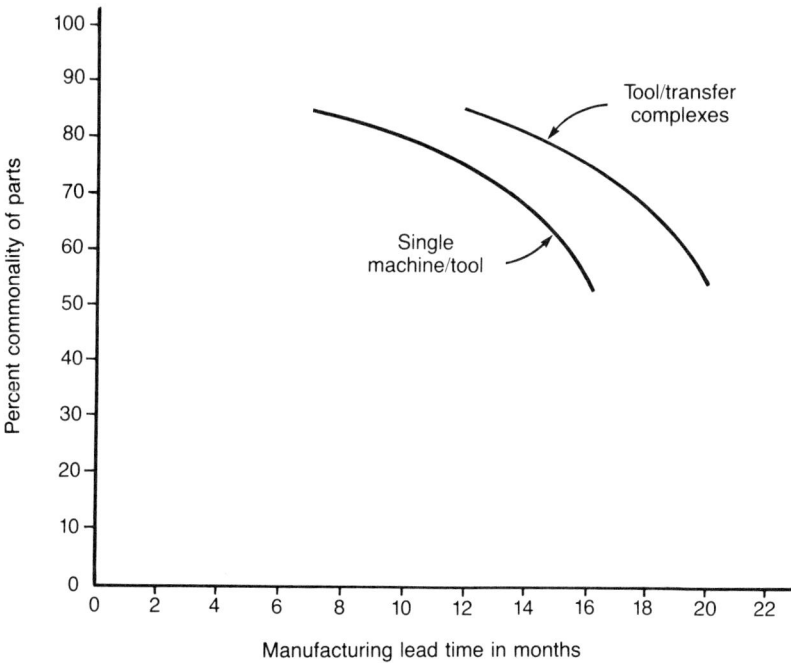

Source: Prepared by Production and Planning Department from historical data.

In 1980, a TTC requiring 4,000 labor-hours of production was composed of:

2,000 labor-hours of common parts.

1,600 labor-hours of specialized parts.

300 labor-hours of national standard parts.

100 labor-hours of factory standard parts.

The principle of product systematization was to be carried out by identification of modules within product lines as standards from which particular design requirements could be adapted. In the case of the TTC and special-purpose lines, more than 250 such modules existed, each subject to dozens of adaptations. In fact, TTC's and the special-purpose machines were essentially unique, as can be seen from the 1980 TTC assembly schedule in Exhibit 8. Some systematization had been attempted within the special-purpose drilling machine group, with the designation of the DU316, DU420, and DU528 units as "typical" and with retention of their designs and molds. In 1980, no person was engaged in systematization work.

THE DESIGN PROCESS

TTC design began in the Research Institute (see Exhibit 5), where "3 sketches and 1 card" were made up; this refers to an overall sketch of the TTC, a "sketch" (rough routing) for manufacture, a "sketch" (rough plan) for assembly, and a labor estimate card. After a more detailed set of plans had been drawn, the design went to the Process Technology Department to check for manufacturability. If problems arose at this stage, they were resolved by the Office of the Chief Engineer. The designs then went back to the Research Institute for editing and copying. They were returned to the Process Technology Department so that routing sheets could be made up for special parts.

At this stage, a part number was assigned to each of the thousand or so special parts. The number indicated the part's parent(s) and the workshops through which the part would be routed. For example:

$$BU311 - 10001 \qquad 17 - 1/2 - 10$$

meant that the part (-001) was part of the body subassembly (10-) of special machine tool BU311; it would start in the foundry (17), go

EXHIBIT 8
NORTH SEA MACHINE TOOL FACTORY
TTC Assembly Schedule for 1980

Jan.	Feb.	Mar.	Apr.	May	June	July	Aug.	Sept.	Oct.	Nov.
BX63:	BK42OCT:	BX75:	850	BX71:	BGT52:	588	BX71:	1112	1241	1261
(2/1)	(27)	(10/1)	856:	(11/1)	(12)	589	(10/1)	1113	1242	1267
BU1060	1127	1036	(7)	1191	BGT52A:	1146:	BU979:	1114	1243	1003
1061	1128	1038:	712	1199:	(12)	(2)	(3)	1115	1066:	1162
965:	1129	(3)	715:	(9)	BX73:	1209:	1157	1116	(2)	1163
(2)		1045	(4)	1143	(5/1)	(2)	1158	1117	BX82:	860
546A		1049:	1034	1056	1173:	1142	922	1118	(23/1)	1217
555:		(5)	1035	1059:	(2)	1141	1139	1119		1220:
(10)		1147	858	(4)		396A	767	1122		(4)
680A		1152:	859	1008		399A:	1005	1123		886
679A		(8)	618	1010:		(4)	1006	1124		887
		1080	661	(3)		648A	1153	1125		1144
		1086:	808	1062		653A:	1159	1126		1145
		(7)	989	1063		(6)	915	1227		1226
		988		1065		BX34A:	916	1228		1271
		1028				(6/1)	1211	(make 2		1282:
						1130	1215:	of each)		(12)
						1136:	(5)			1140
						(7)				1064
										1240

Totals:

Jan.	Feb.	Mar.	Apr.	May	June	July	Aug.	Sept.	Oct.	Nov.
19	30	38	21	34	31	34	30	30	28	32

BU: Special-purpose machine tool (BU is assumed if no letters precede numbers).
BX: Transfer machine.
BGT: Pneumatic tool.
BK: Variable axle boring tool.
Number in parentheses after product number is the number to be produced, assumed to be one if not stated.
Denominator on BX, e.g., (11/1), refers to number of lines.

through the large parts processing section (1) in the #2 workshop (/2), and finish in the painting workshop (10).

Once copies of the design were ready, preparations could start in four areas:

- Mold preparation in the Foundry Department.
- Parts plans in the Production and Planning Department.
- Tool design and manufacture in the Tools Department and Workshops.
- Determination of purchased parts requirements by the Supply Department.

When these activities were complete—approximately one year after receipt of the order—production could begin.

PRODUCTION SCHEDULING

There were four processes involved in the production of all of NSMT's machine tools (see Exhibit 4):

1. Casting (foundry).
2. Machining.
3. Assembly.
4. Painting and packing.

All castings used at NSMT were produced by the Foundry Department—housed in a satellite facility. All other processes were carried out in NSMT's internal workshops. Machining for all five product lines was done by workshops specialized by product line except that done by the specialized workshops—bars and shafts, gears, riveting and welding, forging, painting, hydraulic subassemblies and small-part subassemblies. Assembly was done by workshops specialized by product line. All products came together in the Painting and Packing Workshop.

Universal lathes were produced at a rate of 250 per month, with different models being made each month. Relieving lathes and multitool semi-automatic chucking lathes were scheduled at the rate of slightly more than 30 per month on a rotating basis.

Production of the TTC line was scheduled in "batches" of about 30 each month, notwithstanding the fact that each machine in the batch was different. Upon completion of one step in the production process, a machine waited until the end of the month when it was transferred with its batch to the next process. In order to guarantee that its monthly quota of machines was turned out, each workshop kept a supply of parts or three or four completed machines in stock all the time. Then, if problems arose with the quotas they were supposed to finish, they could substitute with machines on hand, thus avoiding forfeit of all of the workshop's workers' bonus for the month.

INVENTORY POLICY

When the factory first began producing machine tools in 1957, each machine was essentially one-of-a-kind. There was no inventorying of parts except for temporary storage; no distinction was made between common and special parts. In 1960 an order quantity system was implemented for common parts. The order quantity system was nominally used throughout the 1960s but, in fact, the number of common parts produced for inventory was sharply reduced from the 1960 plan. Nevertheless, stocks of common parts accumulated for many years; finally, in 1968, a large number were discarded because they had rusted. At that time, ¥0.4 million in parts was written off.

In 1972 NSMT undertook a five-step program to rebuild common parts inventories. In the first stage, all common parts required for one month's production were made in one batch. Three months later stage 2, which enlarged the batch size to 2 months' requirements, was implemented. Stage 3 enlarged the batch size to 3 months' needs; stage 4 added a 20 percent safety margin to assure that a sufficient number of usable parts were produced to meet a quarter's requirements.

Stage 5 was implemented in 1975; production of small and medium-sized parts was put on a six-month cycle. During the first quarter, half of all common parts needed for the year were produced; the second half was produced in the second quarter. Since the average monthly production of TTCs was about 30 machines per month, the usual batch size (adjusted for the 20 percent safety margin) was 220 machines' worth. This system, which was still used in 1980, was called the "batch cycle system."

The factory adopted a policy of producing one year's requirements of very small common parts like screws, springs, coils, gauge face plates, and so on. Very large common parts such as the tool body housing, which cost several thousand yuan and took up a considerable amount of space, were produced in monthly batches. These policies were credited with a substantial reduction in inventories by 1980. Still, the system had not eliminated the problem of the Assembly Department sometimes having to wait for parts.

The policy for special parts was the same as that for large common parts—a month's worth of parts requirements was calculated, designed, and passed down for production. The time required for production of any special part rarely exceeded 10 days but, since production was based on monthly batches, completed parts waited until the end of the month to be transferred to the batch's next process.

PURCHASED PARTS

Before 1980, purchased parts were ordered twice a year at semi-annual allocation meetings. In 1980, the system was changed so that NSMT could order parts directly from suppliers whenever they wanted to. The factory adopted an order quantity system for 80 percent of their purchased parts, setting the order quantity at half a year's requirements. NSMT would have preferred to order all its purchased parts from local factories; however, most purchased parts came from outside the city because of NSMT's quality requirements. In general, the time from order placement to receipt of goods was about six months.

The remaining 20 percent of purchased parts were classified as difficult to obtain; these were parts in high demand by many industries. Smaller inventories were kept for these parts. The order lead time tended to be from one to three months.

The factory produced one subassembly because they were unable to find a substitute which met their quality standards. The direct current motor made up about 1 percent of the cost of a finished machine tool but tied up far more than its share of working capital. The raw materials necessary for its production—particularly copper and pure iron—were difficult to obtain. To assure steady production of the motors, NSMT maintained inventories amounting to 10 percent of the factory's total work-in-progress inventory.

PROBLEMS

Production Director Shi was convinced that the long manufacturing lead time on the TTCs was the factory's central problem—that it caused NSMT to lose customers to other factories, particularly the National

Research Institute's factory alliance, which was emphasizing customer service and faster delivery. Other customers had chosen to build their own systems rather than wait. Since Shi was confident that NSMT's quality was superior to what competitors or customers could produce, he felt that shortening the time for production would attract customers back. It would also reduce the factory's needs for working capital; in 1980, NSMT's cost of goods sold included interest of ¥0.6 million.

Royal Clyde Biscuit Co., Ltd.

It was February 1987, and the last major section of the factory, filling-making, was soon to be started up. It seemed appropriate for Harry Pitt and Rob Gladstone to reflect on all that had transpired over the previous 3½ years. It had been that long since the idea of a new Sloop plant had been formally broached. Now, £17.1 million later, Harry and Rob wondered what they and their colleagues had learned and what changes could improve the planning and start-up of new facilities at Royal Clyde Biscuit Co., Ltd.

SLOOP AND ROYAL CLYDE BISCUIT CO., LTD.

Sloop was one of the world's major cookies and had been since its introduction in 1928. By unit volume it was the United Kingdom's leading brand, with sales of about 40,000 tons per year. The slogan "Sail away with a Sloop" was second nature to several generations of Britons. Sloop was critical to Royal Clyde Biscuit Co., Ltd.'s, success, especially in the U.K., where it accounted for roughly one quarter of the company's British sales volume.

As cookies go, Sloop was a complicated product (see Exhibit 1 for a brief description of how it was made). Sloop was a sandwich cookie that consisted of 2 chocolate-topped cookie biscuits joined together by a white icing filling. The chocolate had a picture of a sloop molded into it. This made for an elegant and scrumptious cookie. The deposit of the chocolate on just the top or bottom of the cookie itself, with none around the edges, plus the molded impression of the sloop, required more sophistication than was typical for the industry.

Royal Clyde Biscuit Co., Ltd., began as a family-run enterprise in 1869. It manufactured and marketed a number of leading biscuit and snack products but, increasingly, it had been growing outside the biscuit business, largely by acquisition in Europe and North America.

Royal Clyde Biscuit Co., Ltd., pursued a manufacturing strategy that assigned particular products to only one facility within a country. Thus, all of the U.K's production of Sloop was assigned to the original manufacturing complex at Clyde, Scotland. This complex was also responsible for export market production of Sloop (e.g., the Middle East).

EXHIBIT 1
ROYAL CLYDE BISCUIT CO., LTD.
Sloop Basic Process Flow Diagram

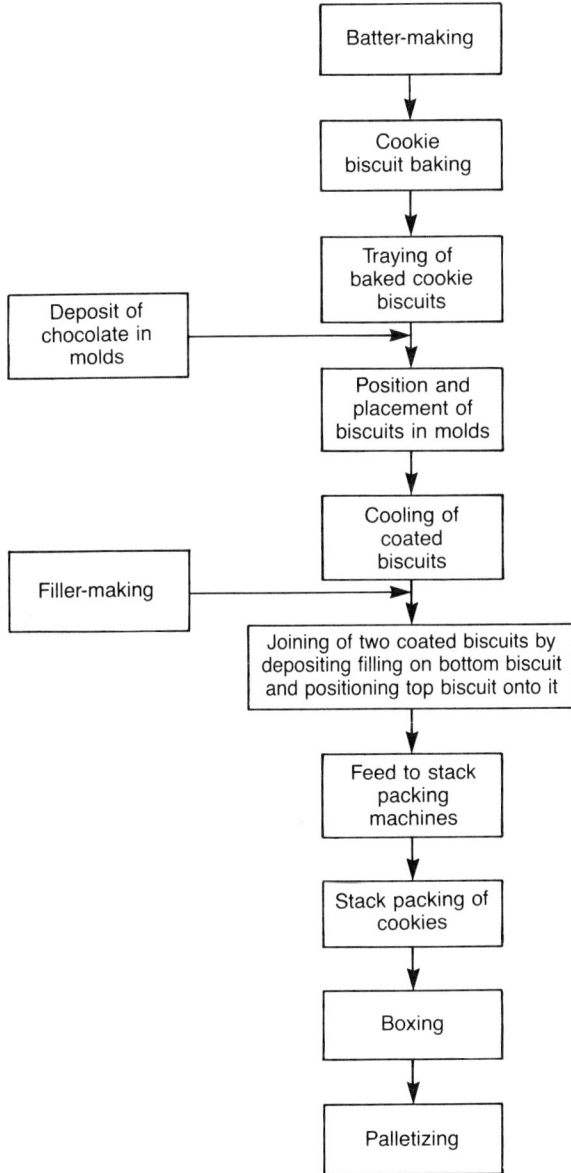

```
                    ┌─────────────────────┐
                    │   Batter-making     │
                    └─────────────────────┘
                               │
                               ▼
                    ┌─────────────────────┐
                    │      Cookie         │
                    │   biscuit baking    │
                    └─────────────────────┘
                               │
                               ▼
                    ┌─────────────────────┐
                    │     Traying of      │
                    │   baked cookie      │
┌──────────────┐    │     biscuits        │
│  Deposit of  │    └─────────────────────┘
│ chocolate in │───────────────►│
│    molds     │    ┌─────────────────────┐
└──────────────┘    │   Position and      │
                    │   placement of      │
                    │  biscuits in molds  │
                    └─────────────────────┘
                               │
                               ▼
                    ┌─────────────────────┐
                    │    Cooling of       │
                    │     coated          │
┌──────────────┐    │     biscuits        │
│Filler-making │    └─────────────────────┘
└──────────────┘───────────────►│
        ┌─────────────────────────────────────────┐
        │ Joining of two coated biscuits by        │
        │ depositing filling on bottom biscuit     │
        │ and positioning top biscuit onto it      │
        └─────────────────────────────────────────┘
                               │
                               ▼
                    ┌─────────────────────┐
                    │   Feed to stack     │
                    │     packing         │
                    │     machines        │
                    └─────────────────────┘
                               │
                               ▼
                    ┌─────────────────────┐
                    │  Stack packing of   │
                    │     cookies         │
                    └─────────────────────┘
                               │
                               ▼
                    ┌─────────────────────┐
                    │      Boxing         │
                    └─────────────────────┘
                               │
                               ▼
                    ┌─────────────────────┐
                    │    Palletizing      │
                    └─────────────────────┘
```

The company, within its geographic sectors, was organized by function rather than by "business" or product line (see the various organization charts depicted in Exhibit 2). That is, a function like engineering or production or quality control was responsible for multiple brands. While particular engineers or production managers, for example, were typically given multiyear assignments to particular products, their advancement was usually through the function. Career moves between functions were rare. There was no general manager for Sloop who might oversee marketing, sales, production, engineering, and finance. Rather, issues of general management were coordinated among the various functions and the company, over the years, had become quite adept at such liaison.

GENESIS OF THE NO. 4 PLANT

The idea for a new Sloop plant first surfaced in late 1981 during a trip south by Harry Pitt, then the engineering manager for Sloop and another brand, and Charlie George, then the assistant production manager for Sloop. The two of them were fresh from the start-up of the No. 3 Sloop plant which was devoted to the larger, export-size Sloop. The new No. 3 plant had been a significant step forward for export production, and Pitt and George began thinking about what might be accomplished with a new domestic production plant. In late January 1982 they drafted a "think piece" for their respective bosses (then Henry Wilson and Clive Macmillan) that argued for consolidating Sloop cookie-baking, chocolate deposit molding, the joining of the two halves of the cookie to the filling (known as joining), and packaging into a new single-floor facility to be built at the main Clyde complex. Their argument rested heavily on saving labor, improving efficiency and waste, and providing easily for more capacity in the future, should it be needed. Having sufficient capacity was an important consideration. Due to aggressive marketing, Sloop sales during the 1970s had grown appreciably (e.g., 10 percent per year), and this had put a strain on Sloop capacity, threatening both quality and cost targets.

Soon after the Pitt-George paper, Harry Pitt became heavily involved with another project and did not resume the push for a new Sloop plant until April 1983. From then on he, together with two other engineers, devoted nearly full time to the project, developing the concept further and identifying its costs and benefits. By August 1983 a provi-

EXHIBIT 2
ROYAL CLYDE BISCUIT CO., LTD.
Organization Chart for the Company (1986–1987)

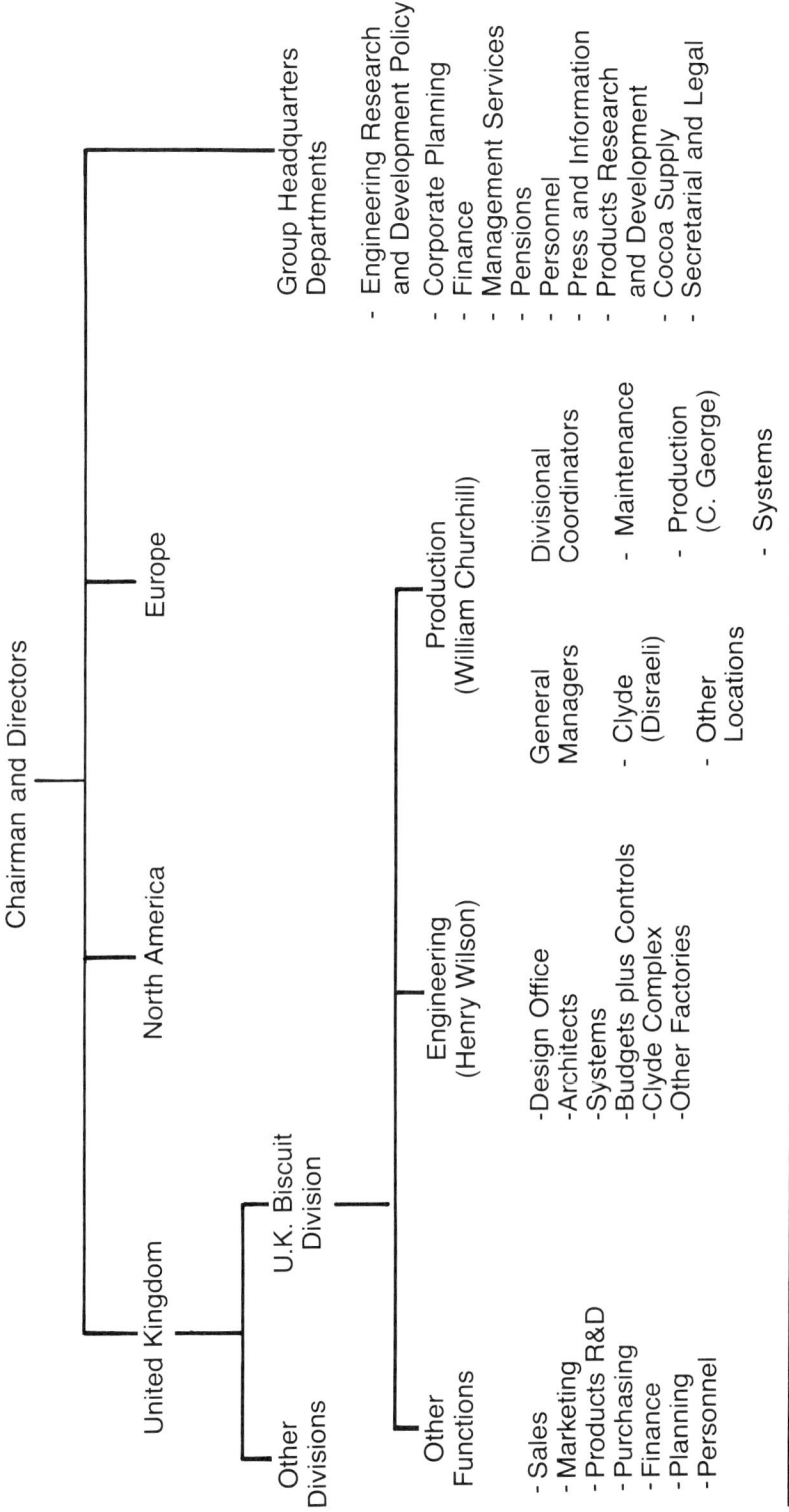

Chairman and Directors

- United Kingdom
- North America
- Europe

Group Headquarters Departments

- Engineering Research and Development Policy
- Corporate Planning
- Finance
- Management Services
- Pensions
- Personnel
- Press and Information
- Products Research and Development
- Cocoa Supply
- Secretarial and Legal

United Kingdom

- Other Divisions
- U.K. Biscuit Division

Other Functions

- Sales
- Marketing
- Products R&D
- Purchasing
- Finance
- Planning
- Personnel

Engineering (Henry Wilson)

- Design Office
- Architects
- Systems
- Budgets plus Controls
- Clyde Complex
- Other Factories

Production (William Churchill)

General Managers
- Clyde (Disraeli)
- Other Locations

Divisional Coordinators
- Maintenance
- Production (C. George)
- Systems

EXHIBIT 2 (concluded)
ROYAL CLYDE BISCUIT CO., LTD.
Organization Chart for the Clyde Complex

1. Production

General Manager
(R. Disraeli)

Factory Manager
for Sloop,
Others
(C. Macmillan)

Other
plants

Chief Maintenance
Engineer

— Factory personnel

Chocolate   Other
brands

Sloop
(R. Gladstone)

Sloop
(C. Eden)

Others

Overlookers (1 per shift)

Chargehands

Operators

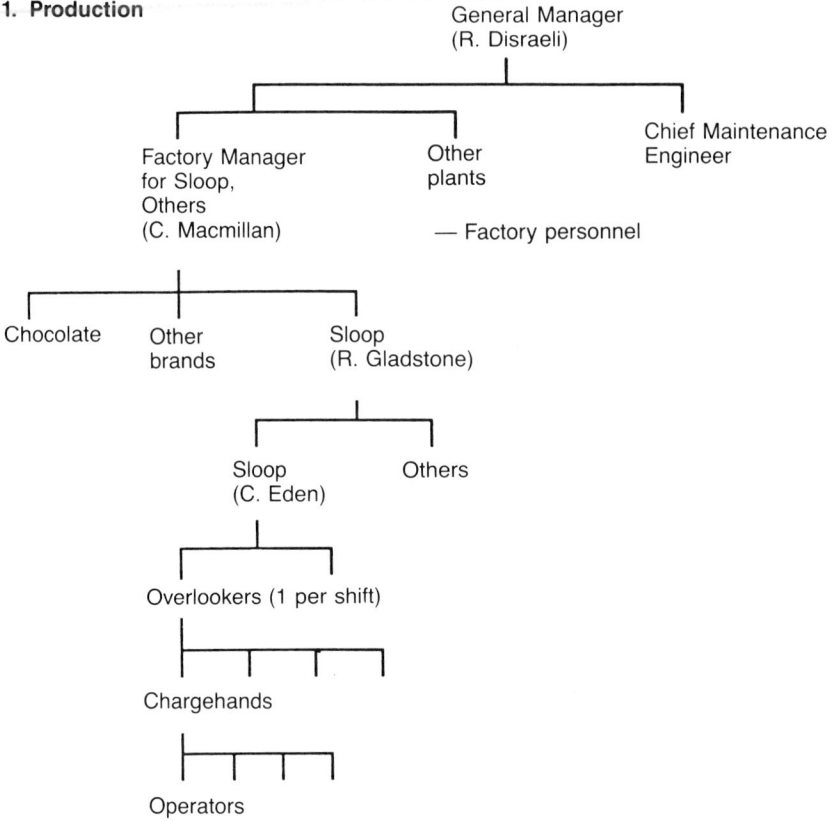

2. Engineering

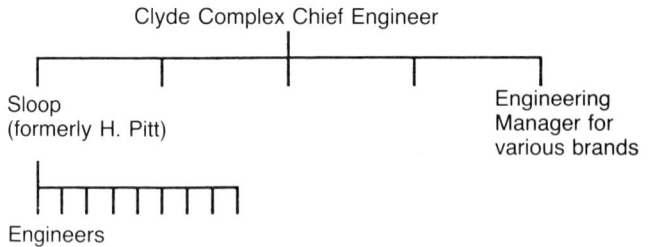

Clyde Complex Chief Engineer

Sloop
(formerly H. Pitt)

Engineering
Manager for
various brands

Engineers

sional timetable had been mapped out. The enabling study was approved by the board of directors in October 1983 with approval of the full project and its capital appropriations request coming in January 1984.

In the two years between the Pitt-George paper and the board's aproval, the project grew in size and ambition. While the original thinking called for a new building, much of the equipment was to be relocated from the old plant and not replaced. Costs were to run at £6.5 million. However, the approved project, as of January 1984, called for £16.4 million of expenditure, with significant funds allocated to replacing equipment, and, indeed, stretching the state of the art. For example, the new chocolate deposit and molding machine (known as the molding machine) was to be wider (1600 mm vs. 1200 mm), handling of the cooking-carrying trays and the Sloop molds was to be significantly automated, the packaging equipment was to be faster, and the molding machine's speed was to vary to match the ability of the wrapping machines to take up the machine's output.

At the time of the board's approval, however, many of the particulars about the new No. 4 Sloop plant were left to be decided. The capital appropriation request itself was rather sketchy about the nature of the new plant. The decisions defining its character were largely left to the engineering-led groups that oversaw the project, once it had been approved.

PROJECT ORGANIZATION

In October 1983, Harry Pitt had dropped all his responsibilities with the other products under his authority to concentrate exclusively on Sloop. By mid-1984, he had gone further, shedding all other Sloop projects except for the new No. 4 plant. At this time there were three mechanical engineers and two electrical engineers working full time with Harry on the plant design. They were aided by an internal team of eight to ten designers and one in-house architect. This, then, was the team that worked day in and day out on the project.

The policy decisions and guidance for this working team was provided by two committees, formed in February 1984, one reporting to the other. The base committee, termed the "Project Management Group," was chaired by Harry Pitt and had the following composition:

Chairman, Engineering (Harry Pitt).

Production (Rob Gladstone—Gladstone had joined Sloop in the fall of 1983 from the Chocolate Department. He was designated as the production manager at Clyde with responsibilities for all export and domestic production of Sloop.)

Product quality (the quality control function).

Chief architect.

Installation manager (the lead craftsman for capital projects at the Clyde complex).

This Project Management Group met every two weeks, on average, for the first year of its existence and then every month for the second year. The last recorded meeting was December 1985. The Project Management Group was charged with keeping a formal record of decisions made, timetables, cash flows, and communications. It was this group that dealt with the many decisions left hanging once the capital appropriations request had been approved. These decisions included, for example, some related to the building itself (roof construction, wall finishes, tiling), some related to equipment choice (which equipment vendor to select), and some related to the concept for the new plant (how the wrapping ought to be linked to the boxing, how the baked cookie biscuits ought to be loaded into trays).

The Project Management Group reported to a more senior-level Project Control Group. Its composition was as follows:

Harry Pitt, as liaison from the Project Management Group.

Chairman, Engineering (Henry Wilson, Harry's boss at the time, with responsibility for the Clyde complex.)

Factory manager (Clive Macmillan, with production responsibility for Sloop and some other brands at the Clyde complex.)

Chief chemist.

Finance representative.

Marketing representative.

THE CONCEPT FOR THE PLANT

As the planning proceeded on No. 4 Sloop, both before and after the board's approval, the concept for the plant became increasingly clear. First and foremost, No. 4 Sloop was to be a plant that integrated cookie-baking, chocolate deposit and molding, joining and packaging, with none of the disjoint operations and materials-handling problems that had afflicted previous generations of Sloop production units. Such an integration would save on the duplication of various overhead functions, simplify materials handling, and facilitate the cleaning of the plant and its equipment. This integration would also foster a smooth flow of product with the accompanying benefits of low stock levels and more efficient materials usage. It would also be a plant on one level, streamlining the layout and permitting utilities to be hidden from normal view.

There were several advances to be made in the production technology embodied in the plant. Some were naturally riskier than others. Among the relatively more risky changes were the following: (1) Automatic filling of trays with biscuits prior to their placement in the molds. (2) Automated feeding of trays of biscuits to the "position and place" section of the molding machine. (3) A wider molding machine (1600 mm vs. 1200 mm). (4) Higher-speed packaging machines where typically 10 cookies would be stacked and wrapped in cellophane packs known as "stack packs." (5) Automatic and instantaneous regulation of the speed of the molding machine to coincide with the prevailing capabilities of the stack pack machines to wrap what the molding machine delivers to them. (6) Mechanical conveyor links between the stack packers and the machines that placed the cellophane packs of cookies into boxes. (7) A new boxing machine for packaging 2, 3, or 4 cookie stacks into different size boxes. Other advances in the design of the plant were not expected to be as risky, although they were new to Sloop (e.g., initial chocolate deposit by a movable depositing head).

In addition to this rethinking of the production technology, there was a rethinking of the organization and management of the plant. The new ideas in this domain were largely associated with Rob Gladstone, although they were in tune with what others in production (e.g., Charlie George and his boss, William Churchill) were thinking. In particular, Rob wanted to adopt more of a "team" concept than had prevailed previously. The new, integrated design for the plant facilitated his approach and the four main production areas (cookie-baking, molding, joining, and packaging) were to report to a single shift supervisor (called an overlooker, as shown in Exhibit 2). More worker participation in management decisions was to be encouraged as well.

Under the old system, maintenance (the fitters) did not report to the plant manager, there were separate foremen (known as chargehands) for the four main production areas, and the output rate was the major criterion for evaluating them. Under Rob Gladstone's proposed system, maintenance would report to the plant manager, and an overlooker would be atop all of cookie-baking, molding, joining, and packaging each shift. The workers in each production area were to constitute a team, and the tasks they were responsible for would be enlarged to include cost, quality, cleanliness, and material usage, in addition to the output rate. Their skills would be expanded, with emphasis on flexibility and quality. Gladstone wanted the chargehands to be part of those teams, to run their particular areas as if they were their own businesses, and to get "their hands dirty." That way Rob felt they could take more initiative in improving costs, quality, and other aspects of the operation.

With the changes in production technology and the improved concept, Gladstone felt that the manning of the new plant could be significantly reduced (Exhibit 3 summarizes what Rob proposed in December 1984 for the packaging area). This change would naturally require a much bigger commitment to training than had typically been made before. Prior training had often been characterized as "sitting beside Nellie"—informal, on-the-job, one-on-one training. Techniques such as statistical quality control had not been pursued.

THE PLAN AND THE REALITY

The step-by-step plan for the construction and outfitting of No. 4 Sloop, as adopted in February 1984, just after board approval, called for (1) the molding and joining equipment to be operational at the end of September 1985, (2) the packaging machines to be operational a month later, and (3) the cookie-baking plant to be up and running by the end of May 1986. However, because of some late deliveries of equipment and troubles with some equipment installations and start-ups (e.g., the molding machine, stack packers), the schedule slipped. The molding operation was not completely cut over from the older plant until the end of April 1986 and was not up to design capacity until October 1986. The batter and oven sections of the cookie plant were not operational until August 1986. The filling-making equipment, because of late equipment deliveries, was not yet started up, nor was the automatic feed of cookie biscuits to the molding machine.

Although late equipment deliveries accounted for some of the start-up's delays and difficulties, they were not the major reason. Trouble getting the equipment to operate as planned was a far greater problem. Here are some of the key areas of difficulty:

EXHIBIT 3
ROYAL CLYDE BISCUIT CO., LTD.
Plant Manning Levels for Packaging

This exhibit compares the traditional manning levels at the Clyde Sloop plant with (1) those proposed in December 1984 by Rob Gladstone, with (2) the levels that would prevail under William Churchill's notion of the "perfect" machine, where quality is so good and reliable that labor for monitoring purposes can be greatly reduced, and with (3) the current manning levels at the plant.

Category for Packaging (February 87)	Traditional Plant	Proposed for Sloop*	Perfect Machine Figures	Present
Direct labor:				
Chargehand	1	2	2	2
12 stack packing machines	12	6	2	8
Remove molding & joining waste	2	—	—	—
Take off and refeed	2	—	—	—
Relief	5	2	—	4
Transport	1	—	—	1
Boxing, pallets	6	6	4	6
Operate reserve machines	1	—	—	—
Total	30		8	21
Indirect labor:				
Cleaning	½	1	1	1
Special boxing	12	1	1	3
Materials input + coding	2	1	1	—
Maintenance	¾	—	—	—
Machine clean	1	—	—	—
Total	16¼		3	4
Packaging total	46¼	19	11	25
Index of production capacity	100	142	213	135

*Note: For Gladstone's proposal, there are two teams of 10 and 9 people each (plus chargehands). The breakdown of direct vs. indirect is therefore not exact for the proposal.

1. Stack pack handling. Getting stack packs in and out of their packaging machines was not initially viewed as risky. However, problems with both electrical and mechanical response times meant that the system struggled to make 24 tons per shift, whereas the target was 32 tons per shift. It took four engineers working three months to solve the problems.
2. Linking stack packing to boxing. Initially, there was to be a

buffer inventory of between 2 and 4 minutes of production between the stack packing machines and the boxing machines that placed Sloop into boxes. Such a buffer inventory was to permit either stack packing machines or boxing machines to go down (e.g., jam) without the other type of machine having to slow down or go out of service temporarily. Building up such a buffer inventory required that stack packs be quickly and effectively rotated into a vertical position while proceeding down a conveyor. Accomplishing this at high speed was more difficult than expected. As of February 1987, there was only a buffer of 30 seconds to a minute of production between stack packing and boxing.

3. Linking boxing to palletizing. A special elevator to move boxes of Sloop between the packaging machines and the palletizer never worked properly. Instead, that system was ripped out and an inclined conveyor was being installed as of February 1987.

4. Automatic feeding of trays of cookie biscuits to the molding machine. This was yet to work well.

The other production technology that was viewed as risky had either worked out beautifully or had worked out well enough so as not to jeopardize the timetable for the start-up. Nevertheless, the unreliability of some of the new equipment during start-up had delayed the achievement of overall target production and quality yield levels.

SUFFERING FROM NEGLECT

In retrospect, for both Harry Pitt and Rob Gladstone the aspect of the No. 4 Sloop project that was most neglected was the management information system (MIS). To the Project Management Group's credit, a sizable number of sensors of various types had been placed at strategic places within the process; there were, for example, 20–30 discrete computer control systems within the process. These systems could indicate such things as the speed of the operation, its output, missed strokes, temperatures, weights, lengths of machine stoppages, and information on breakdowns. However, these separate systems could not talk to each other electronically, thus making troubleshooting more difficult. Especially for Rob Gladstone, a functioning computerized information system was a critical way to improve quality at the plant, especially during start-up; how else could equipment be monitored so that one could know what had gone wrong and where?

MIS had always been the neglected piece of the project. It was at the board meeting to approve the project that MIS was first discussed; it had not been addressed before. Since that time, more had been done on MIS, but it never got the attention other aspects of the project got. Management had even turned down as too costly an offer by Hewlett-Packard to develop an information system, preferring to develop it itself. To Rob Gladstone's mind, however, developing a workable system in-house was likely to be far more expensive and time-consuming than having Hewlett-Packard tackle the job.

Moreover, Rob had a candidate problem for a new MIS system to tackle. Maintaining the consistent quality of the cookie biscuits while using flour from the European Common Market (as opposed to Canadian red winter wheat) was a problem. Knowing how to alter moisture content, fermentation, and so on to compensate for inconsistencies in the flour would increase the efficiency of the cookie-baking area by reducing hold-ups and stoppages caused by problems with the ingredients.

The other area of importance that arguably suffered from neglect was training. The actual production people who were to run No. 4 Sloop were not brought into the plant until rather late in the game (Charlie Eden in July 1985, the overlookers in October 1985, and the charge-hands in December 1985), with insufficient time to train with equipment that, in many cases, was quite different from and more sophisticated than what they were used to. It was generally acknowledged that a more formal approach to planning training at the start of the project would have been of significant benefit.

THE LINGERING PROBLEM OF FLEXIBILITY

Over the years, production had always seemed to guess wrong about the mix of packaging that was required for Sloop. The fact that marketing did not do any better at guessing did not make things any easier. The multipacking of Sloop into big boxes (e.g., 4 stack packs to a box) had been on the rise, and had far outstripped expectations. In 1977, there was none done. By 1984, 6 percent of Sloop was packaged that way. By 1987, 15 percent of Sloop was packaged in the big box. Production had done its best to sniff out trends, but marketing's future requirements for packaging were apparently difficult for even marketing to identify far enough in advance to influence plant design and equipment purchase.

One aspect of No. 4 Sloop, therefore, was specifically designed to facilitate packaging flexibility. The conveyor between the stack packing and boxing machines was capable of diverting stack packs to locations other than the established boxing machines. These other locations could house packaging equipment with other capabilities. What more might be needed for Sloop was not known. While this design modification was an undisputed advance, for Bill Churchill, the director of all U.K. cookie production, this approach was probably not radical enough a solution to the chronic problem of packaging flexibility. He encouraged the pursuit of significantly different packaging concepts that could free production from the scrambling and high-cost off-line packaging of special marketing demands.

REFLECTIONS: HARRY PITT

As Harry Pitt looked back on the previous 3½ years, he was struck by several things. Of course, there were the hardware problems that had been encountered (described above) and the relative neglect of the computer control and information systems, but there was also a measure of pride in all that had gone well and that had improved the efficiency and flexibility of the plant. After all, they had succeeded in building the largest molding and joining machines ever, and were producing Sloop in greater volumes with better quality and huge gains in productivity.

Engineer that he was, Harry still thought about how the hardware problems could be solved. But he also wondered how the decision-making process itself could be improved. In retrospect, Harry wondered if the company might have been better off by delaying the date on which the board was expected to approve the capital appropriations request. It seemed to him that many key decisions for the project were taken after the board's approval, and perhaps on a timetable that was too quick. Indeed, the project team had to approach the board two more times during the term of the project for additional requests that totaled another £0.7 million in expenditure. A more complete preparation of the capital appropriation request, with more details surrounding the concepts proposed, held an attraction for Harry.

The two-tier committee structure for the project also seemed suspect. It did carry some advantages. Notably, it forced the Project Management Group to record its decisions and to present them for regular, formal review. On the other hand, the two-tier structure meant that two groups were trying to do the same job, and that led to some friction and the need to communicate across too many levels of management. Harry did not feel that the two-tier structure actually achieved the stated objective of controlling the project; Harry was his own auditor.

If he were to have to do the project again, he would not involve marketing any more than they were, but he would involve production to a greater extent. In particular, he would involve the person who would have to run the plant on a day-to-day basis (e.g., Charlie Eden, a direct report to Rob Gladstone) in the planning phase, and not simply in the start-up phase of the project. This would have necessitated the early appointment of the plant production manager, something company policy did not encourage, but Harry felt that it would have more than paid for itself.

REFLECTIONS: ROB GLADSTONE

For Rob Gladstone, especially now that the plant was up and running to capacity, although with higher manning levels than he felt should be the case (see Exhibit 3), the biggest disappointment was the lack of an information system that could spot problems and assist in their diagnosis. This promised to be a thorn in production's side for quite a while.

There were also some hardware complaints from production. For example, production preferred a different, more expensive, vendor for the machines that fed the stack packers than the one that was chosen, and would gladly have traded off costs elsewhere in the project. On the whole, however, Gladstone was very pleased about many aspects of the new factory, notably the cookie-baking and molding areas.

Like Harry Pitt, Rob Gladstone had concerns that transcended individual decisions. Chief among these concerns was the excessively functional management structure at Royal Clyde Biscuit. Rob was not convinced that the start-up of the plant was best controlled by engineering. To his way of thinking, the production manager should be in charge; after all, the production people would run the plant after the start-up. Indeed, Rob's ideas went further. Why not structure management into a Sloop business unit? Reporting to the Sloop business general manager would be production, maintenance, engineering, and product quality. Such an arrangement, in Rob's eyes, would foster teamwork at all levels. For example, Rob had a list of 140 unfinished, mainly minor, items from the plant start-up that he had taken up with engineering. Yet he knew that they would be worked on by engineering according to their priorities and not his; he would be reduced to pestering. How much better, he reasoned, for production to have more of a hand in deciding what engineering projects ought to be attacked first.

PART 2

OPERATIONS PLANNING AND CONTROL

The cases in this section deal with the development of plans for conducting activities and the execution of those plans. The planning process involves establishing the conditions under which future activities are going to take place. This can set heavy constraints on the operations. Within the plans, the day-to-day activities of an organization can reach the desired objectives or stray from the mark. This requires managerial control and detailed evaluation of the execution of the plans. The interaction of the planning and execution processes form the basis for most of these cases. As you might suspect, however, there are often other issues of a broader nature that arise.

The introductory case, The Geneva Technical Institute (B), describes the control mechanisms that have been put in place for the duplicating facilities of the institute. The case describes a capacity plan that covers the average demand, and details the activities of staff because of the peaks that occur. It raises the question of matching the system to the needs of the organization.

The Olivetti case explores the planning system for a line of computers introduced by this Italian multinational company. The impact of the planning system on the production activities is discussed in some detail. The next case moves from broad global planning systems to the execution concerns at a Finnish company, Kumera Oy. Kumera makes heavy speed reduction equipment and is facing pressure for improved profitability. The focus is on the activities on the factory floor and how to improve the company's deteriorating performance in the market-place.

The Acme Chemical case returns to broad issues of planning—in this instance, organizational. The company has created an organization with responsibility for managing global logistics operations. It is considering techniques to make the activities of the group more effective as it manages the material flows from raw material source to final customer. In Stewart Instruments, Ltd., the focus again shifts to inside the organization. The company makes scientific equipment for small laboratories. It has a fairly new material requirements planning (MRP) system in place. Since the installation, however, things have not improved and may even be getting worse.

The Geneva Technical Institute (B)

Dr. Albu realized that the duplicating facilities had been severely strained since the high-speed machine had been taken out and replaced with a lower speed duplicator. As department chairman of the Physics Department at the Geneva Technical Institute, he was very concerned that this change would delay substantially the distribution of material to classes and in general reduce the service of the duplication facility to his department. He had read several memos from the duplicating department asking for more lead time, better planning, and more reliable due dates for duplication work. They had stressed that the capacity of the equipment was sufficient for the average workload, but when the work came in peaks, it was very difficult to satisfy all persons. In order to understand the situation somewhat better, he gathered some information on the administrative process concerned with duplication requests.

INITIATING DUPLICATION REQUESTS

The duplication requests came primarily from the faculty directly to the secretaries in the department. The secretaries said the most common method was that a faculty member would come out of the office with a letter, article, or laboratory result and say, "Please get me four copies of this as soon as possible." Sometimes the faculty member would attach a handwritten note requesting copies and the number of copies required, but mostly it would be a verbal request. In these instances the original from which the copies were to be made would be handed to the secretary at the same time. Many of these requests were to provide a copy of something for a visitor in the office, to include in a letter to a colleague, or for distribution at an imminent committee meeting.

Sometimes there would be no original with the request. Such requests came mainly from the faculty but occasionally from the graduate students as well, and were for duplication of an item in the files or in the library. These would often take the form of a note or verbal request for a copy of an article by someone in the latest issue of the *Interna-*

Background information is contained in The Geneva Technical Institute (A) case, page 3.

tional Journal of Physics or for duplication of lab instructions from the files. In these cases the secretaries would have to go to the library to look up the article (often coming back for clarification) or to pull the instructions from the files and make it available for duplication.

In all cases, the reproduction of material in the duplicating department required filling out a request form which was available in the duplication department. This form required the specification of the number of pages to be duplicated, the purpose of the duplication, very explicit references if it was to be taken from a book, and the requesting professor's signature. It was on the duplication request form that the due date was specified. The secretary would fill out the form and then return it to the professor for signature. There were occasions where the secretary would sign the professor's name in order to get copies done quickly, but this was discouraged. Sometimes several days could elapse while waiting for the professor's signature authorizing duplication of the material.

APPROVAL OF MORE THAN 10 COPIES

The institute had been concerned about the increasing costs of paper and duplication. As a result of this concern, a general procedure had been developed which specified that department chairmen should approve long duplication runs. Dr. Albu had interpreted this to mean all runs of material to be distributed to the students. The secretaries, on the other hand, had occasionally asked him to approve runs of 10 or more copies of papers since other departments had been requesting chairman approval for runs over 10 copies each. The duplication center generally used the copier for up to 10 copies and the duplicating equipment for more than 10 copies.

There had been many times when delays of several days had occurred while waiting for the department chairman's approval for duplication of more than 10 copies. In a few instances this had created some real difficulties for a faculty member who was interested in getting a current article or news item distributed to his class. Dr. Albu called one of the institute administrators about the duplication capacity and was told it was unlikely to change in the near future. The cost of paper had continued to increase but requiring approval had already reduced the number of copies being made. The administrator reinforced the idea that he would like to see approval of any runs of more than 10 copies. Dr.

Albu knew, however, that some of the faculty were submitting multiple requests for 10 copies each, since it could be quicker to get copies that way.

THE DUPLICATION PROCESS

Once all the paperwork had been completed and the signatures obtained, the secretaries physically carried the material down to the duplicating department. There the duplicating request and originals were turned over to a clerk who filed the material by due date. The duplicating machine operators tried to work on the material in the order in which it was required. In some cases, however, the secretary was able to persuade the clerk that the request was "urgent." In such instances the secretary might wait until the duplication was complete before returning to the department. In other cases the secretary would return occasionally to the duplication department to see if there was any duplication ready.

In the normal course of events the duplication would be performed on the day required (or earlier if possible, but this was increasingly less frequent). After it was completed, it would be put into a mail box for the Physics Department and the secretaries would pick it up from there on one of their trips to the duplicating area. They would return it to the departmental mail box or desk of the requesting faculty member. Occasionally since the entrance to the building in which the Physics Department was located was right by the duplicating facility, faculty coming in from the outside would pick up the material for the department.

In some instances, if the material was late or the faculty member was concerned about its getting "lost," the secretary would have to go down to the duplicating department and check to see if the material was completed. If it was complete, it would be delivered to the professor. If not, the secretary would need to return at a later time, perhaps after changing the due date or indicting the urgency of the request to the duplicating department.

As Dr. Albu turned to the analysis of the duplication process, he was aware of the concern that several of the faculty had expressed over the delays. He was concerned with the administration's tough stand on duplication approvals, but he still hoped that he could build a case that would help the administration decide to return to the larger, faster equipment.

Olivetti—The Scarmagno Plant

"How can we make products which were not forecasted?" asked Mr. Pescarmona, manager of Olivetti's Distributed Processing and Office Automation Systems plant at Scarmagno, nine kilometers from the company's administrative headquarters in Ivrea, Italy.

Smiling ruefully, he complained about the difficulties that Intel Corporation in California was having in meeting surging demand for its 16-bit microprocessor chips. In a newspaper article, it described how the company had been "caught off guard by the huge surge in demand . . . (when) the economic recovery, combined with an increase in the use of microprocessors in many segments of the industry, turned a semiconductor surplus into a shortage." The chips in demand were the heart of IBM's personal computer (PC) and of the majority of IBM-compatible machines produced by other manufacturers, including Olivetti. Mr. Pescarmona continued:

> Failure to make long-term commitments can cause future shortages when the market gets tight and delivery lead time for microprocessor chips is eight months. We know that IBM has made commitments through June 1985. Supplier capacity is being gobbled up. Alternative sources of supply are available, but these are limited since quality is an issue. All of our purchased components must meet stringent quality control criteria.
>
> Last year, due to economic conditions, we were not experiencing component and part shortages. Today it is a different story. For components having an eight-month delivery lead time, we need to make purchasing commitments this month at the latest (February 1984) in order to satisfy production requirements for the first six months of next year. How can this be done when the forecast of demand used as a basis for those requirements is not due until the end of this month? Furthermore, the forecast itself is likely to be revised twice before being considered final as of September 30!

At Olivetti headquarters, Mr. Samaja, director of Sales and Marketing elaborated:

> To me the issue is clear. How can the company balance the need for economies of manufacturing with the realities of a marketplace in which products, markets and competitors are constantly changing? When the life of a product is limited to 2–4 years, we need to re-think the way we do things.

More and more competitors in our industry are relying on the same handful of component manufacturers and software houses for their basic hardware and software. Also, in the future, most new products will be compatible with the de facto "IBM standard" and will run identical or similar applications software. To differentiate ourselves in this market, we will have to understand customer requirements and be able to respond quickly to change.

This is especially true where large systems and customers are concerned. A contract with a bank for the computerization of its operations is signed only after several months of negotiation.

Once the contract is signed, a branch bank is often chosen for the pilot installation. Invariably, the customer then makes systems and configuration modifications, for example, in printers, in memory capacity, or in magnetic storage media. Thus, the mix of systems options which are actually installed can differ substantially from those originally specified in the contract.

Under these circumstances, defining the product mix in the long term, particularly for our larger configurable[1] systems, is very difficult. Inevitably this affects the accuracy of the forecasts that we make.

We cannot afford to let ourselves be constrained by manufacturing lead times. Our personal computer, the M20, was announced in March 1982 and was demonstrated at the Hannover Fair a few weeks later. In order to be competitive, the M20 had to be developed and introduced in a fairly short time period. Manufacturing had to respond quickly.

COMPANY BACKGROUND

The Olivetti group of companies was one of the world's major producers of office automation and data processing equipment. The group was organized under a parent company, Ing. C. Olivetti & C., S.p.A., named after Camillo Olivetti, who founded the company in 1908. Approximately twenty-five Italian subsidiaries and a holding company, Olivetti International S.A., were held by the parent company. Thirty-two foreign subsidiaries were held, in turn, by Olivetti International S.A. These included sales companies in major international markets and manufacturing plants in six countries other than Italy. In addition, agents and distributors represented Olivetti in over 100 other countries.

---

[1]A configurable system is one in which the customer must make a choice among several options for most of the elements in the system.

While tracing its roots to the manufacture of typewriters, by the 1950s Olivetti had become a major producer of a broad line of office equipment and furniture. In the 1960s, the company expanded into electronics with the introduction of a line of computers, terminals, and peripheral equipment. In 1965, Olivetti introduced the world's first electronic desktop computer, the Programma 101. It was the first "microcomputer," 12 years ahead of the Apple II.

In 1982, the group achieved consolidated net revenues of lire 3,341,400,000,000 and before-tax profits of lire 145,500,000,000 (in mid-1982, 1000 lire = 0.73 U.S.$). Over 70 percent of Olivetti's revenues were accounted for by distributed processing and office automation equipment.

In addition to investing in its own R&D operations in Italy and five other research centers throughout the world, Olivetti was an active investor in several high-technology companies operating in the information handling sector. These investments were designed to give Olivetti rapid access to new products and technologies and to give the company a more effective commercial presence in important U.S. and European markets. As of June 1983, Olivetti owned a minority interest in 21 high-technology companies in the United States and four in Europe, and was aggressively seeking additional investment opportunities.

GROUP STRUCTURE AND ORGANIZATION

Olivetti group activities were administered from Ivrea. A simplified organization chart is shown in Exhibit 1. The group was structured by function, with each director reporting to Mr. Fubini, the chief operating officer. Manufacturing operations were structured on a divisional basis: The six divisions manufactured distributed processing and office automation equipment, cash registers and calculators, office copiers, typewriters, peripheral equipment, and telecommunications devices.

Marketing activities, under the direction of Mr. Cassoni, comprised product management, marketing, and several marketing support functions. Product management responsibilities were structured along lines similar to the manufacturing divisions. Four product managers were responsible for distributed processing systems, office products, cash registers and other point-of-sale equipment, and telecommunications equipment.

EXHIBIT 1
OLIVETTI—THE SCARMAGNO PLANT
Simplified Corporate Organization Chart

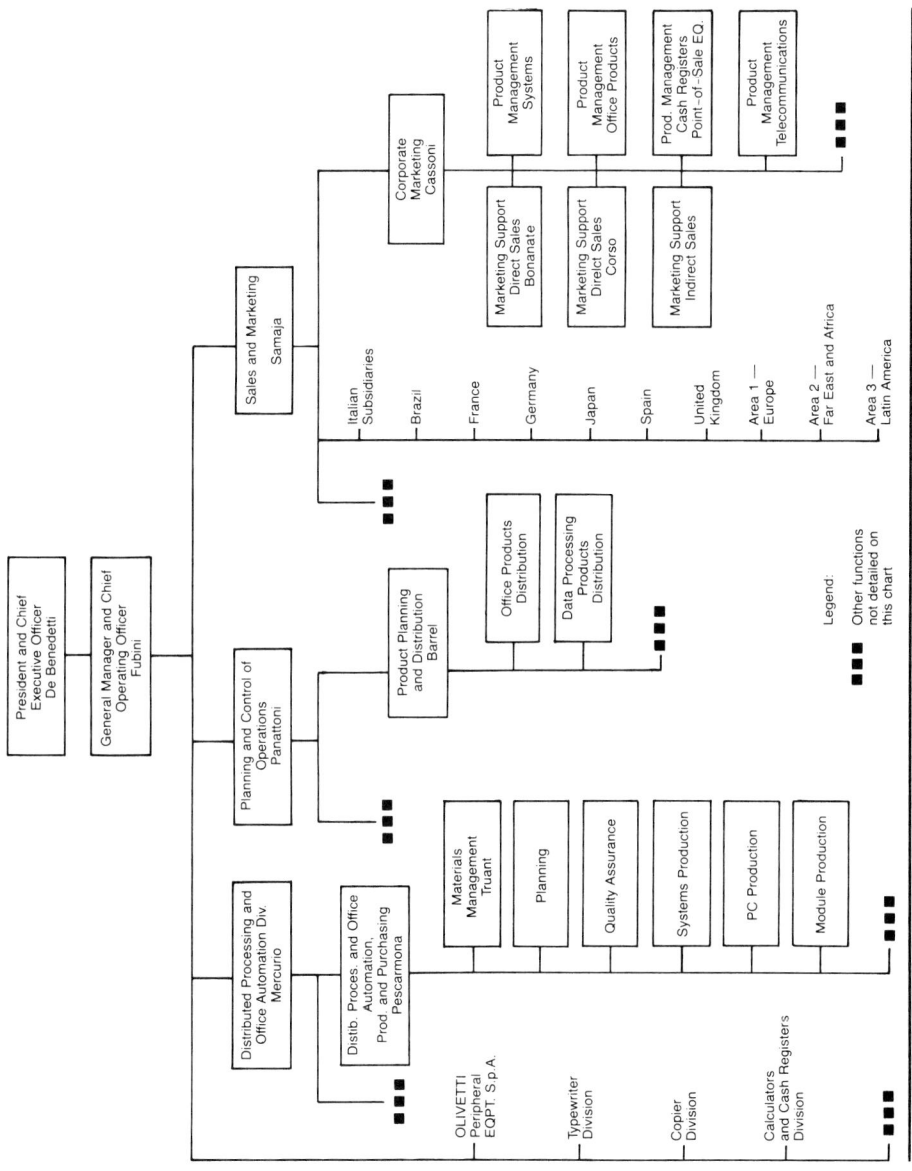

The marketing function was organized by type of account, with three classifications:

1. Large accounts which generated, or had the potential to generate, significant sales volume through multiple purchases of equipment for automating office procedures. These large accounts built complex telecommunications and distributed processing networks which might include a mainframe computer made by another manufacturer. For example, a bank might have as many as 2,000 workstations of various types within a network.
2. Medium to small accounts, generally including companies for which an Olivetti minicomputer would be sufficient to support a distributed processing system. Individual sales made to such accounts would usually be for no less than 30 million lire (U.S.$ 20,000).
3. Indirect sales to small accounts, handled through agents and distributors rather than the direct sales force.

Planning and Control of Operations was under the direction of Mr. Panattoni. This department played an important role in providing the linkage between Olivetti subsidiaries and OEM (original equipment manufacturer) customers, on the one hand, and manufacturing and OEM suppliers on the other. To accomplish its planning function, the department generated aggregate production plans based on the consolidation of requirement forecasts submitted by the various sales subsidiaries. On the control side, the department processed orders received from the subsidiaries, consolidated and communicated these orders to the factories, and arranged for the accumulation and shipment of finished goods to the subsidiaries from a centralized warehouse.

SCARMAGNO PLANT AND PRODUCT LINES

The plant itself was a large, modern complex on an open site just outside a small village near Ivrea. It consisted of four large buildings and several smaller structures totaling 150,000 square meters. In early 1984, over 2,400 hourly workers and approximately 1,000 managerial and technical staff were employed there.

In early 1984, the Scarmagno plant's primary mission was the production of Olivetti's distributed processing and office automation systems, referred to as the Linea 1 or L1 family of products, which it accomplished in one of the site's four buildings. Accounting systems, data processing systems and terminals, word processing systems, and printers were also manufactured on-site.

The L1 line, most of which had been introduced in 1982, was designed as a multifunction group of products for technical, scientific, or business computing, or for distributed data processing applications such as data entry, transmission, and real-time processing. The extensive range of configurations and options available, and the compatibility of most products within the line, made it possible for Olivetti to offer L1 systems as a solution to a wide variety of data processing problems—from single workstations in a small business setting to large, multistation systems with Olivetti micro and minicomputers communicating and sharing tasks with large mainframe computers manufactured by other companies. The four major groups of products, built around four different central processing units, are described briefly in Exhibit 2.

Although the M20 personal computer was designed to fit into the L1 line (it could operate as a multifunction workstation for another system), it differed from the rest of the L1 family. First, because it was sold primarily as a stand-alone unit with a U.S. $2,000–3,000 price that was much less than the smallest M30 system, the M20's unit volume was double that of the rest of the L1 line. Secondly, far fewer options were available for the M20 than for the other systems, as the M20 was itself a "complete" system. The M30/40/60 systems required a number of customer decisions to "configure" the system, including type of keyboard and display, storage media, and interfaces. Finally, over 90 percent of M20 sales were made "indirectly," through dealers or agents. The M20 personal computer relied heavily on software developed and distributed by outside firms.

In contrast, the rest of the L1 line was usually sold directly to the final customer by the Olivetti sales organization as part of a "total office automation solution." By early 1984, Olivetti had developed specialized software packages for scientific and technical, general business, distributed data processing, and banking applications. New or adapted hardware and peripheral equipment was developed for many customers to complement and enhance the specific software applications' effectiveness. As systems applications became more numerous and as Olivetti

EXHIBIT 2
OLIVETTI—THE SCARMAGNO PLANT
Brief Description of the L1 Product Line

M20: A 16-bit personal computer with keyboard and storage media (floppy and/or hard disk) integrated into the system unit. Competitive with other personal computers such as the IBM-PC and the Apple II or III. There are interfaces to connect the unit with peripherals such as a printer or a modem (communications device), or to a network of other computers (in which case the M20 could perform as a workstation or a "smart" terminal).

EXHIBIT 2 (continued)
OLIVETTI—THE SCARMAGNO PLANT
Brief Description of the L1 Product Line

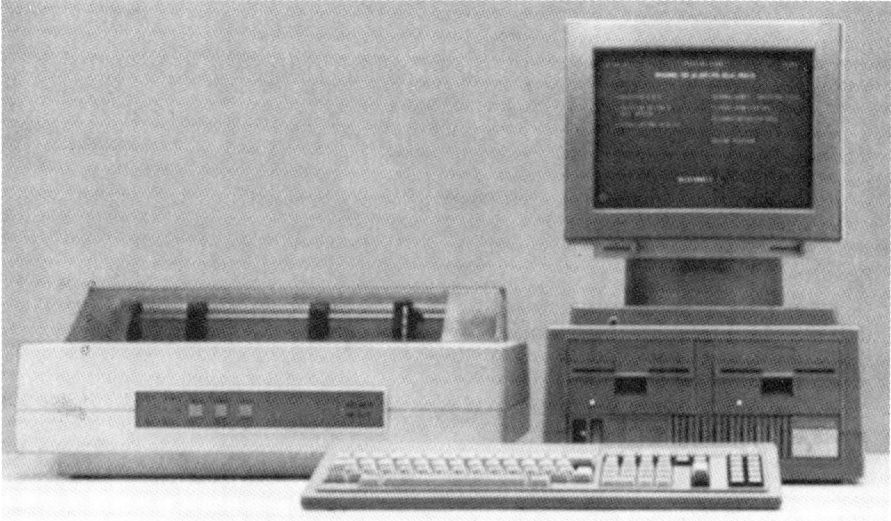

M30: A desktop cabinet housing a CPU with 256 to 512K of memory, two storage devices (floppy disk or hard disk units), and all interfaces and control units necessary to handle from one to four workstations, including keyboard, video display unit and printer.

and its customers gained experience with the machines, the M30/40/60 line grew and evolved.

INVENTORY

Extensive inventories of electronic components, electric parts, and OEM components were maintained under tight physical and quality control. Inventory information was readily available to DPDP[2] and plant management. In early 1984, the Scarmagno plant maintained an inventory equivalent in value to approximately 50 days of plant shipments,

---

[2]The Product Planning and Distribution Department name is translated from the Italian title Direzione Programmazione e Distribuzione Prodotti, or DPDP.

EXHIBIT 2 (concluded)
OLIVETTI—THE SCARMAGNO PLANT
Brief Description of the L1 Product Line

M40: A desk-sized cabinet housing a CPU with 256 to 512K of memory, three types of storage media (floppy disk, hard disk unit, or streaming tape for backup storage of data files), and a more complete and sophisticated array of interface and control units. The M40 can handle dozens of workstations through direct connection and network connection working with mainframe host computers or other M30 or M40 computers.

M60: A still more powerful model approximately the same size as the M40. More sophisticated networking capability, and supporting a wider range of disciplines for controlling workstations through dedicated or switched lines.

Completing the M30/40/60 lines was a large variety of keyboards, display and storage devices, printers, and other peripherals. All of these were compatible across the entire line and could be used with any of the central processing units.

with parts, components, and other material accounting for 30 days and work-in-process inventories for the remainder.

PLANNING CYCLE

Olivetti's fiscal year corresponded to the calendar year, with the planning cycle for any particular year beginning as early as mid-April of the previous year.

Between mid-April and the end of June, the Planning and Control of Operations Department in Ivrea provided each sales subsidiary with an "input budget." This document described the products, hardware and software options, and marketing strategy for the next calendar year. Once they received the input budget, sales subsidiary managers, usually in consultation with members of the Product Management Group, prepared a supply plan and budget for the next year. The supply plan contained a detailed list of the hardware, software, supplies and other product items required to meet the sales forecasts upon which the sales budget was based.

The complete supply planning document for 1984 was 68 pages long and included about 1,700 line items. However, not all of these items were sold by a particular subsidiary. For instance, while the supply plan listed all keyboard options in the product line, only a small number were used by any single subsidiary.

The supply plan (see Exhibit 3) consisted of a 12-month forecast of requirements, on a rolling 4-month basis. The plan was due on three distinct dates during the year: September 30, February 28, and May 20. These dates constituted the beginning of a new planning cycle. A fourth forecast, due July 31, provided an opportunity for the sales force to revise forecast requirements for the last 3 months of the fiscal year (October–December) based on actual results achieved during the first 6 months. However, this revision did not affect the 12-month rolling forecast.

In the first three cycles of this supply planning process, the subsidiaries filled in the quantities of each item desired in each of the three 4-month periods. The forecast of requirements for the first period (January–April) was considered binding on the subsidiary; the subsidiary was committed to sell those items. However, the forecast for the two remaining 4-month periods could be modified in the subsequent cycles of the planning process.

After consolidation of the individual sales subsidiary supply plans

EXHIBIT 3

OLIVETTI—THE SCARMAGNO PLANT

The Supply Plan and Parts Ordering Cycle

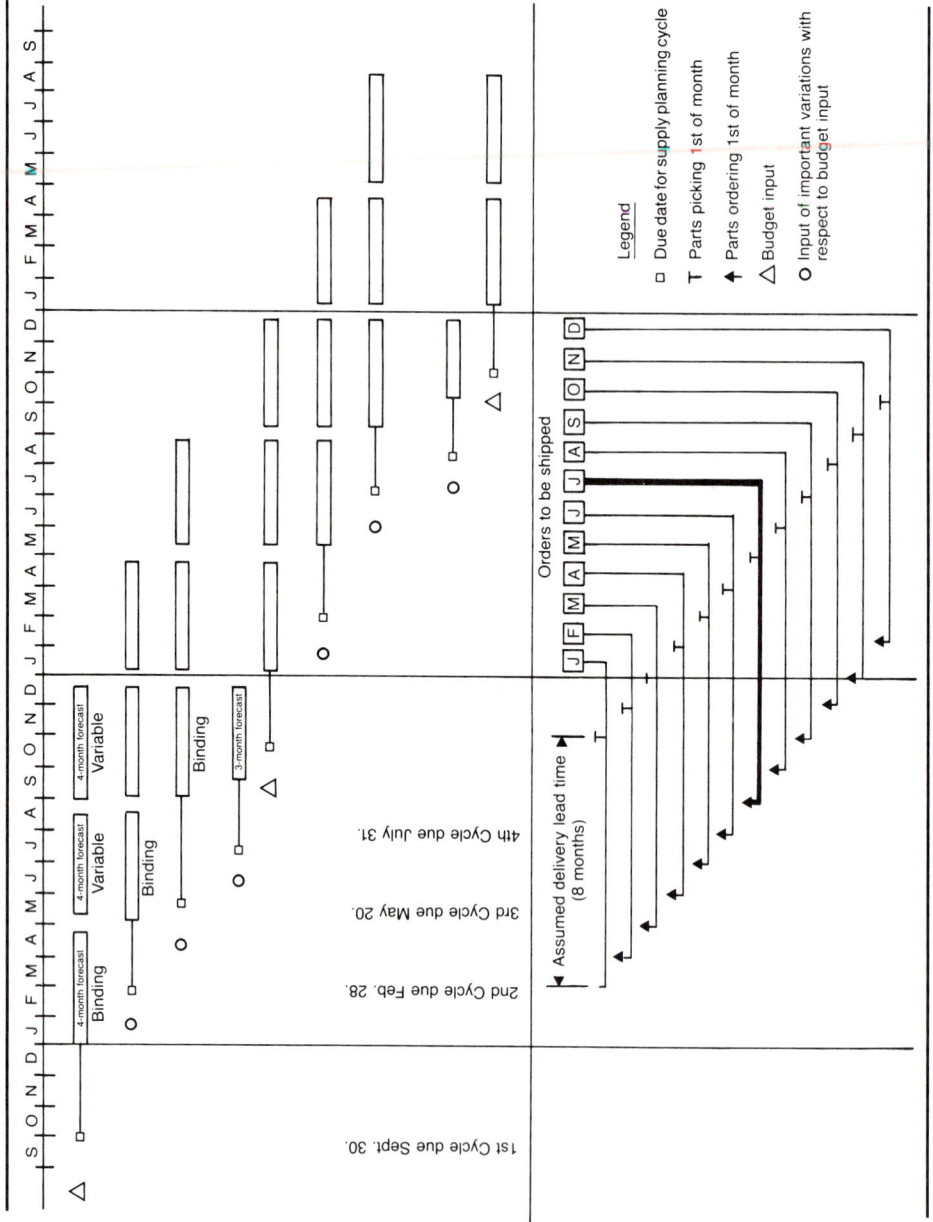

Legend

□ Due date for supply planning cycle

T Parts picking 1st of month

◄ Parts ordering 1st of month

△ Budget input

○ Input of important variations with respect to budget input

submitted in the first planning cycle, Mr. Barrel, manager of the DPDP, prepared a production request which was submitted to senior management for review. Changes were made to reflect specific marketing or manufacturing objectives and to yield desired capacity utilization and inventory objectives.

The approved production request, which indicated the total production requirements by product group (e.g., M20, M30) for the fiscal year, was used to develop a production program. This, in turn, formed the basis for planning within the manufacturing divisions.

In the production program, the annual requirements for each product group specified in the production request were restated as uniform monthly requirements and represented the projected load on the plant. It was on the basis of this load that manufacturing budgets and budgetary controls were established. These remained unchanged throughout the year.

The production program also served as a guide for the acquisition of parts, components, and materials. As the supply planning process moved through successive cycles, the production requests and production programs were revised accordingly.

ORDER PROCESSING

Subsidiaries, dealers, and agents were instructed to telex their orders to the DPDP by the fifteenth of each month. Orders were batched by the DPDP and transmitted to the manufacturing divisions for eventual inclusion in a detailed assembly schedule.

Orders were not confirmed, however, until manufacturing committed to the delivery dates specified. Such a commitment was dependent upon anticipated parts availability and capacity utilization. It was not until the end of the month that orders were considered firm.

The volume of orders varied significantly during the year, increasing from 20 percent of annual sales during the first 4-month period to 50 percent of sales during the last four months. Thus, orders arrived in a nonuniform manner.

PRODUCTION ASSEMBLY AND SCHEDULING

Following order confirmation, approximately 3 months remained for planning and execution. (The production scheduling procedure for the L1 line, including the M20, is shown in Exhibit 4.) Parts requirements

EXHIBIT 4
OLIVETTI—THE SCARMAGNO PLANT
Scheduling Production and Assembly

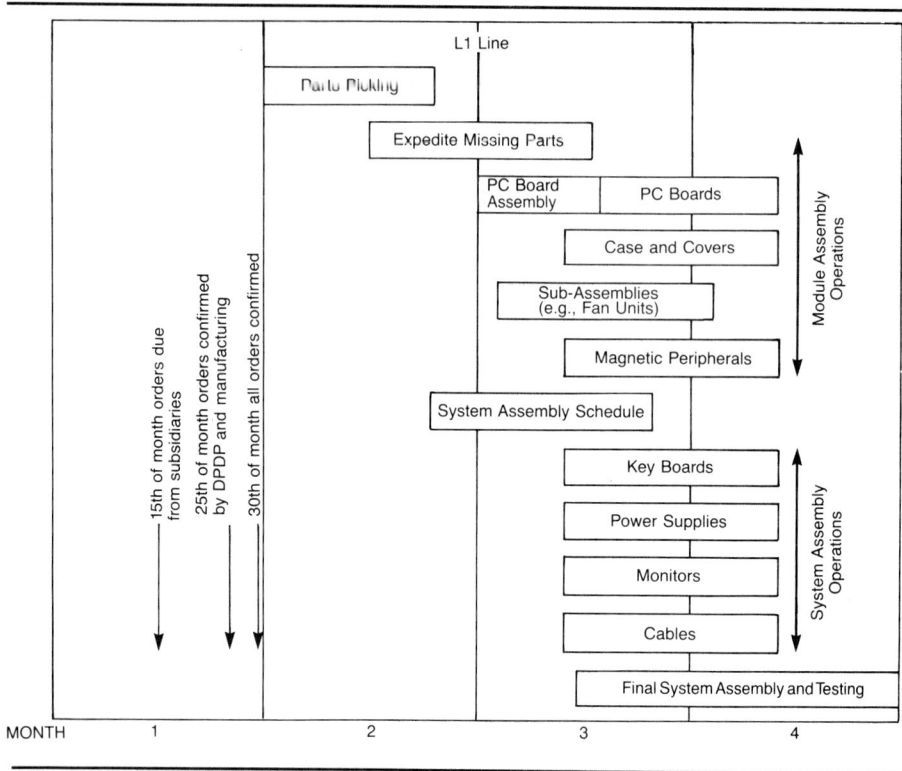

to meet the shipment commitments were determined using COPICS[3] software. These requirements were cross-checked against parts availability. Unexpected shortages were communicated to the Materials Management Department, where every effort was made to cover them by placing rush orders on suppliers. However, costs could increase sometimes twofold if parts and components were expedited. To improve its position, Olivetti used multiple sources of supply wherever possible.

By the beginning of the month following the confirmation of orders, necessary parts were physically removed from stock so that module assembly and system assembly operations could begin one month later.

---

[3]COPICS (Communications-Oriented Production and Inventory Control System)—an IBM software package to manage bills of material, to determine the availability of parts and materials, and to control short-term schedules.

Module assembly operations began on short assembly lines that operated independently of each other. These operations included the insertion of electronic components into printed circuit boards to form the main operational part of the computer (the mother board) and several smaller boards to control the video display, the magnetic storage device(s), printers, etc. Also included were the assembly of the plastic parts to form the case and covers, the completion of assembly and wiring of magnetic storage devices (floppy and hard disk drives), and the bringing together of "kits" of parts and components for supply to the final system assembly area.

System assembly lines were larger than those used for the previous operations since more and bulkier materials had to be handled. Although these lines were interchangeable and could be used to assemble almost any product in the L1 line, in practice each line tended to be dedicated to the assembly of one particular product.

There was a strong emphasis on inspection and quality control throughout all assembly operations. Parts, subassemblies, components, and finished systems were checked and rechecked at several stages of the process to eliminate defective items and to ensure that finished systems met rigorous quality standards. All finished products were shipped from Scarmagno to the central DPDP warehouse before being batched for delivery to the subsidiary or agent (see Exhibit 5 for a diagram of the information flows from planning to shipment).

PARTS DELIVERY PROBLEMS

The time relationship between the supply plan and the 8-month delivery lead time is shown in Exhibit 3. For example, the parts for products required on July 30 would have to be ordered 8 months before the 3-month assembly lead time began. In total there was, therefore, an 11-month supply and assembly lead time, with parts having to be ordered in September of the previous year (see the dark line in Exhibit 3). Furthermore, at the time that this purchasing decision was made, the most recent information available from a supply plan was from the third cycle (the plan submitted on May 20). Therefore, the entire forecast horizon was actually 14 months (the 3-month assembly lead time, 8-month delivery lead time on parts, and the 3 months since the supply plan was submitted). This number varied depending on how recently the supply plan had been submitted at the time that the parts had to be ordered. The long forecast horizon led to recognized problems in several areas.

EXHIBIT 5
OLIVETTI—THE SCARMAGNO PLANT
Planning—Information Flows

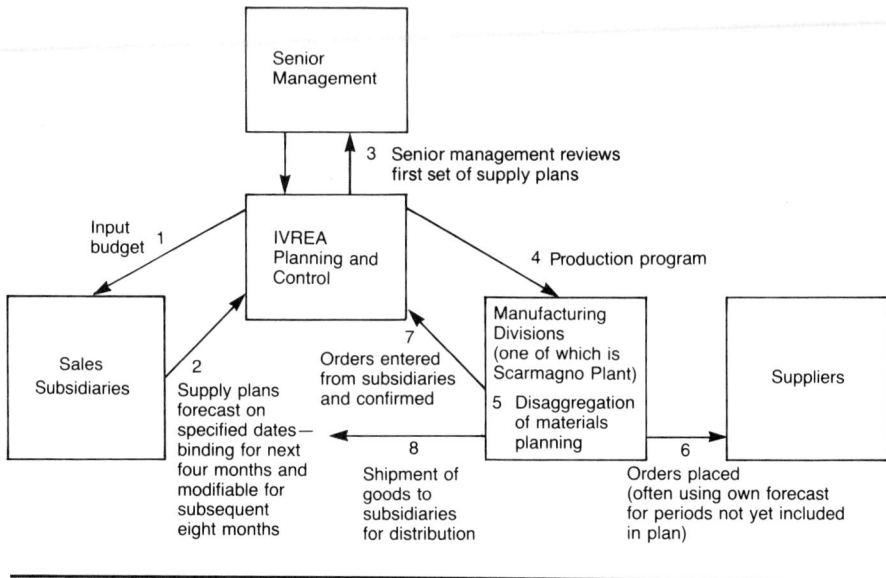

Supply Planning Process

Individuals in both the Sales and Marketing Department and at the Scarmagno plant had expressed some misgivings about both the supply planning process and the usefulness of the data derived from it. Mr. Corso, one of the directors of Marketing Support for Direct Sales, explained why, in his view, the supply plan was subject to a considerable degree of variability from cycle to cycle:

> The supply plan is the principal output of the sales forecasting process. To develop the inputs to the process, sales managers have to evaluate both the market and the competition. Although their evaluations of these factors may not appear in an explicit way, they do have an important influence on the forecasting process. In addition, sales managers have to assess the attractiveness of the Olivetti product line, comparing, for example, our prices and features with those of our competitors. Finally, our specific marketing strategy, which inevitably stresses some geographic areas or product lines more than others, must be considered as an important input to the forecasting process.

Of the four marketing inputs (market evaluation, competitive evaluation, Olivetti products, and Olivetti marketing strategy) the first two were the most volatile. If the market situation changed, the supply plan could be upset. For example, if a competitor reduced prices, the competitive evaluation would change and might affect the products and the marketing strategy. These changes were unpredictable, so that the four inputs were always evolving, and a "technically perfect" forecast was impossible.

Mr. Corso continued:

> This type of dynamic behavior is frequently observed in the PC market, less so for the larger systems in the L1 line. However, software changes or delays can cause major problems in the case of larger systems. Although the larger L1 systems comprise both hardware and software, in most instances the software "justifies" the use of the hardware. If, for example, we bring out a new printer and there is a delay in the development of the software to "drive" it, then we are obliged to specify the older model. The supply plan must be modified accordingly.

Mr. Bonanate, the other director of Marketing Support for Direct Sales, voiced a common concern:

> The supply planning process itself has become overly bureaucratic. Everyone knows that the reliability of the detailed forecasts is poor. The subsidiaries have been given an unmanageable task. Eliminating much of the detail might help. This could be done by reducing the number of items that have to be forecasted.

Mr. Bonanate conceded, however, that the quality of the forecasts did vary by subsidiary and by system type:

> Forecasting demand for large accounts in our smaller subsidiaries is extremely difficult. Because of constantly changing customer specifications and configuration details, a subsidiary is going to wait until the last possible moment to commit a large order to the supply plan.
>
> Forecasting the demand for an increasingly large number of our products which are sold indirectly is also a difficult problem for us. We're getting more competition in some of these markets, and forecast errors and supply problems can hurt if we can't deliver and the competition can.

At the Scarmagno plant, Mr. Caldi, a material requirements planner, spoke about the shortcomings of the supply plan from his point of view:

> Once I receive the production request, the annual requirements by product type are broken down into requirements for the various options such

as memory capacity, type of disk drive, etc. These data were, of course, in the original supply plans, but I prefer to develop my own breakdown. I can show statistically that it is more accurate.

The problems that I have with configurable systems are caused by forecast errors and mix changes in the supply planning process. The customer frequently "trades up" after gaining experience with the first few machines in the system.

With the nonconfigurable systems, our problems are less. Production is flexible. We can move people from line to line. However, we do have to maintain a fairly level rate of output. You can write off inventory, but not people!

Parts/Components Purchasing

Although, in principle, part and component purchasing decisions were supposed to be based on information derived from the supply planning process, in practice this was not the case. As delivery lead times began to lengthen in 1983 and early 1984, many suppliers insisted that their customers provide forecasts of parts requirements well in advance of placing specific orders.

Mr. Truant, materials manager at Scarmagno, explained the problem as follows:

> Our ability to develop a valid forecast of requirements for parts and components is a key factor in negotiating a privileged agreement between ourselves and our suppliers. Such an agreement not only concerns parts and component allocation, service, quality, and price, but also gives us preferred access to advanced product technology as it becomes available.
>
> Currently, in order to ensure a minimum delivery lead time of, say, four to five months on monitors and many electronic components, I have to provide some of our suppliers with a forecast of requirements well in advance of placing an order. For instance, next month, I will start discussions with several of our suppliers concerning our requirements for the first six months of 1985, yet the second cycle of the supply plan that the subsidiaries are to submit by the end of this month (February 1984) only extends out as far as April 1985. All this is done to obtain a 4- or 5-month delivery lead time once I place an order. Without these kinds of agreements, some suppliers are quoting lead times of eight months to one year.
>
> Right now, I could place orders for monitors without a privileged agreement or without providing a forecast, but the delivery lead time would be at least six months, and the price would be perhaps 10 percent higher than I would normally pay. I estimate that we are paying, on the average, a 10–20 percent price premium on the materials which are not covered by negotiated long-term agreements between our suppliers and us.

Production

Since the arrival of orders was nonuniform and the plant based its production program on a uniform production rate, an obvious conflict existed. To deal with this, DPDP and manufacturing planners "pulled" some orders forward in order to produce them in advance of the specified shipment date. Since orders were received three months in advance, this meant that some orders could be produced as much as two months in advance of the specified shipment date provided, of course, that the necessary parts and components were available.

However, it was rare that a subsidiary would accept advance shipment of an order, since the subsidiary's inventory level was one of the criteria upon which the incentive plan for sales managers was based. Indeed, at the subsidiary level, finished goods inventory had been reduced from seven months of sales in 1978 to less than three months of sales by early 1984.

Kumera Oy (A)

Mr. Vesa Kumpulainen, managing director of Kumera Oy, hung up the telephone and shook his head. "Why is it that our inventory continues to increase and we still can't get the right parts? I just tried to find out where the order for Makinen Oy is and got the same old story. It's been partly assembled but we still lack one part. We are already three weeks late on the order and there's no way I can tell them how long it will be before we can deliver. It looks like I'll have to authorize production to use overtime to make the part."

The problem with the Makinen order was typical of what seemed to be happening at the company. Customer complaints had been increasing, costs were rising, and the disputes between departments were becoming more intense. Mr. Kumpulainen knew that something had to be done to get control of the situation. As he reviewed the financial statements for 1975 and 1976 (shown in Exhibit 1), he realized that he must begin soon.

BACKGROUND

The company was founded in Helsinki in 1947 by Mr. Veikko Kumpulainen, father of the current managing director, Mr. Vesa Kumpulainen. The mood in Finland in 1947 was very optimistic. There was a considerable backlog of war indemnity supplies to be delivered to the Soviet Union, and the production of these goods would provide a base for industrial development. Finland was to supply products for the heavy metal industry, an industry which had not been very significant for the country before. It was against this background that the firm started manufacturing small bench lathes.

Two years after starting, the company began to produce a new product: lifting mechanisms for dump trucks. The manufacturing expertise gained by the company in building these mechanisms enabled them to expand the product line. Over time they added mechanical power transmissions, helical gear boxes, worm gears, and clutches. Some of these products brought the company into direct competition with a large, well-established gear manufacturer, E. Santasalo Oy., that had been in operation since 1934 in Finland. Even with this competition,

EXHIBIT 1
KUMERA Oy (A)
Financial Statements–Income Statements (1000 Finnish Marks)

	1976	1975
Sales	17,853	16,250
Cost of goods sold		
Direct labor	4,194	3,711
Material	6,227	5,462
Manufacturing overhead	3,043	2,487
Gross margin	4,389	4,590
General and administrative	1,547	1,423
Depreciation	1,503	1,487
Interest	1,249	937
Profit before taxes	90	743
Taxes	20	214
Profit	70	529

Balance Sheets (1000 Finnish Marks)

	1976	1975
Current assets		
Cash	660	1,803
A/C receivable	3,213	3,462
Inventory	8,756	6,019
Prepayments	303	486
Net plant and equipment	3,897	3,572
Total assets	16,829	15,342
Current liabilities		
A/C payable	4,184	3,573
Notes payable	1,500	1,287
Accruals	2,714	3,206
Long-term debt	6,439	5,354
Capital stock	120	120
Earned surplus	1,872	1,802
Total liabilities	16,829	15,342

however, the overall growth in the market provided growth for Kumera, and by the middle of the 1950s, the company was firmly established in the new line of products.

During the next few years the company continued to grow. This necessitated acquiring new locations to provide additional space. In 1964, they consolidated all operations into one location about 40 kilometers from Helsinski. By the early 1970s, the company was facing another shortage of space. In addition, there was an acute shortage of skilled labor in the area near their plant and in Helsinki. To provide more space and better access to skilled labor, they built a factory in Riihimäki, a small town about 60 kilometers north of Helsinki. The experience was so favorable that the company consolidated all their activities in Riihimäki in 1975 and have remained there to date.

The Kumera product line evolved over this period as well. Under the shadow of the E. Santasalo company, Kumera never attained a leading position in helical speed reducers. They increased the engineering staff and set them to work on developing new products. The result was a series of high-quality worm gears and shaft-mounted speed reducers that form the basis of their current product line.

As late as 1968, most new products of the company were being created in response to customer requests. There was only a small effort to develop a coordinated line of standard products. In the early 1970s, however, the product line was standardized and a catalog printed. Since then, new products have been added that build upon the gear-machining capability of the company. They have produced gears as small as 50 mm in diameter and as large as 2,200 mm. The gear boxes have ranged in weight from 20 kilograms to 10,000 kilograms. Examples of the company's products appear in Exhibit 2.

MARKETING ACTIVITIES

The company has an active customer base of 200–300 firms, of which 100–150 would place orders in any given year. No single customer is dominant, although just a few customers provide a large share of the company's business. Most customers are engineering-oriented manufacturing firms making wood-processing equipment, paper machines, plywood equipment, and so on, for the wood products industry. About 50 percent of Kumera's production is for export: 10 percent directly, and 40 percent indirectly through their customer's products.

The Soviet Union is a major factor in Kumera's market. Bilateral trade agreements between Finland and the USSR provide for the export of wood products equipment to the USSR from Finland. Kumera's customers are the manufacturers of this equipment. In order to preserve Russia's hard currency there has been minimal participation of other Western countries in this trade. Thus, the international competition has

EXHIBIT 2
KUMERA Oy (A)
Example Products

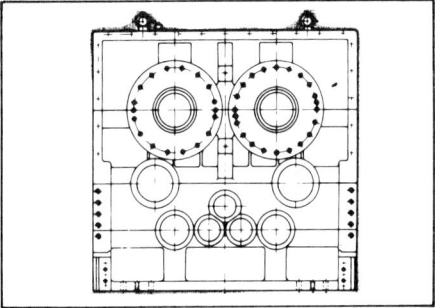

(A)

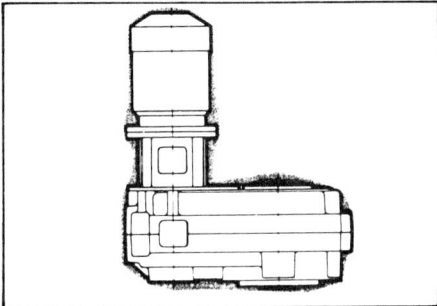

(B)

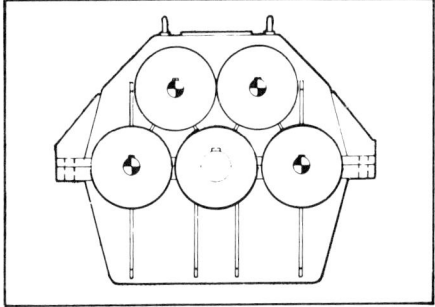

(C)

A. Custom made: VLA-Zx670, for sugar beet presses
B. Bevel and helical gear units: TCM-2000, -3000, and -4000 modular design
C. Marine units: 8FG-250

been limited for this part of Kumera's business. The greatest domestic competition comes from E. Santasalo, but there are other smaller domestic competitors as well. Kumera faces strong international and domestic competition in the Western European and North American markets, however.

The company's products are sold directly through the catalogs and by sales engineers. In many instances Kumera's sales engineers will work closely with the customer's engineering staff in specifying the Kumera products to be used in the customer's equipment. In some cases this can lead Kumera to design special mechanisms to solve difficult technical problems faced by the customers. The sales engineers have a great deal of discretion in promising delivery dates and quantities while working with the customers.

Much of the competition for business revolves around promising quick delivery of products. No published or "standard" delivery times are available. In many cases, therefore, the company accepts the customer request date as the promised delivery date or simply marks the orders for delivery "as soon as possible." The delivery promises range from immediate for some of the stock items to 15 weeks or more for complicated items. The general expectancy is delivery within 2–4 months. For big contracts, the competition is keen and quick delivery is often essential. Kumera has not been very successful in winning a share of these big contracts.

The company has always done well in meeting the technical design aspects of customer service, but the delivery date performance is poor and is getting worse. Actual deliveries for the non-stocked items were taking from 3 to 6 months. Even for the stocked products, requested items were not in stock about 30 percent of the time. This necessitated special runs for stocked items, often using "express" orders to speed them through the factory.

The customer service was a real concern to Vesa Kumpulainen. Past growth of the business had come from sharing in a growing market, not by improved service and market share. Recently, late deliveries had reached the point where more than 50 percent were over 3 weeks late. Some of Kumera's competitors were quoting longer delivery times, but were meeting the promises, and this was taking away some of Kumera's business. The situation had reached the point where Kumera was having to pay penalties on some of the late deliveries. The total number of penalties for this year could reach 30 if something was not done to change the situation.

The impact of the difficulties was felt in other parts of the business as well. For example, the spare parts performance had been badly hurt. Spare parts had always seemed to have low priority anyway, but the situation was getting even worse. Many times critical service parts were not in inventory. If the request was to meet an urgent customer need, the order was made into an express order to the factory. Even with the express orders, however, many spare parts deliveries were late, causing a loss of goodwill.

MANUFACTURING ACTIVITIES

The orders come directly from the customers by mail or phone or from the sales engineers (about half of the orders are from the sales engineers). An internal work order is written for each customer order and delivered to the production planning department. After checking the inventory to see if there are any parts in stock, they manually write out individual orders for all the parts that are to be made to satisfy the customer order. These individual orders are released to the shop with due dates derived from the customer order. The production, however, is scheduled for groups of similar parts. Each part has a card with its shop routing indicated, and as each operation is finished the completion is marked on the card.

A special shop order, an "express" order, had been designed to speed high-priority items through manufacturing. Some express orders are issued to the shop from the production planning department. Others are created as conditions warrant. For example, a group of similar parts being produced as a batch might contain one part needed for an urgent order. That part may get pulled from the group and made into an express order. There are several persons who make these changes in priority. In some cases the sales engineers themselves would go into the shop and pull the cards for the parts for some of their customer's orders. In other cases the loudest complaining customer's order would be expedited by the manager who got the angry call from the customer. Finally, the assembly foreman looks to see what parts will be needed for the assembly schedule. He has a "hot list" of parts which might be short and tries to get them to the pre-assembly inventory area before the assembly schedule calls for them. He uses one of the two full-time expediters to help him. A sample hot list is shown in Exhibit 3.

The use of express cards and constant priority changes means that

EXHIBIT 3
KUMERA Oy (A)
Example "Hot-List"

Expedite Sheet   Date___ June 0
Assembly Shortages

Part Number	Customer Order	Required	Shortage
1555	3117	14	10
16435	3117	24	24
2064	3221	4	4
Other Expedite			
2701	5087E*	1	1

*This is an "express" order for a customer.

only the urgent orders for important (noisy) customers get produced close to the time they are promised. Regular orders for stock items might be in the shop for half a year. There are hundreds of open production orders in the shop at any time, which means that priority changes are difficult to make. First the order must be found and then the express cards or date changes must be made manually. Also, of the hundred or so production orders issued per week, 10 or more are express to begin with. As the priorities are changed and groups of parts are split by making some of the group express, shop disruption is quite high. Many extra-cost setups can be required for express parts, and the grouping of parts does not provide as much efficiency when some parts are pulled out and run separately.

Key to much of the shop scheduling is the stock accountant. She tries to maintain sufficient stock on hand of the inventoried parts. She does this by ordering extra whenever an order is needed or by scheduling a stock order whenever a machine center is about to run out of work. She is also responsible for keeping inventory records and checking inventory balances. The production order in Exhibit 4, for example, is for 50 of the part #16435.

An inventory record for part #16435 is shown in Exhibit 5. There have been both service and assembly disbursements for this part. A physical count was made on May 7 and a 20-unit error was found. The May 23 production order for 50 pieces is shown, even though only 4 are needed to complete the customer order (customer order 3097, the Makinen order, needs 24 pieces, and only 20 are available). On June 3 there was not enough stock for another assembly requirement. This shortage is shown on the hot list in Exhibit 3.

EXHIBIT 4
KUMERA Oy (A)
Order Form for Parts

Work Order No.	P2998		Due Date	ASAP*
Part No.	16435		Quantity	50
Customer Order	3097			
			Stock Acct.	OK
			Date	May 23

*As soon as possible.

EXHIBIT 5
KUMERA Oy (A)
Stock Record for Part No. 16435

Date	Balance	Receipts	Disbursements	Remarks
January 7	33		10	Order No. 2067*
February 10	23	47		Order P2742†
February 11	70		24	Order No. 2563
March 21	46		1	2953E (spare)
May 5	45		Physical Count Correction – 20	
May 10	25		5	Order No. 2892
May 23	20	Order No. 3097 requests	24	Order P2998 50 pieces
June 3	0		0	Short for #3117

*Customer order number.
†P signifies production (work order) number (50 pieces were ordered).

On following up the part needed by assembly to complete the Makinen order, Mr. Kumpulainen found it in the lathe department (see Exhibit 6). There were several express orders in the lathe department at the same time. They would need to be finished before the Makinen order part could be started. Some of the express orders were spare parts, some were changes made by sales engineers for a special customer, and some were for parts needed by the assembly foreman. Mr. Kumpulainen decided that he would not create an express order for the part, but would go back and tell the people at Makinen that their order would be finished in a week—but he knew he was just guessing.

The Makinen order had also been affected by the long lead times for purchasing. The foundry that supplied the gear housing casting for the order promised it to Kumera in 4 months and it was *only* 2 weeks late. In the last few weeks, lateness was increasing and the foundries had lengthened their lead times significantly. To protect themselves, Kumera increased their purchases of castings for inventory, buying substantially more castings against a forecast instead of for specific customer orders. Special castings, like that required for the Makinen order, were requiring increased lead times, and shortages in the quantities delivered were increasing. Some foundries were taking 13 months to deliver special castings. The standard delivery quotation was 4 months.

Even blanket-purchased items were creating difficulties for Kumera. Their general rule for blanket contracting is simply "this year plus 15 percent." This meant significant contracting errors for some items as the product mix changed. The formula worked reasonably well for forgings, steel rods, and much of the hardware, however. Special purchased bearings required 4–6 months lead time for delivery to Kumera.

EXHIBIT 6
KUMERA Oy (A)
Routing Sheet for Part No. 16435

Work Order P2998	Due Date ASAP	Quantity Requested 50	
Work Center No.	Description	Quantity Complete	Date Complete
02	Saw	50	May 26
05	Lathe		
03	Boring		
07	Grinding		
04	Inspection		

"We work with several simple principles here," said Vesa Kumpulainen. "One of the first is that the machines should be kept busy. If a machine center is nearly out of work, the stock accountant, or someone, will try to get work to that center even if it means producing parts for inventory. Secondly, we try to take care of the important customers. Unfortunately, this really means the noisy ones. We make our quiet customers wait. Finally, we have not been concerned about our inventories until now. The high inflation rate seems to favor high inventories, and the Finnish tax law allows inventory adjustments to be used to level tax burdens. Besides, our inventory turnovers have been right at the industry average—2 to 3 times per year."

"We have been brought up short by the energy crisis, however. All of a sudden it became clear that, even with the inventory, our ability to get the right part at the right time was just about nil. In my present view, it seems to me that we must get some more people. The people in production planning do both manufacturing and purchasing planning. Compared to other firms, we have too few people. I think we should increase the staff there from four to six people. In addition, we could add one more purchasing person. It would only raise the total to three but could help with the expediting of purchase orders. In addition to these new people, we need another expediter. With these additions, I think we could cope with the problem."

Acme Chemicals Europe

It was the third day of the meeting in Madrid, Spain. The meeting was one of several called by Acme Chemicals Europe's product flow group to consider aspects of their responsibility for managing the flow of all materials and product for the company. The Madrid meeting had the specific objective of discussing ways to support the focal point, a title given to some of the people in the group. The title had been devised because the position these persons held was a central "focal point" in the material flow coordination process. In speaking of the meeting, Rolf Chop, field service manager, said: "We have made great progress in our discussion of a variety of tools to help the focal points do their jobs. We have introduced the supply train concept and shown how it links raw materials to finished goods and parallels our responsibility to coordinate material flows from raw material through the plants on to distribution and the final customer."

Mr. Chop continued: "It's important that we support the focal points in their part of the job of managing the material flows of the company. It will also be necessary for us to outline the scope of the focal points' activities in a way that will help them do the job. We hope the supply chain concept will help us do that." Ton Netlocks, European product flow manager, added: "We have located our focal points at manufacturing shipping sites. That puts them in the middle of the physical flow of material from raw materials to finished product. We have identified supply chains for all our products and want to eventually have a focal point managing each one. It is clear, however, that we need to provide them the proper tools if we are going to meet our task of balancing market demands with production capabilities."

BACKGROUND

Acme Chemicals Europe (ACE) is a subsidiary of the Acme Chemical Company headquartered in the United States. Founded in 1897, the company has grown into a worldwide producer of basic chemicals, basic plastics, and specialized products for the industrial and consumer markets. The company's financial performance in each of these categories for the last three years is shown in Exhibit 1.

EXHIBIT 1
ACME CHEMICALS EUROPE
Financial Results for the Acme Company by Product Group (in millions)

Industry segment results for the three years were:

	Basic Chemicals	Basic Plastics	Industrial Specialties	Consumer Specialties	Unallocated	Corporate and Elim.	Consolidated
1984							
Sales to unaffiliated customers	$5,337	$1,671	$2,583	$1,675	$152		$11,418
Intersegment transfers	1,552	125	17	14		$(1,708)	
Operating income	252	173	316	132	(25)		848
Identifiable assets	4,968	1,095	1,582	1,513	13	2,261	11,419
Depreciation	602	72	124	97			908
Capital expenditures	397	82	211	87	4		781
1983							
Sales to unaffiliated customers	$4,938	$1,613	$2,411	$1,496	$493		$10,951
Intersegment transfers	1,511	116	16	14		$(1,657)	
Operating income	149	81	316	59	(89)		516
Identifiable assets	5,439	1,147	1,396	1,452	523	2,024	11,981
Depreciation	521	77	109	77	57		841
Capital expenditures	349	57	138	60	26		630
1982							
Sales to unaffiliated customers	$4,646	$1,434	$2,237	$1,528	$773		$10,618
Intersegment transfers	1,390	116	12	13		$(1,531)	
Operating income	(54)	4	270	93	43		356
Identifiable assets	5,444	1,111	1,253	1,430	614	1,955	11,807
Depreciation	543	72	110	85	60		870
Capital expenditures	514	79	89	94	53		829

Aggregation of products is generally made on the basis of process technology, end-use markets and channels of distribution. The Basic Chemicals segment embodies inorganic chemicals, organic chemicals and hydrocarbons and energy. The Basic Plastics segment is comprised of plastic materials and products. Industrial Specialties encompasses functional chemicals, polymeric materials and fabricated products. Consumer Specialties includes agricultural chemicals, human health care products and household films and cleaning products.

Transfers between industry segments are generally valued at standard cost. Sales and operating income for geographic areas and industry segments have been restated for minor product and geographic area realignments.

The Acme Chemical Company is divided into six geographical areas. In addition to the United States and Europe, there are areas for Latin America, Canada, the Far East, and Brazil. Of the non-U.S. areas, Europe generates the greatest level of sales, an amount that exceeds the total for all other non-U.S. areas. Overall, ACE contributes about one third of the total company business. The area financial results for the last three years are shown in Exhibit 2.

ACE is headquartered in Käpfnach, Switzerland. European activities started in 1950 with the importation of products produced in the United States and Canada for resale to customers in Europe. One of the first facilities was a terminal built in Holland in 1957 to facilitate these importing activities.

Manufacturing in Europe was started in Greece in 1960 with a polystyrene plant and continued with other polystyrene plants built in 1962 and 1963 in Holland and Italy. The establishment of a chemical and plastic complex in Holland laid the groundwork for what has become ACE's largest facility, Northcoast. In the entire company, only one Acme complex in the United States is larger.

From the outset, the manufacturing facilities were designed to supply a broad geographical area and not just the country in which they were built. At the present time, ACE operates more than 30 plants in 13 countries. These plants serve customers in more than 60 countries in Europe (both Western and Eastern), the Middle East, and Africa.

PRODUCTS

ACE products are produced for both the industrial and consumer markets. Basic chemicals are the foundation for all ACE's activities. Some basic chemical production is used as raw material (feedstock) for other ACE products, some is used to meet particular customers' needs, and some is sold directly as a commodity. Basic and special plastics are sold as films and granules to other manufacturers. They are used to produce things like food packaging, children's toys, telephones, and drinking cups.

The specialties involve products that are designed to meet certain customers' requirements. Industrial specialties range from plastics suitable for car bumpers to water purification chemicals. These products require formulation and manufacturing expertise to solve specific problems. In the consumer specialties, the range includes agricultural prod-

EXHIBIT 2
ACME CHEMICALS EUROPE
Financial Results for the Acme Chemical Company by Area (in millions)

Geographic area results for the three years were:

	United States	Europe	Rest of World	Corporate and Elim.	Consolidated
1984					
Sales to unaffiliated customers	$5,293	$3,845	$2,280		$11,418
Transfers between areas	851	227	261	$(1,339)	
Operating income	379	301	168		848
Identifiable assets	6,073	2,588	2,658	100	11,419
Gross plant properties	6,521	2,485	2,250		11,256
Capital expenditures	433	203	145		781
1983					
Sales to unaffiliated customers	$5,225	$3,568	$2,158		$10,951
Transfers between areas	824	173	286	$(1,283)	
Operating income	219	177	120		516
Identifiable assets	6,547	2,602	2,731	101	11,981
Gross plant properties	6,916	2,377	2,231		11,524
Capital expenditures	386	139	105		630
1982					
Sales to unaffiliated customers	$5,074	$3,358	$2,186		$10,618
Transfers between areas	826	105	199	$(1,130)	
Operating income	249	38	69		356
Identifiable assets	6,441	2,569	2,691	106	11,807
Gross plant properties	6,678	2,327	2,194		11,199
Capital expenditures	427	274	128		829

The Company conducts its worldwide operations through separate geographic area organizations which represent major markets or combinations of related markets.

Transfers between areas are valued at cost plus a markup. There were no direct sales to foreign customers from domestic operations.

ucts like herbicides, human health products like antibiotics, and household goods like plastic "cling" film. Many of these are branded products, and some are sold at the consumer level.

The ACE product strategy has changed greatly from its initial focus on basic chemicals and plastics. Much of the research and development effort of the past was devoted to manufacturing processes and, indeed, the company is still a recognized industry leader in chemical and plastics manufacturing technology. In implementing their strategy for the 1980s, however, the company embarked on a major program of new product development. The objective for 1984 and beyond was to launch 15–25 new products per year. This represents a substantial increase over the historical average of nine new products per year. In addition, the thrust is to favor specialty products for industry and new consumer products. No diversification of technology was sought, however. The new products would be based on the company's expertise in basic chemicals.

ORGANIZATION

Historically, the Acme Chemical Company has given a great deal of autonomy to its operating divisions. This is true for ACE and is reflected in the ACE organization. The basic structure of ACE is a matrix. Along one dimension there are seven commercial departments forming the basis for the strategic business management of the company. Some of these departments' businesses correspond to basic processes like petrochemicals or plastics. Other businesses involve specialty product groupings such as agricultural products or pharmaceuticals.

Another dimension of the organizational matrix is geographical. There are 14 regional general managers overseeing a country or group of countries in the ACE area. Some of these regions have more than one manufacturing facility and some none. Scattered throughout the regions are the 60 sales offices for the company.

The third dimension of this matrix structure is the functional element, which includes activities like purchasing, manufacturing, marketing/sales, distribution, and research and development. In describing the ACE organization matrix cube, Ton Netlocks said: "God made the geography, man made the functions, and Acme created the businesses."

The top management structure of ACE is shown in Exhibit 3. The primary responsibilities for each of the functional people in the organi-

EXHIBIT 3
ACME CHEMICALS EUROPE
Organization Chart

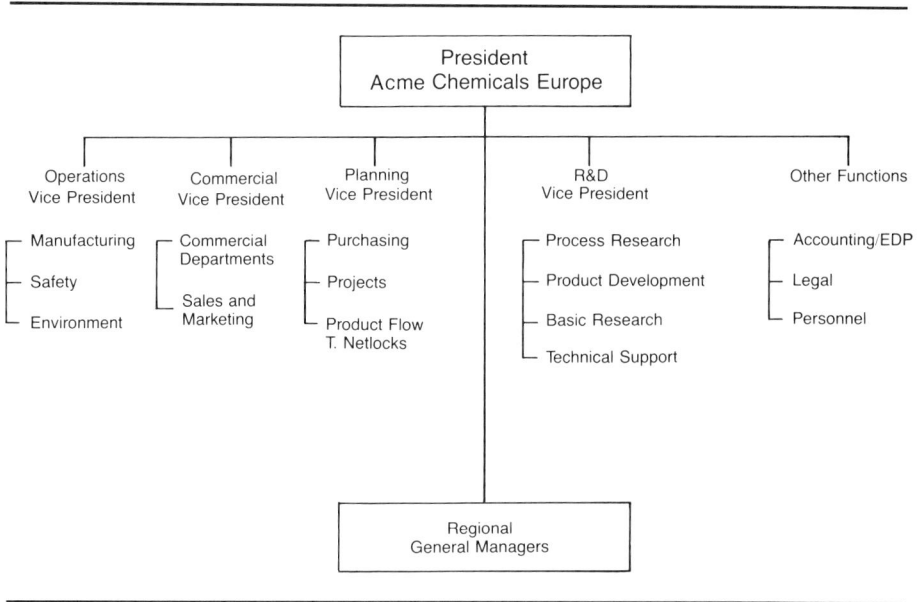

zation are quite different. The operations people are responsible for producing the products at low cost, safely, and within specification. They are also concerned with the utilization of the capital equipment required for the manufacturing process. The commercial organization is concerned with the strategic development of the businesses. The sales group is primarily concerned with the maximization of sales, while the marketing group is concerned with profitability, mostly through the pricing function. The purchasing people have responsibility for contracting for raw material and feedstock supplies both within Europe and around the world. Their primary objective is to secure multiple suppliers who can provide supplies of the right specification at the lowest possible landed cost. The research and development group is busily involved in contributing to the objective of increasing the number of new products developed each year.

In addition to the diversity of each function's objectives, the Acme "culture" encourages a great deal of autonomy and independence in the operating units. Consequently, there's a substantial amount of creativity in pursuing a particular functional, geographical, or business objective.

Because of this, a great deal of effort is spent on coordinating the interfaces between activities. Material crosses many boundaries as it flows through the processes, and the responsibility for coordinating the material flows has fallen to the product flow group which is headed by Ton Netlocks.

PRODUCT FLOW MANAGEMENT

The responsibilities that had fallen to the product flow organization were quite broad. They all, however, revolved around that idea of "balancing" supply and demand. To get the right quantities produced, product flow was responsible for planning and scheduling production. They also were responsible for planning, scheduling and executing the movements of raw materials and the distribution of the finished products. Implicitly this meant responsibility for the inventories created and the service levels provided to the customers.

The product flow organization is shown in Exhibit 4. Ton Netlocks reports to the executive vice president of planning and is responsible for the coordination of all material movement, as well as having direct responsibility for the European distribution function. The commercial department product flow managers are responsible for product groups that are roughly the same as each of the businesses of the company. The regional product flow managers oversee the product flow activities in each of the geographical regions. The focal points, however, manage a supply chain that could cross regions and businesses.

The responsibilities for product flow activities are often shared. For example, both a regional product flow manager and the European distribution services manager would be involved in the distribution activities in a region. Also, the production planning and scheduling activities are shared with the appropriate commercial product flow managers.

This can also mean organizational reporting lines involving more than one person. A focal point, for example, would report to a commercial department product flow manager for functional direction concerning his or her products. For administrative purposes, the reporting line would go to the regional product flow manager in whose region the focal point was housed. Similarly, a plant scheduler would report functionally to a focal point and administratively through operations. Chris Terlinde, a commercial department product flow manager, explained: "Most people have two bosses: a functional boss, someone who over-

EXHIBIT 4
ACME CHEMICALS EUROPE
Product Flow Organization

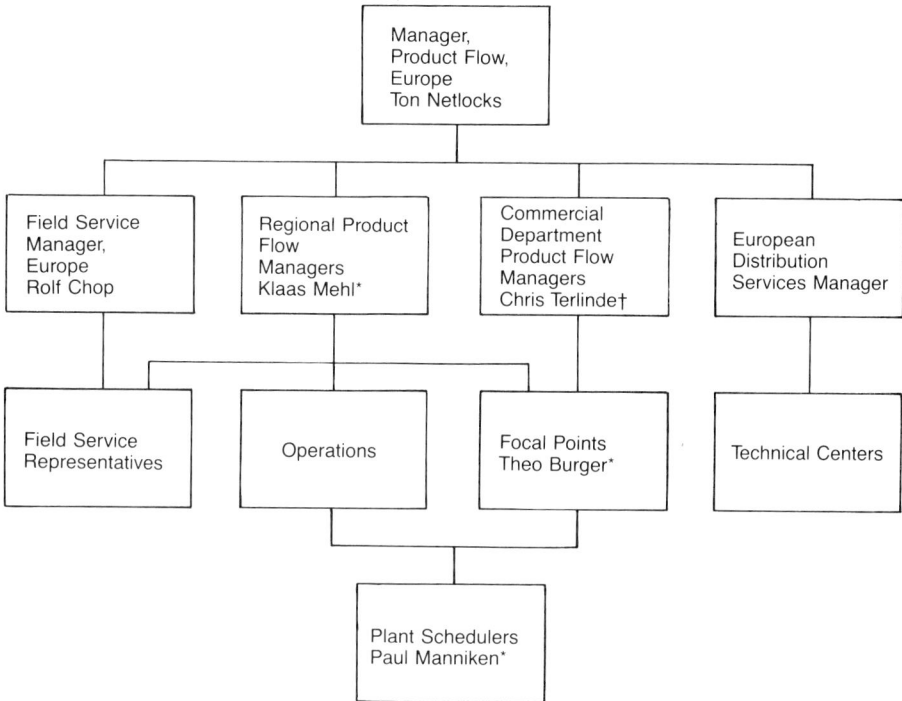

*For the Northcoast facility.
†For the business that includes the styrene monomer.

sees their professional/technical performance, and an administrative boss for geographic reasons."

The activities inside the product flow group are divided by level of product aggregation and time horizon, as shown in Exhibit 5. The product flow managers are responsible for producing plans for aggregations of products over a five-year planning horizon. Geographically they are concerned with Europe, but work worldwide to solve problems or to take advantage of special opportunities. The focal points are concerned with annual plans for the products in their supply chains. They determine sources of raw material and feedstock, and where production takes place in Europe. They also work on a monthly rolling plan for a few

EXHIBIT 5
ACME CHEMICALS EUROPE
The Product Flow Concept

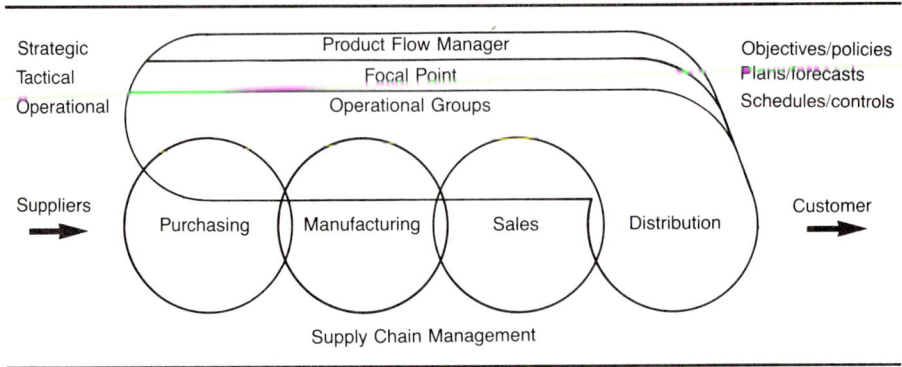

months into the future to manage inventories. The operational people prepare production schedules for a plant for a few weeks into the future for individual products and schedule shipments into and out of a single facility.

The second dimension of product flow management activities is also depicted in Exhibit 5. It is the "horizontal" dimension, the movement of material from purchasing through manufacturing, sales, and distribution to the customer. It is the geographical or spatial dimension. While the "vertical" dimension comprises the activities that move from strategic longer-run plans for coordinating the material flows, through the tactical coordination of those activities, to the day-to-day purchasing, scheduling, and transporting activities, the horizontal dimension parallels the supply chain.

MATERIAL FLOW

Typical of many companies in the process industries, ACE faced very complex material flows. The production processes for many of the basic chemicals produced a variety of co-products. The demand and supply of each of these was not necessarily balanced, however. Some of these co-products could be used for feedstocks in other processes and had markets of their own. Others only had outside markets, while others might be totally consumed internally. Feedstocks for any particular plant could come from sister ACE plants, other Acme Chemical plants around the world, or from outside producers. Similarly, the final products could be basic chemicals or plastics, intermediate products, or specialty finished products. The diversity and dynamics of geographical sources and markets further complicate the material flows.

To provide an indication of the complexity of the material flows, a partial flow diagram for some of the products is shown in Exhibit 6. At the very bottom of the diagram are products that are recognized by consumers, things like brake fluid, polystyrene foam, and plastic household films. These products, however, can be at the end of long processing sequences. Intermediate products like ethylene oxide and polystyrene, which require less processing, also have markets of their own. Some of these intermediate products have Acme trade names, while others are commodities. The basic feedstocks shown at the top of the diagram, like

EXHIBIT 6
ACME CHEMICALS EUROPE
Partial Product Flow Diagram

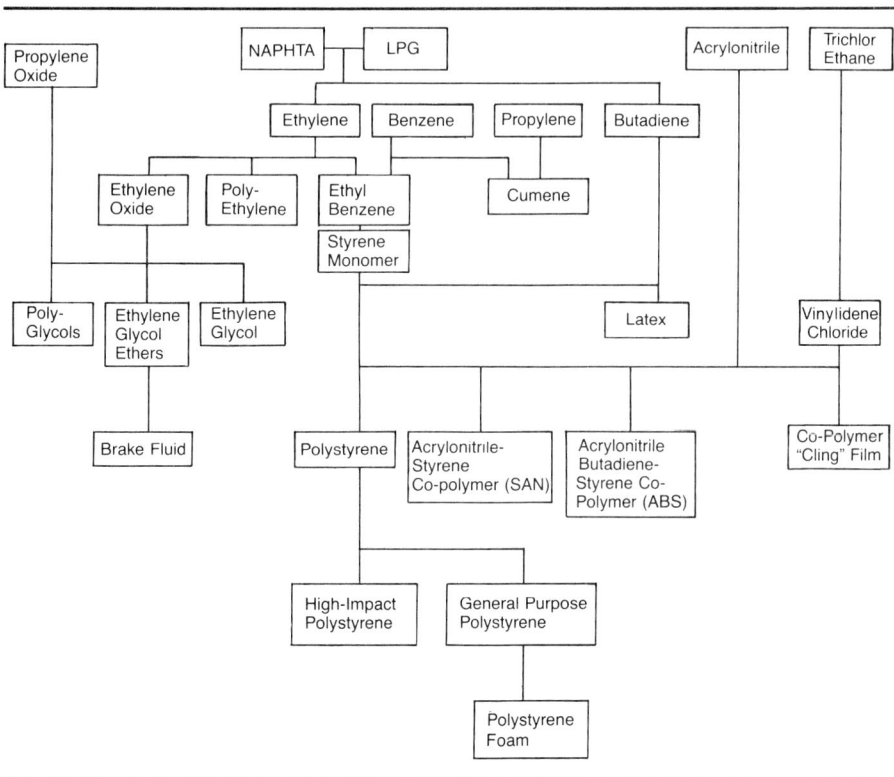

acrylonitrile or the naphtha-cracker outputs (ethylene, benzene, propylene, and butadiene) are almost always commodities.

To facilitate the coordination of the material flows, the product flow
group has introduced the concept of supply chain management. One
aspect of this concept is the flow of product through the processing
steps. This means the supply chain follows the product from purchasing,
through manufacturing and sales, to final distribution to the customer.
A second aspect involves the physical manufacturing characteristics. A
physical supply chain would encompass a product or group of products
and the raw materials and intermediate products necessary to produce
them. A final aspect defines the boundaries for the supply chain around
a group of products for which there is a coherent strategy.

The supply chain concept is primarily to support focal points. As
Ton Netlocks described it, "We have a fairly clear view of what the
scope of activities for product flow managers should be. We tried to
align each of them with one of the commercial departments, the 'businesses' of the organization. After all, that's the unit for our strategic
business planning. Even at this level, though, we have some exceptions.
We had to be sensitive to workload, complexity, and so on, so there is
not a complete correspondence between product flow and the businesses.

"At the operational end of things, it is even clearer. Every operational plant scheduler or distribution scheduler has a specific plant site
or shipping/receiving point to be concerned about. Within the site there
may be different product groups or transportation modes that allow further division. Each of these is fairly straightfoward though, and does
not cause any problems in defining the scope of activities. The focal
points, however, are between the product flow manager and the operations people, and there it's not so clear. That's where we think the supply chain notion will help us. Each supply chain should represent a
grouping of materials for which we need a coherent strategy.

"We're still feeling our way in this," continued Rolf Chop. "The
need for considering workload, complexity, experience and personali-
ties means that we may not be able to do what might be theoretically
nice. We have one supply chain that encompasses ethylene, propylene,
and butadiene, and one that covers benzene and its co- and by-products.
On the other hand, we have a supply chain just for latex and another for
extruded polystyrene foam. We hope to have a focal point for each supply chain, but we have several vacancies at the moment. We are changing some of our existing people to facilitate bringing some new people
on board."

FOCAL POINT

Theo Burger is one of the focal points at Northcoast in Holland. He has been performing the material flow coordination task for several years. He currently is responsible for "plastics": polyethylene, high-impact and general purpose polystyrene, SAN, and ABS. He is slated to take over a supply chain that will have all his current products except polyethylene, and he will also have the styrene monomer (including ethylbenzene) as well as polystyrene, SAN, and ABS. A simplified flow diagram along this supply chain is provided in Exhibit 7.

"As you can see, it's fairly complicated," said Theo Burger in describing the supply chain in Exhibit 7. "My functions will be much as they are now, but I'll talk with several different people and I'll need to learn the market for the styrene monomer." Currently his functions involve the planning of production rates and inventory levels. Once a year, after management has approved the sales plan, Mr. Burger decides the source for styrene monomer for each of the six polystyrene plants. This sourcing plan takes into account the economies of purchasing, producing, transporting, and paying duties or taxes in both the customers' countries and in the production sites all along the supply chain. The sourcing plan also indicates which plants will produce which products and at what levels.

"After the sourcing plan is completed and everyone is notified, I start regular updates and handle the coordination necessary to maintain my supply-demand balances," said Mr. Burger. "Monthly I collect the forecast data for all my products from sales, aggregate the data and issue the production plan for the next five months that will achieve the inventory balances I need. This goes to purchasing so they can provide the purchased materials and supplies, and to the focal points that provide my basic raw materials. I always assume that the focal points will have stock for me, just as I must have stock for the extruded polystyrene foam focal point.

"I have product flow operations people for the six plants that produce polystyrene products who will do the detail scheduling," he explained. "They will do the actual colors for the customers, the packaging and any other special requirements that are needed. They'll also schedule pilot products, routine maintenance, etc. They are constrained by my plan, the cost pressures from manufacturing, and the demands of the market." Paul Manniken, one of the product flow operations people, added: "Of course manufacturing would like full capacity and no changes, while sales would like very high levels of service and great

EXHIBIT 7
ACME CHEMICALS EUROPE
Supply Chain for Polystyrene

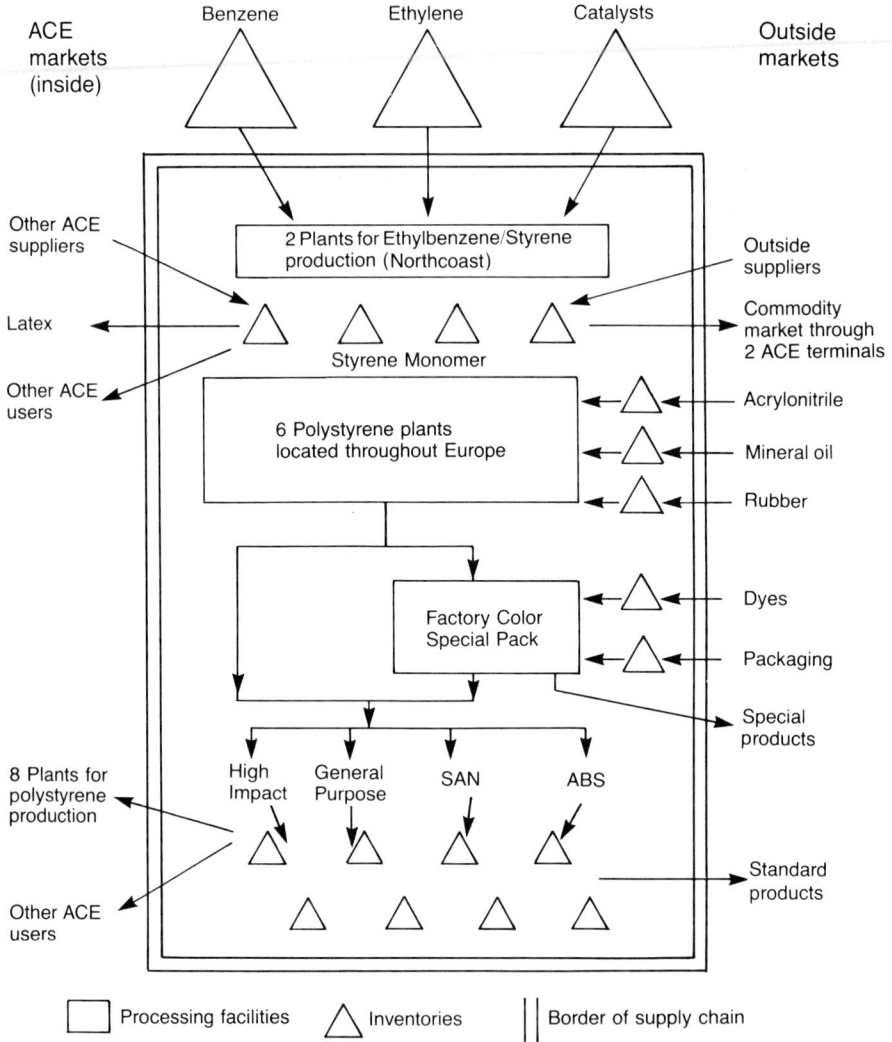

variety. It's a real balancing act to do the best for the company overall, particularly with the increases in specialties and new products."

Theo Burger continued: "I talk to just about everybody in the company to do my job, but I'm functionally responsible to Joze Poncho (plastics product flow manager) in Käpfnach, and administratively responsible to Klaas Mehl (regional product flow manager at Northcoast). When I start managing the new supply chain, I'll get a second functional boss at Käpfnach, Chris Terlinde. He is product flow manager for the business that includes the styrene monomer. Up until now I've had horizontal responsibility for plastic products that sold in similar markets. Now I'll need to learn about a vertical commodity market for the styrene monomer. I guess we'll just have to try it and see how it works."

Stewart Instruments Ltd.

"Psychologically it's important to start off the New Year on the right foot. It's now mid-October. For our plans to be in place and moving the first of the year, we have about eight weeks to analyze our problems and decide what to do about them." The speaker was David Thornton, newly appointed general manager of Stewart Instruments Ltd. (SIL). He had accepted the position several weeks earlier, moving over from his previous job as general manager of one of the parent company's other subsidiaries, which manufactured a specialized line of small electric motors.

Thornton had planned to take up his new appointment in January 1981. His expectations of a smooth transition were shattered on October 13, 1980, by the death in a car accident of Edward Bentley, the man he was to succeed. Under the circumstances he was expected to assume his new position immediately. Four days later, after long discussions with key personnel at SIL's head office and factory in Islington, a stone's throw from the City of London, Thornton was sitting in his office reviewing his notes.

Manufactured products were a present cause of concern. For 1980, SIL expected to lose £1.1 million on sales of £12.7 million of manufactured goods, including spare part sales of £3.0 million. (Exhibits 1 and 2 show selected financial data.) Paradoxically, the business climate during recent months had been favorable, with SIL reporting a third-quarter order backlog of over £2.4 million. But as Thornton put it:

> We have got to get manufactured products out the door. For 1980, we were budgeting production of finished goods and spare parts at £52,000 per day; we averaged only £38,000 per day in September. Deliveries to distributors, even on standard products, are as much as seven weeks overdue.

COMPANY BACKGROUND

SIL traced its origins to 1839 when Alan Stewart, a Glasgow pharmacist, established a company to design and manufacture a limited line of laboratory equipment for pharmacists. Fueled by the Industrial Revolution, demand for general purpose laboratory equipment increased.

EXHIBIT 1
STEWART INSTRUMENTS LTD.
Selected Income Statements
(in pounds sterling, 000 omitted)

	1978	1979	1980*
Net sales	£12,101	£11,112	£12,741
Cost of sales			
Direct material	3,639	3,542	4,612
Direct labor	914	822	1,142
Direct overhead	2,357	2,433	3,556
Total cost of sales	6,910	6,797	9,310
Gross profit	5,191	4,315	3,431
Sales overhead	1,499	1,351	1,859
Other overheads	1,981	2,260	2,601
Management charges	482	418	566
Operating profit (loss)	1,229	286	(1,595)
Other expense	165	69	16
Interest expense	—	37	28
Capitalized variances	—	—	(517)
Profit (loss) before tax	1,064	180	(1,122)

*Projected 1980 results.

The company broadened its line and prospered. By the early 1920s, the company had moved its location to Islington, where it manufactured a complete line of general purpose laboratory equipment. Items such as medical and laboratory glassware, bunsen burners, clamps, incubators, ovens, and water baths made up the bulk of SIL's line.

In 1965, SIL was acquired by a larger corporation seeking to diversify. In 1980, SIL operated as a wholly owned subsidiary within the parent company's Scientific Division. Fabrication and assembly of laboratory apparatus and scientific instruments were still carried out at the Islington factory for distribution to the United Kingdom (UK) and export markets. SIL still distributed but no longer manufactured glassware or supplies. Due to increased demand for space, SIL had been forced to lease a warehouse in Romford, 15 kilometers to the east. The Romford warehouse was used primarily for storing and shipping finished goods. As of October 1980, SIL employed 476 people, 312 of whom were hourly workers.

EXHIBIT 2
STEWART INSTRUMENTS LTD.
Selected Financial Data
(in pounds sterling, 000 omitted)

	1978	1979	1980*
Fixed assets	£4,089	£4,040	£4,006
Current assets			
Stock			
Raw material and parts	2,226	2,206	3,308
Work-in-process	352	1,569	657
Finished goods	1,180	677	825
Prepayments	31	34	40
Cash and accounts receivable	1,874	1,810	1,649
	5,663	6,296	6,479
Less: Creditors			
(Falling due within one year)			
Current liabilities	1,033	1,114	1,638
Intercompany accounts	5,135	5,465	6,126
Net current assets (liabilities)	(505)	(283)	(1,285)
Total assets less current liabilities	3,585	3,757	2,722
Less: Creditors			
(Falling due after one year)			
Long-term debt	139	212	141
Deferred tax	99	104	0
	3,347	3,441	2,581
Capital and reserves			
Share capital	3,347	3,441	2,581

*Projected 1980 results.

PRODUCT LINE

SIL's catalog listed over 7,000 line items comprising 1,100 manufactured products and accessories, complementary products purchased from other manufacturers, and many semidurable and consumable items. Semidurables included separator tubes, reusable glass and plasticware, clamps, and wire screens. Consumables included disposable glassware, filter papers, syringes, pipettes, and reagents.

SIL's manufacturing operations specialized in the production of electromechanical devices. These items were classified into three major segments: constant temperature products, and accessories, vacuum pumps, and laboratory apparatus. Some product examples from each segment are listed in Exhibit 3.

GENERAL PURPOSE LABORATORY EQUIPMENT

The water bath line was representative of the items manufactured by SIL. It consisted of 17 models divided by application into general purpose, special purpose, circulating, and shaker baths. Exhibit 4 shows two such baths and Exhibit 5 gives product details. Each bath consisted of three major components—an outside body, pan assembly, and temperature control unit.

EXHIBIT 3
STEWART INSTRUMENTS LTD.
Example Products from Each Segment

1. Constant Temperature Products
     Water baths and circulating systems
     Ovens
     Incubators
     Refrigerators

   Constant Temperature Accessories
     Digital thermometers
     Circulating systems—remote control
     Replacement parts

2. Vacuum Pumps
     Direct drive vacuum pumps
     Belt drive vacuum pumps
     Vacuum pump oils
     Vacuum pump accessories

3. Laboratory Apparatus
     Timers
     Stirrers
     Centrifuges
     Hot plates
     Immersion heaters

EXHIBIT 4
STEWART INSTRUMENTS LTD.
Two Water Bath Models

MODEL SB-50 SHAKER BATH, 17-liter.
Could hold 25 test tubes or the equivalent. Includes a shaker tray and digital control.

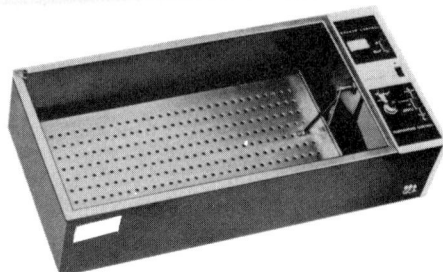

MODEL SC-121 WATER BATH, 2.8-liter.
The smallest general purpose bath. Applications include warming reagents and cell samples.

Water baths were used in laboratories to provide a controlled temperature in which to perform a variety of organic and inorganic procedures and reactions. Flasks or test tubes were simply lowered into the water bath on a rack or tray after selecting the desired temperature. It was important to maintain the specified temperature within a certain tolerance (i.e, sensitivity) and also to insure that this temperature was maintained throughout the bath (i.e., uniformity). General purpose water baths differed one from another only in physical dimensions.

EXHIBIT 5
STEWART INSTRUMENTS LTD.
SIL's Water Bath Line

General Purpose Water Baths

Model Number	SC-121	SC-122	SC-123	SC-124	SC-125	SC-126	SC-128‡	SC-130
Capacity (litres)	2.8	6.4	14	21	20	57	24	32
Power volts	120/240	120/240	120/240	120/240	120/240	120/240	120/240	120/240
Watts	280	560	560	560	560	1120	1120	1120
Adjustable shelf	YES	YES	YES	YES	YES	YES	YES	YES
Chamber dimensions*	12.5 × 11 × 14	12.5 × 27 × 14	29 × 26.5 × 14	30.5 × 25.5 × 18	43 × 23 × 14	65 × 34 × 18.5	21.5 × 27 × 14 / 29 × 27 × 14	30.5 × 25.5 × 29
External dimensions†	19 × 23 × 20	20 × 38 × 20	37.5 × 38 × 20	46 × 39.5 × 25	55 × 37.5 × 20	80 × 51 × 25	64 × 38 × 20	36 × 44 × 35
Maximum temperature	100°C	100°C	100°C	100°C	100°C	100°C	100°C	100°C
Sensitivity °C§	±0.15	±0.10	±0.10	±0.08	±0.12	±0.07	±0.08/ +0.10	±0.10
Uniformity °C§	±0.3	±0.03	±0.3	±0.3	±0.3	±0.3	±0.3	±0.3
Options/accessories	Plastic cover Test tube rack	Stainless cover	Stainless cover	Stainless cover Concentric ring cover	Stainless cover	Stainless cover	Stainless cover	Stainless cover Concentric ring cover
Applications	Warming reagents, Cytology research	Tissue culture, Serology, Coagulation tests, Food QC	Tissue culture, Virology, Genetic studies, General laboratory use	Enzyme reactions, Immunology, Genetic studies, Water QC	Bacteriology, Incubation, Metallurgical analysis	Serology, Hormone studies, Metallurgical research	Virology, Incubation, Protein studies	Deep chamber applications

*Length, width, depth (centimeters).
†Length, width, height.
‡Double chamber 10/14 litre.
§Both at 56°C.

EXHIBIT 5 (continued)
STEWART INSTRUMENTS LTD.
SIL's Water Bath Line

Model Number	Special Purpose Water Baths				Circulating Baths		Shaker Baths		
	Tissue Bath HM-1800	Boiling Bath HM-1900	Incubator Baths HM-3400	Incubator Baths HM-3600	CM-2600	CM-2800	SB-50	SB-100	SB-150
Capacity (litres)	3	20	34	19	28	94	17	34	95
Power volts	120/240	120	120/240	120/240	120/240	120/240			
Watts	280	1120	1100	580	1170	1730			
Adjustable shelf	YES	YES	—	YES	—	—			
Chamber* dimensions	30×18×3.5	43×23×14	71×27×18	30×25×18	46×35.5×16	91×45.5×24	33×27×15	71×27×15	91×46×19
External dimensions†	32.5×27×8	55×38×17	90×33×24	46×39×25	63×40.5×21	109×51×28.5	53×32×24	90×32×24	110×51×27
Maximum Temperature	100°C	100°C	45.5°C	44.5°C	100°C	100°C	100°C	100°C	100°C
Sensitivity °C	At 50°C ±0.15	—	At 44.5°C ±0.003‖ At 45.5°C ±0.003‖	At 44.5°C ±0.15	At 56°C ±0.005	At 56°C ±0.015	At 56°C ±0.06	At 56°C ±0.09	At 56°C ±0.06
Uniformity °C	At 50°C ±0.3	—	At 44.5°C ±0.045‖ At 45.5°C ±0.040‖	At 44.5°C ±0.20	At 56°C ±0.06	At 56°C ±0.09	At 56°C ±0.18	At 56°C ±0.30	At 56°C ±0.30
Options/ accessories	—	—	Stainless steel cover Test tube rack Petri dish rack		Stainless steel cover Concentric ring cover	Stainless steel cover Concentric ring cover	Stainless steel cover Cooling coil and cover Gassing hood		
Applications	Tissue procedures, Toxicology, Radiography	Estrogen procedures, Vitamin B-12 testing	Coliform testing of water at 44.5°C E. Coli testing of food at 45.5°C	Coliform testing only	Research and quality control requiring exceptional temperature uniformity		Applications requiring controlled agitation in addition to temperature uniformity (e.g., germination, digestion, enzyme, and tissue studies)		

Note: Coliform tests designated by DHSS and DOE. E. Coli Tests designated by RIC.
*Length, width, depth (centimeters)
†Length, width, height
‖With test tubes.

EXHIBIT 5 (concluded)
STEWART INSTRUMENTS LTD.
SIL's Water Bath Line

Catalogue descriptions of SIL's Water Bath Line highlighted the following:

General Purpose Water Baths

1. One Piece Interior—stainless steel corrosion-resistant, easy to clean
2. Heaters—time and energy savings by rapid heat transfer
3. Circulation—gravity convection
4. Control Panel—compact, easy to use, sensitive hydraulic thermostat

Special Purpose Water Baths

These baths were designed for special laboratory applications and constructed to rigid specifications.
1. Incubator Baths
   Designs meet official standards for testing of fecal coliform content of water and/or E. Coli content of food samples under stringent temperature criteria. The baths featured:
   (*a*) Unattended Operation
   (*b*) Solid State Push-button Control—two preset temperature selections
   (*c*) Construction—stressed quality components, ease of use and durability
2. Circulating-Water Baths
   Digital solid state temperature control was standard for both models, with an unrivaled temperature uniformity of 0.05°C guaranteed at 37°C. Features included:
   (*a*) High Efficiency Heating Elements—fast, efficient, uniform heat transfer
   (*b*) Stainless Steel Interior—corrosion resistant, easy to clean
   (*c*) Platinum Temperature Sensing Device—ultrasensitive
   (*d*) Built-in Agitator/Circulator—rugged stainless steel impeller
   (*e*) Modern Exterior Design—bold new styling
   (*f*) Set and Forget Temperature Control—digital readout, solid state
   (*g*) Long-life Motor—dependability
   (*h*) Diffuser Shelf—ease of use

Shaker Baths

These reciprocal motion baths were ideal for applications needing constant, controlled agitation in addition to temperature uniformity. Features included:
1. Solid State Controls—performance and reliability
2. Built-in Tachometer—shaker speed control
3. Glassware Flexibility—glassware could be intermixed
4. Construction—stressed quality components, ease of use and durability
5. Five-year warranty

Circulating water baths were similar to general purpose water baths, but were designed to maintain operating temperatures to within closer tolerances for both sensitivity and uniformity. They included an electromechanical impeller which was mounted inside the pan assembly and continuously circulated the water.

Special purpose water baths were designed for specific applications where predetermined levels for sensitivity and uniformity were critical. An example of such a bath was SIL's Incubator Bath HM-3400. It met official standards of both the Department of Health and Social Services (DHSS) and Department of the Environment (DOE) for bacterial testing of water by incubation at 44.5°C $\pm$ 0.2°C and the Royal Institute of Chemists (RIC) standards for bacterial testing of food samples by incubation at 45.5°C $\pm$ 0.05°C.

Shaker baths were designed specifically for applications such as enzyme reactions and tissue studies which required controlled agitation in addition to temperature uniformity. Shaker baths featured a tray mounted inside the pan assembly and fitted with a reciprocating motor. When in use, the tray moved in such a way as to shake any flask submersed in the bath, thus stirring its contents.

Evolution of the product line was in part dependent upon SIL's maintaining close contact with professional bodies and government departments which established standards for various testing procedures. SIL was a founding member of the Scientific Instruments Manufacturer's Association of Great Britain (SIMA) and was represented on associated committees which, in conjunction with the British Standards Institution (BSI), established industrywide performance standards for constant temperature control equipment. These standards became the basis for defining technical specifications or performance criteria for new equipment. Some products, like the HM-3400 incubator bath, were designed specifically for certain applications. The shaker bath line was another example, designed to meet special testing requirements in the field of biotechnology. Exhibit 6 shows shipments for the water bath line for the period 1978–80.

COMPETITION WITHIN THE INDUSTRY

SIL was one of the three largest companies manufacturing and distributing general purpose laboratory equipment in the UK. The other two companies were A. Gallenkamp & Co., Ltd., and Baird & Tatlock, Ltd. All three were characterized by the breadth of their product lines. These

EXHIBIT 6
STEWART INSTRUMENTS LTD.
Water Baths: Orders and Shipments (1978–80)

Model	1978 Units Ordered	Units Shipped	1979 Units Ordered	Units Shipped	1980 Units Ordered	Units Shipped
General Purpose Water Baths						
SC-121	530	522	489	510	537	504
SC-122	659	664	659	658	679	639
SC-123	465	489	359	359	303	290
SC-128	315	316	290	271	269	293
SC-124	858	739	845	907	1029	878
SC-125	143	141	179	161	175	200
SC-126	494	467	477	490	424	421
SC-130	54	47	81	85	57	58
Special Purpose Water Baths						
HM-1800	159	120	85	127	70	68
HM-1900	66	56	63	72	49	51
HM-3400	290	268	260	283	175	165
HM-3600	56	56	85	73	110	73
Circulating Water Baths						
CM-2600	303	305	395	314	219	296
CM-2700	85	101	122	93	76	101
Shaker Baths						
SB-50	280	360	239	238	215	196
SB-100	224	239	208	185	234	229
SB-150	34	33	31	28	—	5

companies had among them 35 percent of a market estimated at £235 million. The remaining 65 percent of the market was divided among more than 100 different companies belonging to the British Laboratory Ware Association. Grant Instruments (Cambridge), Ltd., for example, specialized in "controlled environment equipment for laboratories." It offered a line of products which included baths and accessories, thermostatic control units, incubators, circulators, and recording apparatus. Grant's sales were estimated to be £4–6 million.

The Gallenkamp catalog was considered "the Bible" of the industry. It was a bound, 900-page volume printed in four colors and revised every three years; 20,000 copies were distributed to customers in the UK, and an additional 20,000 copies were distributed overseas. A loose-leaf version, which accommodated routine additions and deletions to the product line, was used within Gallenkamp and made available to its largest customers.

Some 8,000 items were listed in the Gallenkamp catalog. These included products and accessories manufactured by Gallenkamp, complementary products (often offered on an exclusive basis), semidurable goods, and consumable items. Baird & Tatlock's catalog was similar, although it included only 6,000 items and was not revised as regularly. By comparison, Grant's catalog ran to only 36 pages and listed 400 items. SIL's catalog listed 7,000 items.

DISTRIBUTION CHANNELS

In the UK, the majority of general purpose laboratory equipment was sold in two ways, either directly to the end user by the manufacturer or through a network of regional distributors. Some specialist wholesalers also existed who sold only to other, smaller distributors. Specialist wholesalers stocked a wider range of laboratory apparatus, glassware, and instruments than would be possible for the smaller distributors.

Gallenkamp sold directly to end users, offering 24- to 36-hour delivery to its largest customers. It relied heavily upon computer-based order processing, inventory control, and invoicing systems. Customers communicated their orders directly to a Gallenkamp salesperson or through a regional sales office. Orders were then relayed to a central Gallenkamp warehouse where the goods were removed from stock and shipped to the customer.

SIL and Baird & Tatlock each relied on regional distributors which they supported with a small company sales force. Although SIL and Baird & Tatlock each had computerized order-processing systems, neither was linked to its regional distributors. Distributors attempted to satisfy a customer order from stock. Due to their size, distributors did not carry appreciable stocks of items other than consumables. They relied upon prompt delivery of equipment from manufacturers or suppliers in order to maintain high levels of inventory turnover. An average markup of 112 percent by distributors on ex-factory cost was typical (i.e., an item shipped from the factory at £100 was sold by the distributor for £212).

THE END USER

SIL products were used by scientists and laboratory technicians working in research and clinical labs belonging to universities and medical institutions. They were also used wherever general purpose laboratory equipment was needed, such as in corporate research and development, and quality control labs. Thornton was interested in knowing about end users and how they initiated a purchase requisition. He took his request to John Crispin, SIL's sales manager. Crispin had been with SIL in sales for fifteen years and had worked previously as a laboratory technician for a pharmaceutical firm.

A typical medical research laboratory occupied 120 square meters and served two doctors and four lab technicians. Laboratory benches, sinks, shelves, and appliances like refrigerators or sterile chambers were built in. Other general purpose equipment, like water baths, balances, hot plates or centrifuges, were either built into the counters or located on top. Bunsen burners, pipettes, graduated cylinders, and other glassware were arranged on shelves. Specialized equipment like a high-speed centrifuge or a mass spectrometer was installed if the lab's particular work required such equipment. Crispin described two SIL water baths located in such a lab.

The SC-121 was a constant temperature bath, a table-top model which measured 19 cm long by 23 cm wide and 20 cm high. Temperatures could be maintained from 20 to 100°C by turning a single knob with markings from 0 to 10. The technician verified the desired temperature with a standard thermometer. The bath was filled manually with distilled water and topped off when necessary. The lab kept this particular bath set at physiological temperature, 37°C, and used it in experiments with cells or for warming reagents and enzymes. No cover, shaker, impeller, or digital display was needed.

The SB-50 was a shaker bath, considerably larger than the SC-121 and more sophisticated. Instead of a mechanical knob, temperature was set and controlled by using a numeric keypad. A digital display allowed actual water temperature to be verified at a glance. The lab kept this bath set to exactly 56°C, and used it to stop reactions among proteins by raising their temperature. The shaker mechanism provided agitation to maintain an even reaction.

Crispin differentiated between sales of new and replacement equipment. For new equipment, the scientist or technician using the apparatus was primarily interested in meeting the performance criteria demanded by a specific experiment or testing procedure. Water baths had to meet their requirements for temperature sensitivity and uniformity. End users were also concerned with ease of use and with price. For example, the digital display was a useful feature on a water bath but cost more. In some labs, space was at a premium, in which case a compact design or the ability to perform several functions was sought.

In making a choice between different pieces of equipment, the end user consulted one or more of the equipment catalogs which distributors and manufacturers made available for reference purposes. Apart from performance criteria, prompt delivery was expected, and promises of one or two weeks were common. To initiate the purchasing procedure, product description and catalog number were given to the lab's buying coordinator, typically a lab technician or secretary who accumulated weekly orders for reagents, glassware and equipment. Orders were then transmitted directly to the sales representative of the relevant manufacturer or to a distributor's regional office. In some end-user organizations, orders had to be forwarded via the purchasing department. The need for scientists and technicians to have authority over most material and many capital equipment purchases was recognized, but many universities, government institutions, and hospitals were becoming increasingly cost conscious.

Purchase of replacement equipment was limited due to the long life of most products. When equipment was replaced, SIL's reputation for reliable equipment performance, which had been established over the years, promoted brand loyalty. SIL's reputation also depended on the quality of its repair service. Service and spare parts had to be readily available. When a piece of equipment broke down (for example, the heater element of a water bath might burn out), a replacement part could be ordered from a distributor. For more serious problems, an authorized service representative would call to fix the problem or return the equipment to the factory for repair. In any case, SIL depended on its distributors to help maintain a reputation for dependability in responding to customer service requirements.

THE ISLINGTON PLANT

Shortly after Thornton's arrival, Jack May, manager of manufacturing, accompanied him on an extensive tour of the plant. May described the production system in terms of the three related processes which took place at the Islington plant. First was purchase of raw materials and parts, second was fabrication of parts and subassemblies to stock, and third was assembly and release of products to finished goods inventory. The plant floor was divided into separate areas for raw material stores, parts stock, fabrication and assembly. (Exhibit 7 shows the Islington plant layout.)

Products were assembled from fabricated sheet metal or mechanical parts and purchased electrical or electronic components. Sheet metal parts and subassemblies (e.g., outer bodies, pans, covers) were manufactured in the Fabrication Department. Small lots of sheet metal were withdrawn from raw material inventory and cut to size on a shear. Each part was shaped on a punch press or press brake. Parts were then welded together, buffed, and painted to make components. These were then inspected, placed in containers, and transferred to the stock room for storage until required by the assembly department.

Machined parts were manufactured from purchased castings and bar stock. A number of general purpose machine tools were located in the machine shop—screw machines, drill presses, milling machines, and lathes, some of which were numerically controlled. Machining took place in small lots, following the sequence of operations specified on a "Production Operation Sheet." The Production Operation Sheet moved with the parts as they were transported from one work station to the next. Machined parts were inspected when completed, then transferred to the stock room, where they awaited final assembly.

Purchased parts accounted for 40–50 percent of standard manufacturing cost. These parts were purchased from over 600 vendors. For example, the stainless steel pans used in SIL's constant temperature product line were purchased parts. SIL could not justify manufacturing these pans in-house. The tooling and equipment required were sufficiently specialized that it had proved cheaper to buy the pans from outside suppliers. Upon receipt, parts were inspected and placed in parts inventory. Raw materials required by the Fabrication Department were handled in a similar fashion.

Final assembly was performed by approximately 80 specialized workers. The same workers were always assigned to assemble particular products. For this reason, the assembly shop was divided into sections with designated areas for pump, oven, and water bath assembly and a general assembly area for bulkier equipment. After final test and inspection, the equipment was packed and shipped to the Romford warehouse for storage.

EXHIBIT 7
STEWART INSTRUMENTS LTD.
The Islington Plant Layout

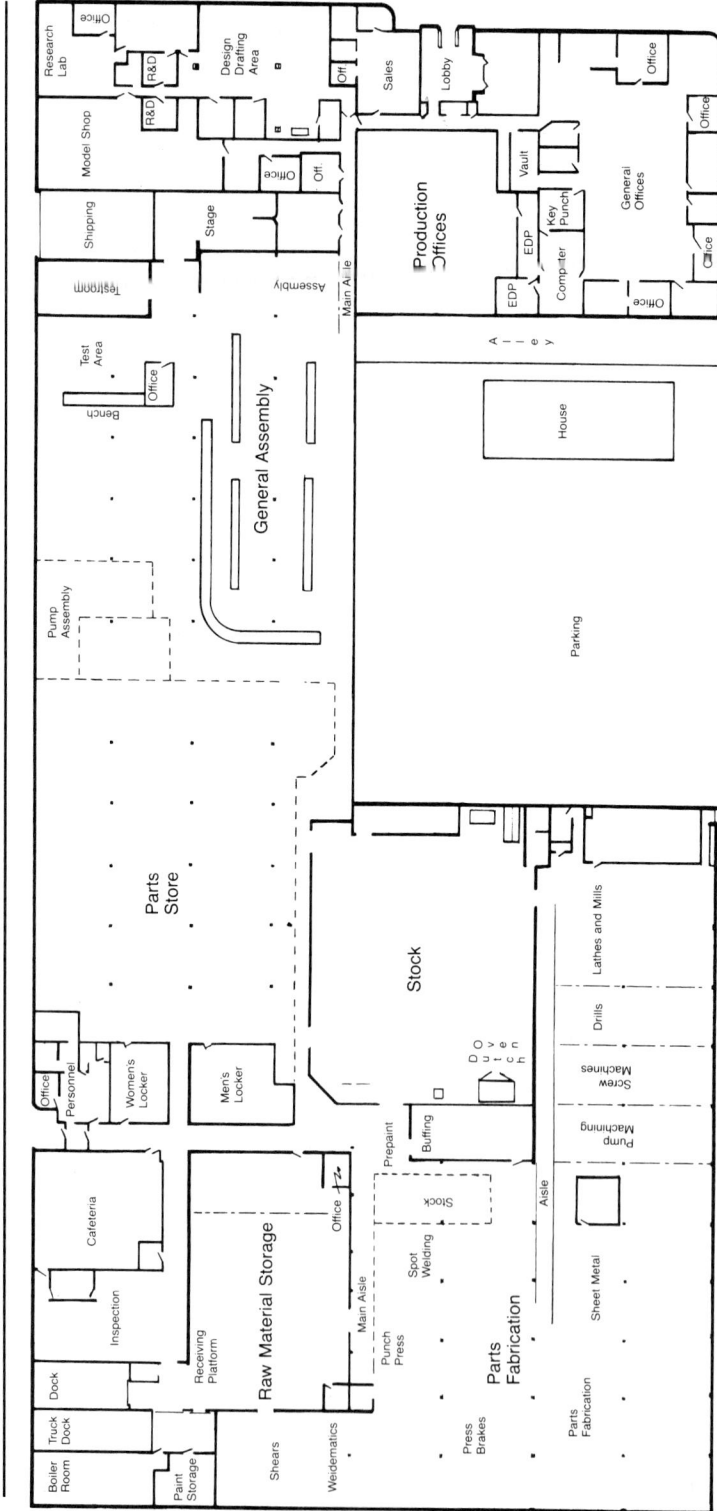

MANUFACTURING PLANNING AND CONTROL

Manufacturing planning and control at SIL was based upon a computerized material requirements planning (MRP) system which had been installed in 1978. Tony McNeil, materials control manager, had been responsible for the implementation of the system and explained its operation to Thornton. Each of the 1,100 products which SIL manufactured was described, for production purposes, by a bill of material (BOM) showing five separate levels of description, the top (Level 0) being the finished product. The BOM listed all the parts and raw materials needed to build one unit. McNeil showed Thornton the BOM for the Model SC-121 water bath. It used all five levels and included 60 different parts, each having a unique part number (PN). The number of units of each part needed were indicated on the BOM, as well as the relationship among parts, subassemblies, assemblies, and the final product. Exhibit 8 shows a simplified version of the BOM for the SC-121 in which only one of the six assemblies used to build the final product is shown in detail. The standard manufacturing costs for both the SC-121 and the pan/top body assembly are given in Exhibit 9.

For the SC-121 ("Level 0" or "end-item") to be assembled, six assemblies, each identified by a unique part number, had to be available, together with an instruction manual, packaging, and miscellaneous other parts. All of these were designated as Level 1 items. The six assemblies were in turn comprised of 38 uniquely identified subassemblies and parts, some in multiple quantities. One of the six assemblies was the pan/top body assembly (PN539338). It was made up of three subassemblies and several other parts, all designated as Level 2 items. The three subassemblies were further broken down or "exploded" into components which appeared as Level 3 items. Raw material used to fabricate the components were specified on Level 4.

Parts or subassemblies frequently were used in more than one product and therefore appeared in multiple BOMs. For example, the SC-121's thermometer (PN31459C) was a component in 50 products or subassemblies carried in the catalog (subassemblies were often listed as replacement parts). Similarly, the thermostat (PN239137) found its way into 43 items and the heater (PN247339) into 19.

The production schedule for parts, subassemblies, and assemblies was derived from a master production schedule (MPS). The MPS specified which end-item products were to be manufactured, the quantities of each, and when these quantities were to be ready for shipment from Romford. For a given schedule, the material requirements planning

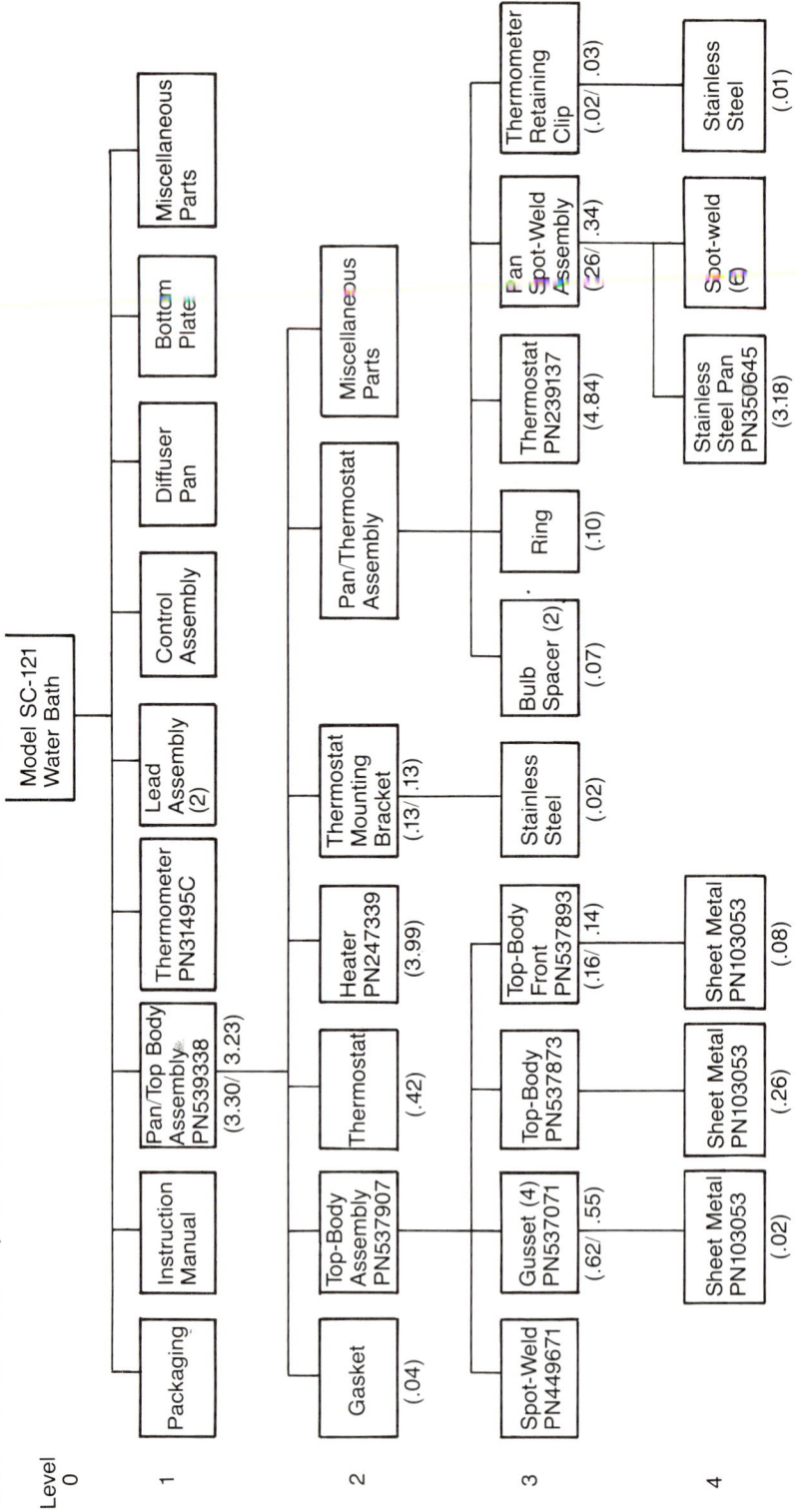

EXHIBIT 8
STEWART INSTRUMENTS LTD.
Model SC-121 Water Bath Bill of Material

Note: Material cost shown by ( ).   Units = £Sterling.
Labor/overhead shown by (/).

EXHIBIT 9
STEWART INSTRUMENTS LTD.
Model SC-121 and Pan/Top Body Assembly Standard Cost

Level	Item	Standard Manufacturing Cost		
		Material	Labor	Overhead*
0	Model SC-121 Total	19.28	7.54	8.37
1	Pan/top-body assembly	—	3.30	3.23
2	Subassemblies/parts	4.45	.13	.13
3	Parts fabrication	5.03	1.06	1.06
4	Raw material	3.55	—	—
	Total pan/top body assembly	13.03	4.49	4.42

*Overhead is applied on the basis of direct labor cost, but the rate used varies by department.

(MRP) system then determined the quantities and timing of material required at Levels 1 through 4, referencing SIL's 1,100 BOMs and 20,000 separate part numbers.

Time phasing was accomplished by taking into consideration manufacturing lead times for manufactured parts and delivery lead times for purchased items. The MRP logic was such that on-hand inventory of assemblies, subassemblies, and components was subtracted from gross requirements to determine net build and order quantities. Allowances were made for scrap losses on those items manufactured from raw material. The MRP system was updated weekly, at which time all the transactions which had taken place during the week (receipts and withdrawls from inventory, scrap losses, etc.), as well as schedule changes (early or delayed shipments), were consolidated.

MANUFACTURING OPERATIONS

As they walked past the paint shop, McNeil drew Thornton's attention to a lot of SC-121 top-body assemblies (PN537907) which were about to be painted with SIL's distinctive blue finish. With the assemblies was a packet of "shop paper" which he withdrew and showed to Thornton. The first sheet was the production bill of material. This document (shown in Exhibit 10) was more detailed than the end-item BOM which Thornton had seen earlier. He noted that each top-body assembly was built using four items: spot weld (a supply), four gussets, the top-body

EXHIBIT 10
STEWART INSTRUMENTS LTD.
Production Bill of Material for Top-Body Assembly

```
07/04/80                 P R O D U C T I O N   B I L L   O F   M A T E R I A L                    PAGE 1

CAT. NO. / PART NO.      537907                    ISSUE DATE  00 / 00 / 00      JOB NO.         72553

DESRIPTION:              TOP BODY ASSY             SUPERSEDED  00 / 00 / 00      QUANTITY          106

SIMILAR TO               DATE JOB                  QUANTITY                      SCHEDULE
RUN WITH  _____        COMPLETED  _____        COMPLETED  _____           DATE      29/04/80

QUANTITY    PART      MAT'L                         NUMBER                          MATERIAL   LABOR
REQUIRED    NUMBER    CODE  DESCRIPTION             REQ'D   WT. LGTH. & BL. SIZE        COST     COST


                            SHEET METAL WORK
    106     449671    P     6-032X1 / 2 SPOTWELD S    1                       PC        ...      ...
    424     537871    S     GUSSET TOP BODY           4                       PC        ...      ...
    106     537873    M     ( I ) TOP BODY            1                       PC        ...      ...
    106     103053    PR    36 X 96 ARMCO GRIP CRS    1      27.343 X 6.421   IN        ...      ...
    106     537893    S     ( I ) TOP BODY FRONT      1                       PC        ...      ...

---------------------------------- MATERIAL REQUIRED FOR 1 UNIT ---------------------------------

      6     103053          36 X 96 ARMCO GRIP CRS   .049                     SH        ...      ...

---------------------------------- DRAWINGS REQUIRED --------------------------------------------

                            B537873
                            C537907
END OF BILL NO.     537907   1 PAGES
```

front and the top body itself. The first three items were all stocked in inventory. The top body, however, was not. It had to be made directly from 24-gauge cold rolled steel (PN 103053) which had a special surface finish. Six "36 × 96" sheets of metal were required to make the 106 parts.

Thornton asked how workers knew what to do. McNeil showed him the production operation sheet (Exhibit 11). This detailed six operations performed at six work stations. A seventh and final instruction transferred the completed parts to inventory. The first three operations involved fabrication of the top body (PN537873). Sheet metal was to be cut to size, then shaped using first the punch press and then the brake press. Once the required number of parts had been fabricated (106 in this case), each was spotwelded to four gussets and a top body front (parts which had been withdrawn from inventory) to form a top body assembly. After welding it was necessary to hand grind the welded seams to insure an appropriate finish. Finally, the 106 top body assemblies were moved over to the paint shop, ready for the last operation.

EXHIBIT 11
STEWART INSTRUMENTS LTD.
Production Operation Sheet for Top-Body Assembly

07/04/80		P R O D U C T I O N O P E R A T I O N S H E E T							PAGE 1
PART NO. 537907		PART NAME: TOP BODY ASSEMBLY		JOB QTY. 106			JOB NO.		7255300
LOT SIZE 100									
DEPT. NO.	WORK CENTER	OPERATION NO.	DESCRIPTION	PHANTOM NO.	TOOL	PIECES PER HOUR	STANDARD RUN	HOURS SETUP	TOTAL ENG. TIME STD.
090	530	01	SHEAR (BLANK SIE 18CM X 70CM)	537873		125.0	.0080	.3000	1.1480
090	580	02	PUNCH N/C	537873		33.0	.0300	.5000	3.6800
090	620	03	BRAKE PRESS	537873		2.0	.5000	1.5000	54.5000
140	660	04	SPOTWELD		14216	5.0	.2000	.3500	21.5500
160	760	05	HAND GRIND			25.0	.0400		4.2400
150	772	06	PAINT LINE			29.0	.0350		3.7100
700	980	999	TO FINISHED STORES						

The time elapsed to complete a job depended on the actual run and setup times at each station. The operation sheet gave the standard run and setup times, which were used to calculate labor variances. Operators were obliged to report, on a prepunched computer card, the start and finish time of each operation. Punch clocks for this purpose were located in each department.

The actual time taken between operations also depended on the time taken to move the containers from one work center to another and on the queue time (time the container spent sitting at the work center before the operation actually commenced). A move time of one working day between centers was used as a rule of thumb. Queue time was determined on a machine by machine and department by department basis. McNeil explained that queue time was based upon the average run time of jobs on the machine, as well as on an a priori assessment of how much work should be ahead of any machine in order to provide departmental foremen some scheduling flexibility. The manufacturing lead time for the order of 106 units had been calculated as four weeks. Normally, in moving from one level to another through the bill of materials, the lead time would be specified as either the calculated lead time or two weeks, whichever was the greater. Thornton had discovered that the lead time for an assembly lot of 50 units of the Model SC-121 water bath was two weeks, provided of course that all necessary Level 1 items were in stock.

COST CONTROL

SIL had implemented a standard cost system at the beginning of the fiscal year. It was used to compare actual production costs to standard and was to serve as a measure of job performance. Unfortunately, the system was not operating as smoothly as Stewart Foster, the controller, would have liked. In fact, he had complained to Thornton that while the system was basically sound, many individual standards—in particular the labor standards—were only approximate. Foster explained that due to time pressure he and his team had been forced to estimate standards for "families" of similar components rather than to determine precise standards on an item by item basis. In following up on some singularly large variances, he had furthermore discovered that the production operation sheets were often out of date, with product design changes or new procedures not reflected. It was obvious to Thornton that Foster was becoming increasingly concerned about the approximations he had been forced to make and the increasing skepticism that his colleagues were voicing about the utility of the system.

PRODUCTION PLANNING

His first meeting with Derek Brown, production planning manager, had made a significant impression on Thornton, for it was obvious that he was working under a great deal of pressure. Thornton soon discovered that Brown was attempting to cope with an increasing number of production scheduling changes at the end-item level and that recently these changes had risen to an average of 287 each week. Brown explained that when the MRP system had been installed, a decision had been made to keep finished goods inventory to a minimum by establishing a zero inventory/zero backlog goal. He wondered now whether the idea had been a good one.

During the third week of each month, SIL's four product managers revised a twelve-month rolling forecast for each product. Revisions were influenced by projected inventory at month's end. For example, when reviewing most recent demand figures, projected receipts for the month, and current on-hand inventory, if the projected on-hand inventory at month end was considered to be "too high," the product manager would not only reduce the demand forecast for the following month, but might also modify the forecast for succeeding months. The reverse was true if the projected on-hand inventory was considered to be "too low." They determined the meanings of "too high" and "too low" among themselves.

Forecasts formed the basis for the master production schedule and ultimately the time-phased material requirements. Translating the forecast into a master production schedule was a difficult task. Brown had to be mindful of three constraints. First, the production lot size could be no greater than forecasted demand over the next six weeks. This was because Marketing considered six weeks to be the maximum time that should elapse between two successive lots of the same item. Next, the 1980 production plan called for shipments averaging £52,000 per day. Third, capacity in the fabrication and machine shops was finite, and bottlenecks could arise at machine centers depending upon the mix of parts scheduled through them.

ACKNOWLEDGED OPERATING PROBLEMS

As Thornton thought back over the conversations he had had with management and hourly personnel during the past four days, he realized that continual reference had been made to the plant's overloaded and overcrowded condition. Morale was being affected. He sensed problems were severe in four areas: fabrication, inventory control/recordkeeping, production planning/purchasing, and quality control.

Fabrication

Workers in both the sheet metal and the machine shops were critical of the time standards being used. In their opinion, the time standards did not reflect the actual time required to complete the various operations. Work was piling up in front of the machines to such an extent that it was difficult for the material handlers to move about the shop floor in their small forklift trucks. Containers of work-in-process and completed parts or subassemblies seemed to be stacked wherever there was space available.

Overtime work had alleviated the problem to some extent, but the demands of frequent schedule changes, of expediting rush and rework orders through the shop, and the continual disruption of engineering changes contributed to a pervasive atmosphere of crisis and resentment. Some workers resented being told to work compulsory overtime week after week.

In order to reduce the load on the Fabrication Department, work had been subcontracted out to local machine shops. During 1980, this had amounted to £240,000 of labor charges at standard rates. Problems arose when it was discovered that critical design changes communicated verbally or informally to machine operators by engineering had not been incorporated into updated engineering drawings due to the pressure of work. As a result, subcontractors were shipping parts which did not meet current specifications. Not only did these parts cost more initially, they then had to be reworked in fabrication.

After assembly, units were transferred to the Test Department for final test. Once this transfer had been made, the Assembly Department received credit towards the daily shipment target. Even if the unit was defective, or indeed could not work since parts were missing, the Assembly Department received credit. Such units were completed in the final test area and the work was reported as "repairs."

Inventory Control/Recordkeeping

Discrepancies existed between inventory levels according to MRP records and a physical count. How such discrepancies occurred was unclear. It was suspected that paperwork was not being completed properly due to the crisis mode of operation. Further, discrepancies tended to be masked by the way in which the cycle count of inventory was conducted. Actual inventory levels were verified upon the receipt of an order. Accuracy was reported as a ratio of the actual on-hand plus receipt to the reported on-hand plus receipt—rather than the ratio of the actual on-hand to the reported on-hand. This procedure inflated the accuracy of the figures which were being reported.

In October, only 40–50 percent of jobs had been "picked clean." To be "picked clean" the required number of all Level 1 items had to be physically on hand to meet the Level 0 requirements specified in the master production schedule. Before an assembly schedule was released to the Assembly Department, it was possible, using the MRP system, to check to see if, according to the Level 1 MRP records, all the Level 1 items required to meet the schedule were on hand. If this check was affirmative, then the stock pickers were authorized to physically remove the parts from inventory and transfer them to the Assembly Department.

Discrepancies between the computer records and physical inventory were discovered during actual stock picking. When this situation arose, parts already picked were set aside. Missing items were then expedited through the required department, either Fabrication or Purchasing. The process could take several days, even weeks, depending on the parts. A physical count of all items in inventory had been taken twice during 1980 in an attempt to reconcile the differences between MRP records and physical inventory.

Production Planning and Purchasing

SIL's buyers attempted to secure deliveries which would meet the weekly production schedule. Planned purchase orders together with any expedite or de-expedite changes were transmitted to Purchasing each week after the MRP run. However, the volume of these messages was such that the buyers were able to complete only 70 percent in any given week. The remainder carried over into the following week, by which time the MRP system had been updated anew. Apart from attempting to expedite an increasing number of requests for missing parts, buyers were affected by the frequent changes in the master production schedule. This made for an increasingly strained relationship between Purchasing and Production Planning.

SIL's buyers had little bargaining power with their suppliers because the typical purchase order was for a relatively small number of units. These were almost always single-sourced and placed upon a vendor significantly larger than SIL. Several vendors had recently refused SIL's business, incensed that having attempted to meet a rush order, it had been cancelled a week or so later. Buyers were now uneasy about cancelling or de-expediting any order.

Quality Control

Due to the overcrowded conditions at Islington, parts and subassemblies were being shipped to the Romford warehouse in addition to finished goods. These were returned to Islington as needed to meet assembly schedules. The transshipments were made in two 40-foot trucks, each of which made two round trips per day between the plants. On-time shipment of finished goods from Romford was being affected, since workers there were spending a significant portion of their time receiving, stocking, and transshipping work-in-process.

Transshipments also resulted in both cosmetic and structural damage to the parts and subassemblies because appropriate palleting and packaging were not available. This created additional rework, reduced effective capacity at Islington, and extended assembly lead times. Space was at a premium as the facility became increasingly clogged. In addition, "shop paper" and other documents used for identification purposes were being soiled, torn, or lost.

SUMMARY

In 1965 the parent company had bought SIL to diversify into new markets and broaden its customer base. SIL had also been generating a significant cash flow. By the late seventies, this was no longer the case. The divestiture of SIL had been discussed on more than one occasion among some corporate staff members. Thornton recognized that it was SIL, his position, and perhaps his future career prospects which were on the line. If only he could get product out the door!

PART 3

MATERIALS
MANAGEMENT

The introductory case in this section, The Geneva Technical Institute (C), is not directly related to materials management, but sets the stage for the section. The issue is one of clearly stating the objectives of the institute and directing the department's resources to achieving those objectives. Rational determination of objectives will be presumed in many of the other cases, but will reappear as an issue in the Robert Victor Neher, Ltd. case, the second in the section. The company produces printed aluminum foil packaging, and the case centers on the purchasing department. In addition to concern over the objectives of the department, there are questions of what measures should be used for evaluating the department's productivity.

   An issue of emerging concern is raised in the Inalfa BV case. A Dutch company that produces sunroofs for automobiles questions whether it should become a sole source supplier to the Xerox company. It would require major changes in the quality system and the product mix, and would necessitate opening the books to Xerox. The case describes the trade-offs as seen by Inalfa and asks for an evaluation of the desirability of entering into a long-term contract. The Frisbee Frozen Foods case raises quite different issues. The company supplies a market area in northern Italy with a variety of frozen foods. A proposal for building a new central frozen food warehouse has triggered a study of the physical distribution system of the company. Contracts for raw materials and a potential contract for some delivery services are elements that must be considered in providing a system that can satisfy high service level demands.

In the Biral International (A) case a company that produces pumps in Switzerland is considering a cooperative arrangement with a Hungarian firm. The question is whether to provide some know-how and to source some parts in Hungary in order to get into the Hungarian market. Some of the issues of dealing with the East European countries are raised. In the Vanderbruk Spice NV case a Dutch company's Japanese division has joined forces with a Japanese distributor to reach the Japanese market. A distribution requirements planning (DRP) system has just been approved for Japan, but the board is not very enthusiastic. The case provides some of the details of the proposed system and the presentation to the board.

The Geneva Technical Institute (C)

After a long and trying faculty meeting, Dr. Richard Albu felt he was no closer to a solution for the secretarial problem. As chairman of the Physics Department at The Geneva Technical Institute, he was concerned that any further delays would lead to very serious morale problems among the staff. Nonetheless, he felt he should take the time to perform a careful analysis of the situation before making any changes. That would increase the chances of the changes really improving the secretarial support. He reluctantly decided to start at the beginning and review all objectives and activities of the department.

To the best of Dr. Albu's knowledge, the objectives of the department had never been clearly defined, although broad goals—like expand knowledge, provide education, and serve the public had been used. It was generally accepted that the department's activities fell into three major categories: teaching, research, and service (with service involving both internal administrative activities and external public relations tasks). Information on each of these areas would be a prerequisite to deciding where the secretarial, professional, and other resources might best be used in accomplishing the department's mission.

TEACHING ACTIVITIES

The conduct of classroom teaching by the department faculty is guided by two key considerations. The first of these considerations is whether the class is comprised of undergraduate or graduate students. The graduate classes were further divided into masters or doctoral levels. The reputation of the department and the degree-granting authority required that the graduate-level courses be taught by one of the 12 full-time faculty members of the department. The undergraduate classes, however, could be taught by part-time faculty or by qualified graduate students under the supervision of full-time faculty members. The department rigidly adhered to these requirements, even though it occasionally meant

---

The Geneva Technical Institute (A) and (B), pages 3 and 87, contain background and additional information.

large classes, alternate-year scheduling, or decreased course offerings in the department.

The second consideration that guided teaching activities was the distinction between courses that were required of students and those which were optional for them. The required courses contained basic material from all the major areas of physics, while the optional courses tended to specialize in areas of particular faculty interest. The required courses involved departmental discussion, to agree on the basic material to be included, and coordination between different sections of the same course that might be offered at different times by different people. The department first made sure the required courses were staffed and then offered optional courses as the faculty resources permitted. Only on rare occasions would an advanced graduate student teach an optional course.

There had been few complaints about the quality of the teaching among the full-time faculty members. There had been several instances, however, when the undergraduates had expressed concern about the quality of the instruction by the graduate students. The faculty member currently responsible for the coordination of graduate student teaching, Dr. Jean-Pierre Moran, expressed real concern about this. "It is difficult to find enough time to talk with the graduate students about their teaching. Most of them have had no training in teaching at all. We seem to expect their knowledge of the subject will be sufficient for them to teach well. Our recent attempts to help in the teaching area have been very frustrating. Any suggested changes, instructions, handouts, or improvements are delayed in the typing queue for so long that it is not worth trying to do much. In addition, the real rewards around here are for research and not for helping the graduate students improve their teaching."

The teaching activities involved a great deal of clerical support. There were course outlines, examinations, handouts, instructions for experiments, and special materials for the classes that were constantly in need of preparation. The clerical activities involved typing, proofing, duplicating, and distribution (usually handed out in class, but occasionally placed in the student mailboxes). Since physics was a constantly changing field, the faculty felt the introduction of new, current material into the classroom was very important.

In some instances, faculty members had elected not to prepare fresh new material for the classes. Dr. René LaForte explained the problem. "The last time I had some current material that was relevant to the topic I was covering in the course, it coincided with an exam in another course. The delay in getting the material ready for me to hand out was so long that we were on another topic by the time it was available. Much of the impact was simply lost. I feel that many of my colleagues have not spent the amount of time they should in providing new material to their classes or in revising their course outlines partly because of the secretarial situation. I don't want to think of the number of times I have done my own duplicating on a commercial machine in town or have carried work home to type myself or have my wife type for me."

Dr. Albu staffed the courses with 12 full-time faculty, 8 graduate students, and 1 part-time professor from a local manufacturing company. All of the graduate students were involved in teaching required undergraduate courses, and the part-time professor was offering a special optional course in his area of expertise. It seemed unlikely that there would be any opportunity to increase the number of faculty or graduate students in the near future. Dr. Albu was also concerned that any success in expanding would further complicate the secretarial situation. As it was, one graduate student said: "Frankly, we all rely a great deal on the secretaries to help us learn the system and prepare the material for our classes. After all, most secretaries have been here longer than we have."

RESEARCH

A variety of research was performed in the department and an outstanding international reputation for quality research was enjoyed by the faculty. Some of the faculty specialized in laboratory research using the extensive equipment available to the department. The laboratory equipment was utilized fairly heavily by graduate students and full-time faculty. A part of the laboratory equipment was used for experiments performed by undergraduates in their required courses. The maintenance of the laboratory was conducted by institute personnel, and there were occasional comments in the department concerning the lack of quality and speed with which the maintenance was performed. Dr. Albu noted wryly that the department had an insatiable appetite for new laboratory equipment. "Much of the equipment has been provided by grants that the individual faculty have won for specific research projects, but we always have requests to purchase more equipment than the budget will allow."

Another part of the faculty specialized in theoretical research, utilizing the library and computing facilities to accomplish their projects. Both laboratory and theoretical research usually resulted in a series of discussion papers, followed by presentations at meetings and publication in learned journals. The discussion papers were duplicated and distributed among colleagues for comment and criticism while final versions appeared in proceedings of the meetings of academic societies and in published journals. It was not uncommon for a single experiment to require ten different drafts of written material from proposal through final publication.

The department had seven research assistants to help in this research. These were generally young graduate students, who were not yet qualified for teaching but had an interest in physics as a career. They performed all kinds of assignments for the faculty, from library research to assisting in the laboratory experiments. In talking with several of them, Dr. Albu found that the workload was quite variable among them, however. In some cases the assistants said that they very rarely had anything to do for their faculty member, while others were concerned that they were working more than they should be. Those that were heavily involved with the faculty, however, were quite pleased with their work and enjoyed it very much. Often the research assistants could be found sitting in the office with the secretaries waiting to see their faculty supervisor or to be assigned work to do.

The publication and dissemination of research findings were felt to be important in maintaining the reputation of the department and providing new knowledge from which future class material would evolve. It was also the means by which faculty were made known to other educational institutions and industry. This visibility meant that most faculty could change jobs quite easily. Also, high-quality research was essential in providing grants for the institute. In addition to laboratory equipment, the grants provided contributions to general overhead and administrative expenses.

SERVICE

The institute was engaged in public relations activities beyond the publicity that came from the research results. Besides winning grants, the department supported the institute and its public image in a variety of ways. The faculty, with the help of the institute's public relations department, was expected to provide information for the press, TV, and general public. This might involve granting interviews, giving speeches to local or national groups, and generally keeping the image of the department and institute in front of the public. While a number of the faculty engaged in these PR efforts, some felt that there was really no reward for spending their time this way.

Inside the institute there were also a number of activities that involved faculty time. For example, the students who were interested in physics were assigned to the department for advice. This counseling took a great deal of the faculty's time. The faculty determined which courses the students were eligible for (by reviewing the courses completed), suggested which they should take next, and explained some of the options within the department. The institute required that all student class schedules be approved by a faculty member before the student could register.

Perhaps the most frustrating thing that Dr. Albu found in talking with the various people in the department was the reaction to committee meetings. There was generally good attendance at the departmental committee meetings, but he learned that much of the attendance at the department-wide faculty meetings was concern for the immediate problem of secretarial support, rather than an interest in the long-term direction of the department. The institute faculty and committee meetings were very infrequently attended by members of the Physics Department. Even new faculty would generally attend only one or two meetings before finding excuses to stop going. Most faculty seemed to feel that the issues were essential, but the meetings were a real waste of time.

There were committees for setting policy at each of the levels of the department's classes (undergraduate, masters, and doctoral), for the coordination of the laboratory facilities, for the management of the institute's library, for reviewing institute policies, and so on. The institute had always placed a great deal of the administrative activities in the hands of these committees, which were almost exclusively comprised of faculty.

As Dr. Albu tried to put into perspective all of the undertakings of the department, he was aware that the relationships between activities and objectives should be beneficial instead of competitive. His first task, however, was to better understand the relationships between various tasks and the objectives as the basis for evaluating alternative ways of improving the situation.

Robert Victor Neher, Ltd. Co.

"We produce everything to order here, and that says we must remain flexible. For purchasing, that means we must know our suppliers well and be able to locate those that can meet our delivery requirements. I do not really want to turn into a formal computer department; it might slow us down. We are a small producer that needs quick, creative solutions for our customer's problems. At the same time we are under pressure to improve productivity. In purchasing there are no good measures to show the productivity improvements. Still, we must contribute to the needs of the company."

Mr. Alfred Eugster, manager of purchasing at Robert Victor Neher, Ltd., had just summarized his feelings about the purchasing activities of the company. The company produces various thicknesses, finishes, and widths of aluminium foil at its plant in Kreuzlingen, Switzerland. The aluminium used by the plant is produced by sister plants of the Alusuisse Group. "We are constantly squeezed between the market price and the cost of the aluminium, which we don't control," said Mr. Eugster. "This means we must continue to look for ways to improve our operations. We have not established a formal productivity program, however."

BACKGROUND

The company was founded in 1910 by Robert Victor Neher. Mr. Neher's interest in producing thin aluminium sheet stemmed from his attempts to produce a balloon lining that would not leak gas during flight. This led to the development of aluminium rolling techniques that produced very thin foil to quite close tolerances. In 1912, a subsidiary was established in Singen, Germany, about 25 kilometers from Kreuzlingen. In 1939, both companies were sold to the Alusuisse group.

Alusuisse is a Swiss group involved in virtually every aspect of aluminium production. Within Switzerland alone, Alusuisse owns 50 percent or more of 21 different companies. They own 50 percent or more of 35 firms in the rest of Europe and 25 in the rest of the world. In addition to this, the company has some ownership interest in about 50 other companies. The role of Neher in this group is to convert aluminium produced by sister companies into aluminium foil products sold to the market outside the group. These products include packaging for food and pharmaceutical products, electrical condenser insulation, and household wrap.

Neher is one of five plants within the Alusuisse group that can produce foil. The other four are located in Germany (the former subsidiary of the Neher company), the United Kingdom, Italy, and the United States. Of the somewhat more than 100,000 tons of foil produced annually by the group, the Neher company produces 13,400 tons. Each of the plants within the group has a form of "exclusive" territory in its marketing area. Within the Switzerland territory, however, the Neher company faces the competition of three aluminium foil plants that do not belong to the group.

THE PRODUCT LINE

The process used for producing aluminium foil products at Neher is shown in Exhibit 1. The process starts by annealing (step 11) rolls of aluminium sheet from Chippis, Switzerland. The aluminium is annealed to provide the correct hardness before rolling it into thin aluminium foil in the mill. The various finishes required by the customers are applied in the converting operation. Lamination bonds the foil to special papers or plastic films. Lacquering both colors and seals the foil. In addition, the foil can be printed with complex, colorful designs or be embossed with a variety of patterns before it is slit to the width required by the customer. The growth in variety of finishes has meant that the number of special papers, plastic films, lacquers, and inks has increased. Exhibit 2 shows a foil butter wrapper. It is laminated to a special oilproof paper, lacquered for color and sealing, and is printed with the design. The holes and vertical bars are for orienting the wrapper in the butter wrapping machine.

The annual product volumes are shown in Exhibit 3. "As a carryover of the Alusuisse interest in aluminium tonnage, we measure everything in tons of aluminium, although this can be deceptive. For example, one ton can make considerably different volumes of product, depending on thickness. Also, one ton of aluminium will make more than a ton of product when it is lacquered or bonded," explained Eugster.

EXHIBIT 1

ROBERT VICTOR NEHER, LTD. CO.

The Production of Aluminium Foil Products

(the basic processes involved in manufacturing and converting aluminium foil)

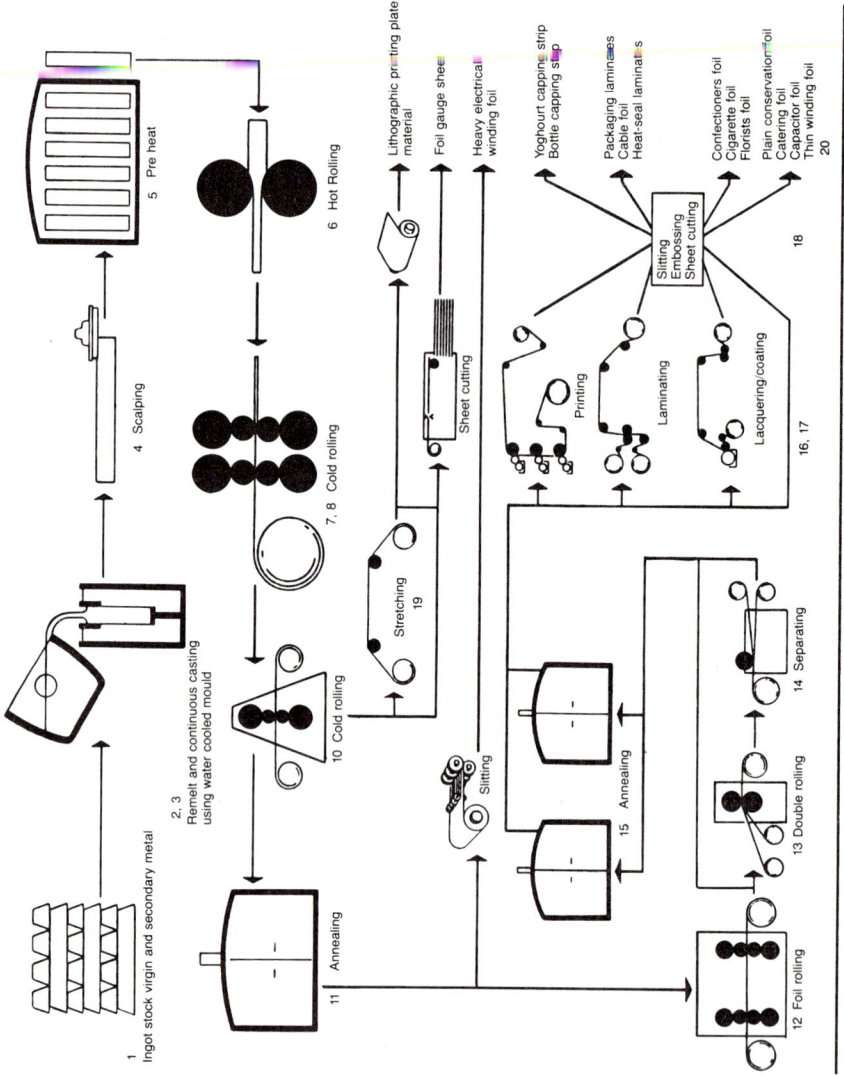

1 Ingot stock virgin and secondary metal

2, 3 Remelt and continuous casting using water cooled mould

4 Scalping

5 Pre heat

6 Hot Rolling

7, 8 Cold rolling

10 Cold rolling

11 Annealing

12 Foil rolling

13 Double rolling

14 Separating

15 Annealing

16, 17

18

19 Stretching

20

Slitting

Printing

Laminating

Lacquering/coating

Slitting Embossing Sheet cutting

Sheet cutting

Lithographic printing plate material

Foil gauge sheet

Heavy electrical winding foil

Yoghourt capping strip
Bottle capping strip

Packaging laminates
Cable foil
Heat-seal laminates

Confectioners foil
Cigarette foil
Florists foil

Plain conservation foil
Catering foil
Capacitor foil
Thin winding foil

EXHIBIT 2
ROBERT VICTOR NEHER, LTD. CO.
Converted Product

Irish Creamery Butter
PACKED UNDER
FRANCHISE FROM
AN BORD BAINNE
GRATTAN HOUSE, DUBLIN Z
BY BALLYCLOUGH CO-OP CREAMERY LTD.

REGD No C 327

EXHIBIT 3
ROBERT VICTOR NEHER, LTD. CO.
Annual Product Volumes from Process

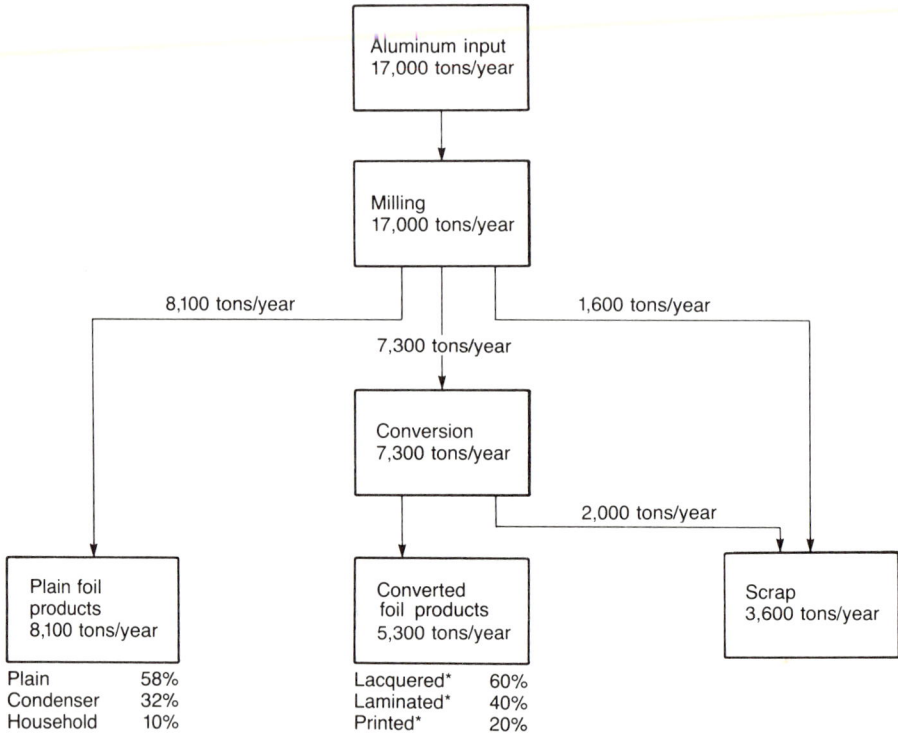

| Aluminum input 17,000 tons/year |
| Milling 17,000 tons/year |

8,100 tons/year   7,300 tons/year   1,600 tons/year

Conversion 7,300 tons/year

2,000 tons/year

| Plain foil products 8,100 tons/year | Converted foil products 5,300 tons/year | Scrap 3,600 tons/year |

Plain	58%	Lacquered*	60%
Condenser	32%	Laminated*	40%
Household	10%	Printed*	20%

*Totals to more than 100 percent because many products go through more than one of these processes.

"Our scrap looks high in absolute terms, but it compares to rates of as high as 30 percent in similar firms. Our efforts in this area have reduced our scrap from an average of 27 percent in 1970 to as low as 21 percent for the current year. We can influence the scrap rate in purchasing through the quality specifications. Although we cannot check all properties of arriving aluminium, we can usually tell if it's okay in the first rolling operation. It is important to catch the problems early, since poor quality aluminium in converting can spoil the whole lot. Even though we claim refunds from Alusuisse for the bad aluminium, plus value added, it is a problem to reschedule," he continued.

THE MARKET

The company markets its products worldwide, with about 75 percent going outside of Switzerland. This has led the firm to develop an expertise in exporting, including an export packing department. The materials to crate product for international shipping are purchased by the purchasing department. The firm also maintains food and drug certificates for their products and components. This helps customers meet international standards for wrapping materials. Getting these certificates can take a long time for a new product or component, so having some available is a valuable competitive factor.

The market for aluminium foil products is highly competitive, and high Swiss labor rates make it difficult for Neher to compete in the plain foil market. To provide the technical knowledge for solving each customer's particular problems, the company has built up their capability in the supporting functions like chemical analysis, artwork and design, bonding methods, and so on. Thus the firm can provide "in-house" service from initial design through pilot test to final production and shipping. These integrated activities have, among other things, made the company one of Switzerland's largest lacquer manufacturers. The impact on purchasing has been an increasing number of support items required.

The technical capability is not enough, however; the company must also respond to the needs of its customers for product. For instance, a lack of wrapping paper could stop an entire packaging line at a major customer's location. Thus service is extremely important. Since the company produces to order, this means that the purchasing department must continually be in a position to locate sources of supply that can deliver quickly to Neher. A combination of the desire to produce to order (in order to keep the inventory levels reasonable) and the desire for rapid, flexible responses to customer requests means the purchasing department must be in constant touch with the suppliers.

PURCHASING ACTIVITIES

To put the purchasing activities at Neher into perspective, Exhibit 4 shows a breakdown of sales into the purchased material costs, personnel, overhead, and profit. Purchasing costs represent about 67 percent of the company's sales. Aluminium is the largest percentage of the pur-

EXHIBIT 4
ROBERT VICTOR NEHER, LTD. CO.
Breakdown of Sales and Purchasing

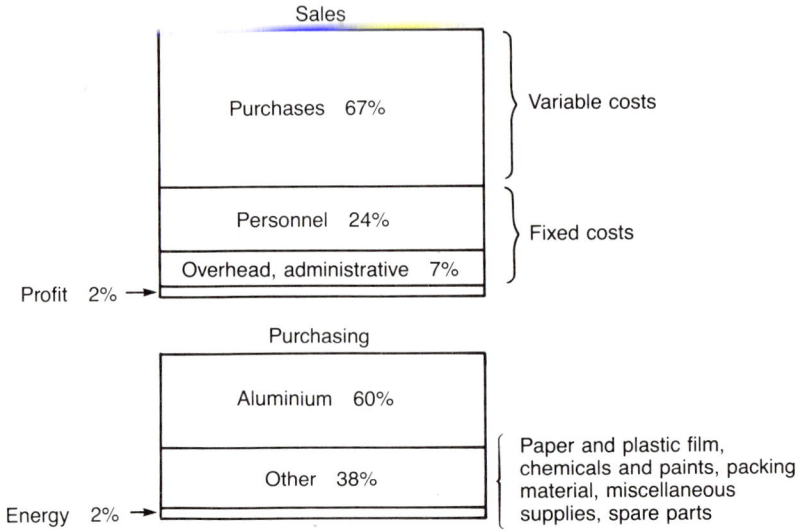

chasing costs, but the price is set outside Neher and is rarely negotiable by purchasing. The energy costs are also outside the control of purchasing, and very little can be done to change them without significant changes in the equipment used by the firm. It is only in the "other" category that purchasing can exercise much discretion. This other category is broken further into paper and plastic film, chemicals and paints, packing material, miscellaneous supplies, and spare parts. The purchasing department also is involved in buying machinery and other capital items, but these are rare and special activities.

The organization chart for the company is shown in Exhibit 5. Besides Eugster, the persons directly involved in purchasing are Forrer, Althaus, Stoffel, and a young man serving an apprenticeship. These five people do not have the detailed expertise to manage the nearly 4,500 active material numbers. As a consequence, they work with "satellite" groups. For example, the responsibility for maintaining the inventories and requesting purchases of the chemicals and paints lies with the lacquer department foreman. Similarly, the warehouse supervisor requests purchases of the packaging material, miscellaneous supplies, and spare

EXHIBIT 5
ROBERT VICTOR NEHER, LTD. CO.
Organization Chart

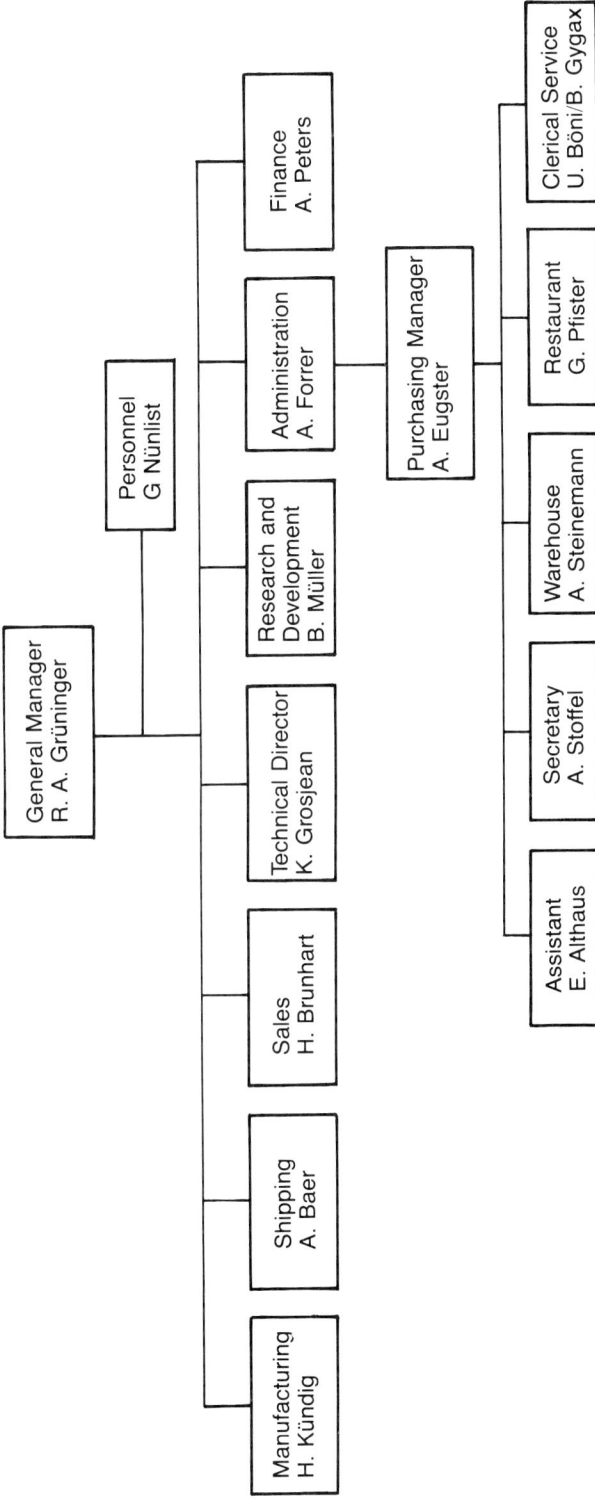

```
                          General Manager
                          R. A. Grüninger

                                │
                                │
                          Personnel
                          G Nünlist

    ┌──────────┬──────────┬──────────┼──────────┬──────────┐
    │          │          │          │          │          │
Manufacturing Shipping  Sales    Technical   Research and  Administration  Finance
H. Kündig    A. Baer   H. Brunhart Director   Development  A. Forrer       A. Peters
                                 K. Grosjean  B. Müller
                                                             │
                                                      Purchasing Manager
                                                      A. Eugster

                        ┌──────────┬──────────┬──────────┬──────────┐
                        │          │          │          │          │
                    Assistant  Secretary  Warehouse   Restaurant  Clerical Service
                    E. Althaus A. Stoffel A. Steinemann G. Pfister U. Böni/B. Gygax
```

parts (with the help of the maintenance foreman). The planning department monitors the paper and plastic film. Mr. Eugster explained the approach in purchasing. "By using the satellite groups, we have a little knowledge about a lot of things. We are always in touch with the people with their special knowledge. We must be! If we had organized the department by having a person in charge of each category, our people would have to know a great deal about a few things. We much prefer the informality and cooperativeness of our system. Besides, we save the wages of at least three more people which would have to be employed in purchasing."

Because of this contact, the purchasing department has become a center of information. In order to formalize some of this information, the department has files of all past invoices and all past purchase orders that are readily accessible in the office. They also have a tub file of open purchase orders, folders of information on vendors, and current price lists as well. Once a month, the purchasing department also gets a computer listing of the current inventory status for every material number. They use this information to coordinate their activity with the satellite groups.

PURCHASING PROCEDURES

The material categories and responsibilities are summarized in Exhibit 6. The purchasing department also recognizes three different groups of items to which different procedures apply. There are "bulk" items whose use depends mostly upon the volume of business and which are of sufficient value to warrant close attention. Another group, the "special" items, are also of significant value, but their use varies with the mixture of specific customer orders in the plant. A third group contains the low-value items, which are mostly in the miscellaneous supply category.

The management of these three groups differ. For the low-value items, the warehouse supervisor uses fairly simple procedures. He maintains a Kardex file for all 3,760 items under his management (although, after four years of parallel operation with the computer, he will soon stop the Kardex system on all but the expensed items). For the expensed items he uses a reorder point system and a simple color code to indicate all items from a single supplier. When the inventory of any of the items from a supplier reaches the reorder point, the warehouse supervisor writes a purchase request for all the items from that supplier.

EXHIBIT 6
ROBERT VICTOR NEHER, LTD. CO.
Material Categories and Responsibilities

Category	Responsibility for Purchase Requests	Value of Inventory 1,000 SFr	Number of Items (Material Numbers)	Approximate Yearly Inventory Turnover
1. Paper and Plastic Film	Planning Department	2,000	430	Paper: 7.5 Plastic film: 2.4
2. Chemicals and Paints	Lacquer Foreman	1,500	300	6.7
3. Packing Material	Warehouse Supervisor	500	400	6.0
4. Capitalized Misc. Supplies	Warehouse Supervisor	400	2,300	3.0
5. Expensed Misc. Supplies	Warehouse Supervisor		700	3.0
5. Spare Parts	Warehouse Supervisor*	300	360	3.0
			4,490	

*With the assistance of the maintenance foreman who has a small inventory of key expensed, spare parts.

For the other items, the warehouse supervisor uses a min-max system (i.e., when the inventory for an item reaches the minimum, order up to the maximum). These procedures are not applied unthinkingly, however. For example, if the maintenance foreman is planning maintenance that will affect the spare parts consumption or if a large order requiring extra packing material were booked, these would be taken into account in planning orders.

Since the usage of the bulk items is dependent upon the volume of production, it is relatively stable and they are covered by blanket contracts. The blanket contract volume is set by the purchasing department using experience and judgment. For example, one of the solvents, PQ6 (material number 4500183), had a monthly average consumption of 77,000 kilograms in 1978, 75,000 in 1979, and 87,000 in 1980. The 1981 rate is 91,400 kilograms per month, which would be a total of 1,097 tons for the year. After reviewing this, Alfred Eugster estimated he would contract for a total of about 1,100 tons for 1982. This figure is determined from his review of past usage, meetings and conversations with salespeople, his knowledge of economic trends, and his experience in the department.

Since there are six suppliers for this particular solvent, he would contract for approximately 180 tons per year with each of the six suppliers. During the course of the year, the actual orders would be based on personal telephone calls between Mr. Eugster and the suppliers. The supplier offering the best price at any given time would be given the order. "The contract is not to set the price," said Mr. Eugster, "it is to provide us with a capacity commitment. The PQ6 is used at a rate of about one truckload a week. Toward the end of each month I will order 4 to 5 loads for delivery the next month at the best price I can get. Our suppliers understand that when international market conditions change, or currency exchanges shift, they will not get our order until their prices are in line. This means that we are in constant contact with our suppliers and have developed a close working partnership with them."

The special items are those that are required to produce a customer order. Almost all of the paper and plastic film items are of this kind. The purchasing process starts with a written customer order, a telephone call, or a telex received at the plant. A customer order can be written in virtually any country's language and usually has a marketing orientation. For example, the latest order for the product shown in Exhibit 2 came in by telex and said, "1 tonne of Kerrygold 1 lb. Butter Foil." Therefore, the first step is to put the order in "Neher language."

For follow-on orders, this is done by copying a filed document that contains a precise technical description of the product and basic materials. Blank spaces are included for adding the quantity required for the current order, the due date and the price. Any changes in the basic description are handwritten onto the file document. For first-time orders, this document is created in the process of developing the product for the customer.

Once the translation or copy is made, it is sent to the planning department to "pull the order apart." This is based on a bill of material describing the items needed to produce the product. The bill of material is pulled from the files and is checked against the translation. Any necessary changes are marked on the bill of material. A detailed routing sheet specifying the exact manufacturing steps and the expected losses is used to determine the total amount of material required to fill the order. For example, the order for one ton of the Kerrygold butter wrapper required 680 kilograms of Butter Paper B (material number 6310673). The planning department combined this with two other orders requiring the same paper, which gave a total of 2,040 kilograms.

The requirement is checked against the inventory balance on the printout from the computer which is made available to the planning department twice a week (soon to be available on CRT monitors in real time). A sample of the entries on the printout is shown in Exhibit 7. If there is a need to purchase more material, the quantity requested is put on a request sheet like that shown in Exhibit 8.

PURCHASING AND FOLLOW UP

Purchasing requests come to the purchasing department on a day-to-day basis. The requests for an item can come from any of the satellites. For example, the lacquer foreman monitors the chemical and paint levels constantly. When he sees a need to replenish inventory, he sends a request to the purchasing department. The planning department similarly sends a request to the purchasing department when they find an item that needs ordering. A large percent of the requests come from the warehouse supervisor for those items that have reached the minimum inventory or the reorder point, or for which there is a common or unusual need.

After the requests are received by the purchasing department, they are reviewed before making out the purchase order. This involves

EXHIBIT 7

ROBERT VICTOR NEHER, LTD. CO.

Sample of Items from the Inventory Listing of 9/30/81

Category	OG*	Material Number	Description	On Hand Inventory	Usage per Month	Month's Supply	Last Price	Consumption Since 1/1	Last Order	Due Date
Paper and plastic film	S	6024573	Sheet Stock D	4,818.0	1,048.8	4.6	2.04	9,439	5,000.0	10/8/81
	S	6310673	Butter Paper B	1,610.0	1,449.6	1.1	2.63	13,047	5,000.0	10/27/80†
				3 000	(10/14‡)					
	S	6555100	Tobacco Sheet	145.0	5.7	25.4	9.69	470	200.0	12/18/80†
Chemical and paint	S	4100593	Lacquer B	32.0	0.4	80.0	36.56	4	40.0	7/10/79§
	B	4500183	Solvent PQ6	103,087.0	91,403.9	1.1	1.32	822,636	15,000.0	10/22/81‡
	S	4900765	Color P	3.8	0.4	9.5	167.50	4	25.0	7/10/79§
Spare parts	M	3473066	Light Bulb R	0.0	5.6	0.0	2.32	50	25.0	10/12/81
	M	3731147	Cleaner M	11.1	5.9	1.9	57.53	53	18.0	8/10/81†
	M	3731163	Cleaner R	1,389.0	431.6	3.2	1.20	3,885	1,050.0	9/15/81†
Packing material	M	2511219	Brown Paper M	508.0	11.9	42.7	1.56	107	600.0	10/8/80†
	M	2512257	Box, Size J	761.0	977.7	0.8	0.91	8,799	1,000.0	10/7/81
	M	2512312	Carton, Type F	1,868.0	462.4	4.0	0.94	4,162	1,726.0	8/27/81†
Misc. supplies	M	2111069	Center Peg A	544.7	3.4	160.2	0.46	31	25.0	1/11/79‖
	M	2111386	Center Peg M	16.0	344.0	0.0	4.17	3,096	112.0	10/9/81
	M	2122036	Oil, Special X	1,158.0	300.2	3.9	1.74	2,702	1,351.0	10/12/81

*Order group: B = Bulk, S = Special, M = Min-max or Order point.

†Already received.

‡This is the last of four orders to be received in this month (two for 20,000 and two for 15,000).

§Minimum quantities of each of these products were ordered and delivered.

‖An order for 500 had only 475 delivered.

EXHIBIT 8
ROBERT VICTOR NEHER, LTD. CO.
Planning Department Purchase Request Sheet

Date	Due Date	Material Number	Amount	Notes
10/14	11/20	6025139	1,000	For stock
10/14	11/20	6193212	5,000	For order
10/14	11/20	6183296	10,000	For stock
10/14	11/19	6310673	3,000	Butter paper B for export order
10/14	11/26	6348294	3,000	For stock
10/14	11/19	6216498	4,000	For order
10/14	11/26	6268672	3,000	For stock

checking the computer inventory printouts (which are received in purchasing once a month), the vendor information, the reasonableness of the quantity requested, and the status of any open purchase orders. When the order is made, a handwritten entry showing the order date and quantity is made to the computer printout. Such an entry is shown in Exhibit 7 for material number 6310673 (Butter Paper B), which was ordered to produce the Kerrygold butter wrapper. In the event that an order cannot be obtained within the delivery time specified by the planning department, the purchasing department changes the requested delivery date for the supplier on the request sheet from the planning department and informs them of the change.

Once the order is made, the purchasing department writes on their copy of the purchase order the internal customer order number which links to the sales department. This copy is then filed in the open purchase order files in the purchasing department. When everything is complete and the purchase order is ready, the information is sent to the computer. "When flexibility is so important, hours may be critical. That's why we bypass the computer for the first few steps in the process. I can process the purchase requests in a day and we can get back and forth on date changes or any quantity difficulties prior to entering it into the computer. That way it is correct in the computer. If we entered the data first and waited for the next printout, it would slow us down and require a lot more paperwork just to correct the errors that were stored in the computer," said Mr. Eugster.

With all the information at their fingertips, it made it easy for the purchasing department to follow up on customer and purchase orders. When a purchased item is received at the factory, it is first verified by the central warehouse foreman or receiving clerk. It is next verified by the foremen of the manufacturing department and the laboratory before the invoice is released for payment. If there is any problem, the purchasing department is immediately in contact with the supplier about the difficulty. "It may be redundant to check things so carefully, and we have been told many times that we do not need to be so thorough since our vendor difficulties are so few. We do not keep exact statistics on how often a vendor is late, short, or has poor quality, but we believe, as a matter of discipline for our people and training for our vendors, that it pays for us to be careful. If they know how thoroughly we check everything, they will be careful on their shipments to us," explained Mr. Eugster.

"Our knowledge of our business and our vendors allows us to do some very useful things. For example, I often hold requests from the satellites when I know that I can get quick delivery on the item. This allows me to do a little batching here in the office which saves the vendors and ourselves some paperwork. For the last five years we have processed some 4,500 written orders and 1,500 telephone or telex orders per year and currently our average purchase order is about 5,000 SFr. During this same period, our output went up 34 percent, sales 59 percent, and the number of items about 5 percent. The number of new items increased much more than 5 percent, however, since we try to clean out any item that has not had any consumption for two years, and we made significant reductions in our inventory in this period. The number of invoices is much higher than the number of orders, about 9,000 per year. Things like utilities, standing deliveries, local purchase, and so on, result in invoices for which there are no purchase orders.

PRODUCTIVITY IN PURCHASING

"I do not think there is a productivity measure for a purchasing department, but I would be glad if there was a simple and effective one like sales has, for instance. On the other hand, the more you control a purchasing organization, the less freedom it has to perform its functions. I think freedom is necessary to develop a close relationship with suppliers. In our plant we have that with the satellites also. If there were productivity measures used for us, we might stop concentrating on buying and try to make those measures look good instead of serving the organization.

"There are so many things that the purchasing department affects that we have very difficult objectives. For example, we rarely think of quality as a variable. We take high quality as a given, although we occasionally will work to reduce quality if we think it is too great for the application. But we must have a relationship with our vendors that provides the service that we require in order to support our flexibility. Within that we try to get the best price we can and to protect ourselves with multiple suppliers. This system works well as long as there is cooperation among all the people.

"I really do not want to be a fully computerized purchasing department. The computer has already somewhat limited our freedom. For example, I cannot switch vendors for some products as I would like because the procedure to get a new supplier on the computer is rather long. I think we have about the right level of computer application at the moment. The benefits, so far, have outweighed the costs. The main concern with applying a computer in purchasing is that you can lose touch with reality. If you end up running your business with the numbers from the computer, you may be out of step with the real world. We already have some of our suppliers who say they cannot deliver in the time that we want because they are on a computer. I have one friend who went around the computer to make a delivery that we really needed desperately. I have a feeling that he will have some trouble because of that."

Thus Alfred Eugster summarized his feelings about productivity in purchasing, and measuring and controlling purchasing performance. He still was interested, however, in ways that his function could be improved. He also wondered if measures of the improvements could be developed in order to show management that the purchasing department was contributing to company performance.

Inalfa BV (A)

"I know the direction this company should take and I feel we should start *now!* My intuition will lead the way!" Fred Welschen, commercial director of Inalfa BV, never wasted words. He was considering a proposal from Xerox Corporation which would require considerable Inalfa investment, although the exact amount was yet unknown. A "yes" to the proposal would bring Inalfa an increasing share of Xerox's business in exchange for two things: lower prices and much higher quality. A "no" would mean that Inalfa would no longer be a supplier to Xerox.

Fred Welschen was strongly in favor of accepting the Xerox proposal in order to boost historically flat sales. However, many questions remained. Even if he could persuade the managing director, how would the new demands be implemented? At what cost? And if a contract were to be signed, what conditions should he accept or avoid?

INALFA

Inalfa was a manufacturer of fabricated metal parts in Venray, a town in southern Holland near Eindhoven. The company had started as a manufacturer of heating components and control equipment and had subsequently produced oil and gas stoves. In the early seventies, when demand for these products decreased, production shifted to fabricated metal parts, automobile bumpers, radiator grills, and fuel tanks. Inalfa also made more complex parts, including sunroofs, gear switching mechanisms for cars, and protective covers for X-ray equipment.

By 1983, most of Inalfa's products were sold to the automobile industry. Products were classified by Inalfa into four groups: sunroofs, fine mechanical parts, car industry parts, and tractor industry parts. See Exhibits 1 and 2 for a sales breakdown by product group and a balance sheet.

Sunroofs accounted for about 40 percent of sales. Inalfa manufactured sunroofs using a patent granted by Vermeulen Hollandia (VH) in Haarlem, Holland. VH was only interested in aftermarket sunroofs and had granted exclusive OEM patent rights to Inalfa. Due to the limited number of patents available, Inalfa had only three competitors worldwide. Two of these firms were German, and the third was American.

Firm	Location	Market Share
Webasto Werk W. Baier	Munich, Germany	55%
Golde GmbH	Frankfurt, Germany	35
Inalfa	Venray, Holland	7
American Sunroofs	USA	3

Source: Inalfa management.

Webasto was the acknowledged market leader in sunroofs, with the largest market share. Although Webasto was considered very reliable, they were also felt to be rather inflexible, a sharp contrast to the number two player, Golde, the former market leader.

Golde has seen its market share decline from a high of 60 percent twenty years ago to a level of 35 percent. Golde was known to have good ideas but very poor quality and reliability. Having no production facilities, Golde contracted out all manufacturing operations.

Inalfa was a distant third in the OEM sunroof market and was considered a small player with many quality problems. In 1983, Inalfa's biggest sunroof customer was Saab, followed by Rover, Jaguar, and Fiat. Growth had been rapid since entering the market and was expected to continue.

Fine mechanical parts were products for office machines such as

EXHIBIT 1
INALFA BV (A)
Sales Breakdown
(guilders 000)

	1979	1980	1981	1982
Sunroofs	7,478	9,154	14,068	16,458
Car industry parts	11,359	11,021	7,900	8,467
Tractor industry parts	8,250	5,721	5,412	5,407
Fine mechanical parts	7,330	6,445	4,934	2,801
Miscellaneous	1,684	1,497	1,739	2,756
	36,101	33,838	34,053	35,889
Sales attributed to Xerox	10.7%	11.5%	8.1%	3.2%
Gldr/$U.S.	1.9055	2.1295	2.4685	2.6242

EXHIBIT 2
INALFA BV (A)
Balance Sheet
(guilders 000)

	1979	1980	1981	1982
Assets:				
Fixed assets	2,762	2,858	2,592	2,550
Inventory	7,623	7,124	8,491	8,222
Accounts receivable	6,616	3,674	5,887	6,386
Cash	1,024	2,246	843	1,235
	18,025	15,902	17,813	18,393
Liabilities and Equity:				
Own capital	5,433	6,931	7,327	7,255
Capital reserves	1,615	1,651	2,167	2,745
Long-term debt	377	291	248	350
Short-term debt	10,600	6,640	7,676	7,666
Various		389	395	377
	18,025	15,902	17,813	18,393

copier frames, paper trays, and metal cylinders. Xerox was the largest customer in this group, and IBM was second.

The last two groups, car industry parts and tractor industry parts, produced bumpers for automobiles and radiator shells for tractors. Inalfa supplied these products to several European and American manufacturers. With highly fragmented markets, these groups contrasted sharply with the sunroof market.

Purchasing Procedures

Each of Inalfa's customers maintained a preferred list of suppliers. Patent restrictions limited this for sunroof suppliers, but purchasers of other products, such as prefabricated metal parts, usually listed no more than 10 suppliers.

When a new part or design was needed, a company would write specifications and solicit bids for the parts. Inalfa's design staff did occasionally help prepare design specifications, but their capacity to do so was limited. The manufacturing contract was usually awarded to the lowest bidder. By winning a bid, Inalfa could therefore be a single source supplier.

Manufacturing

Inalfa's production engineering staff determined the manufacturing process, which was reduced to a series of different steps in a specific sequence. Numerous possible steps included: punching, cutting, folding, bending, drawing, welding, rolling, lacquering, painting, and greasing.

Once the production process was established, Inalfa's machine tool shop had to design and set up tools for each operation. Tools for machines such as lathes, planing machines, milling machines, and drilling machines were normally designed by Inalfa. However, occasionally tools were made from customer-supplied drawings. Testing the tools to ensure that the products made met original specifications was done in cooperation with Inalfa's Quality Control Department.

Quality Control

The Quality Control Department at Inalfa was quite independent of production. A staff of 18 inspected at four points during the production process: as supplies were received, after a job was set up, when a job was completed, and of course when finished products were being shipped.

The typical quality control inspector was a graduate of a technical high school. Training was on the job, with new employees being taught how to read drawings and use measuring equipment.

The existing quality control technique used at Inalfa was batch sampling. Products were checked visually and then measured. The internal reject rate, from start-up sampling to finished batch sampling, was 3 percent. Depending on the product, Welschen admitted that the internal reject rate even went higher. A sales brochure stated: "Everything is of the highest quality. So much so, that rejects average no more than 3% in internal checks." Inalfa management had been proud of their level of quality performance.

The external reject rate, for products sent back to Inalfa by customers, and the reject rate for Inalfa's suppliers were not officially known. However, the Quality Control Department estimated that 2 percent of goods shipped to customers were returned. They also estimated that Inalfa sent back 7–8 percent of the purchased materials and parts that they received. Certain Inalfa customers usually returned more than the average, depending on product complexity and the customer's own standards. Inalfa estimated that Xerox returned between 3–4 percent.

In short, the Quality Control Department at Inalfa was like a police station; their job was to catch the mistakes. The more that mistakes could be identified on entry from Inalfa's suppliers, the fewer the problems there would be in Inalfa's own manufacture. Therefore an effort was made to catch the mistakes before too much value had been added, making the cost of a mistake very high.

MARKETING STUDY

Soon after assuming his responsibilities as commercial director, Fred Welschen had commissioned a marketing study to determine Inalfa's position in the marketplace. The conclusion of the report was blunt: Inalfa must make changes both in products and in markets in order to optimize its potential. The report enumerated Inalfa's strengths and weaknesses:

Strengths
1. Inalfa was capable of manufacturing a wide range of parts, from design to production, for many industries.
2. Historically, Inalfa had proved it was capable of handling crises and market downturns.

Weaknesses
1. Inalfa's primary production machinery was outdated, was not flexible, and could not produce parts of the highest quality.
2. R&D was almost nonexistent.
3. Production engineering was weak.
4. The sales department was badly understaffed, with only two employees to handle Gldr 36 million[1] a year.
5. Quality was poor.

The report noted that Inalfa's three principal markets, the sunroof market, the office machine market, and the computer market, were growing fast. It recommended that Inalfa shift more of its customer base from the cyclical automobile industry to office machines or computers. At the same time, the report recommended that Inalfa emphasize the service content of its products. Such a change would mean developing

---

[1]Gldr = Dutch guilders: in 1983 3.06 Gldr = 1 $U.S.

its relatively weak engineering, design, and development capabilities—high margin activities that are hard for customers to accomplish. After strengthening these capabilities, they should be marketed aggressively.

There was one final problem area. Product costs at Inalfa were not readily determined. Management did have some information, but for the most part they only guessed at cost figures.

ORGANIZATION OF INALFA

Inalfa's management team was led by a managing director supported by the commercial, the finance, and the production directors. This management team was responsible to two outside bodies, the Board of Supervisors and the Worker Council. The Board of Supervisors served as a board of directors except that, under Dutch law, no member of management could belong to the board.

The Worker Council, made up of representative Inalfa employees, also had oversight responsibilities. Because unions in the Netherlands were national, important negotiations were done in The Hague. Local discussions with the unions were normally on issues of secondary importance. At the end of 1982, there were just over 400 employees at Inalfa.

The managing director had spent his entire 38-year career at Inalfa, 24 years as production director and the last 14 years as managing director. At the beginning of his tenure, he had conducted one marketing survey, but since that time had chosen to steer the company on a low-risk course. His primary emphasis had been on cost control. New projects had been considered on an ad hoc basis, with project selection depending on the total cost required. Under his leadership, the company had been profitable and he had intended to keep it that way. The managing director's salary had been supplemented with a standard bonus in profitable years; this bonus had almost always been paid.

WELSCHEN'S BACKGROUND

After receiving a degree in economics from the University of Rotterdam, Welschen worked for five years at Cargill Soya Industrie BV in Amsterdam, a fast-growing American soybean crushing firm. Welschen's experience there had quite an impact on him. "The environment was hectic and I learned a lot from the Americans. I learned to hustle." At the end of five years, Welschen was Cargill's sales manager for soy proteins.

At Inalfa, Welschen first served as purchasing manager, a position he held for two years. He was promoted to commercial director when his predecessor left the firm. The managing director's retirement was imminent and it was generally expected that Welschen would be appointed to this position.

As commercial director, Welschen had been searching for an opportunity to change the staid pattern at Inalfa; he was convinced the company could be revitalized. He felt that the Xerox proposal would push Inalfa in the right direction, even though Xerox accounted for only 3 percent of Inalfa's current business.

Since his appointment as commercial director, Fred Welschen had spent a lot of time trying to improve customer relations, especially with Xerox. He saw not only great sales potential with Xerox, but a chance to diversify away from Inalfa's traditional dependence on the automobile industry. Xerox was also not far away; one of its four European plants was adjacent to the Inalfa plant.

XEROX CORPORATION

Headquartered in the USA, Xerox was primarily a business equipment manufacturer best known for copier machines and, to a lesser extent, information systems and products.

Since the late 1970s, Xerox's copier business had been dramatically losing market share to the Japanese. The reason was easy to grasp: manufacturing costs were typically 30–40 percent less for Japanese competitors than for Xerox. Even worse for Xerox, the quality of the Japanese products was far higher. Overcoming these differences was critical to Xerox's survival. Xerox was not vertically integrated so an estimated 80 percent of manufacturing costs were for purchased materials.

Xerox had traditionally purchased on a plant by plant basis from more than 5,000 vendors worldwide. As a "first" step toward changing its purchasing practices, Xerox began combining orders for products such as lamps, which were used in all their plants. A major goal was to consolidate the Xerox suppliers and develop them into a global source of supply. Buying larger volumes from fewer suppliers would mean greater volume discounts and less administrative overhead.

The Xerox Proposal

Along with other Xerox suppliers, Welschen had heard about Xerox's new informal purchasing proposal. In general, the plan meant to improve supplier quality performance, but other areas were also included. A long series of meetings between Xerox and Inalfa management resulted in a short document listing four requirements:

1. Inalfa would have to implement statistical process control to eliminate Xerox's need for incoming inspection.
2. The level of rejects must stay below 0.5 percent. This requirement would include implementing and documenting quality upgrade programs.
3. Inalfa would be required to participate in Xerox's "Early Supplier Involvement Program." This meant offering advice to Xerox during product design, thus reducing Xerox's cost and improving product performance.
4. Inalfa's prices would have to be competitive on a world scale. The "competitive" level would be determined from a database maintained by Xerox on a worldwide basis.

These points were the main requirements initially set forth by Xerox. Fred Welschen realized others would be added because the Xerox plan was dynamic. Its actual direction would take shape as the plan progressed and lessons were learned from experience.

Statistical Process Control

Of the four requirements, statistical process control (SPC) would be the most difficult for Inalfa. Although not a new technique, it was being used more and more frequently. A series of statistical techniques would be applied to the production process in order to control quality and reduce costs. All machine tools would be calibrated specifically for each product, so that the mean and standard deviation of critical measurements would be known when considering new work. Thus, work would not be accepted for a process without a known manufacturing capability. In addition, a machine tool capable of a high level of precision would not be used for a process which required a low level of precision.

The process would be monitored by the machine operators who produced charts from measurements of a sample of products. A shift in sample mean would be shown graphically, so that the operator could immediately spot a process out of control.

Implementing SPC would involve considerable expense and organizational change: staff would have to be trained, measuring equipment and computers (to produce graphs) purchased, a system designed, and new employees probably hired. At the same time, machine operators would be taking on additional responsibility, and the function of the Quality Control Department was likely to be eclipsed. On the other hand, SPC was being talked about in the Netherlands and had been the focus of some widely attended management seminars.

If Inalfa agreed to cooperate with Xerox, the initial impact would be on Inalfa's Quality Control Department and its relationship with production. Eventually, the role of the Quality Control Department could be reduced as a result of implementing SPC. In the short term, the department would be obliged to expand if the proposal were accepted.

MAJOR CONCERNS ABOUT XEROX

Welschen knew, in reality, that Xerox expected much more from Inalfa than the original four points listed. Xerox was looking for a close working relationship, almost a partnership, with its vendors, meaning open financial books and close Xerox monitoring of Inalfa.

He was most concerned about statistical process control, the major stumbling block with Inalfa's managing director. Welschen believed it would work; there were numerous successful examples. Xerox claimed that applications of statistical process control had enabled costs—and therefore price—to fall after implementation. Both Welschen and Xerox believed, given the cost differential with the Japanese, that Xerox system prices could only go down. Although the cost of implementing statistical process control was unknown, it would be high. Welschen admitted, "I have no exact idea, but that doesn't matter. I am convinced that the program will be successful."

The Early Supplier Involvement Program was the only part of the proposal that all parties readily endorsed, the managing director having offered no resistance. Neither Inalfa nor Xerox knew exactly what the long-term implications of the program would be.

The open pricing agreement would inevitably mean a sacrifice for Inalfa because it would have to reveal its cost structure to Xerox. This position, while insuring future Xerox contracts and a 10 percent profit margin, did reduce Inalfa's ability to negotiate. In addition, pricing would have to decline until it was below global levels. In other words, Inalfa would have to reach the cost structure of world competition.

Technical cooperation would also entail certain costs, although Welschen anticipated numerous benefits. Inalfa would be obliged to give advice to Xerox on new products from the design stage through production. The amount of technical and management time would presumably be small and sales would be guaranteed.

Inalfa's privacy would be greatly reduced by allowing Xerox to monitor financial statements and advising Xerox on labor activity and pending management changes. In addition, Inalfa was concerned that sensitive information about the company might be leaked to competitors.

Welschen had made the effort to contact several other vendors to whom Xerox had extended the proposal. The response of the vendors was consistent, "We're going to sign. It's not going to be such a terrible burden." Some vendors felt, and Fred Welschen agreed, that the proposal would help smooth out Xerox's erratic demand schedule, something that had been a problem for Xerox suppliers for some time. Welschen concluded, "We have an opportunity we shouldn't pass up; we can help Xerox, they can teach us, and everyone is better off."

Frisbee Frozen Foods

Giorgio Pierrotti, president and CEO of Frisbee Frozen Foods, explained to the group in his office, "Your study is very timely, especially in light of our plans for building a new central warehouse. We have the potential for adding a great deal of value in distribution, more even than in manufacturing. The task is to find the most competitive use of that potential." He was talking to a special ad hoc team that had been assembled to do a thorough review of the company. Frisbee had recently completed a reorganization of the company that involved the sales of a part of the product line and some facilities. The team had been put together to review the entire business and had already made a series of recommendations concerning product strategy, marketing, and finance. The ad hoc team members were receiving a final briefing from Pierrotti before turning their attention to the distribution activities of the company. Pierrotti concluded the meeting by asking, "Can we improve the contribution to profits from our distribution system?"

BACKGROUND

The origins of the company date from just before World War I with the founding of a meat packing business in Como, Italy. The firm, called Cocarna, served retail and catering businesses (grocery stores, supermarkets, restaurants, canteens, etc.) in the area around Como. After World War II, Cocarna diversified into frozen food, creating an affiliated company called Creamfriz. In 1972, Creamfriz joined forces with Frisbee, an independent family-owned company producing ice cream and frozen food, in a 50–50 joint venture.

During the late 1970s top management was faced with a declining meat packing business. They decided on two main strategies to consolidate and strengthen their position in the market:

1. To find a partner to increase market share for the meat packing operation or to sell the business.
2. To emphasize the frozen food and ice cream business, by consolidating activities and by investing in new facilities.

In line with the first strategic objective, Cocarna undertook negotiations with a major competitor in the meat packing business. Eventually a contract was signed by which the competitor bought the product rights and use of the Cocarna brand name. Cocarna agreed to deliver packed meat to them while withdrawing from the meat packing business over a two- to three-year period.

With the stage set for getting out of the meat packing business, the company pursued the second strategic objective. By the early 1980s, Cocarna had bought out their Frisbee partner and merged all activities into Frisbee S.p.A., Como. Frisbee invested in frozen food and ice cream plants, cold storage warehousing, and distribution facilities. In the new company, the product strategy was to center on the creation of high value added products which would have potential for high market share and return on sales.

AD HOC TEAM

The reorganization of the company coincided with the withdrawal from the meat packing business. Wherever possible, the workers from meat packing, frozen food, and ice cream were integrated into Frisbee. At the management level, the Cocarna production and technical operations director, Georgio Pierrotti, became president and CEO. M. Cesaro, who had been leading the marketing team at Frisbee, became the executive vice president of marketing. (An organization chart of the company is shown in Exhibit 1.) The close collaboration and sharing of responsibilities between these two top managers was key to the success of the restructuring and consolidation of the company. This collaboration had become a model for other managers and was ingrained from the top to the bottom of the company.

By early 1985, the last of the consolidation activities was completed. The management of Frisbee wanted to step back and assess their new position in order to plan for the future. They were also concerned by the presence of Minerva, a large chain of hyper- and supermarkets that sold their own private brands exclusively. The chain had the largest share of the frozen food and ice cream markets in northern Italy.

In order to assess Frisbee's position, Pierrotti and Cesaro formed an ad hoc team to do a thorough review of the company. The team had completed some preliminary work by October 1985 and had reported their findings. They had found no areas of major concern, but some

EXHIBIT 1
FRISBEE FROZEN FOODS
Management Organization Chart

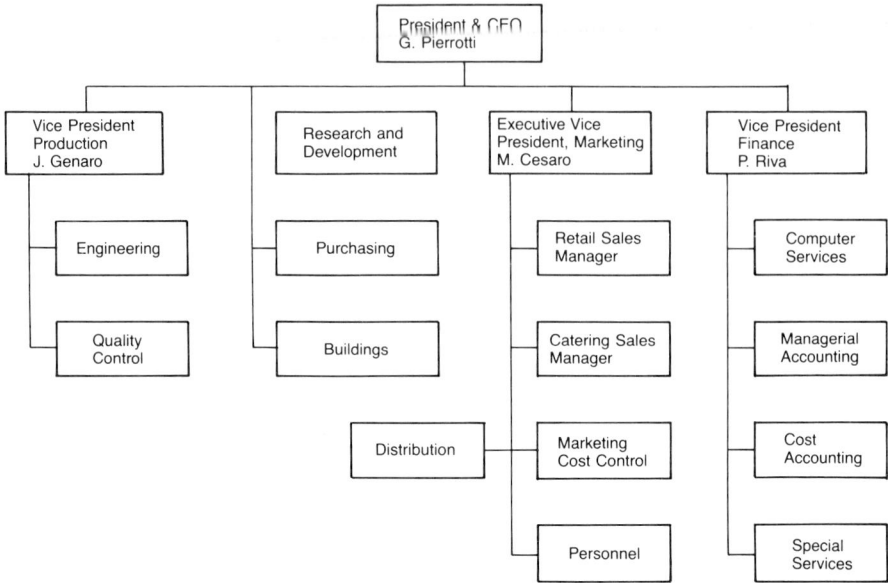

suggestions had been made for product design, marketing, and finance. The team also raised some questions about the level of distribution service and the justification of the planned 17 billion lira[1] automated cold storage warehouse. After having heard the preliminary recommendations from the ad hoc team, Pierrotti and Cesaro decided to ask them to analyze the distribution system in more detail and to present their findings by the end of 1985. Much of the following is based on the team's findings.

FINANCIAL POSITION

The team reviewed the financial position with Riva, vice president, finance. He looked at the last estimate for 1985 and said, "I'm happy that we have had the possibility to consolidate our firm, but I'm glad that

---

[1]In 1985 there were 1,900 lire per U.S. dollar.

it's over. This is the first year, 1985, that frozen food is on its own. I only have a few minor concerns about our financial position. We now have a good base for the future." (Balance sheets and income statements are presented in Exhibits 2 and 3.)

In the past, profits from frozen food had been used to offset losses from the meat packing operations. During the withdrawal from the meat packing business, overall tonnage and assets had decreased, but Frisbee managed to maintain sales and gross operating profit. Funds flow had been very favorable during the last few years, and the company had accumulated the resources to invest in the frozen food business. (A funds flow statement is given in Exhibit 4). The financial position of the firm was strong enough to enable it to borrow funds at the prime rate.

The accounts receivable represented about 45 days' sales. For the moment, Riva didn't see any possibilities to improve this due to the

EXHIBIT 2
FRISBEE FROZEN FOODS
Balance Sheets

	Assets*		
Current assets	*1983 Actual*	*1984 Actual*	*1985 Estimate*
Cash	3.8	11.8	16.8
Accounts receivable	23.4	24.4	27.6
Inventories	41.5	38.1	40.3
Prepaid expenses	11.7	9.5	4.8
Total current assets	80.4	83.8	89.5
Fixed assets, net	80.2	67.6	59.5
Total assets	160.6	151.4	149.0
	Liabilities*		
Accounts payable	31.1	27.2	27.3
Others	4.4	2.0	2.0
Total current liabilities	35.5	29.2	29.3
Long-term debt	48.2	45.3	41.7
Provisions long term (pensions)	16.6	15.2	15.3
Stockholders' equity	60.3	61.7	62.7
Total	160.6	151.4	149.0

*In 1,000,000,000 lire.

EXHIBIT 3
FRISBEE FROZEN FOODS
Income Statements

	1983 Actual		1984 Actual		1985 Estimate	
Metric tons	41,600		37,100		34,200	
	Lira*	Percent	Lira*	Percent	Lira*	Percent
Gross sales	236.9	112.0	232.6	112.0	246.0	111.0
Discounts/ promotions	24.6	12.0	24.6	12.0	26.0	11.0
Net sales	212.3	100.0	208.0	100.0	220.0	100.0
Cost of goods sold						
Raw material	97.8	46.1	94.1	45.2	98.2	44.4
Production	10.9	5.1	10.4	5.0	11.7	5.3
Variable distribution	10.7	5.0	10.4	5.0	11.1	5.0
Other variable	2.1	1.0	2.1	1.0	2.2	1.0
Gross profit	90.8	42.8	91.0	43.8	96.8	44.0
Fixed production	12.7	6.0	11.1	5.3	14.3	6.5
Distribution	17.0	8.0	16.6	8.0	18.6	8.5
Marketing	20.5	9.6	16.3	7.8	23.0	10.5
Depreciation/ amortization	14.0	6.6	21.1	10.1	15.3	7.0
General expenses	10.1	4.8	9.5	4.6	13.0	5.9
Interest	2.1	1.0	1.8	0.9	2.2	1.0
Income before taxes	14.4	6.8	14.6	7.0	10.4	4.7
Federal income taxes	7.1	3.3	7.2	3.5	5.7	2.6
Net income	7.3	3.4	7.4	3.6	4.7	2.1

*In 1,000,000,000 lire.

competitive situation. Some competitors were currently offering up to 60 days to their customers.

Riva did express some concern about the trend in the break-even point. As an indication of business risk, the team had calculated break-even points for presentation to the management. In the calculation it was around 84 percent of sales for 1984 and the estimate for 1985 was 88 percent. Since the market was increasing, it was unlikely that this was a significant risk, but the trend in break-even was of concern. Also, Riva pointed out the business was not dependent on any single customer for more than 10 percent of sales, a factor which further reduced the risk.

Frisbee's biggest investment in current assets was in inventory.

EXHIBIT 4
FRISBEE FROZEN FOODS
Funds Flow Analysis

	1983 Actual	1984 Actual	1985 Estimate
Sources of Funds*			
Net income	7.2	7.2	5.7
Depreciation	14.0	21.1	15.3
Total	21.2	28.3	21.0
Application of Funds*			
Cash	6.2	8.0	5.0
Other working capital	2.1	1.1	0.6
Long-term changes	7.8	13.4	10.7
Dividends	5.1	5.8	4.7
Total	21.2	28.3	21.0

*In 1,000,000,000 lire.

There was heavy seasonality of raw materials, especially vegetables and fruits. The company had a policy of producing the entire sales volume for the following year during crop time. In addition, the high seasonality in ice cream sales necessitated the building up of stocks to meet the summer demand.

In total there is an average of five months' sales in inventory. Even though the company's current facility had been inaugurated in 1982, the growing sales volume and inventory pressures had led to a proposal for a 17 billion (one thousand million) lire central warehouse facility to be built next year. The resources were available, but the team was concerned about the justification and real need.

GENERAL FROZEN FOOD MARKET

The wholesale market for frozen foods and ice cream in northern Italy was about 900 billion lire, which was generally split two ways. One way was by retail or catering channel, where the split was about 50–50. A second was by market segment, either frozen food or ice cream, where the market was split 60 percent and 40 percent, respectively.

The frozen food market segment had been growing steadily albeit slowly (about 3 percent to 4 percent per year) over the past few years and was forecast to continue to do so. Some indication of the potential for future growth was shown by the per capita consumption of frozen food in Italy, which stood at 11 kg per year compared to 20–22 kg in Scandinavian countries. In broad terms, the market tonnage consisted of the following segments: vegetables 26 percent, fish 14 percent, potatoes (largely french fries) 28 percent, prepared dishes (pizza, lasagne, etc.) 12 percent, meat dishes 12 percent, and other (fruit juice, spices, etc.) 8 percent. The biggest sales growth during 1985 was recorded for prepared dishes (+ 16 percent) followed by fish (+ 8 percent).

Growth of the ice cream market segment had stagnated over the last three years, and the market forecast for the years to come remained flat. Ice cream sales were highly seasonal, with 50 percent of all sales concentrated during three months: June, July, and August. Within ice cream, two main product categories had to be considered. The "street items," such as ice cream bars and cups, which are sold from kiosks, small stores, and mobile units. These are sold in towns, at the beach, in tourist spots, and so on. The second category is for in-home consumption, mainly sold through supermarkets and other food stores.

In both market segments, frozen food and ice cream, Frisbee offered a wide variety of products, ranging from simple base products such as frozen peas and plain vanilla ice cream to highly sophisticated meals and frozen desserts.

COMPETITION

There were four major suppliers of frozen foods and ice cream in northern Italy. They had all developed mainly from small traditional family companies in the fresh meat, fish, vegetable, preserved food, or canning businesses. All were now fully integrated manufacturers of frozen foods and ice cream, active across the whole business system from buying the farmers' crops to retailing the finished product.

The biggest competitor was Minerva S.p.A., which controlled approximately 45 percent of all food sales throughout the whole of Italy with its chain of supermarkets and hypermarkets. In northern Italy, they had about 50 percent of the frozen food and 40 percent of the ice cream market. Minerva's business policy was to sell its own brands strictly. They owned their own production facilities for many of the brands, including a frozen food factory and an ice cream factory.

The remaining three companies were about equal in size, but Frisbee enjoyed a brand recognition advantage in the marketplace. The other two companies mainly concentrated on manufacturing private brands for supermarket chains or the catering sector, and producing for some small branded product suppliers. There were also two firms that produced ice cream for supermarkets in the area. One was owned by a large European food multinational, whereas the other was controlled by the North Italian Dairy Farmers' Cooperative.

The retail market segment was dominated by two supermarket chains, with Minerva having about 50 percent and Casa Nuova about 25 percent of the total. Minerva offered a complete range of products from their own factories, from high value added to commodity-type base products. Casa Nuova, on the other hand, sold both branded and private label products. The private label products were mainly base products, such as spinach and fish fingers. They also carried an ice cream manufactured by one of the ice cream companies. The remaining 25 percent of the retail market, which was generally referred to as "open," was mainly comprised of small independent supermarkets and general food stores. Frisbee currently enjoyed a 75–80 percent market share of the open market.

About 75 percent of the catering market was in frozen food and 25 percent in ice cream. Unlike the retail market, there was no single dominant force in catering; it was wide open. Minerva did own a chain of fast food restaurants, which gave it a foothold in the catering business, but Frisbee and the North Italian Dairy Farmers' Cooperative were fighting neck and neck for leadership, with 22–23 percent market share each. French fries accounted for 43 percent of total frozen food in catering, with vegetables coming in a distant second at 27 percent. The other product groups, like fish, prepared foods, meat dishes, and fruit juice, shared equally the remaining 30 percent.

FRISBEE'S PRODUCT RANGE

Frisbee's product range followed the northern Italian market splits very closely. Retail and catering each accounted for approximately 50 percent of sales, while the split between frozen foods and ice cream was 60 percent and 40 percent, respectively. (The 1984 monthly sales are shown for frozen food and ice cream in Exhibit 5.) Although the range was very wide and had grown, in spite of periodic housecleanings, to 530 different items, all products had an excellent quality reputation. Some of the products, such as french fries, spinach, and fish fingers, were almost of

EXHIBIT 5
FRISBEE FROZEN FOODS
Monthly Sales in Metric Tons, 1984

Month	Frozen Food	Ice Cream
January	1,950	480
February	1,950	610
March	2,210	830
April	1,890	1,590
May	1,820	1,760
June	1,590	2,280
July	1,260	2,920
August	1,420	2,020
September	1,560	800
October	2,110	540
November	1,920	540
December	2,120	930
Total	21,800	15,300

a commodity nature, locked in fierce price competition with the private brands of the leading supermarket chains.

The ad hoc team found that a large part of the product range was nearing the maturity stage in their respective life cycles, especially vegetables, ice cream and some of the simpler fish products. (Exhibit 6 depicts the findings.) Furthermore, only about 30 percent of the retail market products (22 percent for catering products) accounted for some 70 percent of sales. The team suggested that some of the smaller contributing items could be eliminated from the line and that more effort be devoted to reducing the portion of low-value, commodity-type products. The timing of such moves, however, would have to be planned in light of developments in distribution and the need to cover the substantial fixed costs. (The average sales contributions by various product groups are shown in Exhibit 7.)

Frisbee management felt that a very comprehensive range was necessary. In the open retail market (the 25 percent not covered by the two supermarket chains Minerva and Casa Nuova), the competition for display space in freezer cabinets was at a premium. Therefore Frisbee needed to be able to offer a full line of products and needed to keep the freezers full. They felt any gaps would permit entry of competitors into the freezer space, thereby providing them the chance to gain a foothold with that customer.

Sales growth for Frisbee in the past had come from new product

EXHIBIT 6
FRISBEE FROZEN FOODS
Product Life Cycle Positions

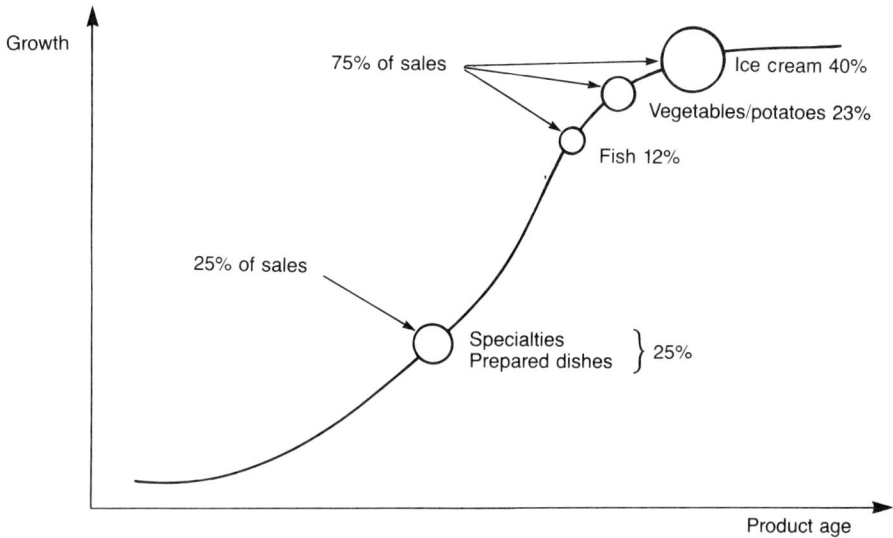

introductions. These new products consisted primarily of high added value prepared dishes and base products. They not only served the retail needs, but specialties were created for the needs and equipment of the professional chef in the catering sector. Frisbee had developed culinary and technical expertise that would lead to new products, and the projection was for continued net increases in the number of products. For the street ice cream, for example, the range was reviewed every year in its entirety, like collections of designer fashions. Some of these items had very short life cycles. Ice creams for home consumption were more stable, but also were expected to experience net increases in flavors and pack sizes.

PRODUCTION

The production area was headed by J. Genaro. He told the team he was concerned about productivity improvement and production line flexibility. He made plans to decrease the number of employees in the factory year by year, over the next few years. This would improve produc-

EXHIBIT 7
FRISBEE FROZEN FOODS
Tonnage, Sales, and Contribution by Product Category

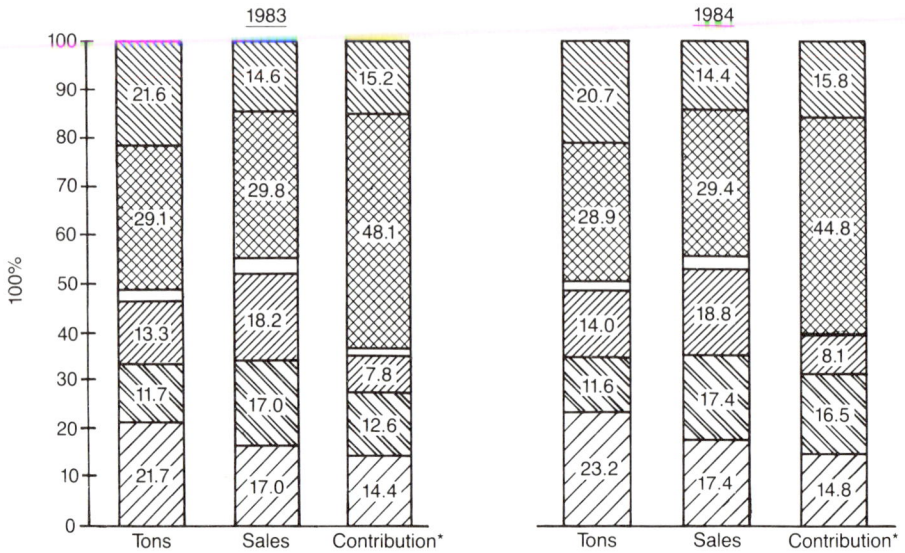

1983

21.6	14.6	15.2
29.1	29.8	48.1
13.3	18.2	7.8
11.7	17.0	12.6
21.7	17.0	14.4

Tons Sales Contribution*

1984

20.7	14.4	15.8
28.9	29.4	44.8
14.0	18.8	8.1
11.6	17.4	16.5
23.2	17.4	14.8

Tons Sales Contribution*

100%

* Contribution to overhead and profit.

Legend

Ice cream

| Vegetables | Fish | Specialties | Others | Street | Home |

tivity, as shown in Exhibit 8. He felt constrained, however, by the heavy seasonality of both raw materials and sales.

In general, Genaro produced the single vegetables during the harvesting of the agricultural raw materials, largely in the spring and fall. His production activities for 1984 are seen in Exhibit 9. Some flexibility had already been developed to cope with the seasonalities. For example, the amount of ice cream sold in summer 1985 was significantly larger than expected owing to the exceptionally warm, sunny days in most parts of northern Italy during September and October. To meet demand, the factory put on an additional shift, moved operators between the ice cream plant and the frozen food plant, and engaged temporary employees. Genaro was also considering a 4.3 billion lira invest-

EXHIBIT 8
FRISBEE FROZEN FOODS
Productivity Plans

	1985	1986	1987	1988
Number of factory employees	534	534	524	511
Tonnage output per factory employee	46.4	48.4	50.4	52.5

EXHIBIT 9
FRISBEE FROZEN FOODS
Monthly Production Output in Metric Tons, 1984

	Frozen Food	Ice Cream
January	480	856
February	711	1,870
March	560	2,277
April	590	1,853
May	942	1,933
June	840	1,981
July	683	2,579
August	663	1,054
September	768	523
October	1,095	243
November	862	511
December	529	397
Total	8,723	16,077

Grand total = 24,800

ment in facilities to improve flexibility of the plant and to produce package sizes down to single serving portions.

Also adding to the flexibility was the potential to purchase frozen food directly for resale or to use as ingredients in special products in the factory. For example, Frisbee did not even make frozen french fries any more; they were all purchased from outside suppliers. This represented about 7,000 tons of the sales in 1984; the remainder of the purchased products amounted to 6,600 tons. Genaro estimated that he could buy about 7,400 additional tons per year of single vegetables and fish. This would require a contract at the beginning of the harvest season, but deliveries could be made throughout the year. That way there would not only be a reduction in manufacturing capacity required during the raw material season, but no need for storage either. The cost of purchasing the items in this way would be approximately 6 percent more than Frisbee's own costs.

It was expected that in the foreseeable future the production division would become even more flexible, with operators to be cross-trained at various jobs. Together with the new investments and existing manufacturing expertise, the greater flexibility should allow an increasing variety of products to be produced without adversely affecting the quality or the high perceived value of the items.

Genaro was pleased with Frisbee's product quality reputation. He also felt that his production costs were quite comparable with competitors. He was frustrated by the accounting system, however. A transfer price had been established between production and distribution that led to zero "profits" by production. They had, therefore, been treated more or less as an outside co-packer rather than a partner in producing high value added products.

SALES/MARKETING

Frisbee marketed its products in a variety of ways. They used some advertising direct to the final customer, promotions and discounts for retailers, some trade advertising, and some general information publications. The company was known for their high-quality but somewhat expensive products. A significant sales and merchandising effort supported the marketing effort and helped maintain the company's market share in the retail sector.

There were at least four persons involved with each order executed: a salesperson, telephone clerk, driver, and warehouse worker. A salesperson visited each customer at least once a month to discuss sales and promotional campaigns, but generally did not take orders. They were also responsible for securing new customers. The telephone clerks worked out of the distribution warehouses, taking orders by phone. They called all customers on a prearranged schedule, using a special card as a guide and recording sheet. In addition to product information, the sheet gave information about the products the customer usually ordered, all previous purchases for the year, and other customer information.

Some 80–90 percent of all orders were taken by the telephone clerks. They were also supposed to sell and inform the customer about new products and articles on promotion. The team found that very little selling was done by them, however. They did prepare a written delivery sheet for each customer, sorted by route and passed to the warehouse for picking. Warehouse workers assembled all orders and put them together customer by customer, after which the van was loaded by the driver.

As a service, Frisbee sometimes would price-mark orders for big customers. Price-marking was done at the warehouses for around 20 percent of the products delivered. Another special service to big customers was product merchandising. Often housewives living near the customer were paid by the hour to carry this out and occasionally permanent employees were used. Merchandising involved arranging the freezer display and restocking the shelves in the stores. The driver also had merchandising responsibilities at some stores.

DISTRIBUTION

The team gathered some additional data from interviews with customers and some of the depot personnel. They learned that the company had developed a high service image since the consolidation. The investments in distribution were apparently paying off. From Frisbee's system of 12 facilities, including the large central warehouse at Como, they could reach any customer in a maximum of a few hours. They had the reputation of accommodating some very difficult delivery requests on short notice. (A map of the locations is provided in Exhibit 10.)

Drivers followed a single fixed route, which could vary each day. Each route had an average of 60 calls, including both retail and catering customers. In addition to ordered quantities, each truck also carried extra items to sell in case items were forgotten during ordering. A customer was always visited by the same driver in order to form a personal relationship.

As the majority of customers, both on the retail as well as on the catering side, were very small and competition fierce, deliveries were frequent and order quantities were small. The situation was further aggrevated, especially in the smaller remote towns, by the limited display space available in freezer cabinets. This necessitated small, frequent deliveries. An indication of the distribution of delivery sizes is provided

EXHIBIT 10
FRISBEE FROZEN FOODS
Location of Central Warehouse and Depots

Legend:
● Depot Locations
▣ Central Warehouse

□ COMO

in Exhibit 11. (Some operating data for individual depots are provided in Exhibit 12, and cost details are given in Exhibit 13.)

The total distribution system consisted of 11 depots (some of which were rented and some of which were owned) and a semiautomated central warehouse next to the factory. Many of the bulk deliveries from the central warehouse to the depots were done by an independent third party freight forwarder. Company vans delivered the product from the depot to the customers. Organizationally, distribution had been placed under the responsibility of marketing, reporting directly to the sales manager, as shown in Exhibit 14.

EXHIBIT 11
FRISBEE FROZEN FOODS
Delivery Statistics, 1984

	Distribution of Delivery Sizes			Number of Deliveries during Peak Month	
Size of Delivery*	Sales (billions of lire)	Deliveries (000)	Sales per Delivery*	Depot No.	Deliveries
< 150	15.7	117.4	130	1	3,200
101–300	45.4	172.4	260	2	6,500
301–1000	79.6	139.4	570	3	9,100
1001–2000	41.5	33.7	1230	4	4,900
>2000	50.3	12.5	4030	5	8,900
Total	232.5	475.4		6	2,200
Average			489*	7	5,000
				8	2,900
				9	5,400
				10	3,600
				11	1,900

*In thousands of lire.

To get additional information for management, the team visited Mario, an independent distributor who had an exclusive contract with one of Frisbee's competitors. Mario purchased the product from Frisbee's competitor and sold it along with noncompeting frozen products in the Eastern region. The product range sold by Mario was similar to Frisbee's and included retail and catering items. Mario performed all of the services of order taking, delivery, merchandising, billing, and some marketing. He took delivery of the product at his warehouse and made all arrangements for further distribution.

For his services, Mario received a discount on the wholesale price of from 10–18 percent (the average was 14.3 percent), depending on the products. In addition, he received a sales volume bonus that ranged from 1–2¼ percent (the average was just under 1.5 percent). Mario hinted broadly that he would be very interested in establishing a similar contract with Frisbee in the future.

The team was aware of the constant pressure on the central warehouse space. There were several months in which there was a requirement for outside storage. This can be seen in the warehouse inventory

EXHIBIT 12
FRISBEE FROZEN FOODS
Operating Data for Depots, 1984

Depot No.	Sales (billion lire)	No. of Vans	Deliveries (000)	Kilometers (000)	Delivery Costs*	Sales/ Delivery†	Cost/ Delivery†	Sales/ Kilometer†	Sales Lire/ Cost Lire
1	11.36	6	26.0	102	485.94	436.75	18.69	111.33	23.37
2	26.11	13	56.5	242	911.82	462.26	16.14	107.92	28.64
3	50.53	22	91.1	449	1,658.02	554.69	18.20	112.54	30.48
4	16.28	12	34.6	265	632.45	470.41	18.28	61.42	25.74
5	39.18	20	85.5	553	1,522.43	458.21	17.81	70.84	25.73
6	12.68	5	19.7	66	427.70	643.67	21.71	192.13	29.65
7	17.60	11	42.2	214	713.44	417.09	16.91	82.25	24.67
8	15.33	8	23.6	149	505.05	649.58	21.40	102.89	30.35
9	21.76	10	52.0	220	767.13	418.55	14.75	98.93	28.37
10	16.28	9	32.0	235	586.95	508.64	18.34	69.26	27.73
11	5.49	4	12.2	36	208.39	449.88	17.08	152.46	26.34
Totals	232.60	120	475.4	2531	8,419.32				
Averages						489.27	17.71	91.90	27.63

*Costs of vans, fuel, and drivers for the depot (in millions of lire).
†In thousands of lire.
Note: Averages are weighted averages, not depot averages.

EXHIBIT 13
FRISBEE FROZEN FOODS
1985 Distribution Cost Breakdown
(millions of lire)

	Wages	Rent	Vans	Electricity	Fuel	Telephone	Travel Costs	Third Party Transportation	Other	Revenue	Depreciation	Total
Central Warehouse	3,270	2,430	87	36	40	7	47	2,818	784	(180)	3,330	12,669
Depot												
1	893	138	52	16	35	18	34		33		—	1,219
2	1,555	—	126	—	98	47	50		228		767	2,871
3	3,006	—	169	104	150	74	110		216		272	4,101
4	1,083	4	65	12	88	21	43		188		—	1,504
5	2,560	410	182	72	211	74	91		192		—	3,792
6	808	169	39	5	27	12	26		29		—	1,115
7	1,268	237	78	42	72	40	55		81		—	1,873
8	904	—	43	44	60	26	33		61		96	1,267
9	1,343	—	98	53	73	49	50		92		114	1,872
10	1,025	169	52	55	80	33	35		66		—	1,515
11	383	—	20	30	17	16	10		25		25	526
Total	18,098	3,557	1,011	469	951	417	584	2,818	1,995	(180)	4,604	34,324

EXHIBIT 14
FRISBEE FROZEN FOODS
Marketing Organization Chart

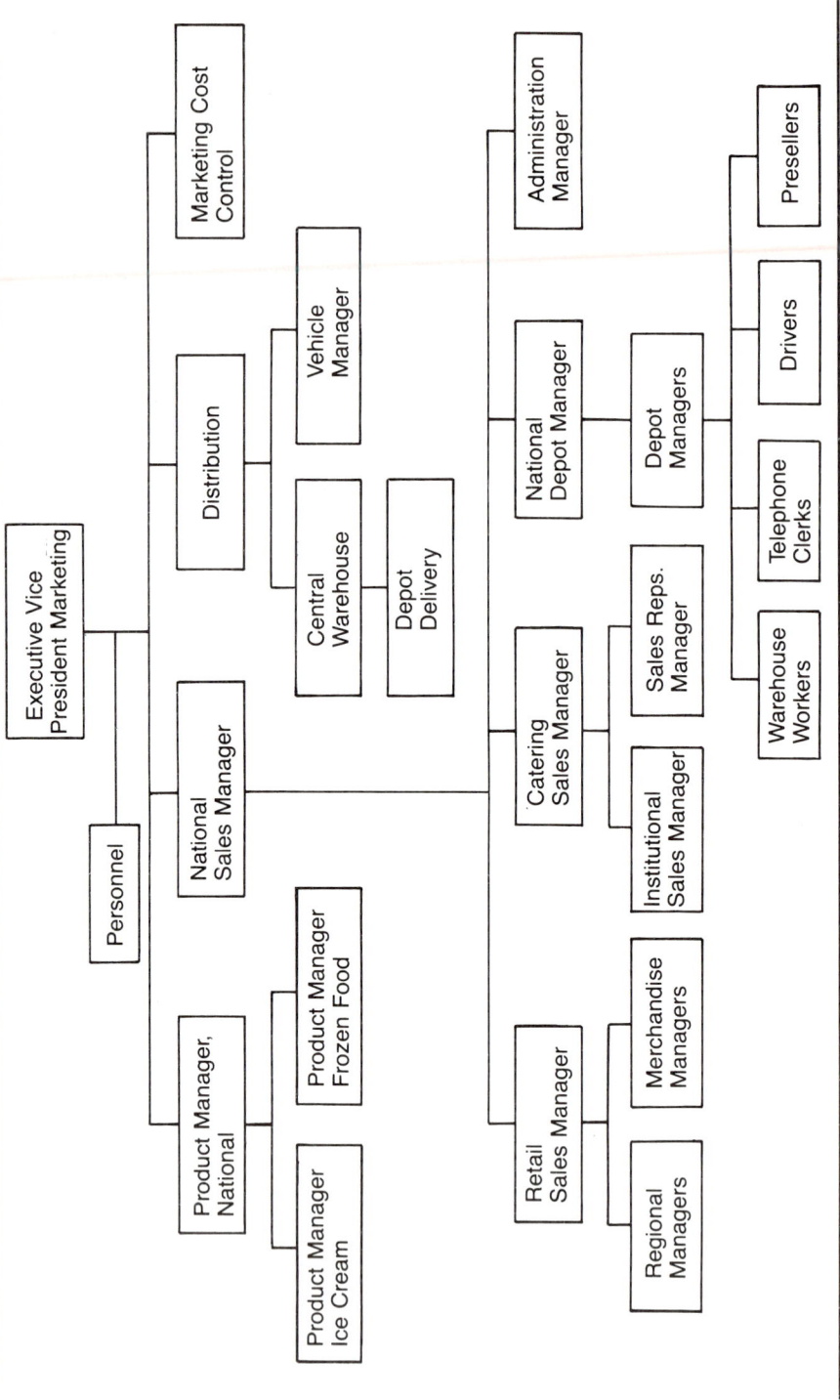

Executive Vice President Marketing

- Personnel

- Product Manager, National
  - Product Manager Ice Cream
  - Product Manager Frozen Food

- National Sales Manager
  - Retail Sales Manager
    - Regional Managers
    - Merchandise Managers
  - Institutional Sales Manager
  - Catering Sales Manager
    - Sales Reps. Manager

- Distribution
  - Central Warehouse
  - Depot Delivery
  - Vehicle Manager

- Marketing Cost Control

- Administration Manager

- National Depot Manager
  - Depot Managers
    - Warehouse Workers
    - Telephone Clerks
    - Drivers
    - Presellers

figures shown in Exhibit 15. This was obviously a key point in the pressure to invest in the new facility. Another factor was the possibility of operating with 13 fewer people (at a saving of about 50 million lire per year per person) and 2–3 percent lower operating costs. The team also learned that Minerva was completing a new large central facility and had plans to dramatically cut back on the number of depots they operated.

Finally, two points kept on creeping back into the discussions. One was a strategic issue relating to the fact that effectively Frisbee had only the 25 percent "open" market segment to play with. Pierrotti had already asked what would happen to their dominant market position if they gave up direct control of distribution activities or possibly allowed one of their competitors to enter some part of the market. The other was an anecdote still fresh in everybody's mind although it happened some 10 years before. The chef of a small restaurant on the edge of Lake Como had wanted an urgent Saturday delivery, just two boxes of frozen

EXHIBIT 15
FRISBEE FROZEN FOODS
Monthly Inventory in Metric Tons, 1984
Central Warehouse & Outside Storage

	Frozen Food	Ice Cream	Total	Outside Storage*
Beginning inventory	7,590	2,272	9,862	
January	7,304	2,607	9,911	
February	7,238	3,776	11,015	
March	6,930	5,113	12,043	1,100
April	6,772	5,286	12,058	1,100
May	6,975	5,365	12,340	1,500
June	7,170	4,970	12,139	1,500
July	7,339	4,503	11,843	1,100
August	7,429	3,485	10,914	
September	7,566	3,183	10,749	
October	7,805	2,874	10,679	
November	7,894	2,821	10,715	
December	7,590	2,269	9,859	
Average			11,189	

*The central warehouse was limited to about 11,000 metric tons of effective storage. Cold storage space was rented in Como whenever this capacity was exceeded.

peas, which the company refused to do. This same man was now food and beverage manager of Italy's leading hotel chain, which to this day refused to buy any product from Frisbee. With this in mind, they turned to the task of assembling the information for their presentation to management.

Biral International (A)

In the fall of 1979, the executive committee of Bieri Pumpenbau AG Biral International, located in Muensingen near Berne, Switzerland, met to discuss the implications of entering into a cooperative agreement with a Hungarian manufacturer to produce Bieri pumps. The committee had to decide if the company should pursue this opportunity along the lines negotiated by Mr. Vacano, the coordinator for sales to the Comecon area.[1] Negotiations had stretched over the better part of the last two years and had reached a critical point. A final decision on the part of Bieri's executive committee was required before the formal blessing of Hungary's Ministry of Foreign Trade could be obtained.

COMPANY HISTORY

The company was formed in 1919 by Bieri to produce a number of different pumps. In later years, the founder's two sons, Franz and Werner Bieri, took over management of the company. Under their direction, the company's manufacturing facilities were expanded in 1953 and 1961, and an entirely new factory was opened in 1971. The company's sales had reached a record of about 52 million Swiss francs (SFr)[2] by 1978, not including sales of the principal supplier of many of Bieri's electrical motors, whose equity was partially owned by the principals of Bieri. In total, the company employed about 400 persons and, since 1978, had been under the direction of the third generation, Ueli and Peter Bieri, the two sons of Franz Bieri, and Hansrudolf, the son of Werner Bieri.

Bieri had been affected negatively during the recessionary period of 1974–76 when residential construction, a major user of Bieri's products, went into a sharp decline in Switzerland. This happened at a time when the value of the Swiss franc moved up sharply against other currencies, increasing the price of Bieri products in its major export mar-

---

[1] Comecon is an abbreviation for Council of Mutual Economic Assistance, comprising the Soviet Union, East Germany, Poland, Hungary, Rumania, Bulgaria, Czechoslovakia, Cuba, North Korea, and a few associated members in Asia and Africa.

[2] In 1979, 1.65 SFr = 1 $U.S.

EXHIBIT 1
BIRAL INTERNATIONAL (A)
Biral's Sales and Profit History

Year	Sales (SFr)	Profit (SFr)	Profit Margin (percent)
1970	37,647,500	NA	NA
1971	42,165,200	191,660	0.45
1972	49,284,000	82,140	0.17
1973	51,225,242	164,280	0.32
1974	51,474,400	10,952	0.02
1975	44,508,928	(39,701)	(0.09)
1976	53,527,900	(12,514)	(0.02)
1977	50,195,754	31,007	0.06
1978	51,917,486	100,518	0.19

kets while these countries also went through a recessionary period. Net profits (computed after funding of various reserves and depreciation) dropped significantly in 1975, but had since recovered. For 1979, Bieri expected its profits to reach the levels of the early 1970s. (See Exhibit 1 for sales and profit history.) The name Biral International had just been added to the company name. Originally, the Biral brand name applied only to a portion of the company's product line, but now described all of Bieri's products.

PRODUCT LINES

Bieri had four major product lines: circulating pumps, general pumps, swimming pool pumps and filters, and control systems. Circulating pumps accounted for 54.8 percent of 1978 sales. These pumps, traditionally marketed under the brand name Biral, were sold both in Switzerland, where Bieri was the undisputed market leader, and in other countries of Western Europe. Negotiations with the Hungarian partner covered exclusively circulating pumps, but the other product lines had to be considered, as additional orders could be expected if the agreement went into effect.

The second major product line, general pumps, or APB for Allgemeiner Pumpenbau, accounted for 33.3 percent of sales. Included were pumps for water supply systems, irrigation systems, and wastewater pumps. These products were produced according to specifications submitted by the client. Sales were strongest in Switzerland, with exports accounting for only about 10 percent of the output.

Bieri's two other product lines were of lesser importance. The swimming pool pumps, or SBF, accounted for 10.3 percent of 1978 sales. More than 90 percent of these sales were to customers in Switzerland. Control systems, Bieri's smallest product line, represented an extension of the company's efforts in the general pump market. Control systems were used for controlling large pumping systems and had been manufactured by Bieri for several years. This capability is also made available to other companies for different control applications. Volume has never exceeded 3 percent of sales, however, and amounted to only 1.5 percent in 1978.

BIRAL CIRCULATING PUMPS

Bieri company had for many years dominated the market in Switzerland with its circulating pumps. The pumps were used to circulate the water of heating systems in both commercial and residential buildings. Biral pumps, while more expensive then competitive products, were considered to be the highest quality and required minimal service. Also, their unique construction with a separating shell ensured that the pumps were effectively protected from penetrating water which could cause short circuits. While the separating shell was, by itself, an easily understood concept, competitors had been unable to produce a competitive design for their own use. Bieri had developed a special 400-ton press to produce these separating shells with high precision.

Other advantages of Biral pumps were their highly efficient electric motors, which ran with a minimum of noise and used little electricity. The electric motors were produced by RCB Elektro-Apparate AG, a small company about 50 miles from the Bieri plant. Bieri was RCB's largest customer and, through the Bieri family, owned a substantial portion of RCB's share capital.

The separating shell technology was the property of RCB. Bieri had the shells produced by an outside contractor who used RCB's technology and Bieri's press on an exclusive basis. All other parts were sourced by Bieri from independent contractors. Final assembly of Biral pumps took place at Bieri's plant in Muensingen. In 1979, Bieri expected to produce 200,000 to 250,000 units. Depending on product mix, output could be expanded by 100 to 200 percent without any substantial investments.

THE MARKETS FOR BIERI PUMPS

Circulating pumps were primarily sold in Europe under the Biral brand name. Forty-seven percent of the pumps were sold in the Swiss market, with the remainder exported to a few European countries with strong sales networks, such as Austria, Belgium, Germany, France, UK, Italy, and the Netherlands (see Exhibits 2–4). These Biral pumps were primarily used for heating systems, but could also be installed in connection with climate control systems and hot water supply systems. The pumps were generally bought by plumbing contractors who installed heating systems. The pumps sold for SFr 50 to SFr 1400, but represented only a small portion of the approximately SFr 10,000 to SFr 20,000 for a complete system. However, the pumps represented a crucial part, since the proper circulation of the heated water throughout a heating system had a major influence on efficiency. Plumbing contractors were particularly interested in trouble-free pumps that required little servicing. Should the pump fail, it was usually the plumber who was asked to service it.

Bieri offered Biral pumps in a large variety of sizes. Depending on the height of a building and the amount of water to be circulated, the contractor could determine exactly what pump was most appropriate. The correct selection was important, since the right pump could run with lower energy costs and noise levels. Since circulating pumps had to run continuously during heating periods, energy consumption and noise level were important considerations for building owners.

Biral pumps were marketed directly by Bieri to a few selected plumbing contractors in the canton of Berne, the particular area of Switzerland where the company was located, and to manufacturers of heating furnaces (OEMs). In the rest of Switzerland, as well as in France, Italy, UK, Netherlands, Austria, and Belgium, Bieri had an exclusive sales agreement with Hoval. Hoval was a well-known manufacturer of furnaces. Since furnaces were sold to plumbing and heating contractors, Hoval was in an excellent position to carry the Biral pumps as an addition to its own product line. Hoval had its own sales force in Switzerland, and operated sales subsidiaries in various European coun-

EXHIBIT 2
BIRAL INTERNATIONAL (A)
1978 Sales Breakdown (SFr)

Country	Circulating Pumps (Biral)	General Pumps (APB)	Swimming Pool (SBF)	Control Systems	Total
Switzerland	13,463,780	15,620,291	5,214,850	545,294	34,844,215
Algeria	—	42,475	7,803	—	50,278
Australia	56,681	—	—	—	56,681
Austria	2,650,860	5,742	38,295	236,522	2,931,419
Belgium	609,094	457	—	—	609,551
Denmark	5,282	11,187	—	—	16,469
W. Germany	3,623,573	167,315	5,899	9,108	3,805,895
France	1,121,639	3,313	—	—	1,124,952
Great Britain	1,627,906	63,747	11,579	––	1,703,232
Iraq	—	855,696	64,340	—	920,036
Ireland	—	79,261	—	—	79,261
Italy	2,813,158	2,097	30,527	—	2,845,782
Morocco	—	3,793	—	—	3,793
Netherlands	2,436,754	57,076	—	—	2,493,830
Norway	14,404	45,118	—	—	59,522
Poland	6,448	—	—	—	6,448
Singapore	—	1,512	—	—	1,512
South Africa	—	13,936	—	—	13,936
South West Africa	22,794	—	—	—	22,794
USSR	—	20,890	—	—	20,890
Hungary	—	306,990	—	—	306,990
Total	28,452,373	17,300,896	5,373,293	790,924	51,917,486
As percent of sales	54.8%	33.3%	10.3%	1.5%	100.0%
Total export	14,988,593	1,680,605	158,443	245,630	17,073,271
As a percent of exports	87.8%	9.8%	0.9%	1.4%	100.0%

tries. Bieri had sales agreements with each Hoval subsidiary. A very close relationship was enhanced through Hoval's small stock ownership in both Bieri and RCB Elektro-Apparate AG. Hoval was also represented on the boards of both of these companies. Hoval's management has made it clear that it considered the Hungarian proposal to be Bieri's decision.

EXHIBIT 3
BIRAL INTERNATIONAL (A)
Geographic Sales Distribution (1977 and 1978)

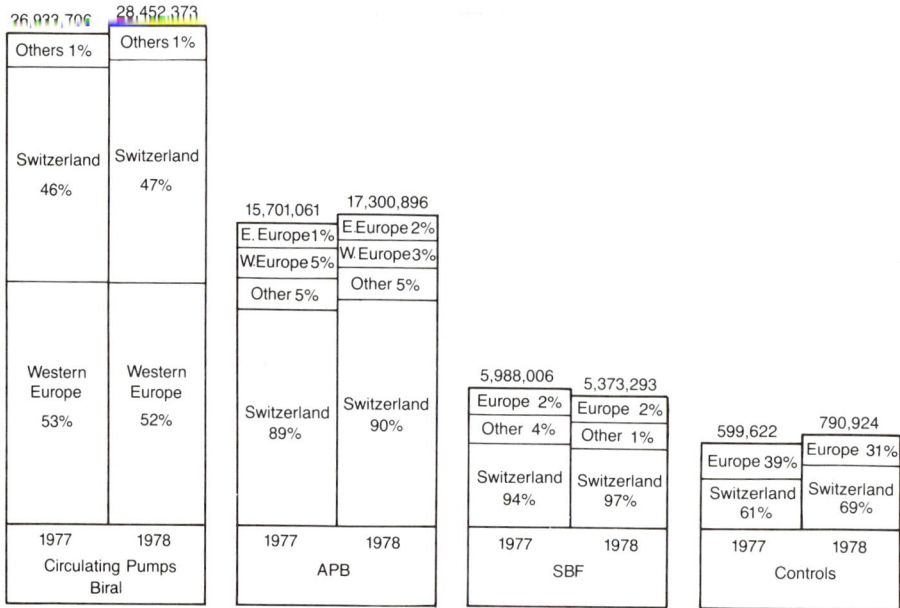

MARKET FORCES IN THE CIRCULATING PUMP MARKET

Sales of Biral pumps depended largely on construction activity and Bieri's competitive advantage. Each new house or building in Bieri's market area required a heating system, and this usually meant an oil- or gas-heated furnace with circulating hot water. Any such installation required a circulating pump. Electric heat, more popular in the United States, was not widely accepted, and in Switzerland a permit issued by the electric company was required to install it. Since electric generating capacity was barely sufficient to cover present demand, few such permits were granted. In other European countries, the situation was not much different from that in Switzerland.

The competitive situation, however, was quite dynamic and subject to rapid changes. Over the past eight years, currencies had fluctuated widely in the world markets. The free float of the Swiss franc had resulted in a marked appreciation against other European currencies.

EXHIBIT 4
BIRAL INTERNATIONAL (A)
Sales Distribution by Region and by Product Line

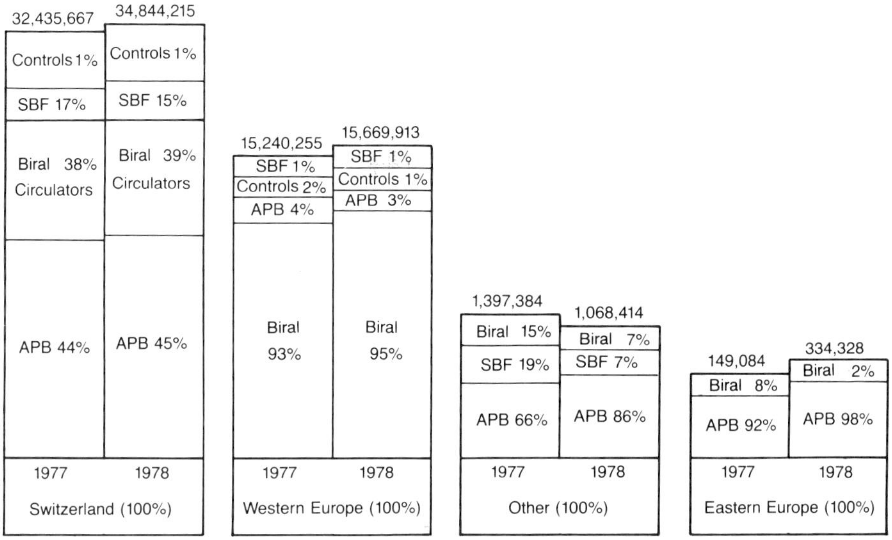

Against the Italian lira, the French franc, and the British pound, the Swiss franc had more than doubled in value. While this was partially offset in these countries by inflation rates of 5 to 10 percent above the Swiss rate, Swiss production costs had increased relative to competitors located in those countries. Against the German mark and the Dutch guilder, the Swiss franc appreciated about 25 percent, but these two latter countries had experienced an inflation rate similar to that of Switzerland. These currency changes left Bieri's prices 20 to 40 percent above those of its competitors. This had a particularly strong effect on Bieri's export markets, where the company did not enjoy the same strong brand loyalty that it had in Switzerland.

While Bieri had no significant competition in the circulating pump market in Switzerland, there were several European companies with substantially larger output and well-entrenched positions in specific countries. The largest one, Grundfos, a Danish company, had operations in all major European countries and a total volume of more than 2.5 million circulating pumps annually. Grundfos had manufacturing costs 20 to 30 percent below Bieri's due to its very large output. Next to Grundfos, there were three other major producers—Wilo in Germany, Euramo in France, and Myson in the United Kingdom. Each of these manufacturers had an annual output of about twice Bieri's volume and maintained strong positions in their home markets, with only spotty coverage of the rest of Europe.

In its latest move, Grundfos started sales operations in Switzerland in 1978. This represented a major competitive threat, since Switzerland absorbed almost half of Bieri's circulating pump output at prices substantially above prevailing levels in other European markets. Grundfos pumps were not produced in Switzerland, so they were priced higher than in other European markets, but still substantially below Bieri's prices. Bieri believed that the Swiss plumbing and heating contractors were unlikely to buy Grundfos products even at a very low price. With Biral's reputation for quality and longevity, Bieri executives believed that the threat emanating from Grundfos was real but not critical.

Still, from a long term point of view, it was important to Bieri to increase annual output to obtain economies of scale and lower unit costs. Reduced costs, combined with the existing quality reputation, would mean the company could look forward to a promising future.

BACKGROUND TO THE HUNGARIAN PROPOSAL

For several years, Bieri had employed a marketing manager for the Comecon area, a position occupied by Mr. Vacano. He had made numerous trips to Eastern Europe to contact the various buying organizations. While each Comecon country had a somewhat different setup, all had from 4 to 25 foreign trade organizations which bought and/or sold merchandise, as ordered by their "clients," all state-run manufacturing or trading companies. Typically, these foreign trade organizations would compete against each other for the same clients or business in their country. During the first phase of Bieri's activities in these countries, it was Mr. Vacano's task to make contact with these organizations. Sales were never large, but had been increasing, as shown below:

Sales of Bieri Products to Comecon Countries

Year	Volume (SFr)	Percent BIRAL	Percent APB
1976	225,923	—	—
1977	149,084	8	92
1978	334,328	2	98
1979 (estimate)	520,220	—	—

General pumps (APB) accounted for the bulk of the business. Sales also tended to be concentrated by countries. In 1976 all sales were to Hungary, and Czechoslovakia accounted for 91 percent of 1977 sales. Hungary again led (92%) in sales to Comecon countries in 1978. Bieri's sales had grown about 50 percent per year despite strong competition from other European pump manufacturers. Direct annual marketing costs were relatively low (averaging 40,000 SFr) and consisted mostly of trips by Bieri executives to the area and participation in trade shows.

Early in 1977, Bieri was approached by a Hungarian foreign trade corporation, Magyarexport (MAGEX) to open negotiations for a cooperative agreement with one of MAGEX's clients, Villamos.[3] The interest centered from the very beginning around Biral circulating pumps. Biral pumps were to be produced in cooperation with Villamos, but payment for manufacturing know-how and licensing fees was, in part, to be made with output from the Hungarian plant, either in the form of finished pumps or parts. Most Eastern European countries, and Hungary was no exception, were in need of Western products and technology, but they were usually unable to pay in hard currency. To alleviate the problem, these countries preferred to pay in merchandise for imported technologies.

Bieri's management quickly realized that such a cooperative agreement could offer an attractive way of increasing the Hungarian (and Comecon) market activity, provided the conditions were favorable. Mr. Vacano was authorized to commence negotiations, and by 1979 he had gone through eight revisions of the original proposal.

Villamos, the manufacturing enterprise, had no experience in producing pumps. It was a relatively small company operating about 15 workshops. In 1979, a new factory was built allowing the company to centralize its operation just outside Budapest, Hungary's capital. The company's operations included an aluminum foundry and manufacturing of garden furniture and camping equipment. The negotiations were carried out exclusively by MAGEX on behalf of Villamos.

An abridged form of the latest version of the proposal is shown in the Appendix. The contract could be summarized as follows:

> Bieri was to deliver to MAGEX-Villamos the documentation and know-how to produce a specified number of Biral pumps. Included were all rights to the patents, including those related to the electric motors, with

---

[3] All Hungarian names are disguised.

EXHIBIT 5
BIRAL INTERNATIONAL (A)
Sample Prices, Biral Pump Parts

	Pump Types		
Item	RB 12 S-1	RB 12 S-2	RB 15 S
Completely assembled	57.65*	76.75	161.70
Motor (complete)	41.09	58.17	132.47
Separating shell (unfinished)	4.20	6.50	15.40
Carbon bearing	1.81	3.50	3.50
Tolerance ring	0.42	0.50	0.67
Impeller	1.22	1.91	8.14
Packing between pump motor	0.32	0.50	0.92
Pump casing	7.08	8.47	10.66
Screw	0.11	0.11	0.11
Control knob for pump settings	0.38	0.38	0.49
O-ring	0.15	0.15	0.15
Screwed plug	0.09	0.17	0.36
Name plate	0.32	0.49	0.78
Label	0.03	0.03	0.03
Connecting parts	2.63	2.63	3.81

*All prices are in SFr, valid for deliveries up to December 12, 1980, and do not include packaging or freight. Packaging and freight will be billed separately after each shipment.

an additional responsibility of Bieri to provide 45 labor-days of training at Bieri and a further possible 30 labor-days at the Hungarian plant. Villamos was obligated to produce a minimum of 30,000 pumps over the 5 years the contract was to be in force and pay a royalty fee of 3 percent of the list price (see Exhibit 5) for every pump produced. The fee could be paid in hard currency or parts shipments.

MAGEX and/or Villamos were prepared to buy pumps and parts from Bieri over the life of the contract and had a contractual obligation to give Bieri preference on such purchases. In return, Bieri would be obligated to buy parts of equivalent value from the Hungarian companies. This obligation would remain in effect until termination of the contract. All money transfers were to take place in hard currency and values would be calculated according to Bieri's price list.

PRELIMINARY EVALUATION OF THE AGREEMENT

For Bieri's executive committee's final evaluation, Mr. Vacano estimated that the direct costs arising from the agreement, such as training, would amount to about 50,000 Swiss francs. While it was difficult to estimate the size of the market for circulating pumps in Hungary, Mr. Vacano believed that 20,000 pumps annually was a "good figure." Sales of other pumps to Hungary had been very slow this year despite the fact that Bieri had submitted quotes for installations totaling more than 1 million Swiss francs. In April 1979, for example, Bieri submitted a bid for a large project, but all the pump orders went to other suppliers. Hungarian sales so far for 1979 had amounted to less than 20,000 Swiss francs.

Negotiations had stretched over two years and were now at a point where he felt that Bieri could not obtain better terms. If Bieri would not go ahead with the contract, Villamos was certain to enter into an agreement with another European manufacturer, possibly even Grundfos.

As far as Mr. Vacano could determine, Comecon countries had for some time bought limited amounts of circulating pumps from Western sources. The major Comecon producer of circulating pumps was Czechoslovakia, but in amounts insufficient to satisfy domestic or Comecon demand. Once Villamos was in operation, it would have to market its pumps through Szerelvenyertekesito, a Hungarian trading company that had the exclusive right to market such pumps in Hungary. No competition existed in Hungary for the pumps covered in the agreement. Once production started, such pumps could be obtained only through Villamos. For larger circulating pumps, Hungarian foreign trade companies would continue to buy from Western firms, including competitors of Bieri.

Under the proposed agreement, Bieri would first supply the parts and Villamos would assemble the pumps. It was planned to phase the parts manufacturing from zero to nearly 100 percent over a two-year period. The pumps covered by the contract ranged in price from SFr 57.65 to SFr 161.70 ex factory Muensingen. Contribution margin (covering variable costs of purchases and direct labor, but excluding factory overhead, depreciation, marketing, sales, and servicing costs) was approximately 50 percent. The contract volume of 30,000 pumps amounted to about SFr 3 million in sales, or about SFr 90,000 in royalties to Bieri. The price per pump would average SFr 100.

THE HUNGARIAN BUSINESS CLIMATE

Ever since the end of World War II, Hungary had been under the influence of the Soviet Union. A member of Comecon, Hungary had a state-operated industry similar to those in other Communist countries in

Eastern Europe. The present political leadership, installed after the 1956 revolution, had over the years liberalized much of the economic activity. With a per capita income of approximately $2,500, Hungarians enjoyed a standard of living that surpassed those of all other Comecon members except East Germany. The country's population amounted to about 11 million. Exports had reached a level of about $8 billion, but were still exceeded by imports amounting to $10 billion.

The negative balance of trade prompted the Hungarian government to take corrective action in 1972. Hungary became the second Comecon government after Rumania to allow joint ventures with Western companies. However, due to restrictions and what Western businessmen considered unclear practices, only three joint ventures had been formed by 1979. Since 1974, the Swedish firm Volvo produced a 4-wheel drive vehicle with the Csepel Company in Budapest that was sold abroad through the Volvo organization.

Siemens of Germany established the second venture and, since 1975, Corning Medical of the United States had produced medical equipment jointly with the Hungarian firm Radelhis. More activity was focused on creating licensing agreements. It was estimated that over the past few years alone, the Hungarian machinery industry had concluded more than 300 licensing agreements with Western firms. Moreover, Hungary had taken the leadership among Comecon countries in creating cooperative agreements. So far, it was estimated that Hungarian enterprises had concluded more than 500 such agreements.

Over the past few years, Switzerland had been an important trading partner for Hungary. Among the countries outside the Comecon area, Switzerland was Hungary's fourth most important trading partner. Switzerland exported goods worth SFr 268 million to Hungary in 1976, up from only SFr 157 million in 1973. Imports from Hungary grew from SFr 155 million to SFr 170 million over the same time period. During the past few years, Swiss companies had signed many licensing and cooperative agreements. At the beginning of 1977, a total of 55 cooperative and 10 licensing agreements were in effect, and by April 1978, it was reported that another 52 cooperative agreements were being negotiated. These agreements, however, still represented only 1.4 percent of Swiss-Hungarian trade, compared to 5.3 percent for German-Hungarian trade and 7.5 percent for Swedish-Hungarian trade. The majority of these agreements were signed by machinery and chemical companies. Among others, there existed an agreement by Hermes Company to have its typewriters produced in Hungary; Sibir for the production of refrigerators; and Brown Boveri & Cie for the construction of steam turbines. Despite several attempts on the part of Mr. Vacano, Bieri had not been able to learn details of the experiences of these Swiss companies' operations in Hungary.

DECISION

The latest version of the agreement had been made available to members of the executive committee. It was Mr. Vacano's strong belief that he had negotiated the best possible contract, particularly when considering the improvements over earlier versions. Should Bieri accept this agreement, it was then up to the Hungarian partners to have it ratified by the Hungarian Ministry of Foreign Trade. Only then would it become available for signature. It was now up to Bieri's management to decide if they wanted to proceed.

APPENDIX:
Licensing Agreement (Abridged)

ARTICLE I: INTRODUCTION

Bieri Pumpenbau AG, located in Muensingen, Switzerland, to be named "BIERI," and MAGEX Hungarian Export Commercial Enterprise, to be called "MAGEX," located in Budapest, Hungary, conclude a cooperation agreement for the manufacture, use and sale of BIRAL[4] circulating pumps and decide to engage in technical and commercial relations as follows:

- MAGEX will acquire from BIERI the know-how for the manufacture, use, and sale of BIRAL circulating pumps type RB12S, RF12S, RB15S, and RF15S. This know-how will be turned over to Villamos in Budapest, a Hungarian manufacturing company, and includes the know-how for the electric motors.

---

[4]The BIRAL brand name is not part of this agreement.

- BIERI is prepared to deliver to MAGEX the technical documentation and manufacturing know-how for the above pumps including the use of all relative industrial patents and rights. The only exception is rights related to the separating shell.
- Within the scope of this agreement, MAGEX is interested in obtaining a yet to be determined amount of components from BIERI.
- BIERI is prepared to accept from MAGEX a like amount of finished pumps, subassemblies, or individual parts manufactured by MAGEX in Hungary based upon the technical documentation of BIERI and provided they meet BIERI's requirements for quality, price, and delivery terms.

ARTICLE II: PURPOSE OF CONTRACT

It is the purpose of the cooperation between the partners of this contract to enable MAGEX to manufacture in Hungary the circulating pumps with the same characteristics and the same parameters of performance as those manufactured by BIERI in Switzerland and to sell these pumps in Hungary and some other countries specified later on.

ARTICLE III: OBJECT OF CONTRACT

BIERI grants MAGEX the following rights:

- The right to manufacture in Hungary the circulating pumps BIRAL RB/RF 12S/15S, including all replacement parts and the electric motors, with the exception of the separating shell that is not part of this agreement.
- The right to all new changes and developments with respect to the pumps under consideration for the duration of this cooperation agreement.
- The right to all industrial protective rights (patents, trademarks, etc.) granted to BIERI in relation to the pumps covered by this agreement.
- The right to sell these circulating pumps in all countries according to special stipulations set forth below.

ARTICLE IV: SALES AND EXPORT RIGHTS

BIERI grants herewith MAGEX the unlimited nonexclusive right to offer and to sell without any restrictions the pumps in Hungary as well as the countries shown below:

Comecon territory: USSR, Poland, East Germany, Czechoslovakia
Hungary, Rumania, Bulgaria, Cuba
Peoples Republic of China
Yemen
North Korea
(Khmer Republic) Cambodia
Laos and Burma

To sell upon consultation with BIERI and after determination of the relative range of export prices in the following countries in the world:

Afghanistan	Finland	Libya	Philippines
Albania	Greece	Malaysia	Portugal
Angola	Iceland	Malta	Sweden
Bangladesh	India	Morocco	Tunesia
Ceylon	Indonesia	Nepal	Turkey
Egypt	Iraq	Pakistan	Yugoslavia

plus in all states of Central and South America as well as in the remaining countries of the world, with the exception of those listed below where MAGEX has the right to export the subject matter upon consultation and solely through the existing sales organization of BIERI to the following countries:

Algeria	Emirates of the	Netherlands	Spain
Australia	Persian Gulf	Norway	Syria
Belgium	France	Saudi Arabia	Thailand
Canada	Great Britain	Singapore	USA
Denmark	Kuwait	South Africa	West Germany
	Luxemburg		

Pumps installed as a part of a turnkey plant may be exported by MAGEX without any restrictions. In the future, BIERI is prepared to enter an agreement about territorial expansion under consideration of the interest of the parties to this contract.

The contract parties will vote upon prices and conditions on the export markets at their regular biannual meetings.

As long as the contract is in force, Villamos may place a label on each pump indicating "Produced under license of Bieri Pump BIRAL International."

ARTICLE V: TECHNICAL DATA

BIERI will turn over to MAGEX the entire technical documentation on the subject matter within three months of the signing of the contract. The total documentation passes into the possession of MAGEX, which may dispose of it at liberty, but with the restrictions of Article IX.

ARTICLE VI: TECHNICAL ASSISTANCE

BIERI will render technical assistance to MAGEX with respect to manufacturing the subject matter. BIERI will specifically instruct specialists of MAGEX at its manufacturing plant in Switzerland for the maximum of 45 labor-days. The group of specialists is never to exceed three people and will have sufficient knowledge of the German language. BIERI will make one of its own specialists available to MAGEX at its Hungarian plant for a period not exceeding 30 labor-days. The entire costs of traveling, lodging, and board for both the Hungarian and Swiss specialists will be paid for by MAGEX. BIERI will pay the Hungarian specialists a daily flat fee, according to Hungarian norms in effect at that time.

For any labor-hours requested by MAGEX in excess of those specified, BIERI will supply the necessary personnel at the typical rates in force in Switzerland for the level of specialists made available. The partners agree to form a group of experts which is to meet twice annually, once in Hungary and once in Switzerland, to treat technical and commercial questions. The group should not exceed three experts on either side.

ARTICLE VII: DELIVERY OF COMPONENTS AND FINISHED PRODUCTS

MAGEX obligates itself to purchase during the course of the contract and, according to its requirements, pumps, subassemblies, or separate parts on the subject matter entirely from BIERI should MAGEX not be in a position to manufacture the subject matter itself. BIERI, in return, will undertake deliveries of entire pumps or parts and subassemblies, in order to assure the sufficient supply of MAGEX with the subject matter of this contract.

ARTICLE VIII: GUARANTEES

Provided that suitable manufacturing shops and equipment for the manufacturing of the subject matter of the contract are existing, and provided that all instructions, statements, and directions contained in the technical documents are strictly adhered to, BIERI guarantees that MAGEX will be in a position to produce the subject matter of the contract in the identical quality and with the same performance parameters as produced by BIERI.

In the case of difficulties, BIERI will indicate suitable measures to be taken by MAGEX to produce as indicated above.

ARTICLE IX: SECRECY

MAGEX obligates itself to treat the manufacturing know-how confidentially during the duration of the contract and for an additional period of 10 years after its expiration. Exempt from this are the manufacturing company in Hungary and Hungarian export trade enterprises with respect to information normally delivered to clients for quotations or orders. MAGEX will assure that the manufacturing company complies with the same rules of confidentiality.

ARTICLE X: LICENSING FEE

As compensation, MAGEX will pay BIERI 3 percent of the sales price for the pumps and parts manufactured in Hungary. MAGEX obligates itself to produce a minimum of 30,000 pumps within the five years of the contract. The basis for computing the licensing fee is the effective transfer price for fully assembled pumps as per Exhibit 5.

BIERI is prepared to purchase from MAGEX, up to the expiration of the contract, pump parts in compensation of the licensing fee at repurchase prices equal to 30 percent below list prices as per Exhibit 5.

In case MAGEX will produce less than the guaranteed minimum quantity, MAGEX will pay the 3 percent fee on the deficient quantity in Swiss francs. The first payments will be made at the end of the second year of the contract, and then annually at the end of each calendar year until the contract expires.

ARTICLE XI: COMPENSATION

BIERI is prepared to accept from MAGEX for the duration of the contract pump parts at the same value as MAGEX bought from BIERI, provided that MAGEX can actually effect delivery. The purchases by BIERI and the sales by MAGEX should be equalized annually as much as possible. Again, MAGEX will purchase parts at the full transfer price as per Exhibit 5, whereas Bieri would repurchase parts at 30 percent below these list prices.

To cover any goods delivered by BIERI, MAGEX will have opened irrevocable letters of credit through a large Swiss bank with payments due upon presentation of shipping documents. To guarantee its purchases, BIERI will establish a bank guarantee for 10 percent of the minimum sales agreed upon. MAGEX may cash the guaranteed amount should BIERI not make any purchases from MAGEX.

ARTICLE XII: PRIORITY AS A SUPPLIER

MAGEX will invite BIERI to tender offers when importing other pumps which are also contained in the manufacturing program of BIERI. MAGEX will exert its entire influence to insure that these pumps be bought from BIERI, provided that BIERI's quotes are competitive with regard to quality, price, and delivery terms. However, these transactions are on a cash basis and are not included in this cooperation agreement.

ARTICLE XIII: HIGHER POWER (ACTS OF GOD)

The contract allows for cancellation given certain acts of God beyond the control of the partners. Any final dissolution, however, is subject to the court of arbitration.

ARTICLE XIV: COURT OF ARBITRATION

Any disputes that cannot be settled by the parties is to be brought before the court of arbitration in Munich, West Germany. Each party nominates one member to the three-person court, with the two selected members agreeing on a third person who is a citizen of Germany. In case an agreement on that third person cannot be reached within 30 days, the chairman of the International Chamber of Commerce in Paris will be asked to nominate the third member. The arbitrators decide by majority vote and their decision is final. The contractual relationship of this agreement is subject to the law of the Federal Republic of Germany. The court of arbitration decides on its own procedures.

ARTICLE XV: DURATION OF CONTRACT

This contract will be in force for five years. It will be prolonged automatically for one year at a time, provided that neither party gives notice by registered letter within six months prior to expiration of the contract.

After expiration of the contract, MAGEX will be authorized to continue to manufacture, use, and sell the products in Hungary according to Article II. However, Villamos is not allowed to use any labels on its exported pumps that may infer any relationship with BIERI.

ARTICLE XVI: SERVICING

MAGEX assumes the entire .servicing duties of customers and obligations of attendance, as well as the entire servicing of replacement parts during the course of the contract, for pumps sold by itself. If MAGEX so desires, BIERI is prepared to offer suggestions and proposals free of charge for creation of a suitable service organization.

Vanderbruk Spice NV

Mr. Jacob Diddens was going over his notes after the board meeting. He had received approval to spend up to 2.5 million guilders[1] on the installation of a new distribution information system for the Japanese operations. The proposal had originated with Vanderbruk's Japanese subsidiary, Nippon Spice. In conjunction with a consultant from a leading Japanese university, the group at Nippon Spice had designed a distribution requirements planning (DRP) system to manage the flow of product through the Japanese distribution system. As director of distribution, Mr. Diddens had followed their work with interest. He realized it was clearly the most advanced of any similar efforts in the company and could serve as a model for other areas of the world.

In making his presentation to the board, Mr. Diddens had presented three benefits from the system: inventory and other savings, better information linkages to customers, and the pilot test of a system that had companywide potential. There was some skepticism from the board and their reaction was split. No one was strongly against the proposal, but there was no one in strong advocacy either. Mr. Diddens felt the conclusion had been, "We'll trust you on this one, but make sure that it's right before you spend the money." With this in mind, he set about drafting a telex to the group in Japan, advising them of the meeting's outcome.

BACKGROUND AND HISTORY

The Vanderbruk Spice company could trace its roots to the late 1700s, when Henrik Vanderveen founded a small grocery store in Rotterdam. Over the years, he began to specialize in some of the exotic food products that came into port from around the world. He developed supply sources and merchandising expertise in essences, spices, and dried fruits from the Caribbean Islands and several countries in Southeast Asia. These products enjoyed a strong demand and the business prospered. The company remained in the Vanderveen family for several generations. Although there were occasional diversions into other products

---

[1] In 1987, 1 $U.S. = 2 Dutch guilders.

(chiefly tobacco, perfumes, and deluxe candies), part of the business was always devoted to the founder's products.

During the early 1900s, with no heirs who were interested in the company, the family turned to professional managers. The professional managers sought to increase the company's international sales and reputation by establishing stronger distribution ties to agents, brokers, and even wholesalers in some countries. During this period, it became clear that developing some manufacturing capability would help the company protect the brand and improve the margins. Around the same time Bruksteen Chemicals, a manufacturer of food coloring products and aromatics for cosmetics and detergents, was looking for opportunities to integrate forward into the market. When managers of Bruksteen Chemicals learned, through a mutual friend, about the interests of the Vanderveen firm, they immediately made contact to discuss the possibilities of a merger.

After a long period of negotiation, the companies agreed to found Vanderbruk Spice, with each management team essentially responsible for the activities they had prior to the merger. The top job went to one of the Vanderveen people. The new company used Bruksteen's manufacturing facilities to make the entire line of products, while distribution was through Vanderveen channels and brands. The business prospered, and there were only minor changes in the product lines, except during the two world wars.

By the early 1950s, the firm was experiencing a rapid worldwide growth in demand for its broad line of food flavorings, food colorings, spices, aperitifs, dessert spirits, and fruit products. A manufacturing capacity increase, to relieve the pressure caused by the demand growth, was financed by issuing stock to the public. The company consolidated all facilities on a new site located near Rotterdam. The company continues to prosper and enjoys a worldwide reputation for high-quality products. The research laboratories have brought out several new products each year, and the engineers have developed processes that have provided competitive advantages. Some financial data for Vanderbruk Spice for the last few years are given in Exhibit 1.

THE JAPANESE SUBSIDIARY

In the early 1970s, the Vanderbruk company made a major effort to increase sales and geographical coverage in the Far East. Japan was one area, in particular, where its efforts were focused. The company tried

EXHIBIT 1
VANDERBRUK SPICE NV
Financial Data
(millions of guilders)

Income Statements

	1986	1985	1984
Net sales	11,930	10,367	9,858
Cost of goods sold			
Labor	3,263	2,915	2,851
Material	3,029	2,684	2,547
Gross margins	5,638	4,768	4,460
General and admin.	3,907	3,341	3,276
Depreciation	564	505	498
Finance and exchange	442	366	248
Net profit	725	556	438

Balance Sheets

	1986	1985	1984
Current assets			
Cash	2,929	2,375	1,860
Receivables	2,742	2,582	2,321
Inventories	2,432	2,318	2,141
Total current assets	8,103	7,275	6,322
Fixed assets	3,341	2,803	2,574
Total assets	11,444	10,078	8,896
Liabilities			
Accounts payable	1,670	1,473	1,329
Notes payable	1,952	1,681	1,264
Reserves	897	725	659
Share capital	415	415	415
Equity	6,510	5,784	5,229
Total liabilities	11,444	10,078	8,896

several times to gain a foothold in the Japanese market, but was only moderately successful. After deciding a presence on the island was essential, Vanderbruk Spice established Nippon Spice, a wholly owned subsidiary, in Tokyo.

Nippon Spice was mainly responsible for packaging bulk product, which was ordered from Holland. In addition to the packaging capability, however, it did produce a few products with mostly local appeal. In fact, some of these local products had been incorporated in the Vanderbruk product line for worldwide distribution. Nippon Spice also mixed some imported product concentrates with local materials before packaging and even handled a few products that arrived already packaged for distribution.

The subsidiary ordered replacement inventory from Holland, using a form of reorder point, order quantity system. As bulk material was withdrawn from inventory to be packaged, the transactions were entered into Nippon Spice's computer system. When a predetermined reorder point was reached, the item was placed on a report which went to a bulk materials clerk. The clerk would pool the items that needed reordering to make up the order that went to Holland three times a week. This order would be timed to coincide with the air shipments that Vanderbruk used for most of its products. (Some lower valued items and prepacked goods still went by sea, but not a large part of the volume.)

Vanderbruk had negotiated, with KLM Royal Dutch Airlines, a very favorable air freight rate to Japan. KLM provided a fixed amount of cargo space three times a week with the stipulation that the space not required by Vanderbruk could be used by someone else. In addition, Vanderbruk had a high priority on additional space, if needed. The clerks at Nippon Spice had a great deal of discretion regarding the items used to fill up the space KLM provided to Vanderbruk. If an order appeared short of the contracted space, a clerk could look for items near their reorder point which could "top up" the order.

Vanderbruk found that, even with the subsidiary, there were still great obstacles to reaching the Japanese market. The grocers and even the emerging supermarkets still relied on traditional, complicated distribution channels. Industrial buyers such as institutional food organizations, department stores, hospitals, the military, and restaurants preferred to use middlemen over buying direct. On the advice of the Nippon Spice president, Patrik Willems, Vanderbruk contracted with Matsumi, a large Japanese food distributor, to help reach the domestic market. In June 1979, Matsumi took over the distribution and marketing of all Vanderbruk products in Japan.

After the distribution contract with Matsumi was signed, sales in Japan increased and the subsidiary began making a profit. Mr. Willems did feel some pressure to improve performance, however. The sales and profit performance had been quite flat for the last few years. (Selected financial data for Nippon Spice are presented in Exhibit 2.) He felt that improved knowledge of the market and careful administration of the

EXHIBIT 2
VANDERBRUK SPICE NV
Nippon Spice Financial Data
(millions of yen)

Income Statements

	1986	1985	1984
Net sales	33,404	35,248	34,457
Cost of goods sold			
Labor	10,176	10,202	9,985
Material	8,481	9,599	9,302
Gross margins	14,748	15,447	15,170
General and admin.	14,432	14,860	14,732
Net profit	316	587	438

Balance Sheets

	1986	1985	1984
Current assets			
Cash	2,408	1,620	1,322
Receivables	2,806	3,106	2,772
Inventories	3,444	3,831	3,627
Total current assets	8,658	8,557	7,721
Fixed assets	2,356	2,481	2,351
Total assets	11,014	11,038	10,072
Liabilities			
Accounts payable	1,546	1,784	1,653
Notes payable	2,561	2,698	2,746
Reserves	1,831	1,796	1,500
Equity	5,076	4,760	4,173
Total liabilities	11,014	11,038	10,072

distribution inventories should make improvements in performance. He fully supported the installation of the DRP system to help accomplish this objective.

MATSUMI

Matsumi had a good reputation as one of Japan's largest food distributors. Over the years, it had established relationships with the most important primary wholesalers in the Japanese food distribution chain.

Recently, Matsumi had also been developing direct distribution arrangements with some institutional customers, such as the Seiyu and Jusco chain stores, the Nichii supermarket chain, and some company restaurants. Matsumi's customers were served through a network of five large distribution centers. Its primary wholesale customers, in turn, supplied larger grocers, some institutional buyers, and smaller distributors. These channels provided access to virtually every grocery store and institutional food outlet in Japan. In 1987, about 85 percent of Matsumi's sales were to primary wholesalers, and the remainder were direct to large institutional customers.

The company had been very aggressive in providing service to the primary wholesale market. All customers received at least two deliveries a week, and some got as many as four. In many instances, the company had made special deliveries when an item was urgently needed by a customer. While not encouraging its customers to make such requests, Matsumi did take advantage of these occurrences to enhance its image. As an extension of Matsumi's service, a sales representative often spent considerable time training warehouse owners in inventory management, freshness control, and delivery planning. A rumor claimed that some Matsumi customers had joined just to get this training.

Matsumi distributed a full line of nonperishable food products, such as canned goods, packaged processed foods, dried fruits and vegetables, seasonings, and so forth. The agreement with Nippon Spice specified that, with the exception of a few locally produced specialty items, only spices produced by Nippon Spice would be distributed by Matsumi.

Also, as part of the agreement, Matsumi reported inventory and demand information to Nippon Spice each month. Matsumi provided summaries of demand (actually, they reported deliveries) and a listing of the month-end inventory balances for each product. In addition, about 10 percent of the items were counted each month (some items were counted more than once a year) and inventory corrections were reported to Nippon Spice. The accuracy of the inventory records at Matsumi was quite good, and there was rarely an error of more than a few units.

Matsumi's inventory management system, like that used for Nippon Spice's bulk products, was based on reorder point, order quantity principles. Records were maintained on all items at each of the five distribution centers. Inventory transactions were recorded during the day and were processed each night at each location. When an item reached the reorder point, an order was sent to Nippon Spice to replenish the item at the distribution center. Nippon Spice made deliveries to each of Matsumi's distribution centers once a week visiting each one on a different day. Matsumi's clerks had on-line access to inventory information at each distribution center through the use of computer terminals in their Tokyo office. They also received a daily report on those items that were below reorder point.

When the distribution requirements planning system was first discussed with Matsumi, no one was aware of the theory. After one Matsumi executive attended a briefing presented to Nippon Spice management by the consultant, he became excited about the prospect. Without grasping the details, he could see the advantages of the system and of extending it to other products handled by Matsumi. Based on such interest, Patrik Willems realized that he could count on Matsumi's cooperation. It was then he started a serious development of the proposal Jacob Diddens took before the board.

NIPPON SPICE'S CURRENT SYSTEM

A reorder point, reorder quantity system was also used to manage the packaged goods inventories at Nippon Spice. Several material clerks were each responsible for a portion of the packaged products, with one concentrating on prepackaged goods from Holland and another on the products manufactured entirely at Nippon Spice. All the clerks have access to packaged inventory status records that show both Nippon Spice and Matsumi inventory levels. (A partial example for a mango flavoring is shown in Exhibit 3.) In addition, every clerk receives a report of all items below their "warning point" (reorder point), including their approximate priority in the packaging sequence.

The packaged inventory status report (Exhibit 3) contains descriptive information on the product, as well as market and status information. The heart of the report is the inventory balance and the commitments to the five distribution centers (On Order For). The result gives a picture of current availability and allocations of that availability against current orders from each location. The net inventory is tested against the warning point to determine whether or not an order should go on the packaging line. The "On Order For" information is updated each time an order comes in from one of Matsumi's distribution centers. It can be used to help allocate an item in short supply.

The information on demand and Matsumi inventories is updated

EXHIBIT 3
VANDERBRUK SPICE NV
Packaged Inventory Status

Product No. C107852-12   Date 4/20/87
  Desc: Mango, Intense Flavor   Last Sales Date: 8/88
  Package, unit 12–25
  Package, Qty. 15   Demand*

last year	43
last month, last yr.	7
last month	2

Warning Point: 5

Matsumi Inventory: 8*

Initial Balance†	On Order For ‡					Net Inventory
6	1	2	3	4	5	4
	0	0	1	0	1	

Notes: Warning point reached with net inventory. No later batches. Packaging priority: no order.
*Reported by Matsumi for all distribution centers in the system.
†Current balance at Nippon Spice.
‡Matsumi Distribution Centers: 1 = Tokyo (North), 2 = Tokyo (South), 3 = Osaka, 4 = Sapporo and 5 = Kitakyushu.

each month when the report is received from Matsumi. The report gives last year's demand, last month's demand, and the demand for the same month last year. Matsumi inventory is the amount last reported by Matsumi for all distribution centers. Right under the current date is the date beyond which this batch of product cannot be sold to the public. Such information helps to manage products with expiration dates. The mango flavoring has a 1988 expiration date. The date of validity is coded into the product number for each batch of product. The next batch will have a different product number, giving a new date for last sale.

The mango flavoring is packaged in lots of 15 boxes of 12 bottles of 25 ml each. The warning point is 5 boxes and the net inventory is 4 boxes, so a message is printed at the bottom of the page. In addition to stating that the warning point has been reached, the information indicates that only this batch of packaged mango flavoring is available. If a batch with a later last sales date was available, a reference to the product number for that batch would also have been printed.

Action should be considered now on the mango flavoring. The messages indicate that there is neither a current packaging order nor a later batch. When the clerk orders another lot to be packaged, the foreman will schedule the order, subject to efficient use of the packaging line. After being scheduled, the order will get a priority number which will inform the clerk of the approximate date the order should be completed.

The clerks all have access to information on each bulk material or packaged item in inventory. They also have grown quite familiar with the products under their responsibility and occasionally check the terminal "just to see what is going on." There is a good spirit of cooperation between the material clerks and the foremen in the packaging area. They would work together quite closely to resolve problems that might arise in trying to meet customer requirements.

Even though no real problems were evident, the decision was made to review the system. "When we started reviewing the system, it seemed that we were getting the material just when we *didn't* need it." said Mr. Willems. "Just after we had sent a bunch of stuff to Matsumi, we'd find our packaging line swamped with orders for the stuff that we had just sent out. We knew they wouldn't be ordering those items again for a while!" Mr. Kiyoshi Hanada, the distribution staff analyst, and Prof. Kenji "Ken" Yoshida, the consultant, did a simulation study of the current system which found that, in general, the contention was true. Unfortunately, however, there were times when an order from one distribution location would create a packaging order. Then some (or all) of the remaining locations would order the same product, and a shortage would result before packaging could be completed.

In general, the service levels to Matsumi were quite high and there was good cooperation between the companies. Sometimes a delay in the bulk arrival *and* packaging would occur; then it would be three or four weeks before an order could be sent to Matsumi. In such cases, the companies would work together (even redistributing the material between locations) to reduce the impact of the shortages. Mr. Willems realized that a shortage at Nippon Spice was not as bad as a shortage in a grocery store or at a Matsumi location which was supplying an institutional account. At those locations, a shortage could mean loss of a sale (or the customer) to a competitor.

Nippon Spice management, however, didn't know the service level to the ultimate customers. They believed it was good, and Matsumi was reported to be better than the competition. On occasion, the Matsumi truck from one of the two Tokyo locations would come by the Nippon Spice plant to pick up items for immediate distribution. Such times were rare, but they made Mr. Willems wonder about the true service levels, especially for the distribution facilities maintained by Matsumi in Osaka, Sapporo (northern Japan), and Kitakyushu (southern Japan).

THE DRP PROJECT

The distribution requirements planning (DRP) project had its beginnings in a middle management program at one of Japan's leading universities. Mr. Kiyoshi Hanada had attended the program and met Prof. "Ken" Yoshida during the course. One course that Professor Yoshida taught was distribution management, and DRP was one of the topics. Mr. Hanada saw the potential for applying the concept at Nippon Spice, where he worked as a distribution analyst. When he got back to work after the program, he invited Professor Yoshida to make a presentation on the concept to a group of Nippon Spice managers.

After considerable discussion in Japan and communication with Mr. Diddens in Holland, there was general agreement that a preliminary study of the costs and benefits of installing a DRP system would be worthwhile. As a basis for starting the project, Mr. Hanada and Professor Yoshida developed DRP records for several example products. An example of the mango flavoring records for both Matsumi's distribution activity and Nippon Spice's packaging activities are provided in Exhibit 4 using a lead time of one week for all activities.

The DRP record includes several features which had been discussed during the program attended by Mr. Hanada. For example, the early part of the record is divided into increments (buckets) of one week, while the latter part is in monthly buckets (indicated at 7/13). The header information for Sapporo includes product data, planning data, and special messages. The order quantity (Ord Qty) and minimum quantity (Min Qty or safety stock) are determined for the product at each location. If the first planned order for a product is later than the age week, a message warning of the risk of exceeding the shelf life is printed. Demand is based on the local estimate of the annual demand and timing is determined by local conditions.

For the Nippon Spice record, most of the header information is the same. The order quantity (Pack Qty) is 15 boxes and the last sale date (Lst Sale) is specified directly. Demand is the total of all distribution locations' annual demand, and the Matsumi inventory (M. Invty) is the total of all five locations. The customer order row is for indicating unusual demands (such as a large hospital or restaurant order) on a distribution location or on Nippon Spice.

The records of Matsumi's distribution system would be coupled directly to the packaging records at Nippon Spice. For example, the planned order by Sapporo during week 6/22 is translated directly into a gross requirement for the packaging activities of Nippon Spice. The to-

EXHIBIT 4
VANDERBRUK SPICE NV
Example DRP Records for Nippon Spice and Matsumi—Sapporo

Product No. C107852-12, Mango, intense flavor

Unit Pack 12-25	Ord Qty 1	Min Qty 1	Age Week 8	Price	Demand 3	Sapporo Special	Date 4/20/87 Notes **

Weekly =>

	Past due	4/20	4/27	5/4	5/11	5/18	5/25	6/1	6/8	6/15	6/22
Forecast		0	0	0	0	0	0	0	0	0	0
Customer orders											
Scheduled receipts											
Projected inventory		1	1	1	1	1	1	1	1	1	1
Planned orders											
Firm planned order	1										

Monthly =>

	6/29	7/6	7/13	8/10	9/7	10/5	11/2	11/30	12/28	1/25	2/22
Forecast	1	0	0	0	0	1	0	0		0	1
Customer orders											
Scheduled receipts											
Projected inventory	1	1	1	1	1	1	1	1	1	1	1
Planned orders	1					1				1	1
Firm planned order	1	1	1	1	1	1	1	1		1	1

Product No. C107852-12 Mango, intense flavor

| | Unit Pack 12-25 | Pack Qty 15 | Min Qty 4 | Lst Sale 8/88 | Price | Demand 43 | Nippon Spice M. Invty 8 | Date 4/20/87 Notes |

Weekly =>	Past due	4/20	4/27	5/4	5/11	5/18	5/25	6/1	6/8	6/15	6/22
Gross requirements		2	0	0	2	1	1	0	0	2	1
Customer orders											
Scheduled receipts											
Projected inventory	6	4	4	4	17	16	15	15	15	13	12
Planned orders				15							
Firm planned order											

Monthly =>	6/29	7/6	7/13	8/10	9/7	10/5	11/2	11/30	12/28	1/25	2/22
Gross requirements	0	0	4	4	3	4	4	3	4	4	3
Customer orders											
Scheduled receipts											
Projected inventory	12	12	8	4	16	12	8	5	4	12	9
Planned orders					15						
Firm planned order											

tal of all the planned activities of the distribution facilities results in requirements that are met by the planned orders for packaging the product. In order to introduce some stability into the package line scheduling, the possibilities for introducing a period of "frozen" orders (via the firm planned order capability) was being discussed.

The volume of mango flavoring is too small to be considered a typical product. It does, however, illustrate several key points about the DRP system. The record for Matsumi's Sapporo location, for example, shows one box in stock, so the next planned order is in the week of 6/22. This date is later than the Age Week (8 weeks from the present date), which means a note (asterisks under the "Notes" heading) is printed indicating that the product extends beyond the "Age Week." This note warns the clerks that the product needs monitoring to make sure it doesn't exceed the last sales date. Even though no immediate action needs to be taken, the clerks can use the information to help reduce the returns of product with expired dates.

Another point regarding the record for the packaging facility can be made by comparing Exhibit 4 with Exhibit 3 for the same product. The record in Exhibit 3 shows that an order for packaging another 15 boxes needs to be released. The record in Exhibit 4 shows that it is not necessary to release an order until two weeks from the current week. Mr. Willems explained: "This is the closest we can come to proving that the reorder point method brings in the material when we don't need it. Our current system is blind to the planned activities in the distribution system. The DRP records will also provide us with immediate information on market activity, not the month end summaries we currently get."

An important part of the system will be the freight consolidation information for bulk shipments from Holland. Exhibit 5 shows an example of the type of information that will be available to the material clerks managing the KLM shipments to Japan. The same record could also help manage distribution to the Matsumi locations.

The record provides information on the weight, space, and special handling needed for various combinations of products to be dispatched on the next flight from Holland. It is derived from the daily packaging schedules of the packaging foremen. The first column simply provides information on past due orders. This information would serve as a reminder to the clerks, although some overdue orders might be caused by shortages in Holland rather than problems in Japan. The second column gives data for shipments which include the planned orders which fall between the present date and the next flight deadline. The third column includes planned orders up to the subsequent flight.

EXHIBIT 5
VANDERBRUK SPICE NV
Load Planning for KLM Space

Date: 4/20/87
Flight: 4/24/87

	I	II	III
	Past Due Only	I + This Trip	II + Next Trip
Weight (Kilos × 100)	120	437	528
Space (Meters³)	0.3	1.8	2.7
Special Handling	No	Yes	Yes

Product No./Description

Past Due by Date	This Trip by Weight	Next Trip by Weight
B327890–34	B213567–89	D456389–09
Mexican Lemon	Orange Tapa	Dried Banana
D47328–17	T515826–18	Etc.
Dried Papaya	Green #103F	
S789654–37	Etc.	
Coffee Liqueur		
End		

The detailed product listings at the bottom of the report will help the clerks make final choices regarding orders from Holland. The past due products are arranged by date (indicating lateness of the item), while the other two columns are arranged by weight. The final aid to the clerks is a simulation capability (not shown) that determines the weight, space, and special handling for any combination selected. This simulation can be used as a final check before transmitting any orders.

THE BOARD PRESENTATION

The presentation to the board was summarized as shown in Exhibit 6. The cost estimates came from the consultant's experience, suggestions from the computer group, and management's knowledge of similar past undertakings. The board had no problem with either the one-time or the annual cost estimates, which in fact they considered thorough and conservative. On the benefit side, Mr. Willems and Mr. Diddens focused on the payoff from "hard" estimates of inventory reductions and savings on product returns in order to sell the project. As the other benefits were difficult to quantify, they were considered as extras.

The details on the savings estimates are provided in Exhibit 7. The

EXHIBIT 6
VANDERBRUK SPICE NV
Summary of Costs and Benefits
(in guilders)

Benefits	Carrying Cost = 20 percent	10 percent
Inventory reduction	2,320,000	1,160,000
Reduced overdate returns	1,330,000	1,330,000
Improved bulk shipments	?	?
Increased market share	?	?
Integration with Matsumi	?	?
Pilot test of DRP system	?	?
Total	3,650,000	2,490,000

Costs	One-time	Annual
Training	250,000	100,000
Programming	600,000	200,000
Equipment	1,450,000	300,000
Warehouse	150,000	50,000
Transportation	50,000	250,000
Additional labor		1,350,000
Total	2,500,000	2,250,000

Approximate return at 20 percent, (1400/2500 =) 56.1 percent
at 10 percent, (240/2500 =) 9.6 percent

estimates of Matsumi's inventory came from the amount reported by Matsumi, as well as from a cross-check with Nippon Spice's shipments and reported Matsumi sales. The disaggregation to the five locations was based on the percentage of total volume in each. To estimate potential savings, the Nippon Spice team prepared records for some items in Matsumi's inventory and studied the accomplishments of other firms that had installed DRP. Using these data, the team concluded that reducing the inventory in the distribution centers by one week could easily be achieved. To calculate the savings, they evaluated the inventory at material cost (again being conservative) and found a week's worth of inventory was 649 million yen (see Exhibit 7). At a 20 percent annual inventory carrying cost rate, this amount came to an annual savings of almost 130 million yen.

There is also a potential for inventory savings at the packaging facility. Better management of the bulk materials from Holland, as well as the packaged materials for distribution to Matsumi, contribute to the total savings. The mango flavoring example shows the potential for delaying orders by one week. Using this example as a guide (again con-

EXHIBIT 7
VANDERBRUK SPICE NV
Estimates of Inventory Activity for Nippon Spice Products—Matsumi Facilities
(millions of yen)

Facility:	Total	Tokyo North	Tokyo South	Osaka (Mid)	Sapporo (North)	Kitakyushu (South)
Percent of volume	100	28	32	22	8	10
Sales est.	60127	16836	19241	13228	4810	6013
Material*	33856	9480	10834	7448	2708	3386
Inventory†	6872	1924	2199	1512	550	687

*Material cost based on first-in, first-out costing.
†From our estimates and their reports.

I. Estimating Matsumi inventory savings (one week reduction):

Material	Mat/Day	Invty	Days' Supply	1-day Invty	1-week Invty
33856	93	6872	74	93	649

Savings per year at 20 percent carrying cost: 129.85. At 10 percent: 64.93

II. Savings for the Nippon Spice inventory (one week reduction):

Material	Mat/Day	Invty	Days' Supply	1-day Invty	1-week Invty
8481	23	3444	148	23	163

Savings per year at 20 percent carrying cost: 32.45. At 10 percent: 16.27
Total = 162.30   81.20
Total in guilders‡ = 2.32   1.16

III. Estimating the savings from a 50 percent reduction in the returns:

Cost of Goods Sold	Return Percent	Cost of Returns	Percent Reduction	Total Savings	In Guilders‡
18657	1.00	187	50.00	93.29	1.33

IV. Summary (in millions of guilders‡):

	20 percent	10 percent
Carrying cost		
Inventory savings	2.320	1.160
Savings on returns	1.330	1.330
Total	3.650	2.490
Annual cost	2.250	2.250
Net annual savings	1.400	0.240

‡One guilder was worth about 70 yen in 1987.

servative), the team calculated the savings from one week's reduction in Nippon Spice's inventory. Valued, again, at material cost, the savings amounts to 163 million yen, or a savings of a little more than 32 million yen per year at an annual carrying cost of 20 percent. The combined savings amount to 2.32 million guilders when the carrying cost rate is 20 percent and 1.16 million for the 10 percent rate.

The second area of hard savings was in product returns that had passed the last sales dates. Currently, about 1 percent of Nippon Spice's products were returned for exceeding the last date. Mr. Willems suspected that many of these returns had never left the Matsumi warehouses, even though he was told the returns were from grocers. Better control of the dates should lead to a 50 percent reduction of these returns. Valued at the Cost of Goods Sold, this amounts to an annual savings of more than 93 million yen per year. These data are shown in Exhibit 7, along with a summary of net savings.

Other potential benefits include the possibility of improved bulk transportation. As Mr. Diddens felt the clerks were already doing a good job, he didn't suggest any explicit savings in that area. Likewise, he didn't recommend increasing demand, although he did feel that better knowledge of the market demand would enhance the job of matching supply and demand. Still, if service could be improved, Nippon Spice should not merely hold its own in an apparently growing Japanese market, especially as the competition's service was supposedly not as good.

The final areas of benefit pertained to the Vanderbruk firm in general. The integration of Matsumi and Nippon Spice provided by the installation of the DRP system could have significant strategic advantages. Other divisions could benefit from such close information linkages with their customers. Mr. Diddens also knew that the Holland manufacturing facility was interested in installing a materials requirements planning (MRP) system which would be logically related to DRP. He felt that the work on DRP in Japan would serve as a useful pilot for that activity, as well as for other DRP installations around the world.

Even though he had received the budget for carrying out the DRP project, Mr. Diddens felt uneasy. He didn't want to let the board down, yet he couldn't put his finger on any one item that really was a trouble point. He also wondered what to say to Mr. Willems and the team in Japan. They certainly were anxious to learn the board's reaction. What should he tell them to do next? As he was musing, his secretary came in with a telex from Mr. Willems saying that the team was waiting to know the results of the meeting and had the whiskey ready for either answer.

PART 4

OPERATIONS STRATEGY

This final section includes cases which center on defining the strategy for operations—that is, determining the manufacturing task or evaluating the impact of proposals on the manufacturing function. The central question is how can operations support overall company objectives? The first case, Kumera Oy (B), considers an investment in CAD/CAM, an application of technology to the process. After just having experienced a major project implementation, the company has extra cash and the CAD/CAM system is suggested as a good use of the funds. In the Labeco case, a North American firm is concerned with a new product. The company currently produces automotive test equipment and is considering entering the medical instrument market. The move would put them into direct competition with some major international firms.

The International Plow case presents an issue faced by many companies doing business in Europe and other parts of the world: How should manufacturing be organized to best serve the firm's markets? Should it produce a broad line of products for a single country or a narrow line for several countries? How centralized should the support functions be? How broad should the plant manager's responsibility be?

The last two cases deal with comprehensive issues. The Maillefer SA (A) case considers product positioning for a producer of plastic pipe extruding equipment. The company has an opportunity to evaluate its competitive position and strengths before laying out the course of its product development activities. In the Sunwind AB (A) case, the use of a just-in-time (JIT) program to enhance the competitive position of a Volvo supplier is suggested. Elements of operations from vendor relations to shop floor activities are involved in the considerations.

Kumera Oy (B)

The installation of a comprehensive material control system had reversed a trend of slipping competitive position, increasing costs, and declining customer service at Kumera Oy. The implementation of the system, which supports order entry, production planning and control, and purchasing, had absorbed a great deal of management time over the last few months. As a consequence, Vesa Kumpulainen, the managing director, was faced with a rather unusual problem—what to do with the funds that had been generated from the improved operations.

One of the proposals was for the installation of a CAD/CAM (computer-aided design and computer-aided manufacturing) system costing about $300,000. Though obtaining capital was not a problem, Mr. Kumpulainen was trying to determine whether the benefits were sufficient to warrant the investment of both the capital and management time required for implementation. He was especially sensitive to the fact that the company had just gone through a major implementation process.

BACKGROUND

The installation of the material control system (the periodic control system) had required substantial management effort. Although the technical aspects of the system were not complex, there were many areas that required substantial management involvement. The greatest degree of management attention was required for implementation. The effort was highly successful, however, in providing a solid basis for future growth, improving operations, and releasing funds for other investments. As an example, the company had already invested in several modern numerically controlled machines to improve manufacturing efficiency.

The production scheduling aspect of the periodic control system provides the basis for improved operations and customer service. Mr. Kumpulainen likened the schedules to a railroad timetable, with specific times for starting and completing groups of products. By fixing the

---

Additional background information on the company is contained in Kumera Oy (A), page 108.

schedules for the production of product groups and then abiding by these schedules, a high degree of predictability and improved planning is provided. This benefit accrues to vendors and customers as well as to Kumera. Further, the "train schedule" approach to scheduling provides a basis for other activities to improve operations. These activities range from bill-of-material processing to inventory control. The planning foundation provided by periodic control was also viewed as an important element for utilizing CAD/CAM.

The periodic control system benefits were not gained without cost, however. Among the difficult management problems encountered during installation were personnel turnover, training, and selling the idea inside and outside the firm. Many of these, of course, have to do with the fact that periodic control changed virtually every aspect of the management of the flow of materials. The pervasive nature of the changes meant that many people had to be sold on the idea and trained to use the new procedures. The high level of discipline expected (e.g., no more production of a few extra pieces just because there was enough material) required vigilance and follow-up to keep the organization from sliding back into the old informal ways.

The success of the system vindicated the proponents. The funds generated by better inventory management, reduced costs, and improved service levels provided part of the motivation for considering the use of a CAD/CAM system. Mr. Kumpulainen was not sure he or the organization was ready for the implementation of another new system so soon after installing periodic control. He realized, however, that CAD/CAM would not make as many changes in the way things are done as periodic control had. In some cases, it would simply provide a way for doing the same things better.

THE CAD/CAM PROPOSAL

Mr. Veli-Pekka Mattila, Kumera's planning director, had been researching the possibility of using CAD/CAM. Several systems were available, and use of them had been growing throughout Europe. Major efforts at developing standards and improving the performance of the systems were underway in Germany and Norway. One of Kumera's competitors had already installed CAD and other competitors were considering CAD/CAM installations. Many metal machining, fabrication, and assembly companies in other parts of Europe had installed systems and were gaining experience in using them.

The system that Mr. Mattila had selected for Kumera performed both drafting and numerical control programming functions. The drafting functions would speed and simplify the basic engineering design process. By storing and displaying the "drawings" for engineered parts electronically, changes could be made and evaluated quickly. The need for manual preparation of paper drawings would be reduced. The potential savings from these functions were estimated to be two draftsmen and one design engineer. Naturally nobody was to be let go. Turnover and the postponement of hiring would provide the savings.

The CAD/CAM system would also support the programming of Kumera's numerically controlled (NC) machines. These machines were controlled by computer programs that specified the rates and directions of movement of both the workpiece and machine tool. Much of the basic information for the NC programs comes from the engineering drawings. The CAD/CAM system couples the drafting programs with the NC programming processor to provide this data electronically. It was estimated that CAD/CAM would save two NC programmers for the company.

Several manufacturing benefits had been attributed to CAD/CAM systems in addition to those in engineering. These all derive from the ability to check designs and NC programs thoroughly before using them in the factory. The cost of raw material could be reduced through better utilization (about $10,000/year) and reduced scrap ($10,000/year). The improved programs for the NC machines would eliminate most of the test runs before production, saving both material and labor costs ($20,000/year). The improved design and engineering of the parts would increase the reliability of the products, resulting in additional savings ($10,000/year) in product support services.

Many other benefits had been claimed for CAD/CAM, but they were difficult to quantify. One benefit, for example, would be the improvement in competitive position due to better and quicker product design. Another strategic benefit would come from improved "image." One claimed CAD/CAM advantage, reduced lead times, was not as great a benefit for Kumera as for other companies. The periodic control system had already improved the lead time substantially. The reductions in drafting time would not change overall lead times appreciably.

The costs of the CAD/CAM system involved not only the basic investment of $300,000, but an annual cost of approximately $30,000

EXHIBIT 1
KUMERA Oy (B)
Summary of Costs and Benefits for the CAD/CAM Proposal

Costs	
Investment	$300,000
Annual service costs (software and hardware)	$ 30,000/year
Benefits	
Personnel costs (2 draftsmen/2 NC programmers)	$ 70,000/year
Material savings (scrap and utilization)	$ 20,000/year
Elimination of test runs	$ 20,000/year
Reliability improvement	$ 10,000/year
Total benefits	$120,000/year

would be required for software and hardware service. Also, the savings from the design engineer would be offset by the cost of a CAD/CAM systems specialist. The technology in the industry was advancing rapidly and the estimated technological life of the system was five years while prevailing rates of interest were in the range of 10–12 percent. A summary of the costs and benefits is provided in Exhibit 1.

DECISION

As Vesa Kumpulainen reviewed the proposal on the CAD/CAM system, several thoughts were going through his mind. He realized that the implementation would require an effort on his part and Veli-Pekka's. He was not sure how to weigh the arguments about the competitive advantage of some of the "image" considerations. The financial aspects of the investment had been documented in the proposal, but they were not the only considerations. He felt a decision should be made quickly, before a great deal of experience without CAD/CAM had been gained on the new NC machines.

Labeco

Ted Englehart, President of Laboratory Equipment Corporation (Labeco) reread the letter from the Indianapolis Center for Advanced Research (ICFAR). It contained a request for more information concerning Labeco's proposal to secure the rights to an ultrasonic breast scanner that had been developed by ICFAR. The letter from ICFAR also indicated that, after Labeco had submitted their proposal, other serious contenders for the rights had expressed an interest, including Elscint, a well-established, international, financially strong medical instrument/equipment firm. Labeco's proposal had indicated the company's interest in producing and marketing the product and specified that ICFAR would continue to do research into the uses and technological improvements of the machine. Considerably more detail was asked for in the questionnaire that accompanied the letter and there was an opportunity to revise the conditions of the proposal.

The breast scanner appeared to be a product that could make up for a projected decline in sales, a problem that had concerned Mr. Englehart for some time. As he stated it, "We need some products that will make us 'bomb proof'. A large portion of our current product line is very sensitive to changes in the Environmental Protection Agency's standards and practices. The breast scanner is an appealing possibility which would take us into a new market. It also seems to fit our manufacturing capabilities very well. There is growing interest in it which just confirms that it is a good product, but I need to consider the total strategic impact before deciding how aggressively to pursue the rights."

BACKGROUND

Labeco was founded in 1943 to produce single cylinder test engines for testing aircraft spark plugs. These engines are made to very demanding specifications in order to provide reliability, long life, and high accuracy in the test measurements. Test engines provide engineers with data on fuel consumption, engine parameters (e.g., oil temperature and air flow) and performance (e.g., horsepower and torque). By 1947 Labeco's engine was adapted as the standard for spark plug rating by the Society of Automotive Engineers.

In 1954 the company won a design competition for a lubricant testing engine. The competition was sponsored by the Coordinating Research Council, an engineering group from the automotive and petroleum industries. The product that resulted from this was a single-cylinder engine which extended the company's manufacturing capability in high-precision moving parts, control and measurement devices, and close tolerance testing. It also took them into the oil industry market, one closely allied with the automotive industry.

After about ten years of strong growth in sales, the market for new test engines stabilized. The highest percentage of current sales related to the test engine line is from spare parts. The single-cylinder test engines, however, still enjoy a worldwide market among automotive companies, oil industry firms, and both public and private test laboratories.

The test engines involve the use of dynamometers, devices for applying and measuring forces on rotating objects. The competence gained in using these devices led to the development of chassis dynamometers for testing cars and trucks. These are products mounted on stationary platforms which apply various road conditions to vehicles through rotating drums which are powered by the wheels of the vehicle being tested. They are used for monitoring fuel consumption, testing engines and drive trains, and measuring exhaust emissions. Labeco's dynamometer line, sold to the automotive industry, is particularly sensitive to changes in the EPA and energy legislation.

In the 1960s the company added a line of "fifth wheels." These are bicycle-like wheels that are trailed behind a vehicle to measure precisely speed and distance. They are used in automobile, truck, and off-road vehicle testing. The fifth wheels are sold to many of the same customers as the company's other products. Other devices for testing and measuring have been manufactured by the company, but none have achieved important sales volumes. Exhibit 1 shows some of the company's products.

Ted Englehart took over as president of Labeco in 1973. He had previously worked for Indiana Gear Works, where he rose from machinist to executive vice president. He later managed Wilson Engineering Company. Both were aerospace gear manufacturing and engineering firms in Indiana. Capitalizing on the engineering talent and manufacturing experience at Labeco, he set about expanding and diversifying the product line. A line of custom dynamometers, requiring substantial engineering to meet customer specifications, was instituted. Using his knowledge of gear manufacturing and the industry, he initiated a line of high-speed gear testing equipment, primarily for helicopter gears.

EXHIBIT 1
LABECO
Sample Products

Mileage accumulation dynamometer for duplicating road load characteristics

Computer control console for engine and chassis dynamometer systems

Precision single cylinder test engine packages - CLR oil test engine, TACOM diesel engine, and 17.6 spark plug rating engine

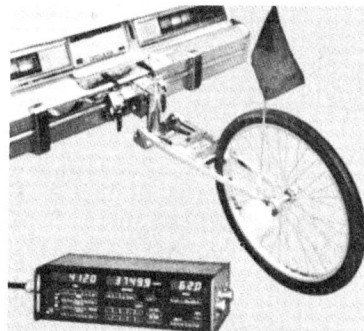

Labeco Tracktest 5th wheel and microprocessor based instrumentation

In 1975 an acquisition provided Labeco with a general-purpose testing machine for use on a variety of automotive and off-road vehicle components. It also gave the company some additional manufacturing capability in the areas of hydraulics, electrical assembly, and specialized gear boxes.

These products opened up a market with the helicopter companies, but also had a great deal of market commonality with the existing line. They were sold to testing laboratories and agencies of the government as well as to automotive and oil companies. To a large degree, much of the new business fit right into the market contacts and experience of the company.

PROJECTIONS AND CONCERNS

The importance of the new product lines in spurring sales and changing the product mix can be seen in Exhibit 2. From 1978 to 1980, sales grew and then remained relatively constant through 1982. The single-cylinder test engines and fifth wheels together maintained a fairly steady rate of sales at about 20 percent of the total. On the other hand, the chassis dynamometers have ranged from more than 40 percent to as low as 5 percent of sales. The generally declining trend reflects the changes that have taken place in environmental protection and energy policies. The slack has been picked up by the custom dynamometers, and the gear and special testing equipment. These two categories have accounted for about 60 percent of sales in the last two years. The miscellaneous products rarely account for as much as 10 percent of sales.

In developing the plans for 1983, even though he expected a moderate increase in the chassis dynamometer business, Mr. Englehart projected a 25 percent decline in sales (see Exhibit 2). This reduction was of concern to him for several reasons.

First and foremost, he was concerned about maintaining jobs for the work force. Secondly, he was concerned that the firm was still not "bomb proof" enough with the current product mix. Despite the broadening of the product line, the volatility of some of the products still had a substantial impact on the total performance of the company. Finally, he was concerned about the profitability which was essential to provide the funds to compete for new business in the current and potential lines of the company.

The pessimistic projections and his concerns for the firm had led Mr. Englehart to look for new product opportunities. He was aware that any new products would need to build upon the company's strengths and utilize the company's facilities.

CURRENT SITUATION

Labeco enjoys a fine reputation in the automotive and oil testing industry. Their single-cylinder test engines are known throughout the world, and virtually no promotion is required for these products. The fifth

EXHIBIT 2
LABECO
Sales History and Estimated Sales
(in $000; percent of total)

Product Line*	1978	1979	1980	1981	1982	(est.) 1983
1	991 (29)	1,077 (21)	1,163 (17)	1,315 (20)	1,327 (21)	1,063 (22)
2	1,057 (31)	1,172 (24)	2,905 (42)	955 (14)	315 (5)	380 (8)
3	627 (18)	1,118 (22)	1,278 (19)	622 (10)	2,100 (32)	1,768 (37)
4	611 (18)	1,571 (32)	1,388 (21)	3,349 (50)	2,089 (32)	1,449 (30)
5	127 (4)	27 (1)	64 (1)	402 (6)	634 (10)	146 (3)
Total	3,413 (100)	4,965 (100)	6,798 (100)	6,643 (100)	6,465 (100)	4,806 (100)

*Product lines: 1. Single-cylinder engines and fifth wheels
2. Chassis dynamometers
3. Custom dynamometers
4. Gear and special test equipment
5. Miscellaneous

wheel is sometimes advertised in the trade literature, and direct mail has been used at times. But this product, as well, sells mainly on its own merits to the automotive industry.

Labeco's reputation is so strong that whenever any firm is considering a dynamometer application, they are likely to invite Labeco to bid on the project. Some of the sales engineers devote a major portion of their time to preparing these bids. In many cases they will become involved early enough in the design that they can help the customer with state-of-the-art specifications for the project. Mr. Englehart estimates that Labeco now bids on about 90 percent of the custom dynamometer applications. The requests come from automobile and truck manufacturers, oil companies, farm equipment companies, and government and private testing laboratories.

Mr. Englehart's experience in the gear industry brought new market contacts to Labeco. The gear and general-purpose testing machines are sold to gear and helicopter manufacturers. In addition, the general-purpose machine is sold to the automotive industry. Both product lines are used in test laboratories as well. The sales engineers prepare proposals and do some solicitation in these new markets.

"Image is very important in our business," explained Mr. Englehart. "Our products tend to sell themselves. We have only four sales representatives, and most of them are overseas. Instead we rely on our reputation for high quality and our ability to help solve our customer's testing problems. We only have seven people on our staff devoted to sales administration and engineering, but we all are involved (see Exhibit 3). From the design of the product, through manufacturing and installation, down to delivery and customer follow-up, we're establishing the reputation that will sell our products."

The company is located in Mooresville, Indiana, about 15 miles southwest of Indianapolis. The buildings in current use are depicted in Exhibit 4. The capacity of the two major buildings is sufficient for a substantial expansion of business before additional space would be needed. Labeco owns another building (not shown in Exhibit 4) about three blocks away from the two major buildings. This building is currently used for storage, but is available for future expansion.

The office/fabrication building contains the administrative offices and the machine shop. The machine shop contains regular, general-purpose machine tools such as milling machines, drills, boring machines, grinders, press brakes, and so on. With this equipment, the company can produce sheet metal parts for cabinets and enclosures, a wide va-

EXHIBIT 3
LABECO
Number of Employees by Department

Accounting		5
Administration		2
Design		11
Engineering		15
Mechanical	10	
Electrical	5	
Manufacturing		36
Machinists	16	
Welding/fabrication	7	
Assembly	9	
Electrical assembly	4	
Maintenance		5
Material control		9
Sales engineers and		7
administration		
Total		90
Sales representatives		4

riety of close-tolerance machined pieces for stationary and moving parts, and high-quality welded parts for bases and frames.

The engineering/assembly building houses engineering, the assembly and testing areas, and inventory. The purchased parts (e.g., electric motors, tires, wiring, and computer components) are received here before being assembled together with company-produced parts to make subassemblies and final products. The assembly activities involve both mechanical and electrical/electronic capability. Included in the company's capabilities is the ability to assemble circuit boards and computer controllers. This came about as part of the computerization of some of the company's products.

In order to assure final product quality, Labeco had developed extensive product testing capabilities. These capabilities included all the mechanical, hydraulic, and electrical testing necessary for the single-cylinder engine, dynamometer, fifth wheel, gear testing and general testing products of the company. In addition, the company had recently added testing capability in electronics to test the computer-controlled products they are currently producing. This testing capability was important in assuring the company's reputation for quality products.

EXHIBIT 4
LABECO
Physical Facilities

Assembly facilities

a. Multiple module assembly
   T-slot floor rails
b. Isolated T-slot base plate
   18 ft × 30 ft
c. 150 ton press
Plus: Overhead cranes (three)
   5 ton and (one) 10 ton
   (two with multiple speed control)
   208A electrical service
   with 4,180V capability
   8,500 sq ft assembly area

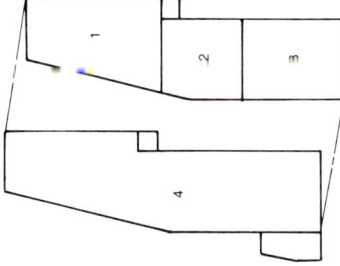

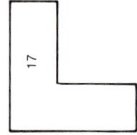

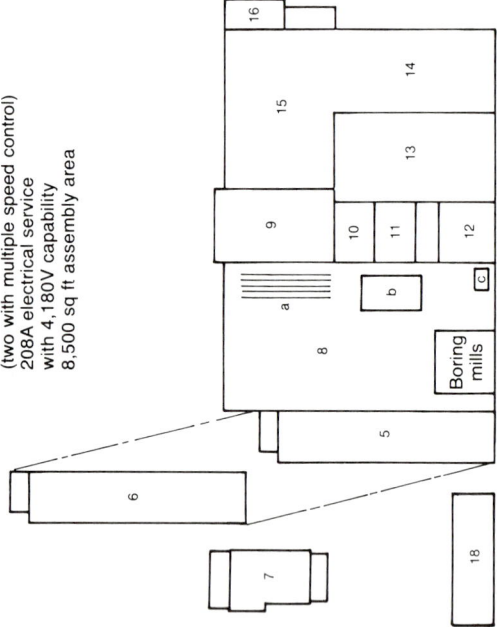

1. Administration and sales department
2. Purchasing department
3. Accounting department
4. Machine shop
5. Dynamometer systems engineering department
6. Design department
7. Aerospace, special dynamometers
   and production engineering department
8. Mechanical assembly and test
9. Stores
10. Electrical assembly
11. Engine assembly and test
12. Electronics laboratory
13. Welding shop
14. Sheet metal and paint shop
15. Storage
16. Sand blast
17. Carpenter shop and storage
18. Maintenance department

The engineering and manufacturing capabilities were carefully monitored by the company management. Mr. Englehart pointed out that the management systems used to perform this task were a primary asset of the company. For example, the computerized manufacturing system controlled the bills of material, product costing, drawings and inventories. The management systems were a major factor in the company's product diversification program and in controlling costs. They also figured importantly in the management of the computerization of some of the company's products.

ICFAR

ICFAR was founded in 1971 as a not-for-profit center to provide a link between industry and academia. Located in Indianapolis, ICFAR draws upon the medical and engineering departments of Indiana and Purdue Universities at Indianapolis (IUPUI), and most professional staff members have academic appointments at the universities. Although ICFAR engages primarily in medical and engineering activities, it is not restricted to these.

The unique role that ICFAR plays is in the gap between pure research and the commercialization of new technology. Its objective is to enhance the research activities of the universities and to promote the incorporation of new technology into business, primarily in the greater Indianapolis area and the state of Indiana. This is accomplished by evaluating the commercial feasibility of the new knowledge created by the universities. Activities range from extending basic research to evaluating specific applications and even to developing prototype hardware for testing commercial feasibility.

The center's support comes from a variety of sources. Private customers that use the center's expertise to answer research questions provide one source of funds. Government and private grants fund some studies and royalties received on commercially licensed products provide additional revenue. ICFAR provides knowledge, technical expertise, and prototypes to industry, utilizing the basic knowledge generated by the universities' research facilities.

The relationship between Labeco and ICFAR grew out of a project involving computers. Labeco had approached ICFAR in 1979 for some assistance in using microprocessors for dynamometer control. ICFAR became involved in the development of the hardware configuration, the software for performing the control functions, and the interfaces between the microprocessors and the dynamometers. ICFAR still provides development support for Labeco in these areas.

The coupling of microprocessors to the dynamometers had been very successful. It enabled Labeco's customers to program a sequence of test conditions and to control those conditions to a much closer degree than was possible with manual control. ICFAR's support in the project to computerize some of the products had been very beneficial to Labeco. Ted Englehart learned of the breast scanner through this association with ICFAR.

BREAST SCANNER

Dr. Elizabeth Kelly-Fry had been directing ICFAR projects involving ultrasonic methods for early detection of breast cancer for about eight years. In the last two years, a team of ICFAR engineers led by Narendra Sanghvi and including Frank J. Fry and Richard F. Morris had been involved in the design of a prototype ultrasonic breast scanner. By 1982 the concept and technology were proved, and two prototypes had evolved. Evaluation and development were continued on the two prototypes, but very little commercial interest had been shown in the device. The evaluations were all very positive, and the staff at ICFAR was convinced that their approach was superior to existing approaches.

To demonstrate the field effectiveness of the scanner, ICFAR made the decision to build and place ten units (at cost) with users who would agree to perform field evaluations. At the same time they recruited an engineer, Steve Morris, with the understanding that he would be employed by the licensee to help in the transfer of the technology, and took the unusual step of applying for FDA certification for the machine in an effort to make it more attractive to a commercial enterprise. This certification is normally not sought for research and development projects, but it is required for medical equipment being produced for commercial use.

By the time Labeco started considering the breast scanner, seven units had been installed, and the field evaluations were providing positive feedback on the machine's effectiveness, as well as useful information on maintenance and servicing. The users paid between $54,000 and $65,000 each for these clinical prototypes. This amount was enough for ICFAR to recover the direct costs of building the machines. No attempt was made to contribute to general overhead or recover any of the research investment in the device, however.

The ultrasonic breast scanner operates much like sonar, using high-frequency sound waves to detect irregularities in the breast tissue. A computer is used to control the progress of the physical motion of an ultrasonic transducer over the patient. The sound waves are projected into the tissue and are bounced back into a receiver, where they are picked up and electronically processed. A video image is formed that is displayed on a monitor, a device that looks like a small black and white TV screen. The computer provides the operator with a great deal of control over the rate of scan, the magnification, the area covered in the exam, and other system parameters. A picture of the breast scanner is provided in Exhibit 5.

EXHIBIT 5
LABECO
The Breast Scanner

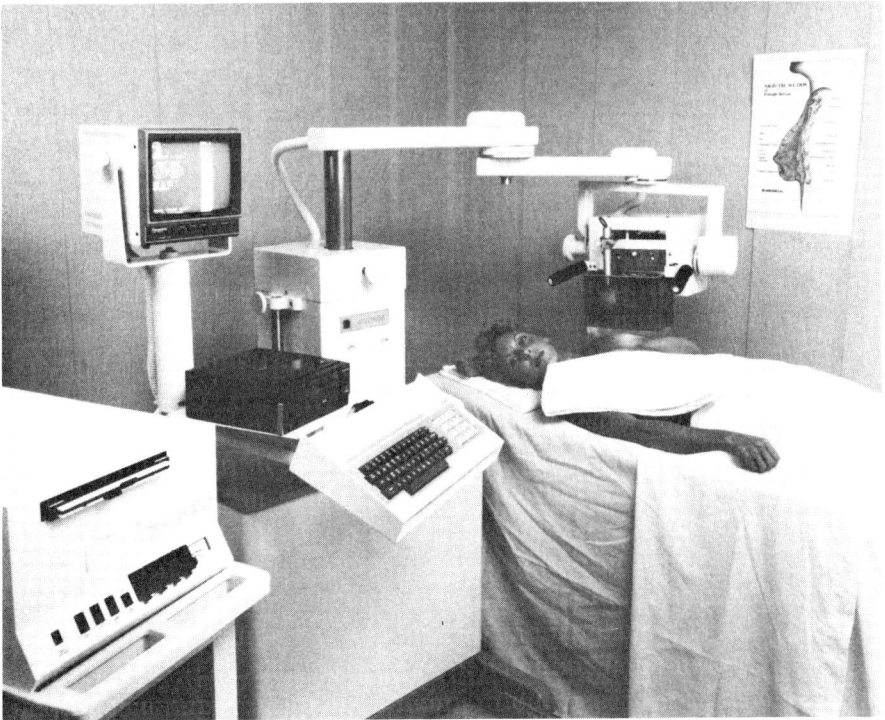

Unlike X rays, high-frequency sound waves produced at diagnostic intensities have no detrimental side effects. This means that they can be used with women for whom exposure to X ray could be dangerous, pregnant women, or women who prefer not to have X-ray exposure. Since there is no need to wait for film processing, the doctor can see and evaluate the results while the scan is in progress, providing opportunities to look more closely at areas of concern or even to take tissue samples from suspect areas.

The application of ultrasonic scanning devices in medicine is growing. They are being used to check unborn babies, provide scans of the cardiovascular system and other body tissue, and provide information on internal organs where X rays could be dangerous.

In addition to all of the advantages of ultrasonic scanning, the prototypes developed by ICFAR have distinct advantages over competing equipment. The unit is small and portable so it can be rolled to a patient and is easily positioned by a doctor or attendant. While the scanner is in use, the patient can lie on an examining table while a small bag of water is placed in position for the scan.

The competing machines, however, involve stationary water-filled tubs to which the patients must be moved. The tissue to be scanned must be immersed in the water, making it very difficult to scan obese patients, pregnant patients, or patients with fractures.

PRODUCT EVALUATION

The breast scanner appeared to be an attractive addition to the product line. The lack of patent protection was of some concern, but the market potential looked good. Breast examinations are conducted in clinics, at hospitals, in physicians' offices and in medical laboratories. Not all of the locations where breast examinations are conducted would use ultrasonic scanning, however. The total annual market range for ultrasonic breast scanning devices was estimated to be 400 to 500 units in any case. A 20 percent market penetration would provide Labeco an annual volume of 80 to 100 units.

An evaluation of the current competition indicated that, at $65,000 per unit, the ICFAR breast scanner had a significant price advantage over all existing products. The portability and patient comfort aspects were important advantages as well. A potential competitor was Siemens, which had been testing its own machine at a clinic in England.

The expected market price was $50,000; the patient could sit up for an examination using the Siemens machine.

Mr. Englehart estimated that Labeco could produce and market 10 units during 1983. Labeco would also take over the 7 units that IFCAR currently had in the field. The sales were expected to grow to 25 the next year, 50 the third year, and to reach the annual market potential of about 90 units in the fourth year. Current capacity was sufficient for assembling some 200 units per year. There was no practical limitation on parts fabrication or subassembly capacity.

The breast scanner required several manufacturing operations. The base and stand were to be welded into a subassembly. Most of the parts required to make the arms and scanning mechanism would need to be machined. Several were moving parts, and many required close tolerances. The sheet metal enclosures for the electronic equipment would need to be fabricated. Subassemblies incorporating circuit boards and wiring would be needed, and additional electronic components would be required during final assembly. The assembly and testing would require both mechanical and electronic skills.

Most of the major purchased parts, such as microprocessors, video monitors, and electric motors, could be obtained from Labeco's current sources of supply. It was important to capitalize on these contacts, since the purchased parts, components, and raw material had run as high as 60 percent of the cost of ICFAR's units. Mr. Englehart recognized that he would have to exercise careful control of costs if he were to achieve the anticipated 40 percent gross margin on the sales price of $65,000. He felt that his engineers could improve the manufacturability of the product and that the company's experience could reduce manufacturing costs below those of the first units made by ICFAR.

LABECO'S PROPOSAL

After the initial evaluation, Mr. Englehart submitted a proposal to ICFAR for licensing the breast scanner. The essence of the proposal was contained in three provisions. Labeco would provide a $20,000 advance payment against future royalties, Labeco was to have exclusive rights to the machine, and the royalty to ICFAR was to be $2,000 per unit.

Shortly after the proposal had been sent to ICFAR, Dr. Tom Franklin, who had just been appointed acting director, wrote to Mr. Englehart and told him of the other companies that were interested in the breast scanner. Dr. Franklin also said that an ad hoc committee of the ICFAR board of directors had been formed to help establish the criteria for licensing the breast scanner. He requested that Mr. Englehart fill out a questionnaire that the committee had compiled to help evaluate the proposals from firms that were interested in the machine. The questions involved topics like:

1. The financial package in terms of flat fees, advances, royalties and equity position offered to ICFAR.
2. Any contract provisions for future ICFAR support in engineering, marketing, providing enhancements, research, and so on.
3. The physical location of the business and intentions for production and employment in Indiana.
4. Estimated annual demand and production of the breast scanners.
5. The perceived mutual value of the arrangement to ICFAR and to the company, and any other factors important to the decision.

After reviewing the request from Dr. Franklin, Mr. Englehart knew that the competition for the rights to the breast scanner would be serious. He was particularly concerned about Elscint. He knew they were well financed and had a good reputation. His immediate task was to decide how aggressive to be in responding to Dr. Franklin.

International Plow

As 1987 dawned, Don Cowles was heartened by Morris Industries, Ltd.'s, performance over the last year and held high hopes for the company's performance over the next 12 months. Still, he harbored anxiety about what might be forced upon him. The last round of redundancies (layoffs) had not gone down well with the work force. Over the past 4 years, the work force had contributed significantly to turning around a difficult situation, and they had swallowed significant attrition and redundancies with aplomb. But, this year, as Morris's chief manager, he felt that they could not approach the work force with any more redundancies without provoking trouble.

MORRIS INDUSTRIES—A SHORT DESCRIPTION

Morris Industries, Ltd., was the British unit of International Plow, a producer of agricultural implements (plows, harrows, balers, and other implements that could be attached to a tractor). International Plow was, in turn, a part of Mesot, Inc., an American-based conglomerate headquartered in Dallas, Texas. Morris had been acquired by Mesot in the late 1970s along with a number of other agricultural implement producers in other European countries. International Plow held about a 20 percent market share in the 11 countries it served.

For the most part, Mesot's acquisitions had been mainly of family-owned and run businesses. This was certainly true for Morris. Don Cowles had been brought into Morris in September 1982, as the operations director. He had started his career in the British automotive industry but had moved to Morris from a position as managing director of a small machine tool company. This was an attractive move for Cowles, considering that it placed him within a large, multinational company that was known for leaving its various operations autonomous. Within such an environment, Cowles felt he could advance and grow.

Upon Cowles's arrival in September 1982, Morris was really a series of small companies, each with its own managing director. About 85 percent of sales were attributable to the companies involved with agricultural implements, but there were other companies that dealt with such products as silos and fences. Within the implement business there were several companies involved, each with a different responsibility (e.g., fabrication of components, final assembly, painting). They shipped components among themselves, incurring significant transport costs among 8 diverse locations and prompting numerous transfer price arguments. Within 6 weeks of his arrival as operations director, Don had proposed a major consolidation which called for manufacturing space to be pared from 407,000 square feet to 222,000 square feet, for the manufacturing headcount to be reduced from 480 to 380, but yet for production to increase from 600 units per week to 1,000 units per week. Cowles went further, as he felt that manufacturing was not only fat, but that it also suffered from a lack of controls. For example, in 1982, part numbers for the various components of a farm implement did not exist; the bills of material were essentially carried around in people's heads. This prompted Cowles to adopt a commercial production and inventory control software package.

The year 1983 was thus one of adapting to considerable change. It also was a year of confrontation with the union representing the warehouse workers (manufacturing was represented by another union). The warehouse union had historically been a strong one at Morris, and the productivity of warehouse workers had not budged much in years. To counter this situation, in negotiations with the union, Don Cowles had insisted on the adoption of an individual incentive pay scheme. In a showdown, the union relented, and within four days, the pick rate in the warehouse rose from 30 pieces/hour to 90 pieces/hour.

Despite such operational turnarounds, business and profitability continued to slip to break-even levels. International Plow headquarters in Copenhagen, Denmark, reacted by removing Morris's managing director, who was a member of the founding family. On December 1, 1983, Don Cowles was named to replace him. In quick succession, the "old order" of management exited, largely of its own accord. Of nine direct reports to Cowles in 1984, only three were holdovers from the prior top management.

THE FARM IMPLEMENT MARKET
IN THE UNITED KINGDOM

International Plow's strength was in the farm implements aftermarket. Farmers interested in replacing their own worn or broken plows, harrows, and other implements often approached dealers marketing International Plow's products, rather than returning to their original equipment dealers. International Plow had historically done little original equipment (OE) business with Europe's agricultural equipment producers, although there were plans to grow this business substantially. The size of the aftermarket depended on several factors, chief among them the tractor population and the performance characteristics of the farm implements equipment for new tractors. The tractor population in Europe in the early 1980s was not growing much at all, and of significant impact for the aftermarket, Ford, Deere, and others began selling longer-lasting implements with their new tractors. These facts combined to change a growth industry into a declining one, characterized by industry overcapacity and severe price competition. The total UK farm implements annual aftermarket sales dropped from 400,000 units in 1979 to 250,000 units five years later. In 1984, the aftermarket's volume decline and price cutting overwhelmed the cost cutting that Morris had initiated, with the result that Don Cowles's first year as the managing director ended with a loss of about £1,000,000.

This bleak situation was exacerbated by the nature of Morris's customer accounts. The United Kingdom was characterized by perhaps the most mature and sophisticated farm implements distribution system in Europe. Almost two thirds of the aftermarket was served by local dealers, as opposed to original equipment farm equipment dealers. These local dealers demanded both low prices and rapid deliveries from the farm implements manufacturers. One dealer chain, Farmers All (FA), was notorious for its lack of loyalty to anyone other than the lowest price supplier, and Morris had the misfortune of tying up about one third of its business with this low-margin customer.

This situation presented Morris with some intriguing strategic choices:

1. Continue to cut costs and hope that Morris could be better at it than the competition, maintaining the price competition in the market.
2. Pull out of the severe price competition by differentiating their products in some way that would be appreciated by the market.
3. Break the hold that FA had on the company, without losing too much revenue, and at the same time giving the FA problem to the competition.

The glimmer of a possible way out of the trap Morris found itself in began to shine through in 1984. Don Cowles, in part to remedy his own ignorance about the marketing and sales side of the business, had commissioned some market research. That market research showed that

British farmers would be willing to pay a slight premium for a product that was longer lasting and more effective than the traditional carbon steel products that then dominated the marketplace. By using alloy steels, the farm implement could be made longer lasting, and if painting, unnecessary with these more corrosion-resistant alloy steels, was foregone, the cost savings would just about balance out the cost increases of using the more expensive alloys. Thus was born the King Steel product. Morris gradually introduced it to the product line, one model at a time over many months, saving the formal launch of the entire product line until March 1985, when its inventories of carbon steel products had been reduced sufficiently.

The introduction of King Steel permitted Morris to begin differentiating its product from the competition. The company's relationship with FA had also put it in the position of having to provide product to local dealers with twice-a-week deliveries where the dealer could place its order as late as the day before delivery. This so-called twice-weekly–next-day service was logistically tough—it took months for Morris to master—and costly—it ate up the hard-won cost savings from the warehouse—but it was yet another means of differentiating Morris from the competition.

Thus, while 1984 was a lousy year for sales volume and profit, it did offer Morris some hope for the future. The King Steel product and twice-weekly–next-day service provided some product differentiation. The poor productivity of the warehouse had been, at least partially, addressed. And manufacturing costs had been slashed with the previous year's plant consolidation and the introduction of some production and inventory controls. Furthermore, Don Cowles had also acted to change the organization. Previously, Morris had been run as a group of four companies, each one evaluated as a profit center, with its own managing director. As the consolidation had proceeded in 1983, Cowles announced a centralization of the organization. Sales and marketing were pulled to the group level, and the managing directors were transformed into plant managers. This was a much cleaner and more effective organizational structure. (See the Morris organization chart, Exhibit 1.)

THE SITUATION IN COPENHAGEN

Mesot's tradition of autonomy for its various European subsidiaries came to an end in 1985 with the arrival in Copenhagen of Charlie Clotfelter as general manager for International Plow. Clotfelter, born in Ger-

EXHIBIT 1
INTERNATIONAL PLOW
Organization Chart for Morris Industries, circa 1984

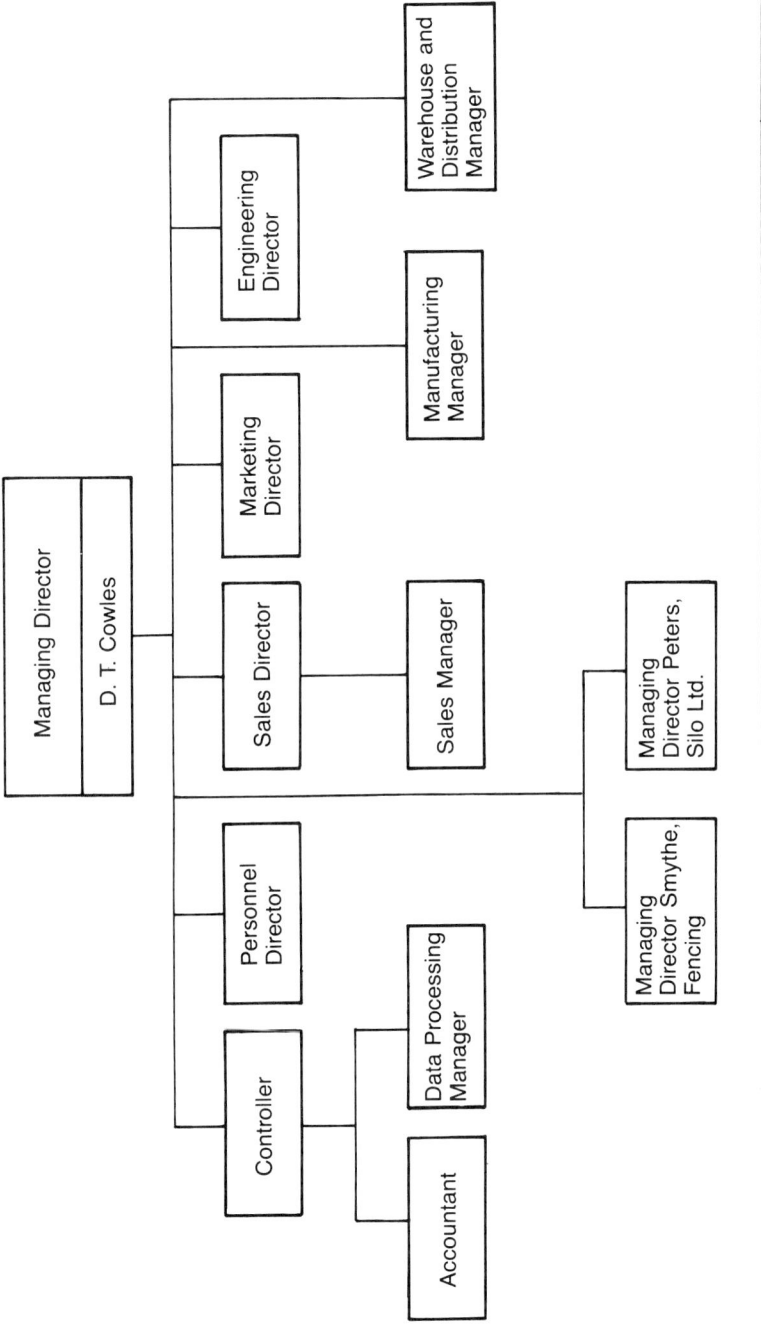

many but raised in the United States, joined International Plow from Ford Motor, where he had been involved in various international operations. The themes of industry overcapacity, severe price competition, and margin-cutting that plagued Morris in the UK were being played out all over Europe. It was clear that some new direction and some concerted action was needed.

Clotfelter was clearly willing to make some tough decisions. In Morris's case, for example, he approved a general price increase in the spring of 1985 that led the entire industry away from the brutal price-cutting that had characterized its recent history. Moreover, Clotfelter tackled the troublesome problem of Farmers All. There too, he approved raising prices, knowing full well that FA would drastically cut Morris's volumes. He was willing to stand firm for production at a profit, even if it meant significantly lower volumes. In fact, FA did reduce Morris's volume greatly (by 15–20 percent), but because prices had been raised, revenues did not decline as much, and furthermore, the low-cost FA products were now the competition's to cope with.

One of the things that struck Clotfelter upon his arrival at International Plow was the duplication of effort and capital among the country-specific subsidiaries, a duplication that was all the more costly in times of industry overcapacity. Each of the subsidiaries was responsible for its own purchasing, fabrication of components, assembly, and painting of farm implements. This decentralization, often with more than one aftermarket manufacturing location within a country, seemed to forego economies that might be achievable with some other arrangement.

It was also clear to Clotfelter that the intercompany shipment of farm implements could be improved. Intercompany shipments (say, from Hansen in Denmark to Morris in the UK) were necessary because a company like Morris did not produce agricultural implements that were compatible with all of the tractors that one might find on British farms. For the rarer or older tractor, often made elsewhere, a company like Morris would have to place an order with one of its sister companies. The sister companies, in part because margins were lower for intercompany shipments, tended to put lower priority on them than on shipments within their own territory, and this spawned ill will, and even some retaliation (e.g., a late delivery for a late delivery). Incoming intercompany shipments currently ran 27 percent of sales at Morris, the largest of any of the sister companies. Intercompany shipments were expected to grow as most European countries were becoming less dominated by their national tractor manufacturers. Moreover, as Copenhagen was pressing for reduced inventory levels throughout International Plow, the failure to make intercompany delivery of implements in timely fashion could easily thwart sales growth plans.

STRATEGIC CHANGES

In late 1985, in response to the prevailing industry trends and the situations within the various International Plow companies, Clotfelter pushed for the "Europeanization" of International Plow. This strategic redirection of the business, which went under the banner "one company, one product line," had three major components: marketing, organization, and manufacturing.

Marketing Changes

The chief marketing change contemplated was to standardize the product line offered throughout Europe. This had a whole host of implications: (1) common appearance and labelling of the product, (2) a common catalog, (3) a common brand name, (4) a common product numbering scheme for order-taking, and (5) fewer models offered. This last point deserves additional comment. The shape, size, and the precise fittings for the tractor were the key determinants of an implement's appropriateness for a particular tractor model. By clever design, International Plow could achieve the paradoxical result of at once having to manufacture fewer families of implements (a reduction from 109 to 27 "families"), but yet being able to cover 95 percent of the tractors on a country's farms, a higher percentage coverage than was currently the case.

Such changes were a lot to consider, and as Ron DeSoto (the Copenhagen-based director for aftermarket sales and marketing and an American who was transferred from Mesot about a year earlier) was quick to emphasize: "Marketing has no interest in commonizing anything unless it helps customers and our local sales representatives." As it was, DeSoto could see several benefits from standardizing the product line:

1. International Plow's coverage in any country would be broader and availability would improve at the same time. This was a plus given the diminishing importance of national makes within most

of Europe's home markets. International Plow could then tout its being the only supplier a retail outlet needs.
2. With common standards, the reliability and consistent quality of International Plow implements would improve. Echoing Morris's success with alloy steel implements, the marketing strategy for a pan-European product line called for an alloy steel line of products, dubbed the "Ally," that could satisfy the most demanding market in Europe (the German). Indeed, getting full European Economic Community (EEC) approval for the Ally in all its families was an important component of the strategy, and was in process. Charlie believed that what had been a "cheap and cheerful" market that was predominantly price-sensitive was in fact changing to value, quality and performance.

Marketing was thus enthusiastic about the standardization and what it could do for International Plow in the marketplace.

Organizational Changes

Consistent with the "one company, one product line" theme came changes to the current organizational structure where each country was its own autonomous unit, with full responsibility for marketing, sales, manufacturing, and distribution. A pan-European approach required a more centralized marketing and sales function. Accordingly, the revised organization called for the sales and marketing managers resident in a particular country to report directly to Copenhagen, although they would have continuing close ties to their fellow managers at their home site. With sales and marketing separated organizationally, the managing director's role was essentially reduced to manufacturing and distribution, and accordingly, the managing director title gave way to that of plant director. (See Exhibit 2 for the current organization chart at Morris and Exhibits 3 and 4 for before and after charts for International Plow.)

Manufacturing Changes

To address the perceived inefficiencies and duplications in manufacturing, the strategic redirection called for the establishment of two "components centers" for Europe that would process castings and forgings and ship them to assembly plants. This would save some manpower (it

EXHIBIT 2
INTERNATIONAL PLOW
Organization Chart for Morris Industries, circa 1987

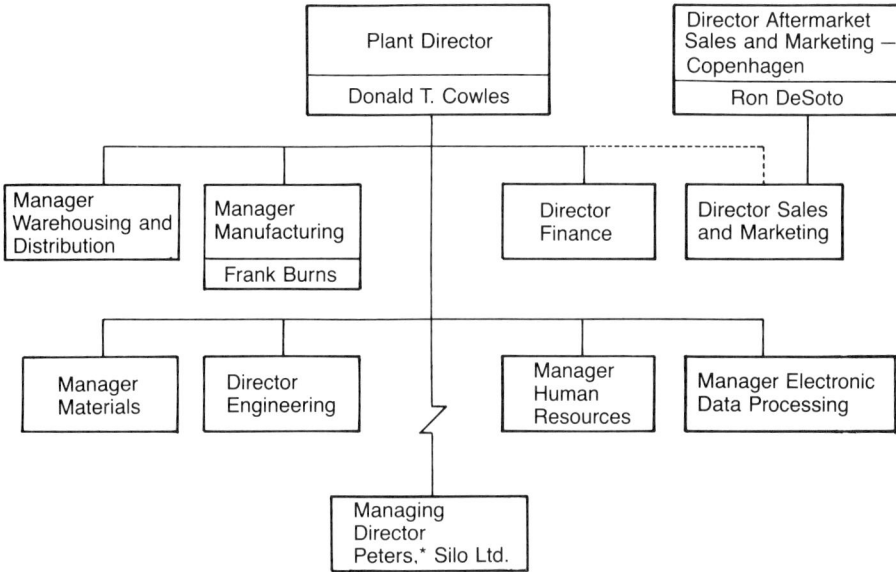

*Peters was scheduled for divestment.

EXHIBIT 3
INTERNATIONAL PLOW
Organization Chart for International Plow prior to June 1986

EXHIBIT 4
INTERNATIONAL PLOW
Organization Chart for International Plow, effective June 1986

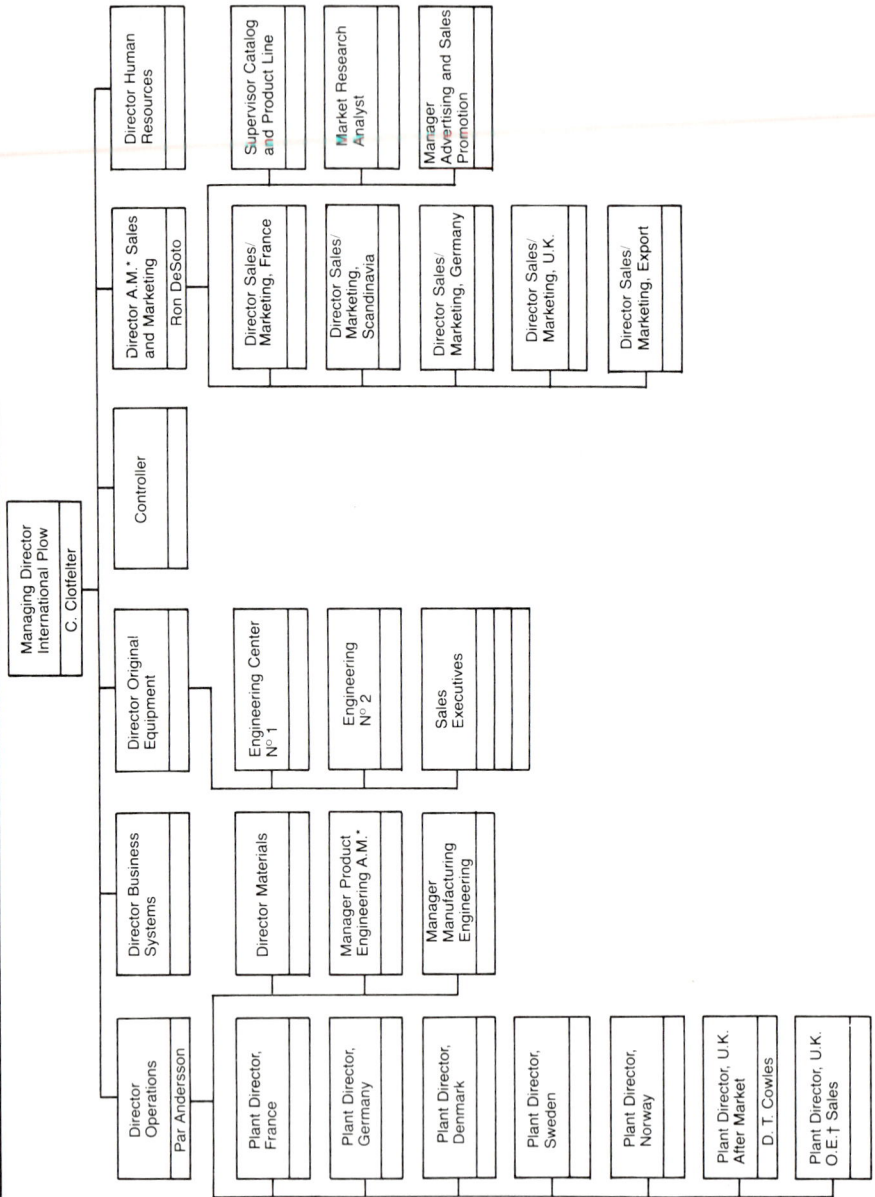

Managing Director International Plow — C. Clotfelter

Director Human Resources

Director A.M.* Sales and Marketing — Ron DeSoto

- Supervisor Catalog and Product Line
- Market Research Analyst
- Manager Advertising and Sales Promotion

- Director Sales/Marketing, France
- Director Sales/Marketing, Scandinavia
- Director Sales/Marketing, Germany
- Director Sales/Marketing, U.K.
- Director Sales/Marketing, Export

Controller

Director Original Equipment

- Engineering Center N° 1
- Engineering N° 2
- Sales Executives

Director Business Systems

Director Materials

Manager Product Engineering A.M.*

Manager Manufacturing Engineering

Director Operations — Par Andersson

- Plant Director, France
- Plant Director, Germany
- Plant Director, Denmark
- Plant Director, Sweden
- Plant Director, Norway
- Plant Director, U.K. After Market — D. T. Cowles
- Plant Director, U.K. O.E.† Sales

*After Market.   †Original Equipment

was estimated that 10 jobs at Morris could be eliminated) and it would concentrate purchases, thereby improving the odds for favorable purchase prices. It would also permit the acquisition of the best equipment possible for components production. In addition, production planning was expected to improve along with a dramatic increase in inventory turns.

The Scandinavian plants had worked on this basis, with components fed to the Norwegian and Swedish plants from the Hansen plant in Denmark. The new plans called for the Hansen plant to feed the German plant as well, and for the second components center to be established in France (The Damade Company) to feed both France and Great Britain. There was little question that France made a better choice than Great Britain for this second components center, as Damade already had casting and forging capabilities. The Morris facilities in the UK did not have this equipment; they had purchased castings and forgings on the open market.

Under the reorganization, the various plant directors reported to the director of operations in Copenhagen, Par Andersson, who had come to this job in October 1985 from his prior position as managing director of the Swedish company. Andersson, working with a group of three engineers in Copenhagen, campaigned across all the companies for inventory and throughout time reductions, for the consolidation of manufacturing and warehouse tasks so that workers could easily shift from one to the other, and for innovations in the process. Par acknowledged that the output per direct worker at Morris was high, but that the indirect labor to direct labor ratio was also high. Reducing that ratio was needed in order to make Morris even more efficient than it had become since Cowles had taken the reins.

THE STRATEGY CHANGE AS PERCEIVED BY MORRIS

Don Cowles recognized the irony of the Clotfelter strategy change. Two years earlier, Cowles himself had led an organizational change whereby (1) the managing directors of the several Morris companies were "demoted" to plant managers, and (2) the marketing and sales function was centralized. In some sense, then, the Clotfelter plan was similar to Cowles's plan but writ large for all of Europe, using alloy steel products that Morris had gained early experience with. Nevertheless, being on the receiving end of this strategic redirection was tough to take. No longer would he be a managing director.

Intellectually, however, Cowles had few gripes about the broad-brush aspects of the plan. He could see the merits of it. Nevertheless, he had some grave reservations about the process of implementing the strategy at International Plow and some of the particulars of the plan. Cowles did not relish having the new strategic redirection "sprung" on him and the other managing directors at a specially convened meeting. There had been no prior debate or opinion soliciting among the managing directors, those who would unquestionably be most affected by the change. Of course, he knew that the various managing directors would be unlikely to alter Copenhagen's stance, but a hearing on the matter seemed to him to be the fair and sporting thing to do.

Some of the plan's particulars were also troubling. For example, it was not clear to Cowles how he was to be evaluated. It did not seem proper that Morris remain a profit center, as marketing/sales were to be split off from operations. Such an arrangement would leave him as the one holding the responsibility, but not the authority. He was also unclear about who was going to manage the warehouse. Was that a manufacturing responsibility or a marketing/sales one? And what of human resources, discipline, and recruitment? Was Cowles to be responsible for these functions for marketing and sales as well?

Despite his initial pique towards the strategy change, Don Cowles was nevertheless committed to making it happen and to proving to Copenhagen that the steps already taken at Morris would lead to significant profitability in the years ahead.

THE CURRENT SITUATION AND SOME
LINGERING QUESTIONS

The year 1985 had seen a turnaround in Morris profitability. From a £1,000,000 loss the previous year, the company rebounded to a profit of £705,000.[1] The year 1986, while even more profitable (£2,550,000), was nevertheless a tough one. Don Cowles, at the suggestion of Jim Adams, Clotfelter's U.S.-based boss, had pursued yet another aggressive consolidation program. Into the former warehouse and paint facility, he

---

[1] In early 1987, £1 = 1.65 $U.S.

moved all of Morris's aftermarket production. In July-August, final assembly was moved to the old paint area and in November-December, fabrication was shifted to the so-called "well" area of the plant. This reduced space to 87,000 sq ft from the then-prevailing 222,000 sq ft used by manufacturing (see Exhibits 5 and 6). This space reduction was accompanied by an adoption of manufacturing cells (metal bending, cutting, and welding grouped together), the introduction of two-shift production, and the sourcing of some forgings from Damade in France. Finished goods inventory had been reduced to 65,000 units from almost twice that number, and work-in-process had been cut even more dramatically, as now there was no place to put it. Production throughput times had been cut from 12 weeks to 3 weeks. Manpower continued to decline through both attrition and redundancies. (Redundancies cost the company approximately 3 weeks' pay for every year of seniority held by the worker affected.) The manufacturing complement at the beginning of 1987 stood at 211. Indeed, the entire company had nearly been halved in size since 1982, from 1,036 to 576. (See Exhibit 7 for some relevant statistics describing Morris's change and progress.)

There had also been another confrontation with the warehouse work force. With the change to twice-weekly–next-day service, it was found that 65 percent of the week's orders came in on Monday and Tues-

EXHIBIT 5
INTERNATIONAL PLOW
Manufacturing Facilities Prior to Consolidation

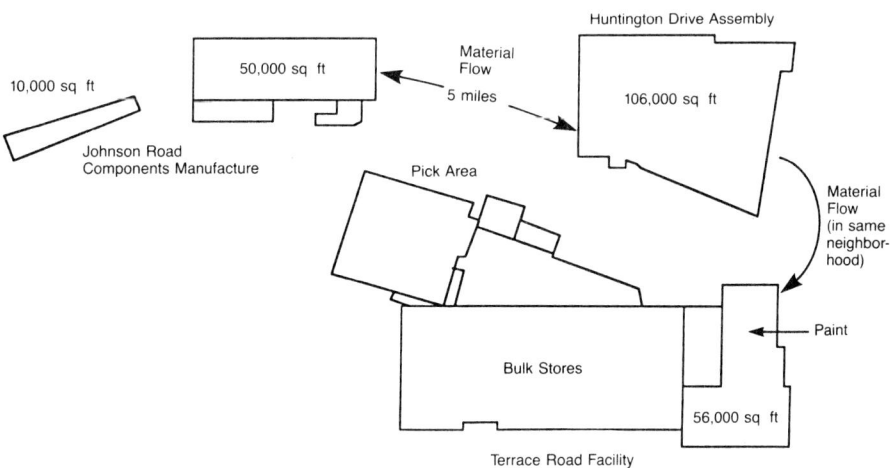

EXHIBIT 6
INTERNATIONAL PLOW
Postconsolidation Layout

Total Manufacturing Space (shaded)

Fabrication	31,000
Assembly	56,000
Total	87,000 sq ft

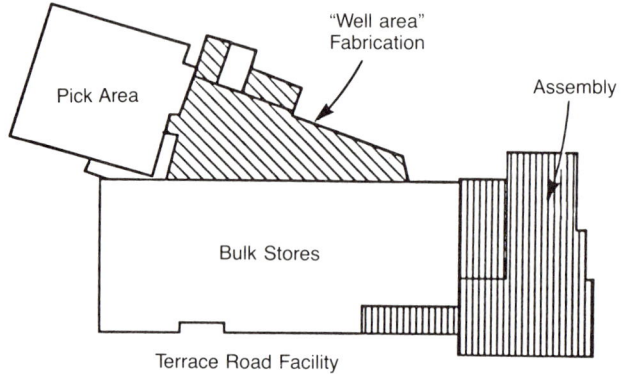

Pick Area — "Well area" Fabrication — Assembly — Bulk Stores — Terrace Road Facility

EXHIBIT 7
INTERNATIONAL PLOW
Some Relevant Statistics on Morris Industries
Headcount, by year, farm implements manufacture and distribution

1982		832
1983		860
1984		556
1985		551
1986	August	501
	December	441
1987	Target	383

Layoffs (redundancies) by date and area affected

Date	Area Affected	Number
December 1982	Manufacturing (2 plants closed)	205
July 1984	Warehouse (incentive scheme)	30
November 1984	Manufacturing (volume decline)	50
November 1984	Sales and marketing (reorganization)	15
February 1986	Manufacturing, warehouse, staff (Farmers All reduction)	40
August 1986	Manufacturing (first phase of consolidation)	10
November 1986	Manufacturing (second phase of consolidation)	40

EXHIBIT 7 (concluded)

Productivity comparisons by year and cost structure

Manufacturing (1982 = 100)

Year	Index of Production Output	Headcount	Index of Output per Worker-Year
1982	100.0	454	100.0
1983	102.5	358	127.5
1984	109.9	296	117.0
1985	123.8	290	193.5
1986	121.4	240	229.0
1987 (plan)	121.2	200	275.0

Distribution (1982 = 100)

Year	Index of Distribution Volume	Headcount	Index of Volume per Worker-Year
1982	100.0	223	100.0
1983	97.6	190	114.6
1984	94.4	161	131.1
1985	105.9	180	131.1
1986	105.5	170	138.4
1987 (plan)	106.1	140	168.9

Cost Structure

Direct material	48%
Direct labor	11%
Overhead	41%
	100%

day (Saturday was the biggest day of the week for the local dealers). In order to satisfy this peak demand without overmanning, it was necessary to alter the hours of the warehouse workers. For example, there was little for them to do in the early hours of a Monday morning, but there was plenty for them to do on a Monday evening. Accordingly, Cowles proposed a change in their hours of work which shifted their schedules to 10:30 A.M. to 7:30 P.M. This spawned a brief job action which forced management into the warehouse to pick parts for a few hours, but in the showdown, the warehouse workers agreed to the new schedule.

The year 1986 was also a year to digest some of the implications of Charlie Clotfelter's strategy change. For Don Cowles and his staff, there were a host of lingering questions. Some related to the nature of the relationship between the country-specific companies and the Copenhagen headquarters:

- What role would the plant managers have in companywide strategy formulation?
- How would innovation in products and processes be maintained?

This latter point was a particular concern for Frank Burns, Morris's manufacturing manager. He had seen his manufacturing engineering staff reduced from 16 to 3 and he wondered how International Plow was going to maintain its technological strengths in the face of both relative austerity and the reorganization. There was little history of sharing technology or ideas among the sister companies.

Other questions related to the relationships among the sister companies themselves:

- The reduction of the many specific shapes, sizes, and fittings for International Plow's products was to be accomplished by the development of a much reduced number of product families. How would the various product "families" be assigned among the sister companies? Not all products (e.g., plows, disc harrows) were likely to be produced by all the plants. Some decisions then had to be made about which ones were going to be made by which plants. What kind of equity would be maintained from plant to plant? Heretofore, Copenhagen had not had to worry about cross-country equity, as each country had been more or less on its own. Now it was, in part, up to headquarters to determine the relative sizes of the various sister companies through the assignment of specific products and the associated decisions of which plants would ship farm implements intercompany to which others.
- There was also concern at Morris for the quality of both parts and finished product being shipped in. Morris did not have any incoming inspection, but there had been some increasing concern about the quality of the goods received, and thus the potential need for some inspection. Once the components center was in place, would costly incoming inspection be necessary?

- There was even more concern about the ability of the sister companies to supply farm implements or components to the UK in timely fashion. Morris had purged its operations of substantial inventories and was moving towards just-in-time manufacturing (for example, through the introduction of bending-cutting-welding cells in final assembly). Erratic supply could destroy some of these gains or imperil the timely distribution of farm implements to the marketplace.
- Don Cowles had his own doubts about the advisability of the components center anyway. Would costs really be reduced, given admittedly higher transportation costs and the vagaries of exchange rates? Don did not think that the case for a French-based components center to feed the UK was airtight. In fact, he reasoned that if components were better off produced in that fashion, then why not entire farm implement assemblies. (The preliminary version of the capital appropriations request for the French component center indicated a payback of four years.)

No matter how these various lingering questions got resolved, one thing was sure in Don Cowles's mind. He could not, in good conscience, ask his work force to sacrifice any more. During the last set of redundancies there had been mutterings about management "letting down" the workers, and he felt that anything more would merely confirm that sentiment, perhaps even in his own eyes. In fact, the Morris human resources manager, Jack Warner, thought that any more than 10 additional redundancies would spark a "crisis."

Don Cowles was not the only one with lingering questions about the "Europeanization" of International Plow. Many in Copenhagen, including Charlie Clotfelter and Par Andersson, were just as concerned about the implementation of this strategic redirection for the company. They too were wrestling with the best way to proceed and how it would affect the sister companies like Morris.

Maillefer SA (A)

It was March 1980, the end of one challenge and the beginning of another for Jacques Bonjour. A party celebrating the end of the intensive Program for Executive Development at IMEDE in Lausanne, Switzerland, was still in progress, but Bonjour's mind was already considering the difficult task ahead of him. He had just accepted a new position as marketing manager for the MP Group (pipe machinery) of Maillefer SA, a leading Swiss manufacturer of equipment for the extrusion of plastic.

Although Maillefer had been for many years a major competitor in the cable machinery market, efforts over the past five years to extend this success into the pipe machinery market had not achieved very satisfactory results. As their new marketing manager, Bonjour was to be responsible for formulating a new strategy for the MP Group in the pipe machinery market. Specifically, his goal was to increase MP Group revenues from SFr 3.5 million[1] to over SFr 7.5 million, while directing activities towards products and markets where Maillefer could compete profitably.

As Jacques Bonjour left the IMEDE party, he thought back over Maillefer's history, how the MP Group came to exist in the first place, and what steps he should take in order to achieve the goals that had been established for the MP Group.

COMPANY BACKGROUND

In 1900, Charles L. Maillefer established a workshop in the old mill at Romainmôtier, a Swiss village in the hills near the French border. Maillefer SA, a privately-held Swiss company, originally manufactured machine-tool equipment for the forming, milling, and grinding of metal. In 1925, M. Maillefer and his two sons began to manufacture cable-making machines which wound multiple strands of wire into a single braided or twisted cable for mechanical or electrical use. Other machines were developed to coat or sheathe the completed cables with one or more layers

---

[1] In March 1980 one Swiss franc (SFr) = 0.57 $U.S.

of insulation, machines which formed the basis of Maillefer's current business.

With Europe at war, plastics became a widely used replacement for rubber. In 1941, Maillefer SA produced its first extrusion machine. This marked the beginning of what was to become a specialty: the manufacture of machines for the cable-making and plastics industries. In 1964, a new assembly workshop was built at Ecublens, ten minutes from Lausanne, and by 1972 all manufacturing, technical, and administrative functions were consolidated there. A subsidiary was established in the United States to manufacture and market throughout North America.

Maillefer specialized in sophisticated extruders and support equipment which originally were sold exclusively to the cable machinery market. Maillefer cable machines extruded a variety of plastic materials to coat or insulate wires and cables. Maillefer's products were known the world over for being able to extrude material which met the exacting specifications of suppliers to the electronics and telecommunications industries. As Monsieur Maillefer said,

> The performance level attained by Maillefer equipment is the result of painstaking research, innovative engineering and diligent attention to detail: the hallmarks of a company which, at all levels, is conscious of its role in the furthering of technological progress.

The high quality of the company's machines was measured by the dimensional precision (diameter and thickness), material homogeneity and surface quality of the extruded product, and the ease with which product specifications could be attained and maintained on line. Customers demanded precision in order to meet strict performance requirements (microelectronic wiring, life-sustaining surgical tubing) and/or to reduce the material cost of products manufactured in high volume (coaxial cable, water conduit). Such results were achieved by means of precise control of temperature, pressure, and rate of flow during the extrusion process. Maillefer extruders had always been known for their ability to accurately process a wider range of thermoplastics than those of other manufacturers.

By 1980, Maillefer was employing 450 people and was averaging sales of 140 extruders annually, 80 of these complete with line equipment. Revenues were approximately SFr 80 million, of which 90 percent was export sales. However, the cyclical nature of the cable industry made specialization risky. Management wished to diversify operations, which had led them as early as 1969 to investigate the market for pipe extrusion machinery, the idea being to adapt their extrusion technology from cable machinery and to generate new sales.

THE MP GROUP

The MP Group was first set up in 1970 as an independent subsidiary which would market equipment to manufacturers of extruded pipe. Since pipe and cable both required extrusion equipment which was similar in design and function, it was presumed that Maillefer could anticipate additional sales of extrusion machines and line equipment by transferring their extrusion technology from one market to the other. Before long, it became apparent to MP's commercial staff and Maillefer's technical people that a subsidiary relationship was impractical; thus in 1975 MP was brought in-house as a small, informally structured group. As one manager in Ecublens put it,

> The main idea in starting MP was to have a broad diversification, beginning with the pipe market segment, then eventually going on to include a range of extruder equipment for additional segments.

In fact, however, the undertaking had proven to be quite complex.

Jacques Bonjour, meanwhile, had been working from 1966 to 1979 as an engineer in the German-speaking part of Switzerland, as well as abroad. Then, in the autumn of 1979, he entered IMEDE's Program for Executive Development. It was at this time that he learned about the interesting and exciting challenge at Maillefer SA as marketing manager for the MP Group. After discussions with Maillefer's management, Bonjour accepted the appointment and moved into his new office in March 1980. He could have no illusions about the task ahead of him, for it had been clearly spelled out in a policy memo issued before his arrival:

> General management has decided not only to keep the MP Group, but to develop it, finding realizable diversification and seeking new growth. This decision has been made despite the fact that sales for the first part of 1980 are weak, 25 percent below the objective.

In 1980 the MP group was staffed by only six people. In addition to Bonjour, Franz Jermann handled sales, assisted by one other person. Three additional people provided technical support. As the organization chart in Exhibit 1 illustrates, MP relied upon the corporate organization for most services. In 1979, MP accounted for sales of 20 installations

EXHIBIT 1
MAILLEFER SA (A)
Organization Chart

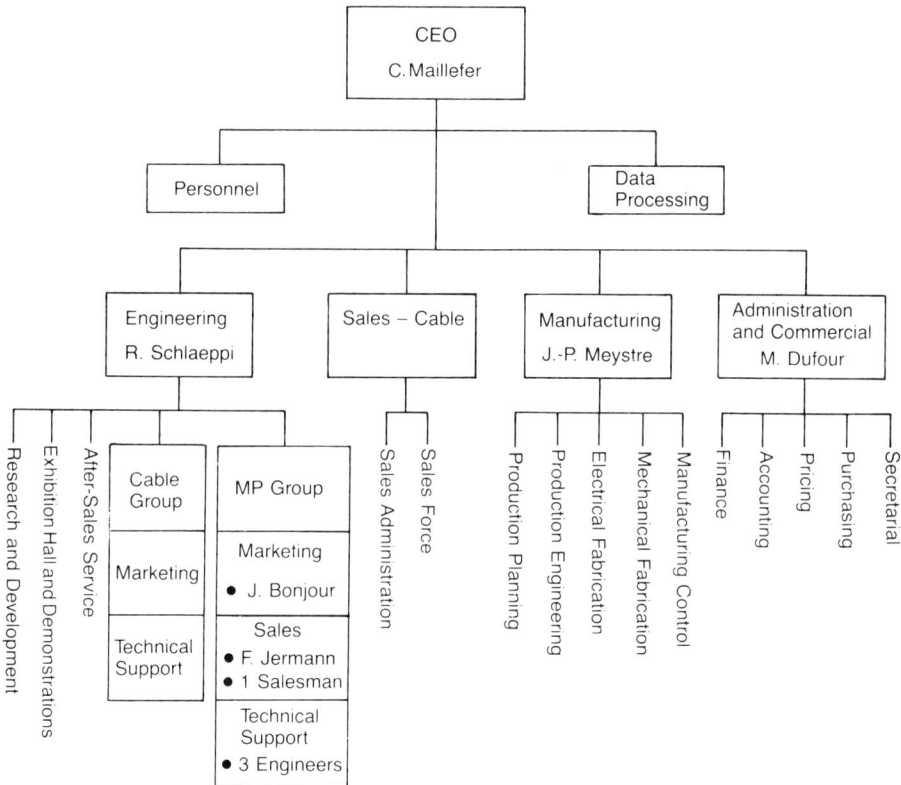

totaling SFr 3.5 million, all for plastic pipe. All the engineering and manufacturing was being done at the main facility in Ecublens.

THE EXTRUSION PROCESS

In plastic extrusion, the raw material first had to be transformed from
a solid to a molten state. As shown in Exhibit 2, an extrusion machine
consisted of a hopper, barrel/screw assembly, and extruder head. The
hopper fed solid plastic pellets into the barrel, where they were heated
to melting point by a combination of controlled heating and cooling ele-

EXHIBIT 2
MAILLEFER SA (A)
Plastic Extrusion Machine

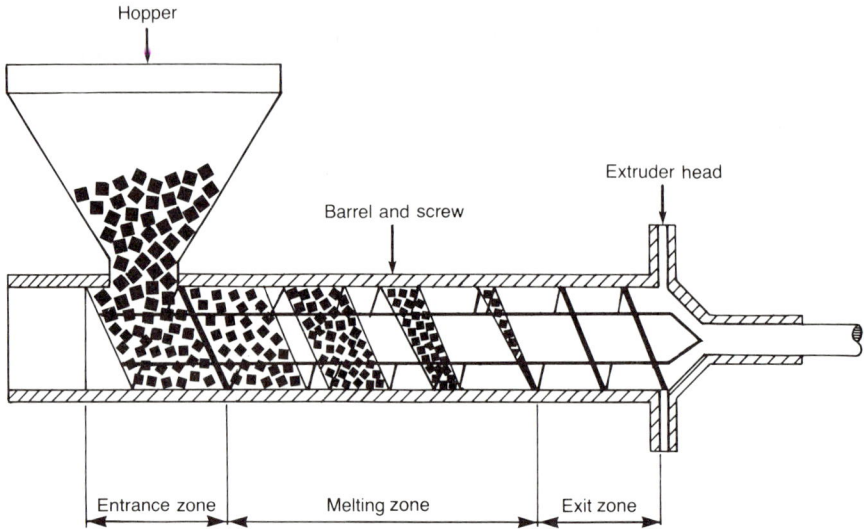

ments as well as by the mechanical energy produced by screw rotation. The screw moved the plastic towards the extruder head while mixing it thoroughly. The head then delivered a controlled flow of uniform, molten plastic of the desired consistency. The shape of the head varied depending on the task, such as coating a wire or forming a pipe.

As shown in Exhibit 3, an extruder operated as the main component of an extrusion line. To extrude pipe, plasticized material was pumped out in a steady flow by the extruder screw. While molten, it passed through the extruder head and vacuum calibration trough which formed the desired size and shape of pipe. The hot plastic cooled and set as it moved through one or more cooling troughs. A motorized haul-off provided the drive mechanism for the line.

The speed at which the haul-off drew the pipe away from the extruder head had to be precisely synchronized with the rate at which the rotating screw fed material into the system. Flexible pipe was then fed to a coiler, where it was wound on large spools while rigid pipe was cut to the proper length and stacked on a dump table. Another option was the application of an identifying stripe or code on line. Alternatively, two or more extruders could be integrated into a single line in order to perform layering of several plastics in a single pass.

EXHIBIT 3
MAILLEFER SA (A)
A Pipe Extrusion Line

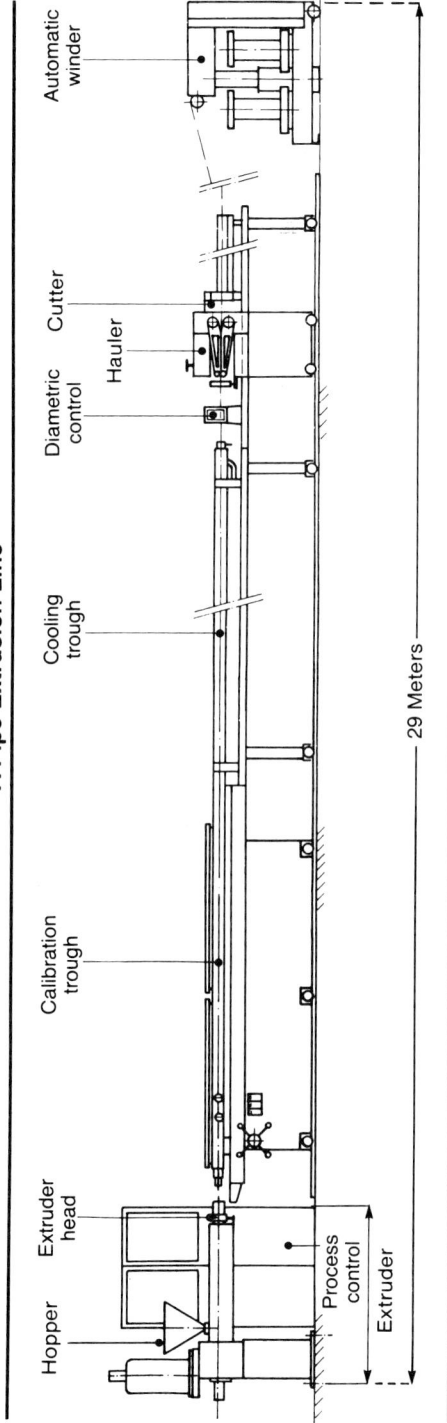

A critical component of plastic extrusion equipment was the extruder screw. The screw performed several functions. In addition to transporting material through the barrel where heating, mixing, and pressurizing occurred, the plastic being processed had to be transformed steadily in order to maintain homogeneity, a precise temperature, and a continuous flow to the extruder head. Screw design was one of Maillefer's recognized strengths in research and engineering.

Maillefer's "BM Screw" (see Exhibit 2) was a patented design which made up the core of all the company's extrusion machines. The BM Screw revolutionized the industry when it was announced in 1960. Maillefer used a double-spiral design which effectively divided the barrel into three zones: entrance, melting and exit. Only molten plastic of the proper consistency could reach the extruder head. Advantages of the BM Screw were its ability to control temperature precisely in the barrel as well as at the extruder head. Even at a high output rate, the BM Screw was able to maintain material homogeneity and allow for rapid changes in materials or colors without shutting down the line. Screw and barrel geometries were custom-designed to accommodate the individual characteristics of each family of plastics and their respective processing rates.

Extruders were also designed to match the processing task at hand. Small extruders processed limited amounts of polymer, while the largest extruders were capable of handling high volumes. Exhibit 4 presents a breakdown, by screw diameter size and number of units, of extruder

EXHIBIT 4
MAILLEFER SA (A)
Extruder Machinery Installed Annually in Western Europe, 1977–1979,
by Screw Diameter Size

Extruder Screw Size (mm)	Units Installed per Year	SFr/Year (millions)	Share of Units (%)	Share of (%)
30–60	1,350	95	30%	18%
60–75	1,045	89	23	17
75–100	903	104	20	20
100–140	800	132	18	26
140–180	300	59	7	12
180 and over	102	37	2	7
	4,500	516	100%	100%

Source: The Extrusion Machinery Market in Europe, Frost & Sullivan, 1979, New York, N.Y.

machinery installed annually in Western Europe during the period 1977–1979. Screw diameters ranged from 25 mm to over 180 mm and corresponded to the raw material processing rating (in kg/hr) of a given extruder.

Two variables were critical in determining how closely extruded pipe met specifications. The first was the consistency of the rate of draw by the haul-off. This had to be synchronized with the rate at which the extruder screw fed material into the system. Deviations in speed resulted in varying wall thicknesses, which reduced the strength of the pipe. Secondly, the vacuum pressure maintained at the extruder head had to be constant in order to insure uniformity in pipe diameter. Any variation in diameter increased the amount of scrap, thereby reducing efficiency and raising the costs of production.

A real-time process control system was used to control these variables during extrusion. The system contained the hardware and software required to monitor production. Sensors monitored barrel and screw temperature, head temperature and pressure, screw rotation speed, and rate of draw by the haul-off. Other sensors measured the

EXHIBIT 5
MAILLEFER SA (A)
Pipe Extrusion Line Components

	Swiss Francs (000)	Percent Total Price
Extruder		
BM-80 extruder	120	27%
Extruder motor and drive	55*	12
Control cabinet and extruder control	25*	6
	200	45%
Line		
Line process control	50*	11%
Extruder head and tooling	20	5
Calibrating trough	30	7
Cooling troughs	35	8
Hauler	35	8
Cutter	20	5
Winder	50	11
	240	55%
Total extruder and line components	440	100%

Note: Example assumes a BM-80 extruder with standard line components.
*Denotes electronic and process control components which could have higher costs for specialized lines.

thickness and diameter of the extrusion. The data were fed to the process control unit which was able to perform the adjustments to maintain tolerances during operation. Process control was a major part of the total cost of an extrusion line (see Exhibit 5) and played a central role in meeting the increasingly strict product specifications being demanded by pipe manufacturers.

THE EXTRUSION MACHINERY INDUSTRY IN EUROPE

As shown in Exhibits 6 and 7, approximately 4,500 extruders per year were installed in European plants during the period 1977–1979. This represented an annual investment of SFr 516 million. (By comparison, an estimated 1,400 extruders were installed annually in the USA during the same period.) Note that the SFr 516 million figure refers only to extru-

EXHIBIT 6
MAILLEFER SA (A)
Extrusion Machinery Installed Annually in Western Europe, by Country

	Actual (1977–79)	Forecast (1980–84)	Forecast (1985–89)
West Germany	107.6*	134.2	180.5
France	78.1	99.6	132.5
Italy	116.0	148.2	185.0
United Kingdom	65.4	83.9	114.0
Belgium/Luxembourg	15.7	19.4	24.7
Netherlands	20.8	25.8	31.5
Denmark	7.6	9.3	11.1
Ireland	3.8	5.0	6.9
Total EEC	415.0	525.4	686.2
Switzerland	10.3	12.5	15.4
Austria	11.9	14.6	18.3
Spain	39.2	53.5	71.0
Sweden	14.6	19.0	24.7
Norway	9.5	11.9	14.8
Finland	3.6	4.2	5.3
Portugal	3.8	4.8	8.0
Greece	6.5	8.8	13.3
Turkey	1.6	2.4	3.2
Total non-EEC	101.0	131.7	174.0
Total	516.0	657.1	860.2

*Million SFr
Source: The Extrusion Machinery Market in Europe, Frost & Sullivan, 1979, New York, N.Y.

EXHIBIT 7
MAILLEFER SA (A)
Extrusion Machinery Installed Annually in Western Europe, by Application

	Actual (1977–79)		Forecast (1980–84)		Forecast (1985–89)	
	Cost*	Units	Cost*	Units	Cost*	Units
Film machinery	130.7	1,141	171.1	1,494	229.1	2,001
Sheet machinery	63.9	557	87.4	763	123.1	1,075
Pipe machinery	118.1	1,031	147.5	1,288	188.5	1,646
Wire and cable	59.2	516	67.2	587	79.3	692
Coating and laminating	45.3	395	53.8	470	65.7	574
Profile extrusion	26.0	226	33.9	296	45.6	398
Compounding/recycling	52.6	459	71.4	623	98.0	856
Other extrusion	20.2	175	24.8	216	30.9	269
Total	516.0	4,500	657.1	5,737	860.2	7,511

*Million SFr
Note: Market size (SFr) counts extruders only in Europe. Counting line equipment and other export markets, Maillefer estimated that the numbers above represented 25% of their available market potential in cable and 33% in pipe. The number of units is calculated by dividing the cost by the weighted average extruder price of SFr 114,455 from Exhibit 4.
   Source: The Extrusion Machinery Market in Europe, Frost & Sullivan, 1979, New York, N.Y.

ders and related control equipment. Additional line equipment offered significant additional sales potential. It was estimated that the extruder represented 30–50 percent of the price for a complete extrusion line, depending on the type, and that half of all extruders were sold as part of a complete line.

   The extrusion market consisted of seven major segments (see Exhibit 7): manufacturing machinery to produce plastic film, sheet, pipe, and profiles; machinery to coat wire or cable; machinery to laminate paper or synthetics; and machinery to perform compounding (preparing polymer or recycling plastic). Maillefer competed in two segments: extruders for coating wire or cable and for extruding pipe.

   The market was expected to grow at an average annual rate of 5 percent during the 1980s. This was down considerably from an average annual rate in excess of 10 percent experienced during the 1970s. The highest individual growth was predicted for compounding equipment and sheet extruders (8 percent), the lowest in wire and cable machinery (4 percent). Pipe extrusion equipment was expected to grow at 6.3 percent. Due to the recession, however, industry forecasts for extruder installations in 1980 had already been revised down to 3,500 units.

PIPE EXTRUSION MACHINERY

Pipe extrusion machinery was the second largest market in the extrusion machinery industry. It accounted for sales of approximately 1,000 machines in 1977–1979, worth SFr 118.1 million. Line equipment accounted for an additional SFr 135 million in sales.

Plastic pipe was extruded in innumerable forms and used in as many different ways. Around one million metric tons of polymer were processed into plastic pipe in Europe each year. Sizes ranged from tiny 1 mm diameter precision tubing to water conduit as large as 1,400 mm in diameter. Industry analysts classified pipe into three main categories: small pipe, 1–50 mm; medium pipe, 50–225 mm; and large pipe, 225–600 mm plus.

Ideally, the scale of downstream line equipment would also be standardized into comparable classifications, so that line equipment would match extruder size, material processing volume and speed, and so on. This was not the case so far, however, and manufacturers had to provide a continuous range of sizes for haulers, cooling troughs, and so on. Even basic dimensions were difficult to standardize. For example, pipe extrusion production lines were much longer than other extrusion lines, since there were so many downstream components which had to be integrated. Integration was especially critical in markets where precise tolerances were required.

Materials

Hard PVC accounted for the bulk of processed tonnage. It was used for the large water mains, simple conduit, and sewerage mains required by the building and construction trades (see Exhibit 8). At the beginning of 1980, hard PVC still remained the most suitable and competitive material in the large-diameter pipe range (225 mm plus). But, especially outside the construction business, other materials were proving to be more suitable.

High density polyethylene (HDPE) was being used more and more frequently for pipe in the medium-size range, such as high-pressure gas or water pipe. At the same time, PA, an expensive engineering plastic, was being used with excellent results for pipe in the small-diameter range, the "precision pipe" needed for automotive and industrial purposes. Flexible medical tubing, requiring precise dimensions for use in expensive, sophisticated equipment such as dialysis machines, also

EXHIBIT 8
MAILLEFER SA (A)

Dimensional Tolerances & Processing Speeds for Four Classes of Pipe Application

Description	Example Raw Material	Raw Material Price (SFr/kg)	Outside Diameter (mm)	Tolerance (mm)	Thickness (mm)	Tolerance (mm)	Line Speed (meters/min)
Water conduit (250–1400 mm range)	Hard PVC	1.90	250	±2.5	10.0	+3.0	5
Pressurized water and gas (10–250 mm range)	HDPE*	2.50	10–32	±0.3	2.0	+0.4	30–60
			110	±1.0	22.8	+2.5	10
			250	±2.3	10.0	+1.2	10
Precision automotive (5–25 mm range)	PA*	12–15	6–11	±.05	1.0	+.03	60
			12–18	±.075	1.2	+.035	60
			19–22	±.1	1.4	+.04	60
Medical tubing (1–10 mm range)	Soft PVC	3.50	1.8	±.05	0.5	+.025	300
			4.0	±.05	0.5	+.025	250
			9.0	±.05	1.2	+.03	250

*HDPE, high density polyethylene PA, polyamide (nylon).

used special engineering plastics, but was increasingly being made with soft PVC.

Customers

Some customers purchased machines for in-house use, while others were custom or contract processors. In-house extrusions were made by manufacturers for use in their own products. This required that they have sufficient volume to justify the large investment in equipment and skilled personnel. Custom and contract processors performed work for smaller organizations and/or specialized in applications requiring high precision or specialized engineering activity. The equipment selected was based on the prerequisites of their customers, who then used the extruded pipe for a variety of purposes: construction, public works, precision products, etc.

Sewerage and Water Conduit

This is a commodity item, available in standard sizes, used for piping water into residential and commercial neighborhoods. Conduit for water mains started at 400 mm diameter and ranged up to the 1400 mm diameter size used in special public works projects. Conduit in smaller diameters (in the 250–400 mm range) was used to link individual residences to water mains, as well as for sewerage, storm runoff, and drainage.

Hard PVC was the material most used for conduit. It was inexpensive, yet also had characteristics which provided strength and excellent resistance to the elements. However, the raw material, which came in powdered form, was difficult to process because of its hardness. To alleviate the problem, manufacturers had developed twin-screw machines.

Large extruders, which had the capacity to process the large volume of material required, had to be used. That meant the line operated very slowly, since no more than 5 meters of pipe could be extruded per minute.

In these large applications, the emphasis was on the efficient use of raw material. A significant amount of raw material could be saved by reducing diameter and thickness within given tolerances. In addition, scrap losses could be reduced by minimizing the amount of production which was not within these tolerances. Line equipment had to be large enough to handle such bulky pipe. In fact, for conduit over 400 mm in diameter, the sheer size of cooling troughs, haulers, and cutters began to outweigh the extruder in engineering, design, and manufacturing complexity.

Pressure Pipe

Pressure pipe was used in buildings, laboratories, and industrial machinery for the distribution of water or gas under high pressure (e.g., circulating cooling water to a diesel engine). Reliability was the end user's primary concern, because a break could result in machinery shutdown, fire, or danger to workers. The material used could be low or high density polyethylene. The superior characteristics of HDPE for flexibility and strength made up for the higher price of these materials as compared with that of hard PVC. Pressure pipe was of medium diameter (32–225 mm) and was produced on single-screw extruders at relatively low speeds (10 to 30m/min). Even over 225 mm, HDPE pressure pipe could be used as a substitute for hard PVC.

The volume of material used for medium-diameter pipe was less than for conduit, but the amount was still significant. Small variations in dimensional tolerance affected material usage; therefore, precise control over production parameters could produce savings. As an example, reduction by 0.1 mm of the average thickness for a tube 32 mm in diameter and 2 mm thick (assume production for 3,000 hours at 12m/min) would save 16,000 kg.

Careful, even mixing by the screw of the material as it moved rapidly through the barrel was essential to ensure a homogeneous result. If it were not homogeneous, the finished pipe would not perform reliably under pressure.

Medical Pipe

This tubing was used by hospitals and surgeons providing care to patients. Uses included intravenous feeding lines, blood delivery, catheters and air or food tubes. During use, the plastic remained in contact with the patient's skin or internal organs. Often, the tubes provided life-supporting functions. Pipe which was thinner than specification or which varied in diameter could burst under use. Pipe with a rough or brittle surface texture was more prone to rejection by the body or could cause infection. Reinsertion of feeding or blood tubes was traumatic for the patient. As a result, users of medical pipe demanded rigorous specifications not only for size and shape, but for composition and surface texture as well.

Medical pipe was of small diameter (1–10 mm), produced at high speed (up to 300m/min), but had to meet strict specifications for inside diameter, outside diameter, and wall thickness. The most frequently used materials were soft PVC and engineering plastics. In production, a consistent output within the specifications had to be maintained for hours of continuous operation. Specifications for material uniformity and surface quality of the extruded pipe made production at a high rate difficult to achieve. However, a high level of output was necessary for an extrusion line producing very small-diameter pipe to be economically feasible.

The amount of raw material processed on medical pipe lines tended to be low, making reduction of raw material consumption a secondary consideration. Nevertheless, economy was possible, depending on how carefully the extrusion line was operated and the level of control maintained. For example a reduction by .02 mm of the thickness of a tube 4 mm in diameter and .5 mm thick (assume production for 2,000 hours at 120m/min) would save over 11,000 kg.

COMPETITION

There were 92 manufacturers of extruders in Western Europe in 1980, but only a dozen leaders in the field with strong international reputations. In several cases, they were part of large manufacturing concerns which built other machinery for the plastics industry in addition to extruders. Others, privately owned and moderate in size like Maillefer, concentrated exclusively on the manufacture of plastic extruders and related line equipment. Some of the producers specialized in supplying one or two extrusion processes, while others would cover the whole range of processes. The trend seemed to be towards specialization in extrusion processes (cable, sheet, etc.), in materials (PVC, HDPE, etc.), and in applications. Other factors differentiating manufacturers' equipment included the ease with which such operations as start-up, shutdown, and material changes could be effected, the control over the process during operation, and the level at which both the extrusion line and process controls were automated.

Most of Europe's manufacturers (78) were located in the four largest countries (Germany, UK, France, and Italy). The 32 manufacturers located in Italy were mostly small firms which mainly produced simple low-cost machines, bought by local processors supplying the building and construction trades. The others all provided some degree of competition. However, in assessing Maillefer's strongest competition, Bonjour directed his attention to the leaders among Germany's 24 extruder manufacturers. He believed it was essential to maintain a performance level as well as a reputation for quality which would equal or surpass German manufacturers in the marketplace. The principal top-of-the-line German competitors were Reifenhauser, Krauss Maffei, and Battenfeld. Exhibit 9 compares the products and prices among these competitors and Maillefer.

Reifenhauser

Reifenhauser immediately stood out as one of the leading companies specializing in extrusion machinery. In 1979 they had 1,100 employees and sales valued at SFr 83.2 million. An estimated 35 percent of this figure was in extruders, the rest auxiliary line equipment. As one of the oldest established producers, Reifenhauser supplied extrusion process equipment from small cable and pipe machines to larger extruders for pipe, film, compounding, etc., concentrating on the higher quality, higher priced end of the market. They also were already well established in a broad-based international market.

In 1979, Reifenhauser produced 288 machines, one quarter of which were twin-screw machines for processing hard PVC. The rest were single-screw machines in the screw-diameter range of 30 mm–150 mm which directly competed with Maillefer's product line. Reifenhauser's prices were, on average, lower than Maillefer's.

Krauss Maffei

Krauss Maffei was part of Fredrich Flick Industrieverwaltung, Germany's 30th largest industrial enterprise and a multiproduct giant among machinery manufacturers. As part of the Plastics Machinery Division, Krauss Maffei accounted for extrusion machinery sales of SFr 27.4 million, an estimated 40 percent of this amount in extruders, the rest in line equipment. In addition to single-screw extruders and complete lines for they had developed twin-screw extruders capable of handling PVC powder in high volume, and had recently manufactured a three-screw planetary extruder.

EXHIBIT 9

MAILLEFER SA (A)

Product and Price Comparison

Manufacturer	Extruder Model*	Screw Diameter (mm)	Output (Kg/Hr)	Price (Swiss Francs)	Extruder Height (mm)	Materials Processed	Applications
Maillefer (single screw)	1. BM-30	30	12–25	57,700	1,000	Soft PVC	Pipe, cable
	2. BM-45	45	35–60	80,100		LDPE‡	
	3. BM-60	60	70–150	125,400		HDPE	
	4. BM-80	80	190–250	200,000		EP†	
	5. BM-120	120	235–550	242,900			
	6. BM-150	150	370–760	288,100			
(twin screw)	BD-84	84 × 2	300–400		1,000	Hard PVC	Pipe, compounding
	BD-112	112 × 2	700–800				
Reifenhauser (single screw)	1. ST30	30	10–15	46,200	1,050	Soft PVC	Pipe, cable film, general extrusion
	2. RT121	50	70–100	62,500	450 or 1,000	LDPE	
	3. RT281	70	120–200	83,100	650 or 1,150	HDPE	
	4. RT801	90	240–320	120,000	750 or 1,150	EP	
	5. RT1651	120	450–800	188,900	750 or 1,150		
	6. RT1801	150	600–1000	224,800	1,150		
(twin screw)	BT70	70 × 2	80–150		1,150	Hard PVC	Pipe, profile compounding
	BT100	100 × 2	300–450				
	BT130	130 × 2	450–700				
	BT150	150 × 2	500–1100				

Maker (type)	Model	Screw diameter (mm)	Output range (kg/h)			Materials	Applications
Krauss Maffei (single screw)	1. EC138	35	10–14	43,300	1,000	HDPE	Pipe, profile, sheet, compounding
	2. EC200	50	30–50	60,900		LDPE	
	3. KME60	60	90–150	80,300		EP	
	4. KME90	90	240–320	121,200			
	5. KME125	125	500–600	187,000			
(twin screw)†	KMD90	90 × 2	300–400		1,000	Hard PVC	Pipe, profile
	KMD120	120 × 2	500–700				
Battenfeld (single screw)	2. Uni-45	45	45–80	68,100	1,160	HDPE	Pipe, profile, sheet, film, compounding
	3. Uni-60	60	50–220	92,300		LDPE	
	4. Uni-90	90	250–350	135,600		Soft PVC	
	5. Uni-120	120	200–700	201,600			
	6. Uni-150	150	250–950	239,200			
(twin screw)	Exi-90	90 × 2	160–600		1,160	Hard PVC	Pipe, profile, compounding
	Exi-130	130 × 2	700–1600				
	Exi-160	160 × 2	1200–2400				

*1,2,3,4,5,6 designate comparable machines.
†Engineering plastics.
‡Low-density polyethylene.

In 1979, Krauss Maffei produced 120 machines, 20 percent of these being twin-screw machines for hard PVC. Their smaller single-screw machines were used to extrude pipe and profiles, while larger machines were also used for compounding and sheet extrusion. Prices were comparable to Reinfenhauser's.

Battenfeld

Battenfeld was part of Schloemann-Siemag, well-known for their heavy industrial equipment used in steel milling and manufacturing. Although Battenfeld was primarily producing injection molding machinery, they had recently moved into extruders suitable for all pipe applications and lines. Battenfeld's sales in 1979 totaled SFr 357 million, of which SFr 71.4 million was in extruders and line equipment. Bonjour estimated that 30 percent of this figure represented extruders, the rest line equipment. Battenfeld's resources for technical and commercial support were extensive: in addition to 2,300 employees, they were able to draw on the experience of Gloenco, a British extruder manufacturer they had acquired in 1978, as well as various other holdings in plastics engineering and downstream line equipment.

Battenfeld manufactured and installed 132 extruders in 1979; 65 percent were single-screw machines in the screw diameter range of 45–120 mm, the rest larger single-screw and twin screw machines. Battenfeld's single-screw extruders performed well processing LDPE and HDPE in small and medium diameters at high speed. Larger single-screw machines (120 and 150 mm) were used to produce pressure and nonpressure pipe in HDPE and soft PVC up to 600 mm diameter.

MARKET TRENDS

Traditionally, small local processors had supplied most of the simple, low-cost plastic pipe (i.e., large-diameter conduit) as well as medium-diameter general-purpose piping such as garden hose. Technological requirements for the design of extruders and line equipment were straightforward, which meant that the delivery of equipment was rapid and the availability of spare parts was relatively assured. Reliable delivery and service influenced the decision to place an order. Manufacturers of extruders for this segment of the market were widely spread, especially in the countries of southern Europe where this equipment was most important. Where advanced extrusion techniques were required, specialization among extruder manufacturers was becoming a significant trend in the market. As a result of the economic decline of the late seventies, many manufacturers in Germany, France, and England were concentrating their efforts on machines for specific applications and with material where they had unique skills. In this way, they hoped to carve out a special niche and achieve growth by gaining a reputation in a field of expertise.

In order to do this, machines had to be specialized, as different raw materials varied with respect to their physical, chemical, and thermal properties. Thus hard PVC tended to be processed on twin-screw extruders which could process this dense powder more uniformly. In fact, the ability to process hard PVC had become a mark of technical distinction among manufacturers supplying the medium- and large-diameter segments. Likewise, auxiliary line equipment, such as winders, markers, or specialized attachments, had to be adapted to the specific dimensions and characteristics of the various extruded products.

The relative trade-off which customers made between cost and performance varied, depending on the application. Producers of generic products such as garden hose or water conduit competed on price. Because they processed large tonnages, high output and reduced scrap were the leading criteria in selecting an extrusion line. Producers of precision extrusions for medical and industrial products were more concerned with an extruder's ability to provide a rigid tolerance for diameter and wall thickness. This tolerance also had to be maintained through long production runs without needing subsequent off-line inspection procedures.

Regardless of the application, adherence to strict tolerances resulted in a reduction in material usage and waste which meant an increased yield per kilogram of raw material. This had always been important on lines which processed large tonnage, but now even on low-volume precision lines, processors were realizing that small improvements in the control of the extrusion process could reduce costs. More and more frequently, precision pipe processors were expecting higher productivity as well as precision through better control of production parameters and less manual intervention. Due to escalating raw material and labor costs, automation of the production process (e.g., computerized process control) and of the line (e.g., automatic winders) began to increase. However, with the plastic extrusion industry continuously changing, processors wanted flexibility as well. One plastics processor summed up his needs:

> We need the possibility to manufacture with a high degree of reproducibility, products which meet more stringent standards, at higher production rates, with less manual intervention, less nominal material consumption and less scrap. In terms of flexibility, the equipment must potentially be able to process a variety of raw plastic materials as new applications are developed.

MP PRODUCT LINES

In 1980, Maillefer's cable and pipe extrusion lines were based on their BM extruders. Their reputation was unsurpassed in the cable field, where the emphasis had always been on machines of reasonable output which could also maintain strict tolerances, as well as on custom-designed line components which could add specialities such as color-coded striping. In order to develop MP's products further, the screw and barrel geometries were reengineered for pipe plastics. New line components were also designed, particularly the extruder heads for pipe and the vacuum calibration trough. Other components, such as cooling troughs, haulers, winders, and hoppers, were common to both cable and pipe extrusion lines.

Meeting tolerances was not achieved by any one component alone, but by the synchronized operation of the entire line. Sensors continually monitored barrel temperature, calibrating vacuum and haul-off speed. Diameter and thickness were checked for accuracy and parameters were automatically adjusted to maintain output within specification. Buyers had become used to requesting customized line machinery. A laboratory simulator called the EXMATE enabled Maillefer to analyze the influence of different screw and barrel geometries on extrusion results. From such analyses, special designs were developed for specific families of plastics and their applications. Maillefer's extruders were among the most sophisticated in screw geometry, and temperature and process control; they were also the most expensive, measured on the simple basis of price-performance (SFr/average kg/hr processed).

Maillefer's single-screw extruders processed a variety of plastics, including engineering plastics (used in cable machines as well). Hard PVC usually was processed on double-screw extruders. Unlike Maillefer's cable business, MP had neither a dominant characteristic nor an established reputation in the pipe marketplace. Most of the extrusion lines sold had been for pressurized water and gas pipe of LDPE and HDPE in diameters of 50 to 225 mm. Lines for HDPE pipe up to 400 mm had also been produced, but they had required some adaptation of the larger cooling troughs and haul-off. A double-screw machine for processing hard PVC was being developed, which would also use the larger line equipment.

In the small pipe market, MP had sold lines for extrusion of pipe as small as 50 mm. Drip irrigation was one application where MP had been particularly successful. Drip irrigation systems supplied water to crops using small-diameter, flexible HDPE pipe fitted with tiny drippers. Drippers delivered a controlled amount of water directly to the base of each plant. In addition to meeting specifications for diameter and thickness, the drippers had to be inserted at precise intervals along the pipe. MP had developed a piece of line equipment which could do this at the rate of one every second. Customers were satisfied, and new inquiries were being received.

MP had introduced a new automatic winder which met with immediate approval as it was capable of operating at the high speeds required by precision lines. In addition, automatic changing of the take-up reels reduced manual intervention and thus saved on personnel.

DELIVERY AND PRICE

From order placement through installation, Maillefer's delivery lead time for a complete extrusion line averaged 10–12 months. After an agreement was signed, as much as 2 months could be spent confirming technical specifications. When the customer did not know or could not decide on a particular specification, the process was further slowed down. Then 4–5 months would elapse waiting for the ordering and delivery of parts. After that, 3–4 months usually were required for manufacturing and assembly. Testing came next and lasted two days for simple lines and a week or two for lines which required multiple trials of materials and/or output samples for customer approval.

MP technicians and engineers helped customers to select the most appropriate system, put it into operation, and train personnel to run it. Customers were able to work before and after the sale with production lines at Maillefer's Exhibition Hall. In this 2,000 square meter facility built in 1978, complete extrusion lines were available for test runs and instruction. Cable and pipe extrusion lines shared both fabrication and assembly at the facilities in Ecublens. Manufacturing occupied 5,000 square meters in the modern, one-story, steel-framed building next to headquarters.

A recent management meeting had reviewed the questions of delivery and price. Catalog prices of both extruders and lines averaged 15 percent above other top-of-the-line competitors. In some cases, prices were as much as 25–30 percent higher. Bonjour made the following recommendation:

> Our cable machines are among the best in the world, and we've also had some success with pipe, but the competition on cost and delivery is more stiff in the pipe market. It's inevitable that in certain applications, there are limits to what the customer will pay. Although I don't want to nego-

EXHIBIT 10
MAILLEFER SA (A)
Pricing Analysis
(SFr 000)

	Status Quo* Scenario	Bottom Line* Scenario
Extruder sales	2,663	4,210
Line equipment	1,090	1,869
Total	3,753	6,079
Less:		
Manufacturing and overhead	3,170	5,458
Profit before tax	583	621

*Status quo: 20 extruder sales, 10 as part of a complete line. 1980 catalog prices.
Bottom line: 40 extruder sales, 20 as part of a complete line. Prices 24 percent below 1980 catalog.

	Extruder Size (screw diameter)				
	45 mm	60 mm	80 mm	120 mm	Total
Status quo					
Extruders alone	2	3	4	1	10
Extruders with line	1	4	4	1	10
	3	7	8	2	20
Bottom Line					
Extruders alone	3	7	8	2	20
Extruders with line	3	7	8	2	20
	6	14	16	4	40

tiate on price with a customer in order to win a contract, I do need enough flexibility to establish a price level which will attract potential customers.

He summarized the issue in a memo which presented two pricing scenarios (see Exhibit 10) which MP could adopt. At current price levels a "status quo" was forecast; i.e., twenty machines in 1981 with sales of SFr 3.75 million. The alternative analyzed the effect of a price level 24 percent lower than current catalog. If the number of extruder and line sales could be proportionally increased, the result would benefit sales without damaging profits.

THE OPTIONS FACING MP

All of the options possible for the MP Group were being weighed in Bonjour's mind. Sales needed to be increased; therefore, a decision on pricing was necessary. However, there was also the issue of positioning to be considered. Lines for medium pipe had provided the bulk of MP's sales, and new sales could still be found in this market. Activities were also underway in both large- and small-diameter applications. The time would come when the customers, as well as Maillefer's management, would expect him to define MP's place in the market. And that time seemed to be rapidly approaching.

Sunwind AB (A)

On November 14, 1985, Lars Olov Larsson, managing director of Sunwind AB, eased back in his seat as the SAS Boeing 747 climbed away from Tokyo's Narita Airport to begin the 17-hour flight to Gothenburg (Sweden). He was returning from a 10-day trip to Japan, where he had visited factories of Nissan Motors and Mazda, as well as a number of their parts suppliers. This visit had reinforced his conviction that Sunwind should initiate a proposal to Volvo, the company's major customer, that just-in-time (JIT) delivery of components be made directly to Volvo's 700 series automobile assembly lines at Torslanda (near Gothenburg), Kalmar (a port city on Sweden's east coast) and at Ghent (in Belgium).

Lars Olov, a graduate engineer from Chalmers University, had previous managerial experience with Volvo, Kockums, Philips, and ASEA. He had joined Sunwind in June 1984, shortly after Perstorp AB (a Swedish multinational with annual sales of Skr 3,500 million),[1] had bought the company from its founders. Sunwind was part of Perstorp Component AB, one of nine Perstorp business area groups.

Perstorp Component AB comprised six companies manufacturing sophisticated wood, wood fibre, and plastic moulded components for the automotive and engineering industries. In fiscal 1985 (September 1, 1984 to August 31, 1985), sales were Skr 521 million. Major markets were in the USA and Nordic countries.

BACKGROUND

Sunwind, with headquarters at Säve, a small village within the Gothenburg metropolitan area, was the second largest of the Perstorp Component AB companies with 1985 sales of Skr 102 million. (Income statements in summary form are given in Exhibit 1.) Sunwind had been founded in 1953 and, at the time of the Perstorp acquisition in February 1984, manufactured a line of interior trim primarily for Volvo. Sunwind did supply parts to Saab's automobile division; however, those sales

---

[1]In 1985, 7.63 Swedish kroner (Skr) = 1 $U.S.

EXHIBIT 1
SUNWIND AB (A)
Income Statements (Summary)
(Skr 000)

	September 1, 1984– August 31, 1985		September 1, 1983– August 31, 1984		September 1, 1982– August 31, 1983	
Sales		102,092		57,693		84,783
Less: Manufacturing, selling and administrative expenses	98,136		54,321		75,696	
Operating earnings before depreciation		3,956		3,372		9,087
Less: Depreciation	2,125		1,266		1,806	
Interest expense	1,347		785		1,327	
Plus: Interest and nonoperating income	484		1,321		5,954	
	290		362		762	
Net earnings before tax and allocations		774		1,683		6,716

accounted for only 5 percent of revenues. Products for Saab included door panels, floor lids and rear shelves. The company had two factories, a 1800 square meter plant at Säve, 8 km from Volvo's Torslanda operations, and a more modern 10,000 square meter plant at Högsäter, 130 km north of Säve. The Högsäter factory was close to the proposed site of a new Volvo assembly plant which, if plans were realized, would be completed by August 1988. In 1985 the Säve and Högsäter plants accounted for Skr 37.6 million and Skr 64.4 million, respectively, of Sunwind's sales.

When Lars Olov joined Sunwind, the company employed 35 people at headquarters, 75 people at the Säve factory and 150 people at Högsäter. Only 75 percent of the available space at the Högsäter plant was used and, at the time of the acquisition, Perstorp corporate management had suggested that Sunwind should consolidate all its manufacturing activities at Högsäter.

Lars Olov was not of the same opinion. He felt that Sunwind could exploit the Säve factory's proximity to Volvo's Torslanda plant. The just-in-time (JIT) approach, if it proved successful, would not only guarantee the viability of Säve operations, but also provide Sunwind with a sorely needed competitive advantage within Sweden's car trim industry and improve profitability which had declined sharply during the previous two years.

Lars Olov not only felt pressure from corporate management to improve performance, but there was also increasing pressure from Volvo and from competition. He realized that Sunwind's privileged relationship as the exclusive supplier to Volvo was threatened.

Volvo had introduced its 700 series of automobiles in 1981. The 700 series, designed to replace the popular 200 series, had proved to be very successful, indeed more successful than Volvo had anticipated. (Past production and forecasts of future volumes for the 200 and 700 series are given in Exhibits 2 and 3.) Sunwind was the only supplier of the floor lid which fit behind the rear passenger seat (see Exhibit 4) of the 700 series station wagon, a 5-door model which represented some 21 percent of the total 700 series production in 1985. This percentage was expected to rise to 37 percent in 1986.

During the latter part of 1985, Sunwind had difficulty meeting Volvo's requirements in terms of both quantity and quality. While Volvo's requirements for 5-door floor lids for the 700 series averaged 650/week in 1985, weekly requirements had increased from 250 in early January to 1,200 by November. Average weekly requirements in 1986 were expected to approach 1,200 units with volumes sometimes exceeding 1,400

EXHIBIT 2
SUNWIND AB (A)
Volvo Production 200 and 700 Series (Sweden and Belgium) Units

| | Actual | | | | | | | | Forecast | | | |
| | Calendar year 1984 | | | | 1985 | | | | 1986 | | | |
Plant*	T	K	G	Total	T	K	G	Total	T	K	G	Total
Model												
200 4 door	81,843			81,843	58,294			58,294	58,000			58,000
5 door	74,540			74,540	58,014			58,014	49,000			49,000
2 door	3,433			3,433								
700 4 door	27,256	19,987	41,792	89,035	40,318	25,599	59,517	125,434	35,000	18,000	52,000	105,000
5 door	915			915	17,050	4,525	12,090	33,665	(no plant designation)			62,400
Total units	187,987	19,987	41,792	249,766	173,676	30,124	71,607	275,407†	142,000	18,000	52,000	274,400

*Assembly plant: T Torslanda
K Kalmar
G Ghent
†November–December 1985 forecast data are included.

EXHIBIT 3
SUNWIND AB (A)
Volvo Production of 700 Series 5-Door Station Wagons 1985–86
Actual and Forecast by Month (Units)*

Assembly Plant			*I*	*K*	*G*	*Total*
Manufactured	1985	Jan.	1,000			1,000
and delivered		Feb.	900			900
		March	1,300			1,300
		April	1,600			1,600
		May	1,200			1,200
		June	600			600
		July	850	75	190	1,115
		Aug.	2,000	0	2,000	4,000
		Sept.	1,900	850	2,500	5,250
		Oct.	1,900	1,000	2,400	5,300
Forecast		Nov.	1,900	1,100	2,200	5,200
		Dec.	1,900	1,500	2,800	6,200
	Total	1985	17,050	4,525	12,090	33,665
Forecast	1986	Jan.				5,800
		Feb.				5,600
		March				5,400
		April				6,100
		May				4,700
		June				5,100
		July to Dec.				29,700
	Total	1986				62,400
Forecast	Total	1987				65,000

*Sunwind's floor lids were used exclusively in 700 Series 5-door station wagons.

units/week. Lars Olov estimated Sunwind's current capacity to be approximately 1,250 units/week.

Actual output varied considerably due to equipment failures and other problems. For example, the gluing machine had proved particularly troublesome and had increased rejects. Other causes of problems included off-spec plywood blanks received from a Finnish supplier and glue seeping through the carpeting which covered the plywood forms. Volvo had also rejected a shipment of floor lids due to differences in the shade of the carpeting covering the four separate pieces which made up a floor lid.

EXHIBIT 4
SUNWIND AB (A)
700 Series Station Wagon

Practical difference

The 740 and 760 with that fifth door are not only luxurious. They are also the most practical cars we've ever made.

Opening the hatch unveils an enormous boot space whose dimensions are 151 cm wide, 82 cm high, 105 cm deep. Putting it differently, you've got all of 1,110 litres at your disposal.

If that's not enough, you can easily convert it to 2,120 litres. With a depth of 182 cm.

Instant transformations of storage space are made possible thanks to the folding rear backrest. Of course, you can fold down the entire backrest. Or, using the asymmetric split, you may fold down only the smaller or larger section. Volvo offers you maximum storage flexibility.

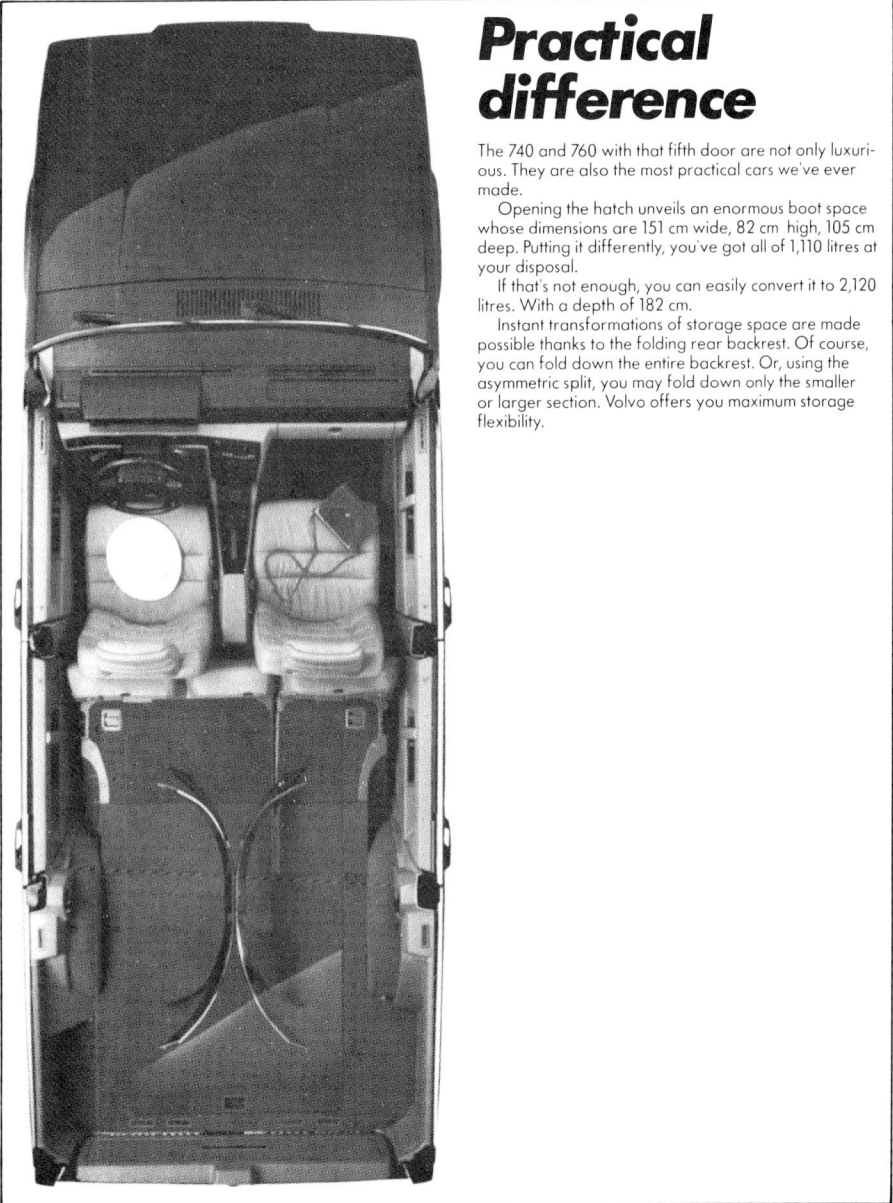

Taken from the VOLVO 760/740 Estates brochure. Shows glass-topped table in the rear of the vehicle. Both rear passenger seats have been folded forward.

Such difficulties could not have come at a worse time, when Lars Olov was already concerned by the worldwide trend of major manufacturers in the automobile industry to rely on fewer suppliers. He knew that Toyota, which industry observers continually cited for its productivity gains, relied on only 320 suppliers, while Volvo had over 600! Headlines such as: "Volvo will reduce number of suppliers; pressure on subcontractors" in *Dagens-Nyheter,* one of Sweden's major daily newspapers, did not help his peace of mind.

He also was aware that JIT deliveries had been implemented recently within the Volvo group. Earlier that month he had read an article in Volvomonitor, a company publication, describing the JIT supply of automobile seats by a Belgian manufacturer to Volvo's plant in Ghent. This manufacturer was a potential competitor with the capability to supply floor lids to the Ghent plant in addition to the seats. Indeed, since assembly of the 700 series, 5-door had started in Ghent, Sunwind found it difficult to meet the demand.

THE PRODUCT

Lars Olov felt that the floor lid for Volvo's 700 series 5-door station wagon would be appropriate for demonstrating Sunwind's capability to be Volvo's first Swedish JIT supplier. In 1985, the product accounted for 17 percent of Sunwind's sales revenue. Forecasts for 1986 indicated that this figure could rise to 25 percent. Also Volvo was likely to be interested in such a proposal, since floor lids were bulky, easily soiled, and offered in several carpet/colour combinations. The floor lid fitted into the compartment behind the rear passenger seat, providing a rigid flat surface for carrying loads, as well as covering the storage compartments for a foldaway rear-facing children's seat and a spare tire. The lid comprised four separate items (see Exhibit 5). The front unit was hinged in the centre. The uppermost section could be opened when the back of either rear passenger seat was folded forward, which also increased the load carrying area. The rear unit was also hinged to gain access to the storage compartments. Two removable panels which fitted left and right of the rear wheel wells completed the lid.

The floor lid was covered with carpeting that matched the interior decor. In 1985 Volvo offered its customers four different colour choices (beige, blue, black, and burgundy) and two different types of carpeting (needle felt and tufted). With four separate pieces making up a floor lid,

EXHIBIT 5
SUNWIND AB (A)
Floor Lid—Schematic

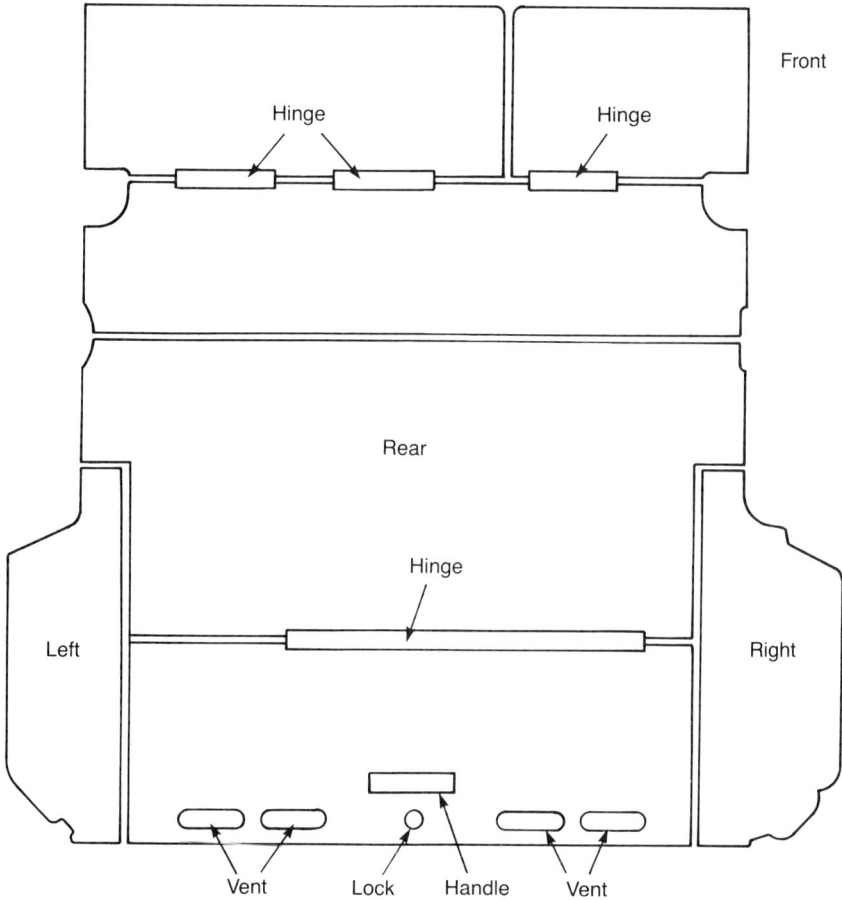

32 part numbers were needed to specify a particular part/colour/carpet combination.

THE PRODUCTION PROCESS

The material requirements for a complete floor lid are given in Exhibit 6. Each lid was manufactured from shaped plywood sections. The three sections comprising the front unit were hinged together as were the two

EXHIBIT 6
SUNWIND AB (A)
Material Requirements: 700 Series Floor Lid

| | Floor Lid Parts, Model 705 | | | | |
| | Rear | Front | Small Left | Small Right | |
Material	1354179	1354177	1354213	1354225	Total
Plywood	2	3	1	1	7
Wooden battens		8			8
Carpet	1	1	1	1	4
Steel fixtures/hinges					
small	3	3			6
large	4	18	3	3	28
Plastic, rubber,	5	12	2	2	21
leather parts					
Screws	10	29	9	9	57
Rivets	14	15			29
Nuts	4	16			20
Staples	AN*	AN	AN	AN	AN
Total					180

*As needed.

sections comprising the rear unit. In addition, plastic parts for the handle and vents, appropriate steel fasteners and fixtures, as well as carpeting were required. Most production operations were carried out at Säve.

The flow of material between operations and the intermediate storage locations at the Säve plant site is shown in Exhibit 7. After being received and inspected, plywood blanks, precut carpeting, sheet metal, fasteners, and fixtures were stored as raw material and parts inventory in two separate locations. The rectangular plywood blanks were obtained from a Finnish supplier. Carpeting, from a Swiss supplier, was precut in Högsäter and shipped on pallets to Säve. Metal parts for hinges were fabricated from sheet steel in a small workshop at Säve and stored in parts inventory. Finished goods were stored in a separate location near the shipping dock, while a 630 square meter tent provided storage for work-in-process inventory.

The production process was divided into separate operations. The standard machine setup time, run time, and batch size for each operation are shown in Exhibit 8, while Exhibit 9 shows the factory layout at Säve.

EXHIBIT 7
SUNWIND AB (A)
The Säve Site

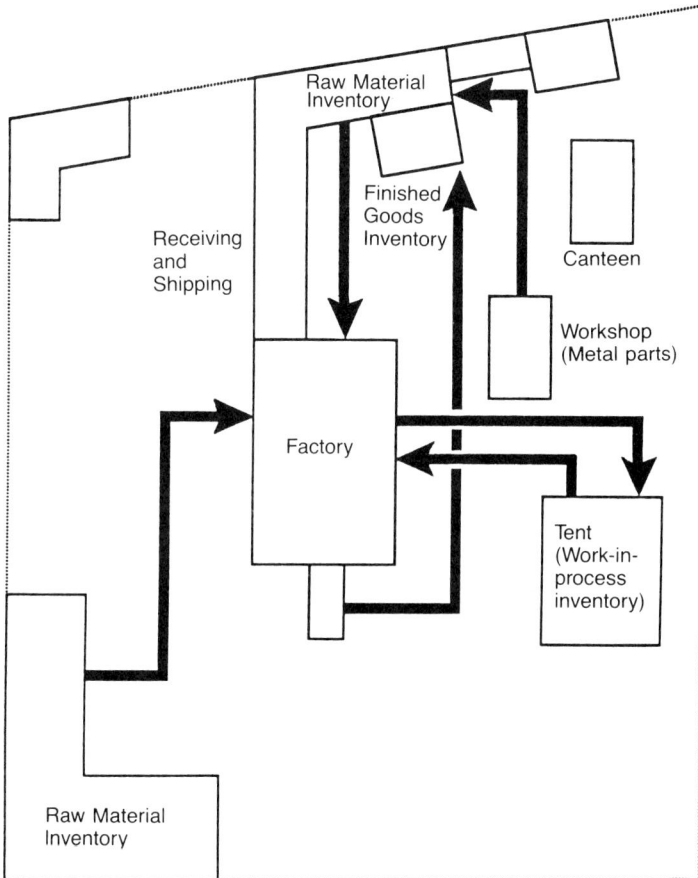

Parts Fabrication

The first stage in the production process was the fabrication of individual parts. Steel parts for the hinges were fabricated and assembled to stock at Säve. The wooden battens, used to hold foam padding in place on the front unit were also prepared at Säve. The precut carpeting shipped from Högsäter was stored on pallets until required. The various plywood sections were shaped on a numerically controlled milling machine which was operated on a three-shift basis (Operation 1, Exhibit

EXHIBIT 8
SUNWIND AB (A)
Production Operations

Operation	Rear			Front			Right or Left		
	S*	R*	B*	S	R	B	S	R	B
Parts									
Carpet preparation (Högstäter)	0	1.35	1200	0	1.35	1200	0	0.45	1200
Steel hinge parts	180	0.80	17,000	240	0.55	30,000			
Assembly of hinges	0	0.65		0	1.35				
Cutting battens				30	0.50	1500			
1 Shaping plywood panels	80	1.60	2500	30	0.85	2500	60	0.35	2500
2 Painting	0	1.00	1500	0	1.00	1500	0	0.30	1500
Assembly									
Preparing subassemblies									
3 Attaching battens,									
4 Riveting, inserting studs	0	1.90	1000	0	4.95	1000			
Assembly of lids									
5 Mounting hinges	30	1.35	1500	30	1.50	1500			
6 Gluing carpet	100	2.00	500	100	2.00	500	0	4.50	
7 Attaching metal and plastic fixtures	0	9.50			12.50	500			
Total†	390	18.80		430	25.20		60	5.15	

*Key: S = Standard setup time (minutes). R = Standard run time/operation (minutes/unit). B = Batch size (units).
†Total does not include carpet preparation.

EXHIBIT 9
SUNWIND AB (A)
Säve Factory Layout and Floor Lid Operation

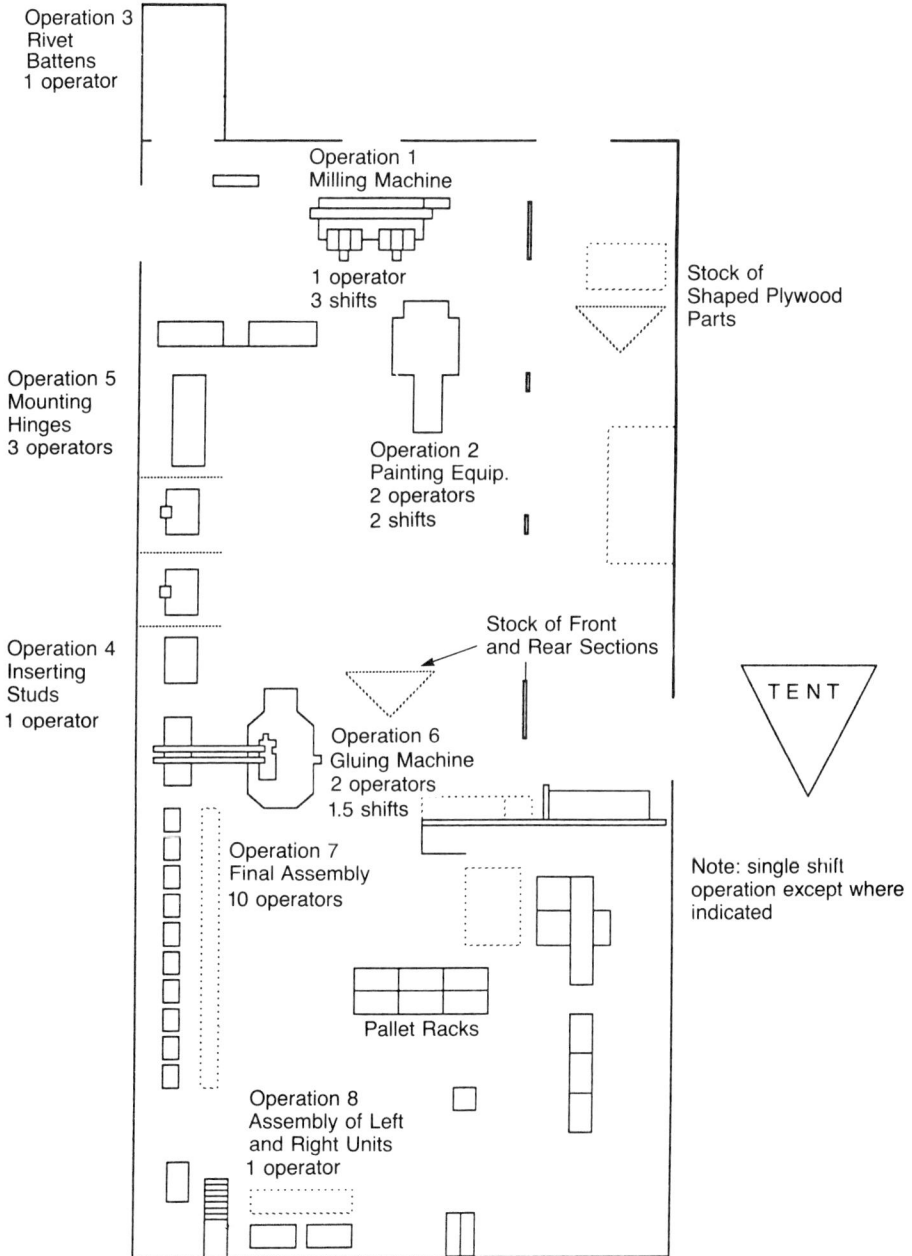

Operation 3
Rivet
Battens
1 operator

Operation 1
Milling Machine

1 operator
3 shifts

Stock of
Shaped Plywood
Parts

Operation 5
Mounting
Hinges
3 operators

Operation 2
Painting Equip.
2 operators
2 shifts

Stock of Front
and Rear Sections

Operation 4
Inserting
Studs
1 operator

TENT

Operation 6
Gluing Machine
2 operators
1.5 shifts

Operation 7
Final Assembly
10 operators

Note: single shift
operation except where
indicated

Pallet Racks

Operation 8
Assembly of Left
and Right Units
1 operator

9). Because of the length of time required to make tool, jig, and fixture changes, parts were manufactured in batches of approximately 2,500. The shaped plywood sections were stored on pallets before being painted (Operation 2).

Assembly Operations

In Operation 3, the wooden battens were attached to the sections of the front unit, while in Operation 4 metal studs were placed in a series of specially drilled holes in the plywood pieces for both the front and rear units. These studs served as anchors for the rivets used to attach the various fixtures in the final assembly operation. The sections were re-stacked on pallets and taken by forklift truck to the tent for storage.

Ultimately, the pallets were removed from storage and, in Operation 5, the sections were hinged to form the front and rear units, respectively. The completed pieces were again stacked on pallets before moving to Operation 6.

Operation 6, where the carpeting was glued and folded onto the plywood units, was carried out in batches of 500. Once the glue had set, the forward and rear units were ready for the final assembly operation (Operation 7), in which additional steel fixtures, plastic, rubber, and leather components were added. The edges of the carpeting were trimmed and then stapled to the underside of the plywood. The left and right units of the lid had few components and were assembled on a virtually continuous basis at three small dedicated workstations at Operation 8. The completed units were stacked in special containers provided by Volvo. Each container held 20 front or rear units of the same colour and carpet type. Left and right units were stacked in similar containers, each holding 200 identical pieces. The containers were taken by forklift truck to finished goods storage to await shipment to Volvo.

Plant Staffing and Inventory

On the first shift, 21 workers and 4 material handlers were assigned to Operations 1–8 on the 700 series floor lid line. The allocation of workers to operations is shown in Exhibit 9. The milling machine operated on a three-shift basis and the gluing machine operated an average of 1.5 shifts/day. The personnel worked 40.7 hours each week (excluding breaks and personal time) on a five-day week, 45 weeks per year basis.

Lars Olov knew that the standard labor content (excluding machine setup time) for a completed floor lid was about 50 minutes. While he did not know the average time it took a batch of plywood forms to move from raw material inventory to finished goods inventory, he did know that raw material, work-in-process and finished goods inventory were 6.0 percent, 4.6 percent, and 1.1 percent of Säve sales, respectively.

Production Planning, Scheduling, and Control

Volvo's order forms, giving firm-planned and planned requirements by part number for each part/colour/carpet combination supplied by Sunwind, provided sufficient information for Sunwind's purchasing department to place orders with Sunwind suppliers and for the production planning department to release production orders to the factory. Production planning also developed the assembly schedules for the final assembly of the appropriate number of front, rear, left and right units to be manufactured in each required colour/carpet combination.

Given the extended delivery lead times of some items (e.g., carpeting), the purchasing department used a 3- to 6-month planning horizon to place orders with suppliers.

In contrast, the production planning department focused on the first four weeks of the delivery schedule. The demand for each front, rear, left and right unit was summed over the eight colour/carpet combinations and divided by the number of working days in the four-week period. This represented the average number of units, irrespective of colour/carpet specification, which had to be produced each working day in order to meet requirements during the four-week period. This provided the production planning department with a quick check on capacity requirements and gross material requirements (i.e., for plywood blanks, hinges, fasteners and fixtures, etc.) needed to fulfill the delivery schedule. Net requirements were then calculated to maintain the equivalent of one week of production in each of the inventories: raw material, work-in-process, and finished goods, a Sunwind rule of thumb.

When releasing orders to production, the planning department was guided by batch sizes (see Exhibit 8). Typically, the batch size chosen equalled two weeks' production, but this could be modified in the factory later where the foremen and machine operators would be guided by the capacity of the pallets.

The four units comprising the floor lids were assembled from stock.

Production planning provided an assembly schedule at the beginning of each week which indicated the quantity and colour/carpet combination of each unit to be assembled and delivered to Volvo during the week.

The production foremen coordinated the flow of material between the various workstations and the intermediate stocking locations. Three of the material handlers used forklift trucks to move pallets of material from one place to another, while a fourth used a manual trolley to maneuver pallets within the more confined areas of the plant.

Quality Control

As a supplier to Volvo, Sunwind was obliged to document its quality control procedures. These procedures were summarized in Sunwind's Quality Manual, which was available to Volvo personnel on demand. The manual detailed, for example, such procedures as inspection (both incoming and outgoing material), production quality control, the processing of engineering change notices and testing. It also specified mandatory documentation procedures to satisfy legislative requirements facilitating vehicle recall procedures and acceptance procedures for new or modified parts.

Lars Olov recognized, however, that relatively few of the procedures were followed in practice. While mandatory documentation requirements and acceptance procedures for new parts were stringently observed, quality control procedures in manufacturing were lax. Processes were not monitored formally; rather, there was a tendency to rely on workers recognizing and reacting to more obvious faults. If parts were rejected after receipt and inspection at Volvo, Sunwind would replace the defective material, identify the cause of the problem, and eliminate it. No summary statistics were available to Lars Olov concerning such rejects.

**VOLVO'S TORSLANDA AND GHENT
ASSEMBLY OPERATIONS**

Volvo's Torslanda plant supplied the Scandinavian market and a portion of the American market. The Ghent plant supplied continental Europe, the remainder of the American market, and all right-hand drive requirements.

The assembly lines operated on a single-shift, 5 days/week, 45 weeks/year basis. Painted car bodies were placed, in strict sequence, on a moving conveyor which snaked through a 500-meter-long assembly shop. At 70 different workstations, parts, components, and subassemblies were added, enabling each car to be built to a specific customer order. Once the body was placed on the assembly line, it took 8 hours before it was transferred to final test and inspection. To the casual visitor, no car on the line resembled another. Each varied in terms of style, colour, country-specific requirements, and options.

In the assembly procedure, the floor lid was fitted exactly 6 hours after the car body was loaded onto the line. As a 700 series 5-door model reached the interior trim workstation where the floor lid was to be fitted, the assembly line worker removed the four required pieces from a special container located beside the line. The front and rear sections were bolted into place, while the right and left panels were snapped into place. There were sufficient containers near the line to meet production requirements for a period of 3 hours. Each container held eight floor lids, which were stacked inside the containers according to the colour/carpet specifications for each 700 series 5-door model on the line.

The containers were prepared at one of several subassembly stations which served a number of assembly line workers with sequenced material, such as instrument panels and seats. When a 700 series 5-door station wagon was loaded onto the line, the colour/carpet combination for the floor lid was transmitted to a printer at the subassembly station. This information was accumulated in batches of eight. The parts, in the appropriate colour/carpet combination, were picked from a buffer stock located in racks placed along the walls of the assembly area. The buffer stock consisted of one pallet box for each of the 32 part/colour/carpet combinations. The containers were taken from the subassembly area to the assembly line workstation by material handlers driving forklift trucks. The buffer stock was replenished from a large central stock on the basis of requests from the workers manning the subassembly stations.

If an assembly line worker discovered a defective part, he or she notified the line inspector immediately. The defective part was placed in a "rejection box" and its replacement obtained as quickly as possible. As an interim measure, the assembly line worker would "borrow" an identical part from another special container. Ultimately the defective part was replaced from the buffer stock used by the subassembly station workers.

VOLVO'S KALMAR ASSEMBLY OPERATIONS

When the Kalmar plant came on stream in 1974, it represented a unique approach to assembly operations. The traditional assembly line was replaced by "team zones" in which each team of workers had responsibility for assembling an entire subsystem within the vehicle; for example, the electrical system, the instrumentation system, and so on. The assembly task was divided into 20 team zones with the work divided so that it could be completed at 4–5 stations. Two assembly workers would move with the car from station to station carrying out all the work assigned to that team. When the work was completed on one car, they would return to the start of their zone to work on the next vehicle. This system required a cycle time for an assembly worker of between 16 to 40 minutes, depending on the zone and whether or not the two workers interchanged jobs. The cars were transferred through the plant on revolutionary computer controlled working platforms.

The Kalmar plant was supplied with painted car bodies produced at Torslanda. The car bodies were transported by rail and carried in a specific sequence. The train left Torslanda each day at 18:00 hours and arrived at Kalmar in the early morning, prior to the start of the shift.

Upon receipt, the bodies were unloaded, washed and dried. Each body was then placed on a working platform and moved automatically through the various team zones.

At Kalmar, the floor lids were fitted by the team responsible for interior trim. This zone was reached 2 hours after the body had been loaded onto the working platform. To fit a floor lid, a member of the team picked the required parts in the appropriate colour/carpet combination from pallet boxes (32 in all) stored in the team zone.

PURCHASING OF FLOOR LIDS

Every four weeks Volvo would send Sunwind an order form which showed requirements over a 60-week planning horizon. This was broken down into seven 4-week periods and a 32-week period, as follows:

1. Requirements by week for the first 4-week period beginning two weeks from the date of preparation. These requirements were considered firm.
2. Requirements by week for the second 4-week period. These re-

quirements were considered "half frozen" (i.e., subject to some small changes).
3. Forecasted aggregate requirements by period for the subsequent five 4-week periods.
4. Forecasted aggregate requirements for a subsequent 32-week period.

The Volvo group of companies had a wholly owned transport company which served a number of its companies in the Gothenburg area. They insisted that the suppliers (which included other Volvo companies) use the transport company, use standard containers, and ship one part number per container. This facilitated storage and material handling in the centralized warehouse in Torslanda and Volvo's other plants. The supplier ordered transportation and empty containers as required.

VOLVO'S RECEIVING, INSPECTION, AND STOCKING OF PURCHASED PARTS

Torslanda's procedures were typical of all Volvo's plants. Some 2,500 standard containers were delivered to Torslanda each day and processed by seven inspectors. Parts and components shipped from the Volvo group of companies were not checked. While goods from other suppliers were subject to spot checks, the stringency of any check depended on the sensitivity of the product (e.g., electrical and electronic components were subject to the most frequent checks).

If a particular shipment was subject to inspection, a container would be chosen at random and the parts inspected according to prescribed statistical quality control procedures. If the parts passed inspection, the total shipment would be accepted and placed in central storage.

If the inspected parts did not meet the quality control criteria, the entire shipment was rejected and the containers set aside. Procedures required that the inspector call the supplier immediately. The supplier could either send a replacement shipment or come to Torslanda to check the rejected shipment and replace the defective parts. The inspector would also call the Material Control Department at the plant to inform them of a potential shortage of parts. Statistics on supplier conformance to specifications were kept by Central Purchasing at Volvo.

The line inspector and receiving inspector examined any parts on the line to determine whether the defect was a supplier or an assembly fault. In effect, the receiving inspector acted as an arbitrator. In either case, the supplier was asked to ship a replacement part. Parts rejected due to supplier faults were either scrapped or returned at the supplier's expense. The supplier ultimately received formal notification of the fault and the next shipment of parts was subjected to 100 percent inspection.

VOLVO'S SUPPLIER CONTACT DEPARTMENTS

As a supplier to Volvo, Sunwind maintained both formal and informal contacts with Volvo managers in various departments both at company headquarters and at the Volvo plants. Among the more important contact groups were those shown in Exhibit 10.

    Volvo's Central Purchasing was split into seven departments. The four buying departments specialized in steel and sheet materials, electrical components, exterior trim, and interior trim. These departments were further subdivided into purchasing groups. Mr. Claes Behrendt was the purchasing group manager responsible for contractual relations with Sunwind. The Material Department performed a material planning

EXHIBIT 10
SUNWIND AB (A)
Volvo Car Company—Partial Organization Charts

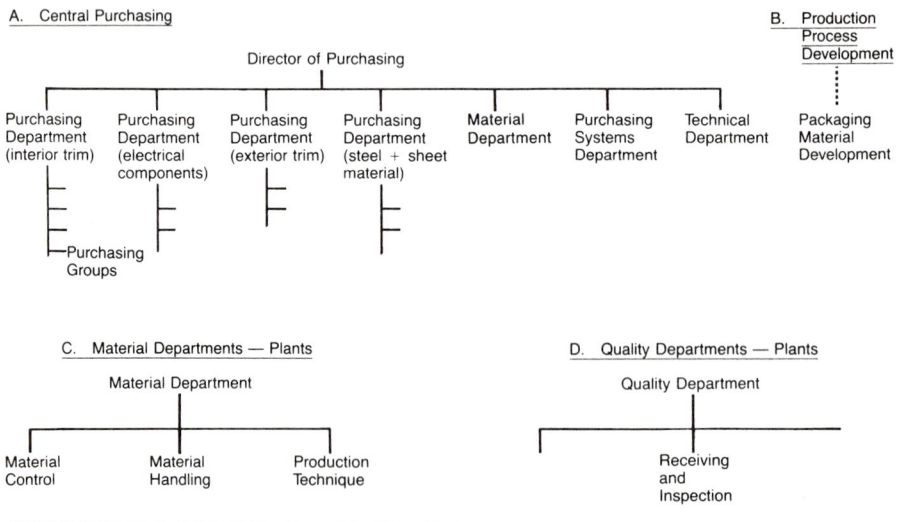

and control function. It ensured that the supplier had adequate capacity to meet Volvo's requirements and was informed of engineering change orders. It provided the detail orders and forecasts for Volvo's suppliers. The Purchasing Systems Department was responsible for developing computer-based purchasing systems, while the Technical Department had responsibility for quality assurance and the testing of initial samples from suppliers.

Within Volvo, the Packaging Material Development group was on the same level as the Purchasing Departments. The group was responsible for designing packages and containers which would ensure the integrity of parts in transit and effective utilization of space available in the various modes of transport used—truck, transporter, container, rail car, and freighter—as well as in storage locations at the plants.

The role of the Material Departments at Volvo assembly plants was to work with qualified suppliers to ensure efficient and effective supply. While Central Purchasing focused on the suppliers' ability to meet quality, quantity, technical development, and price criteria, the Material Departments tended to focus on supply logistics; that is, the physical movement of parts from the supplier to the assembly plants and the maintenance of appropriate stock levels.

The Material Department at Torslanda was representative. It was split into three separate functions: Material Control, Material Handling, and Production Technique. The Material Control Department was responsible for material planning and control at the plant level. Material Handling was responsible for the receipt, stocking, and distribution of materials within the plant. The Production Technique function was responsible for methods engineering, process design, and layout within the plant. The Receiving and Inspection group was part of the Quality Department and independent of the Material Department in Volvo.

THE JIT PROGRAM

As the plane reached cruising altitude, Lars Olov flipped down his tray table and started to work on a list of priorities for implementing JIT deliveries from Sunwind to Volvo's three plants. One possibility was the sequential delivery of floor lids from Säve directly onto the assembly line at Torslanda. After a 700 series 5-door station wagon was loaded onto the line, Sunwind would have 6 hours to effect delivery of the floor lid for that car.

Lars Olov was convinced that JIT delivery could and should be implemented. The system would guarantee jobs at Säve and increase profitability. However, he knew he would have to contend with some degree of scepticism. The existing operations were neither efficient nor effective, and there was always someone asking endless "what if" questions. What if a machine breaks down? What happens if a truck goes off the road? And so on.

To implement JIT deliveries, Lars Olov felt he would have to tackle the capacity and quality problems first. Then there was the headache of getting the information from Volvo regarding the appropriate colour/carpet combination soon enough to launch orders into production. New containers would be needed. He had doubts about relying on the Volvo transport company; it appeared to him that training his own drivers made more sense.

Then, of course, he had to sell the idea to Volvo. Where should he start? Whom should he talk to?